THE WONDER CABINET OF FABULOUS INSECTS

THE WONDER CABINET OF FABULOUS INSECTS

DENIS RICHARD
PIERRE-OLIVIER MAQUART

FOREWORD BY PHILIPPE LE GALL
TRANSLATION BY MARGARET BESSER

CERNUNNOS

CONTENTS

The choice of which insects to present was necessarily subjective—so is the order in which they appear and the division into sections. We beg your indulgence. Arguments could be made for putting this or that portrait in a different chapter, but we have opted for spontaneity: let us take you on a stroll through the world of insects.

FOREWORD

What better metaphor for life itself than insects? Their abundant, colorful swarm connects us to nature: that source of all life which we humans sometimes delude ourselves into seeing as separate from us. Insects are truly fabulous—in appearance, behavior, and their ability to amaze and inspire. This book explores their fascinating world without reducing them to pests or pollinators. At a time when certainty of their ability to survive anything has been replaced by concerns over declining populations, Denis Richard and Pierre-Olivier Maquart bring us arresting images and food for thought as they showcase some of the most iconic species among more than a million known to science. But this book is not just about insects. The authors also introduce us to some of the people who have spent their lives studying insects, and whose work has opened our eyes and hearts to these incredible creatures.

Like many entomologists, my own passion for insects began with the books and magazines I read as a child. To discover their strange and diverse beauty is to plunge into the unknown: from the depths of the rainforest to our own backyards. Every single day, research is adding new pieces to the infinite puzzle that is insect classification. Not long ago, an entomologist interested in small ground beetles discovered more than thirty new species, all in the south of France! Whether it's scouring South American forests in the depths of the night for the massive titan beetle or seeking out the "terrible hairy fly" of Kenya—Richard and Maquart reveal an entomologist's life to be full of unique challenges.

This book is a beautiful homage to insects, entomology, and entomologists. I would not be surprised if, years down the road, I end up meeting young researchers who credit this book with putting them on the path to extraordinary adventure that is the study of the natural world.

Philippe Le Gall
Secretary-General, French Entomological Society (SEF)
Vice-President, Office for Insects and Their Environment (OPIE)

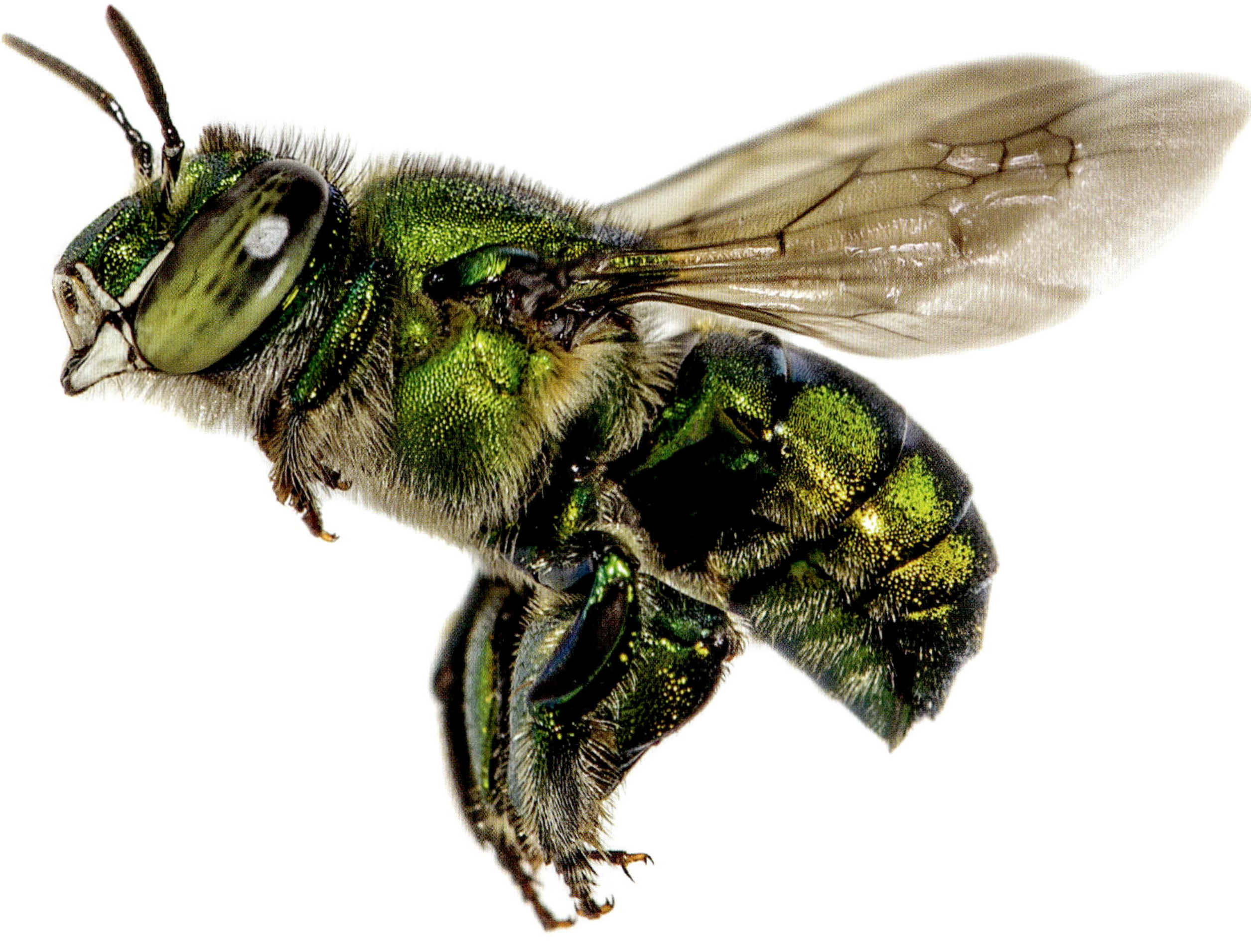

Euglossa dilemma, a solitary bee from Central America, is specialized in pollinating orchids.
(For another famous orchid lover, see pages 130–135.)

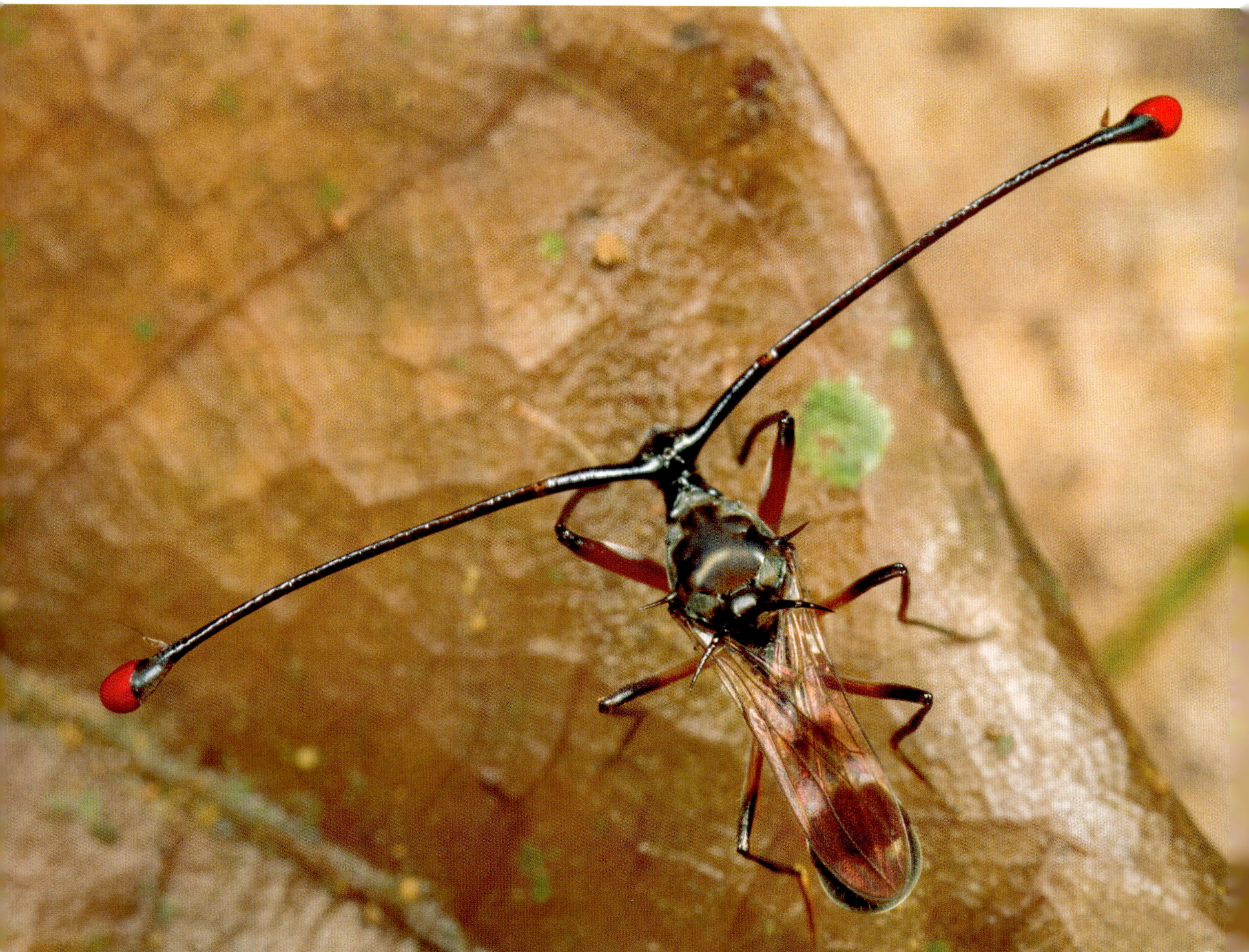

This stalk-eyed fly from Borneo (*Cyrtodiopsis whitei,* family: Diopsidae) has visual receptors on long stalks on either side of its head, like a hammerhead shark.

© Mark Moffett/Minden Pictures/Biosphoto

INTRODUCTION

When our editors at Delachaux et Niestlé first suggested we put together a book of insect portraits, we were left with some tricky questions. Which species should we include? Why them and not others? How do we get novice readers interested in entomology? And how do we convey the vast diversity of the insect world, with over a million described species? Is it possible, in only a couple hundred pages, to get across the profound mystery of these creatures, which are so small they often go completely unnoticed . . . and yet are so indispensable, not to mention sublime?

Whatever we decided, we were bound to be frustrated. Our editorial guidelines limited us to presenting a handful of insects that were emblematic of their world, their connections to humans, and the urgent need to protect them. Painful choices had to be made. So we consulted with other entomologists, drew up several lists, faced up to our own biases, and tried to apply some degree of fairness. Nothing was entirely satisfactory. In the end, we adopted a more personal approach and focused on the species that fascinated us when we were budding naturalists, along with a few that have left their mark on the history of entomology and all humankind. Most of all, we wanted to fill these pages with photos and illustrations that will astonish, intrigue, and enchant the reader.

We hope that those of you who already love insects will forgive us for being somewhat arbitrary and incomplete in our selection (and for the many, many portraits that are more like brief sketches) while finding nuggets of more precise information as you leaf through these pages.

Lovers of nature and fine art books will hopefully find something to pique their curiosity or even spark a new passion. And perhaps they may even take a stand for insects one day.

There is one thing we can all agree on: insects are fabulous. Absolutely fabulous.

Denis Richard and Pierre-Olivier Maquart

We would like to thank the entomologists who were kind enough to provide friendly and judicious feedback, as well as those who contributed photographs, many of which are published here for the first time.
This book would not exist without the trust confided in us by Delachaux et Niestlé via our editor, Stéphanie Zweifel, who once again managed to check our ambitions and who patiently stood by us as we drafted these pages. Nor would it exist without our layout artist, Mathilde Delattre-Josse, who brought all this to life.

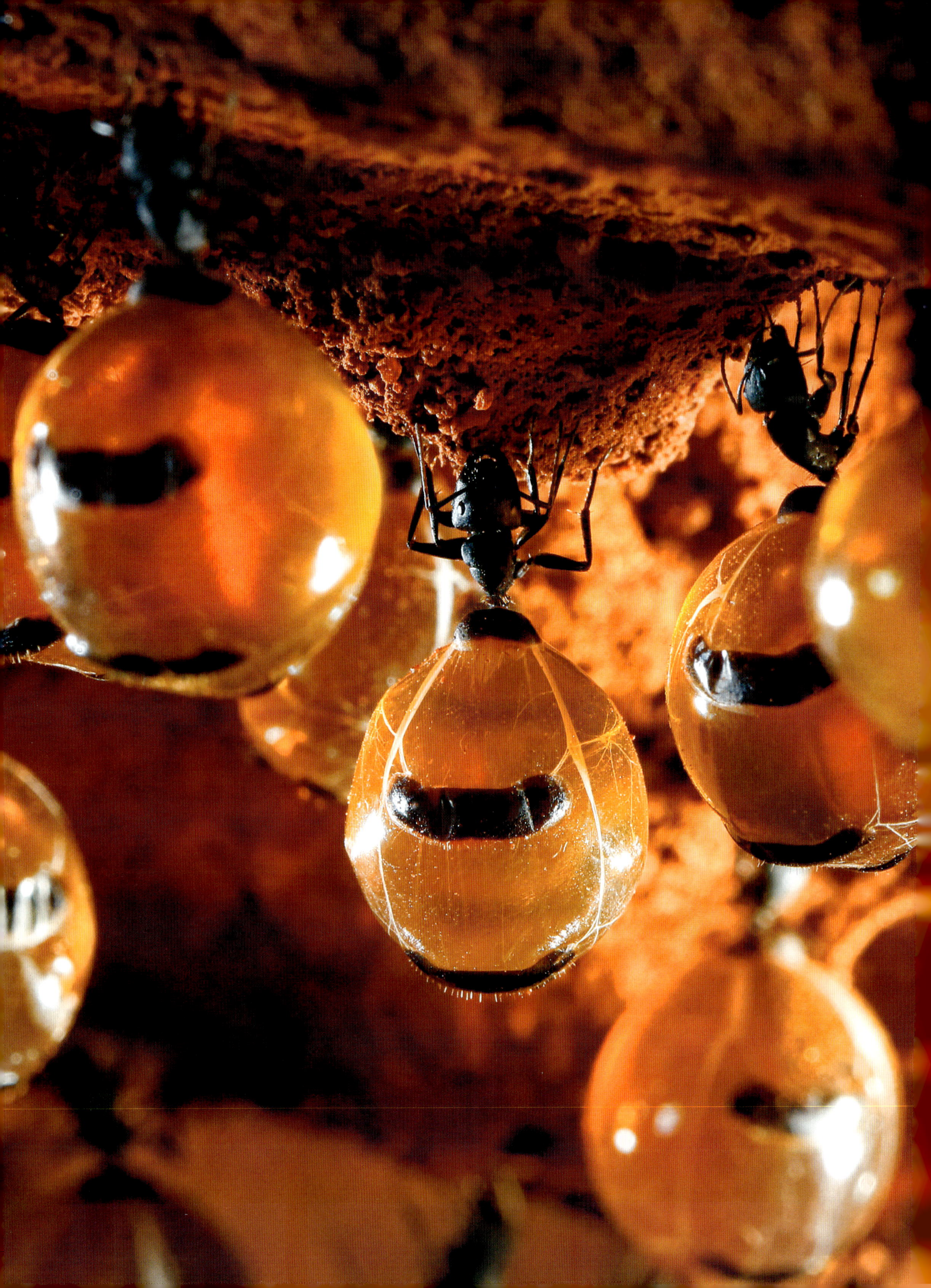

RECORDS AND FEATS

The word "record" might make you think of the largest or heaviest insects, the "mosts" that inspire a lifelong passion in children. But there are other record holders, more discreet but no less astonishing. Some can fly incredible distances, jump to dizzying heights in proportion to their size, or run at unbelievable speeds. Others achieve a different kind of feat: surviving the extreme conditions in which they live. After all, 400 million years of evolution have enabled insects to colonize almost every corner of the Earth. Whether easy to please or highly selective when it comes to habitat, insects face diverse challenges and play an essential role in maintaining ecological balance. They are tireless pollinators, recyclers of plant and animal matter, soil aerators, and, of course, a vital link in the food chain, both as prey for countless predators and as predators themselves. Last but not least, they are an endless source of inspiration for human engineers, providing natural models for new biomaterials, technologies, and pharmaceuticals.

Honeypot ants have developed a truly unique way of surviving drought. Some members of the colony act as "living larders" and spend their lives hanging by their back legs from the walls and ceiling of a storage chamber. They fill their abdomens with sugary liquid collected by workers and feed it back to those same workers when food is scarce during the dry season. This photo of ants in the genus *Myrmecocystus* was taken in a semiarid region of Australia.

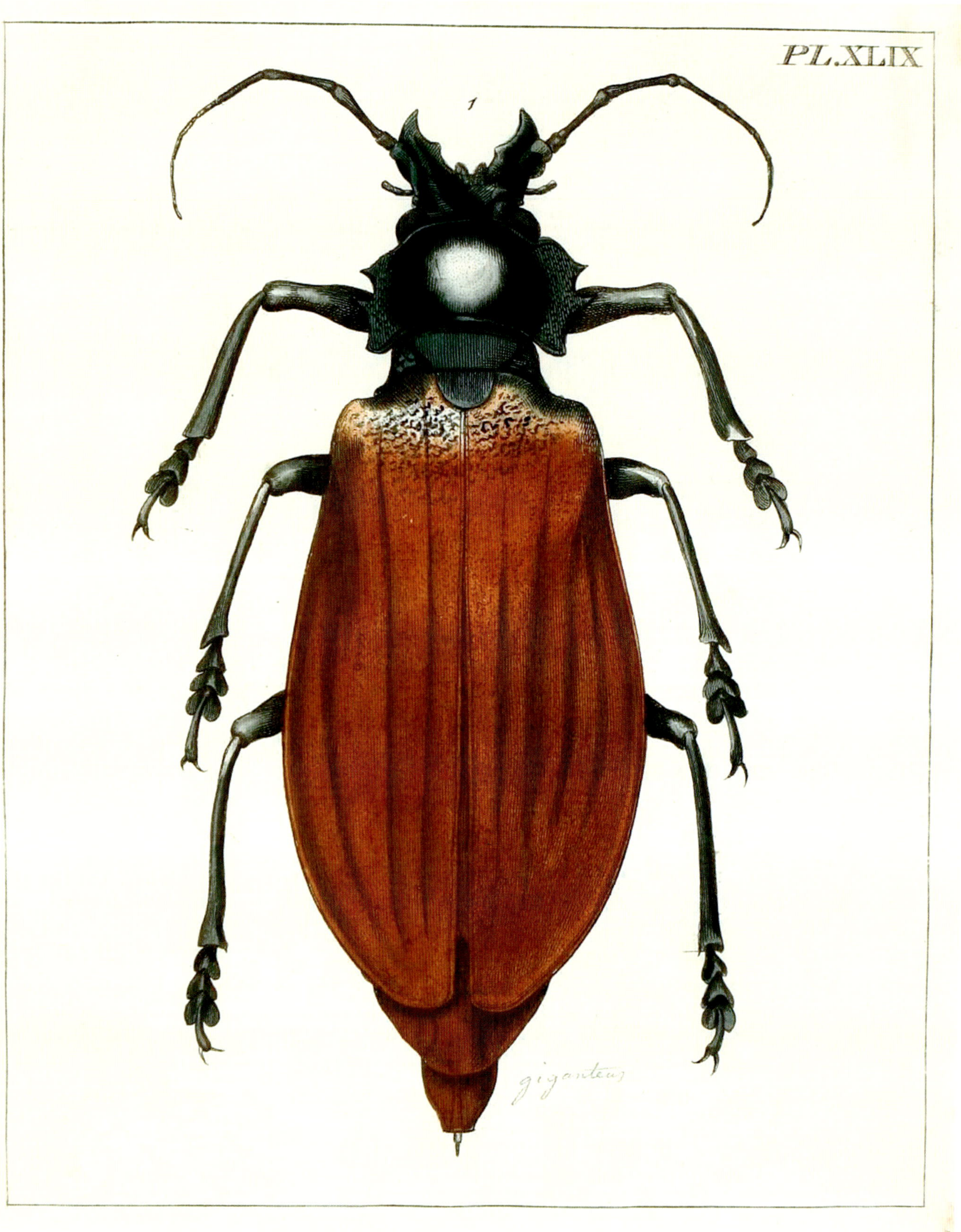

This print of a female titan beetle first appeared in *The Natural History and Antiquities of Selborne*, a major work published in 1789 by the English naturalist Gilbert White (1720–1793).

© Gilbert White

THE TITAN OF THE AMAZON

TITANUS GIGANTEUS
(COLEOPTERA: CERAMBYCIDAE)

This enormous beetle, first described by Carl Linnaeus in 1771 based on a specimen of unknown origin, has long been something of a mystery. Despite its incredible size, and the relative frequency with which it has been observed, its life cycle is still not fully understood.

In centuries past, the rare titan beetle would be found washed up on the banks of the Rio Negro, a tributary of the Amazon, or in the stomachs of large fish caught near Manaus, Brazil. British entomologist Henry Walter Bates (1825–1892) managed to collect only a few damaged specimens during his expedition to the Amazon in the mid-nineteenth century. Up until the Second World War, there were at most thirty specimens in collections worldwide. (An intact titan beetle was worth the equivalent of about $10,500 at the time!) The species became known to the general public thanks to a 1959 *National Geographic* article by American biologist Paul A. Zahl (1910–1985). Zahl had discovered that the males were attracted to light and so was able to capture sixteen in just a few days in the Serra do Navio region of the Brazilian Amazon two years earlier. His expedition proved not only that titan beetles were far from rare, but also that the adults—which are strictly nocturnal, active between midnight and three to four a.m.— live for only a few weeks during the wet season. They do not feed, and die once they have used up the reserves consumed during their larval stage.

Starting in the 1980s, collectors were able to purchase male specimens caught in the old-growth equatorial rainforests of Brazil, Peru, Bolivia, Colombia, Ecuador, Surinam, and French Guiana. Females were harder to find, as they are not attracted to light. While "small" specimens (70–100 millimeters) were relatively common, the largest males (over 150 millimeters, the largest authenticated specimen coming in at a whopping 167 millimeters) remained rare and highly desirable. With passionate collectors willing to pay hundreds of dollars to acquire one, titan beetle hunting was big business. However, English entomologist Max Barclay explains that in French Guiana, at least, the specimens trade did not harm the forest or the animals that call it home. Because female titan beetles were virtually impossible to

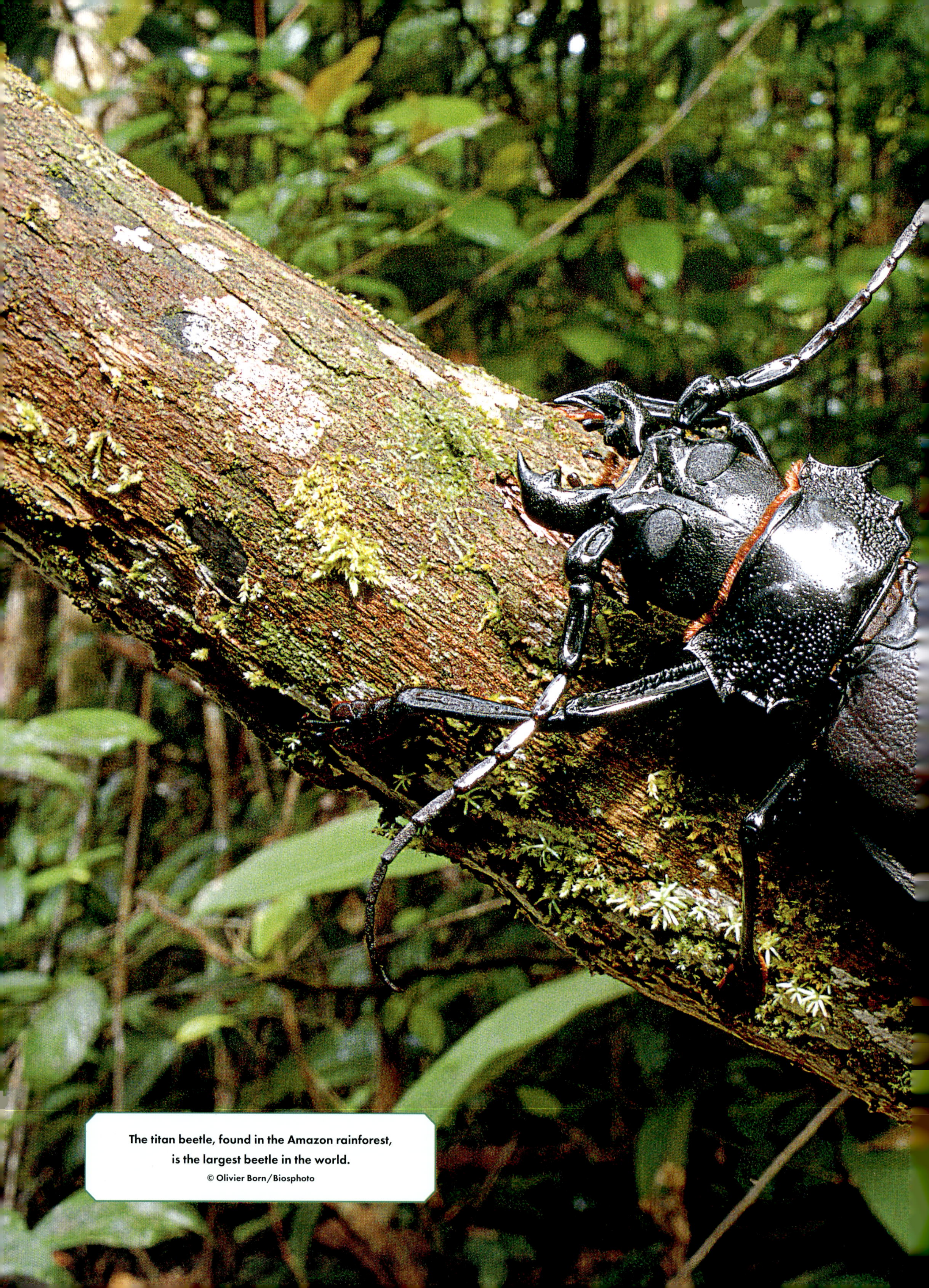

The titan beetle, found in the Amazon rainforest, is the largest beetle in the world.

© Olivier Born/Biosphoto

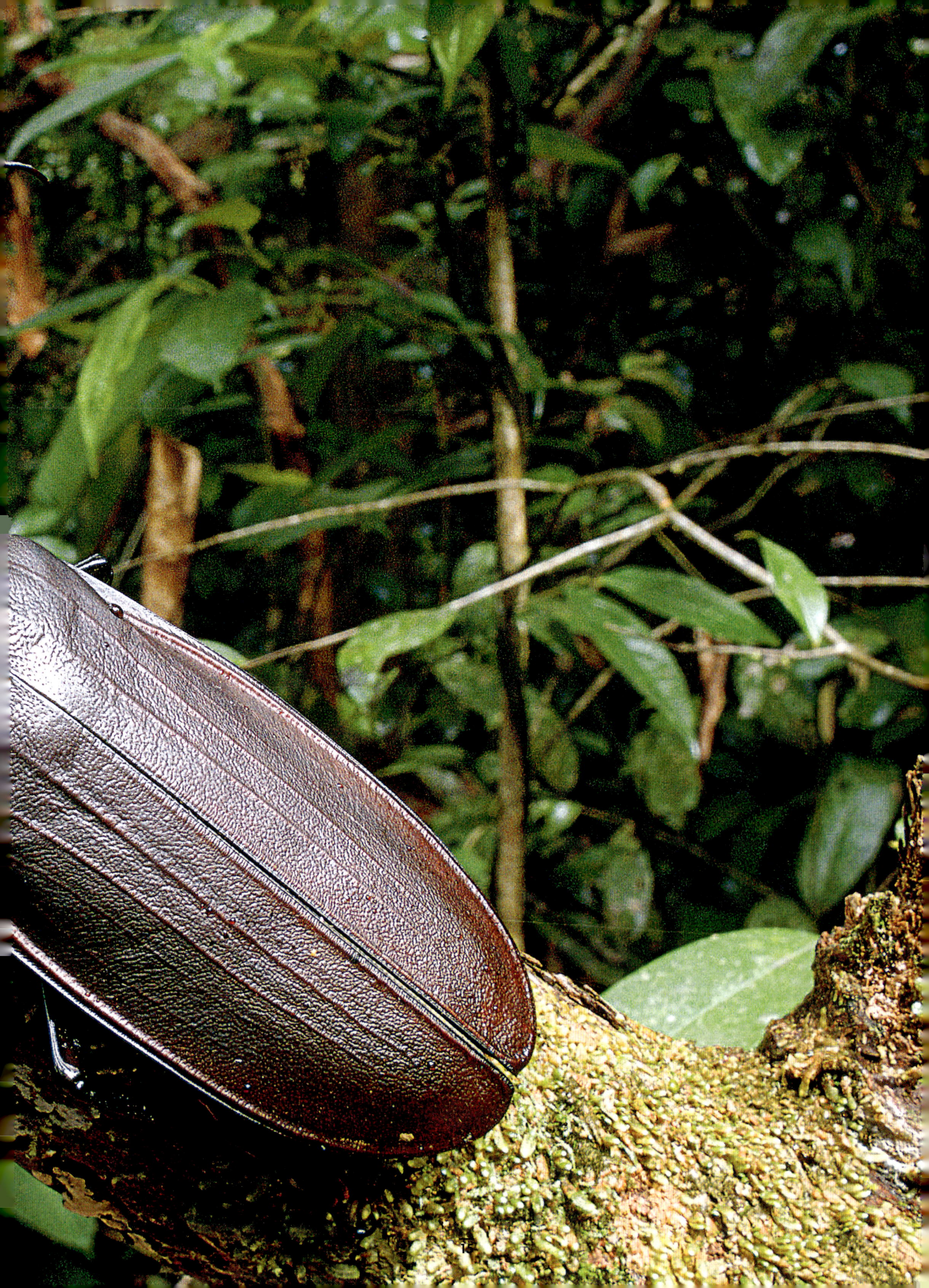

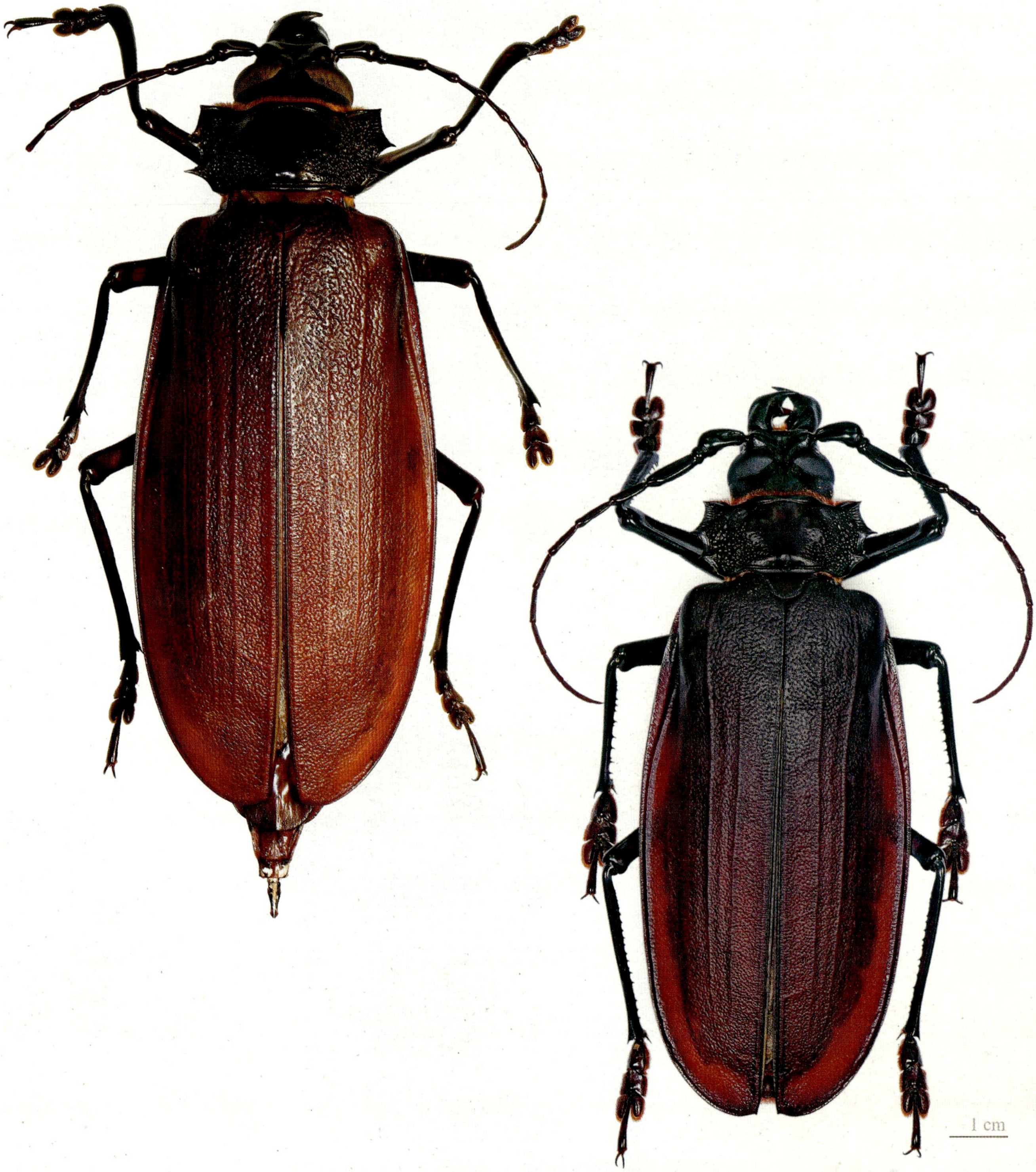

Female titan beetles fly rarely, if at all, and are not attracted to light, which makes them difficult to collect. They probably spend most of their lives laying eggs in the underground parts of the largest trees in old-growth forests. As shown in the illustration above, females (left) have wider elytra than males (right) and no spines on their tibia.

capture, only males were collected. That made the trade sustainable, since a single male fertilizes several females immediately upon reaching adulthood.

Interest from collectors has not stripped these singular and ancient beetles of their mystery. Their life cycle remains unknown, though it is probably similar to that of other large Amazonian longhorn beetles. Titan beetle larvae have never been observed but must be enormous, given the size of the adults. They likely feed on moldy, decomposing wood underground, which would explain why no adult-sized exit holes have been found in tree trunks. (Many adults have also been found with their elytra—the hardened forewings —covered in mud, suggesting they emerged from wet earth.)

In addition to large-scale collection from the remaining wild South American populations, these giant beetles are also threatened by mass deforestation (sometimes carried out with government approval), wildfires, and human incursions into their habitat—an ecological catastrophe that will soon make them much more scarce, or even drive them to extinction.

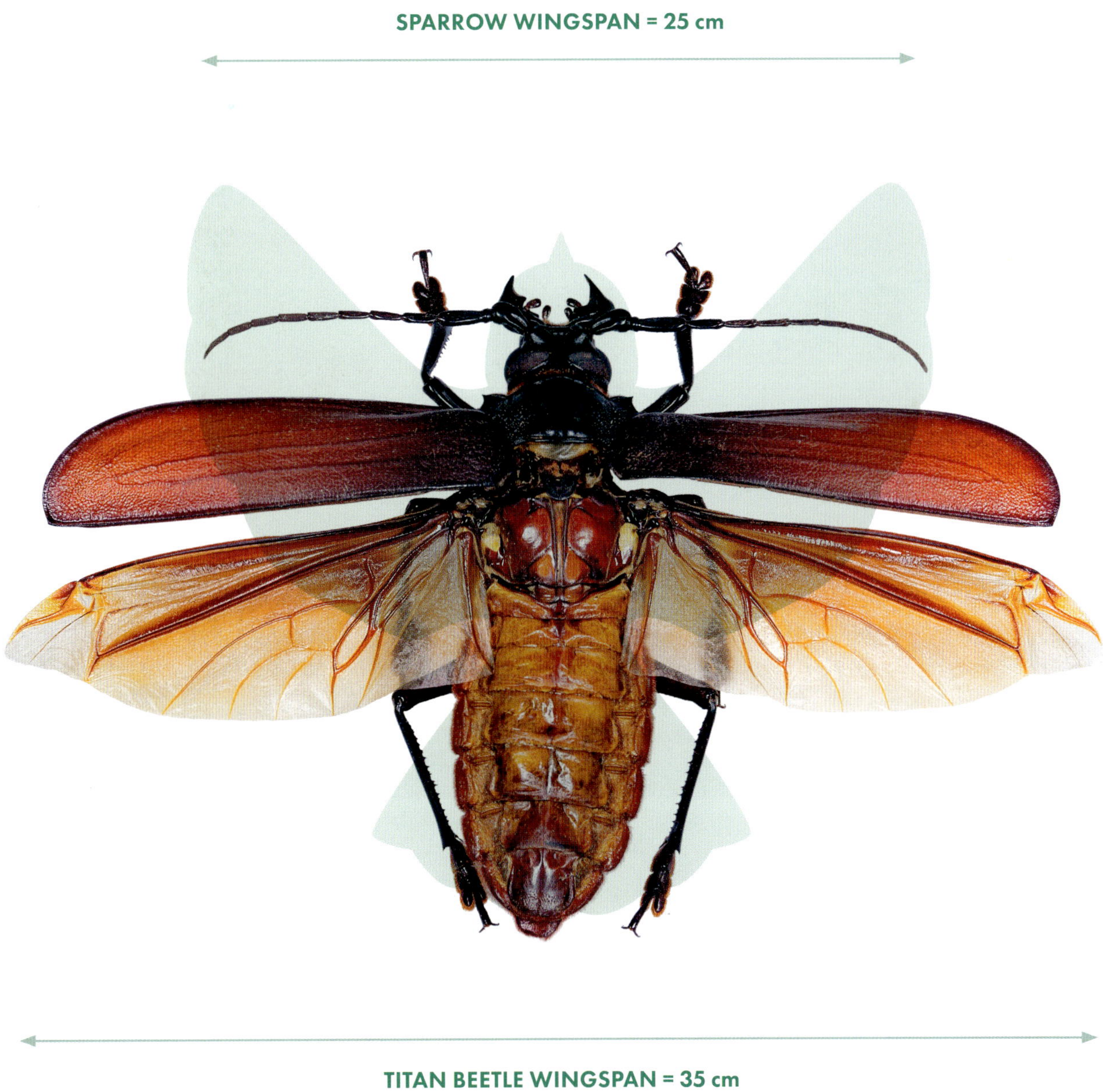

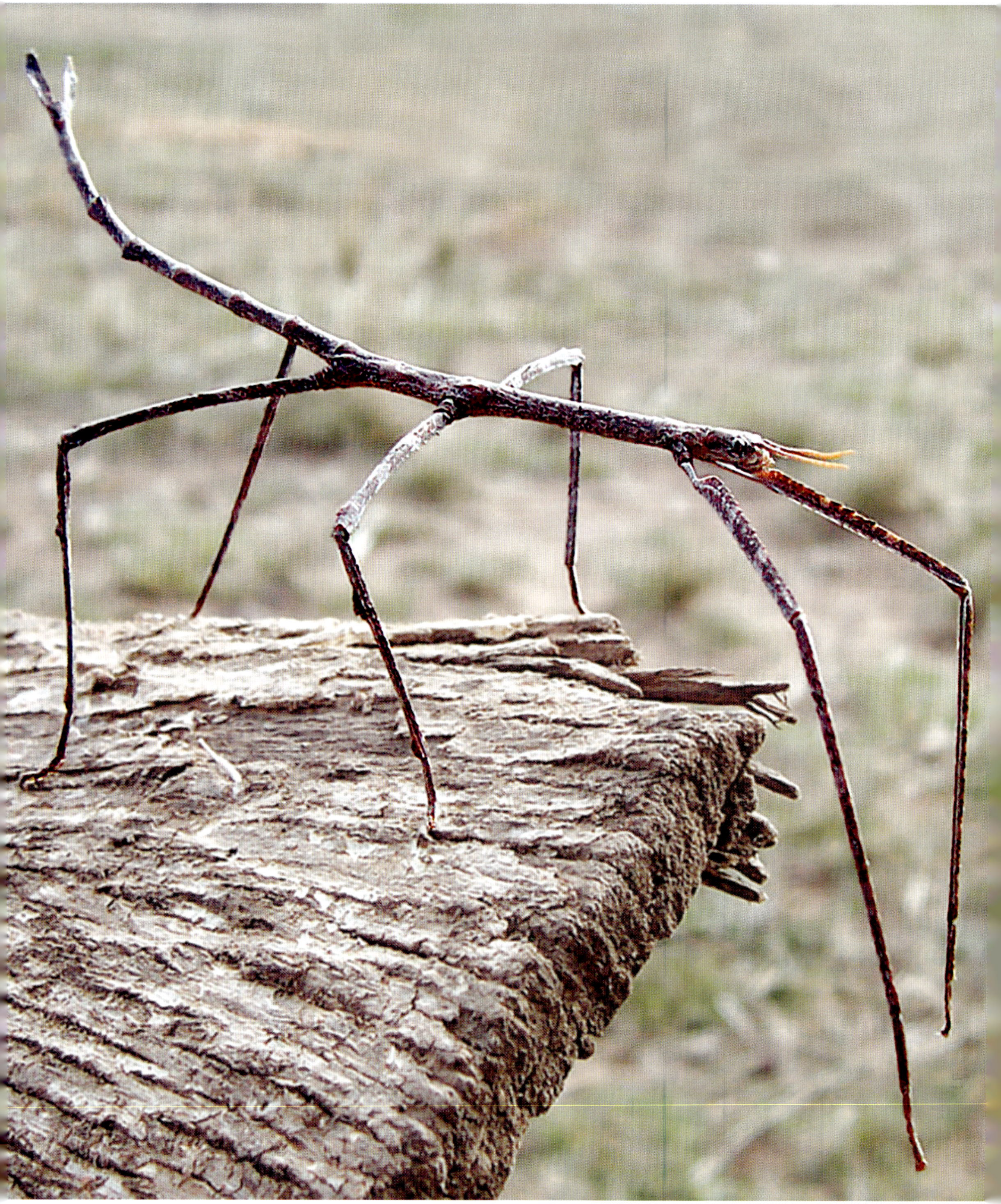

MEET THE MEGASTICK

PHOBAETICUS CHANI

(PHASMATODEA PHASMATIDAE)

Its sticklike body just keeps going, like a stalk of bamboo. *Phobaeticus chani* certainly lives up to its common name: Chan's megastick. This giant insect was discovered in 1989 by a farmer working near Ulu Moyog village in Sabah state, Borneo, who handed it over to a Malaysian naturalist, Chan Chew Lun. When describing the species in 2008, English entomologist Philip E. Bragg named it in honor of Chan. It is the longest insect to be scientifically described.

Judge for yourself: this stick insect looks more like a bamboo shoot than its smaller cousins. The largest collected specimen measures 56.7 centimeters long, if you include the six long legs that sprout off its body like twigs. With a body length of 35.7 centimeters, it beat the previous record holder for longest insect, *Phobaeticus kirbyi* (a close cousin that also lives in the forests of Borneo), by 3 centimeters.

Little is known about the megastick's ecology or biology, as only three specimens have ever been captured in their remote forest habitat. Even observing them is extremely difficult: like other giant stick insects, they are nocturnal and hang immobile from branches when disturbed, making use of their excellent camouflage. Their eggs, like those of some other stick insects, have little winglike fins that probably allow them to scatter in the wind as soon as they are laid, allowing for better dispersal than the sedentary parents could achieve.

Chan's megastick, native to Borneo, was described in 2008.

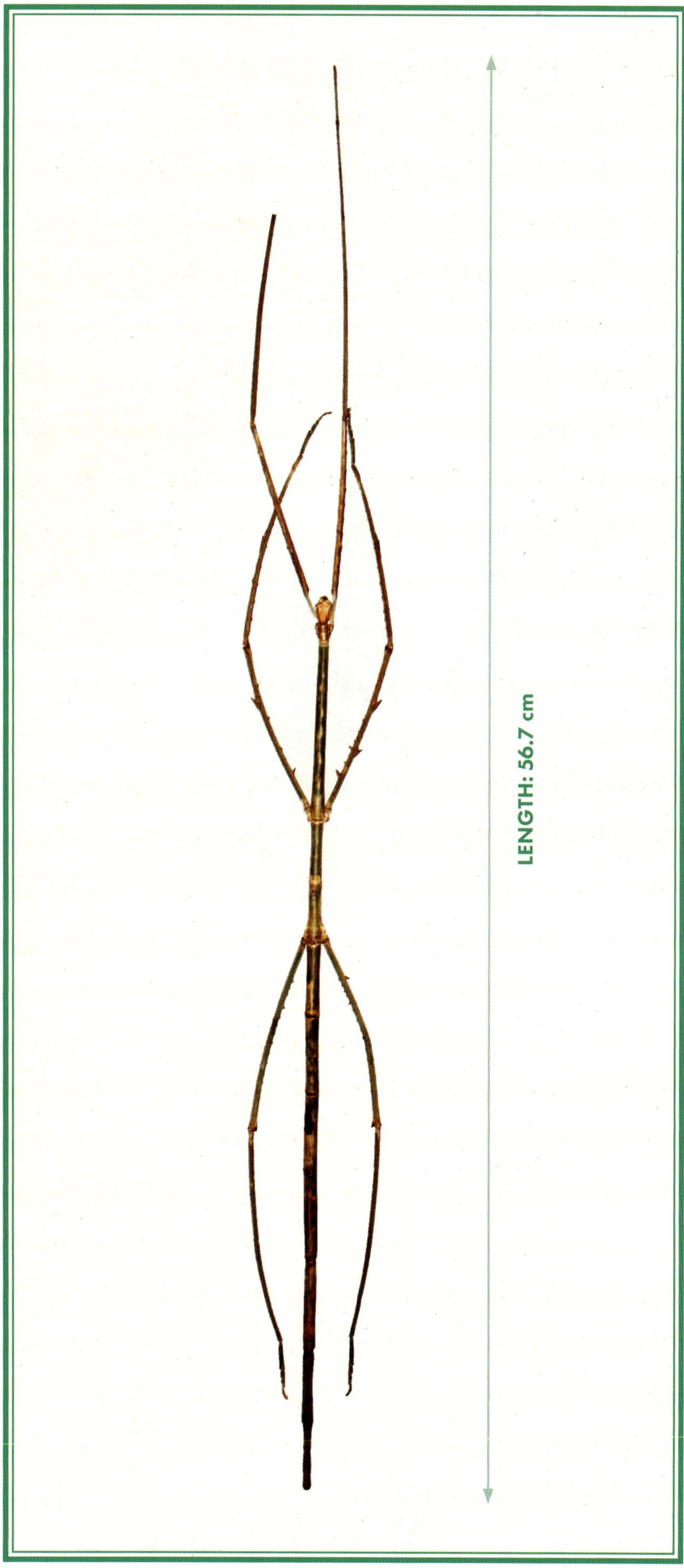

Phobaeticus chani is over half a meter long!

This picture with a human hand for scale is worth a thousand words.

Phobaeticus kirbyi, a close cousin of *P. chani*, is another giant stick insect from Borneo.

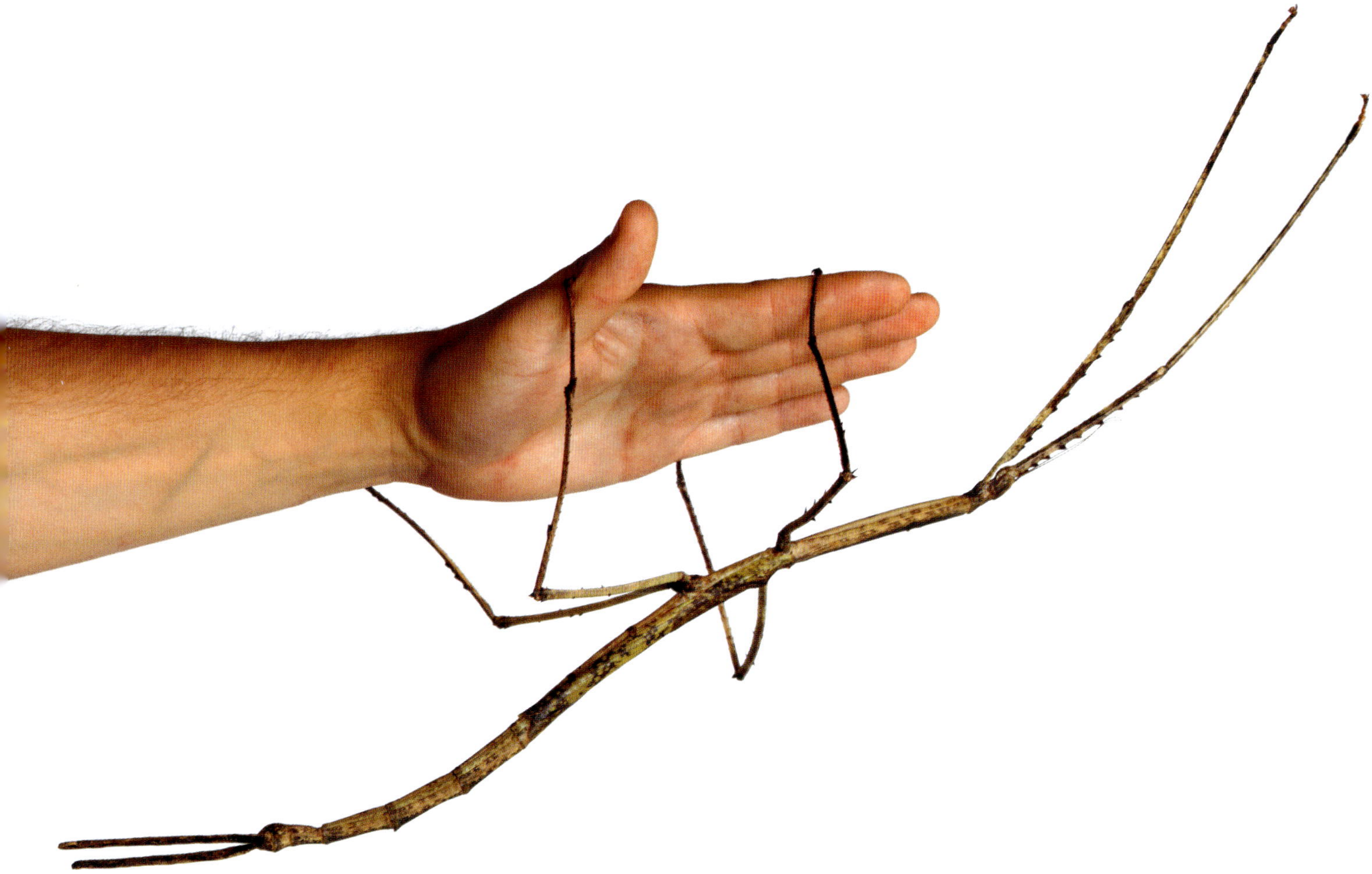

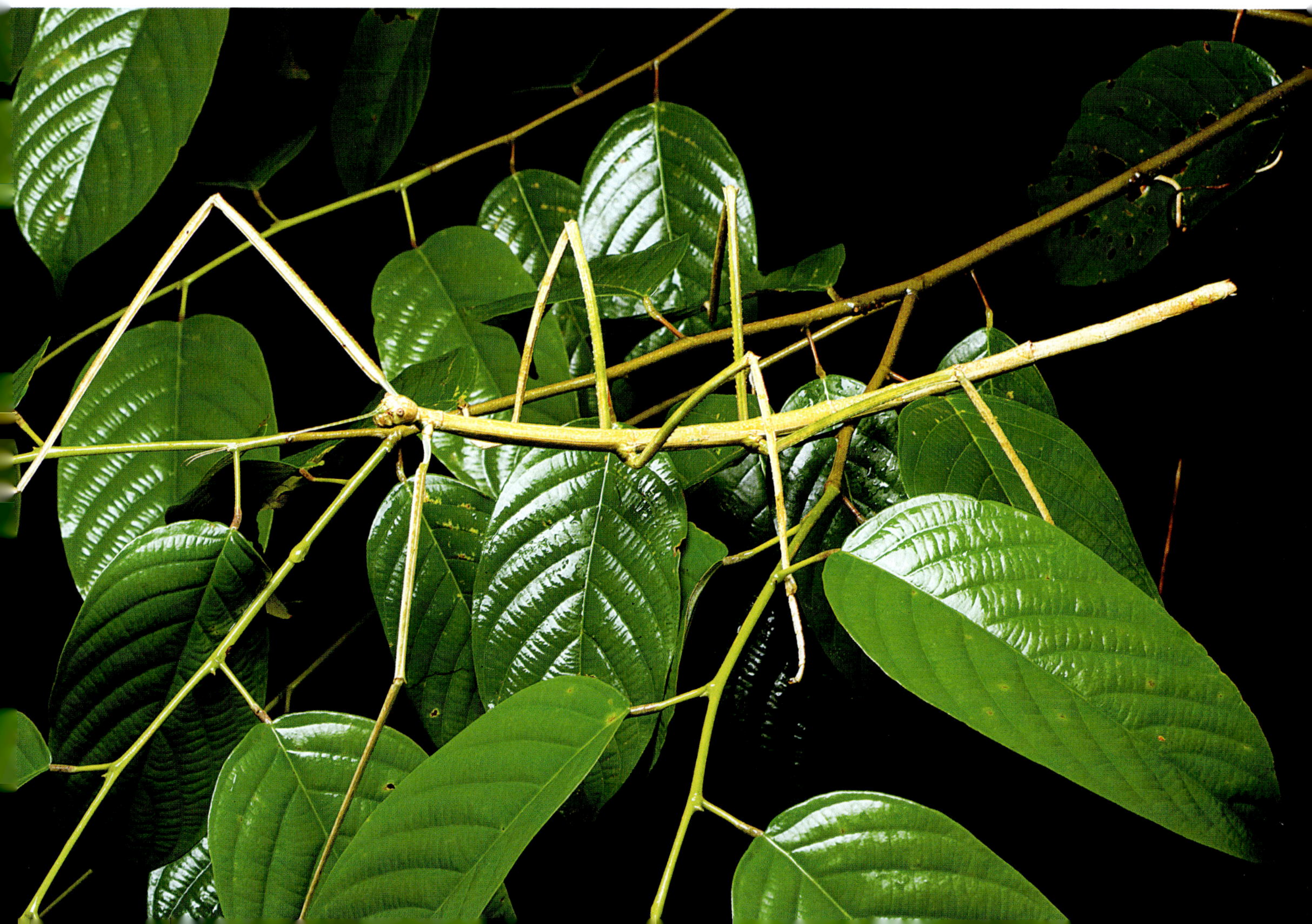

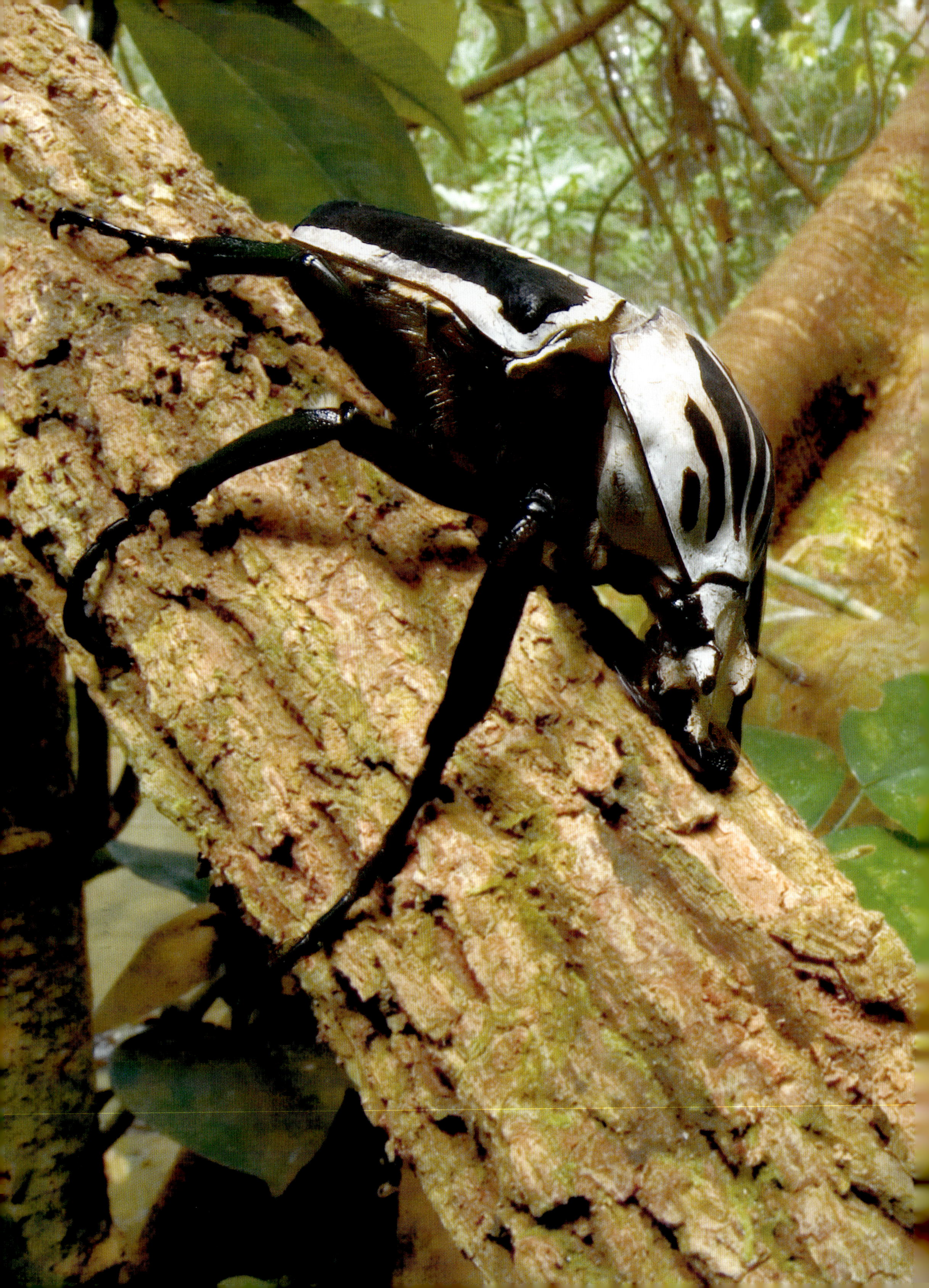

AN AFRICAN GOLIATH

GOLIATHUS GOLIATUS

(COLEOPTERA: SCARABAEIDAE)

In the eighteenth century, the captain of an English merchant ship in the Gabon Estuary spotted an enormous scarab beetle floating down the muddy river toward the Gulf of Guinea. He managed to fish it out . . . and found that it was nearly 10 centimeters long, one of the largest insects he had ever seen!

The captain gave the beetle to David Ogilvie, a ship's surgeon, who preserved it in alcohol and brought it back to Europe with him. The year was 1766, during the period known as the Enlightenment, when educated elites were captivated by naturalists' discoveries. The 96-millimeter-long specimen ended up in the collection of William Hunter (1718–1783), who made it the centerpiece of his cabinet of curiosities. It would long remain unique. In 1770, Dru Drury (1725–1803, a wealthy silversmith with a passion for entomology, used an illustration of the specimen by engraver and color theorist Moses Harris (1731–1785) in the first volume of his *Illustrations of Natural History*. The illustration was included without naming the beetle, and no credit was given to Hunter—as the latter would later complain. Carl Linnaeus described the species in 1771, based on the engraving in Drury's *Illustrations*, and gave it the name *Scarabaeus goliatus*, but Jean-Baptiste de Lamarck moved it to the genus *Goliathus* in 1801. Hunter's specimen is now conserved at the University of Glasgow. A similar beetle was found in 1775 by British naturalist Henry Smeathman (1742–1786) during an expedition to Sierra Leone funded by Drury and naturalist John Fothergill (1712–1780). Drury mistakenly took this second specimen for a color variant of the same species. In 1837, however, it was described as a new species: *Goliathus regius*, the royal goliath beetle.

The enormous goliath beetles of sub-Saharan Africa have attracted lovers of natural curiosities since the eighteenth century. This male *Goliathus regius* was photographed in Guinea.

© Piotr Naskrecki/Minden pictures/Biosphoto

Goliathus goliatus specimens remained extremely rare for nearly a century, making them all the more valuable to collectors. In the early nineteenth century, only a handful were held in collections. That number did not rise until the 1870s, when insect hunting in the African rainforest intensified as European colonists and missionaries began to take an interest.

There are five species of goliath beetle, all of them striking in size and color, which can vary greatly among individuals. They are cousins of June beetles and rose chafers. The largest specimens of *Goliathus goliatus* and *Goliathus regius* are up to 11 centimeters long.

The males are territorial and use their forelegs and Y-shaped horns to fight off rivals. They are

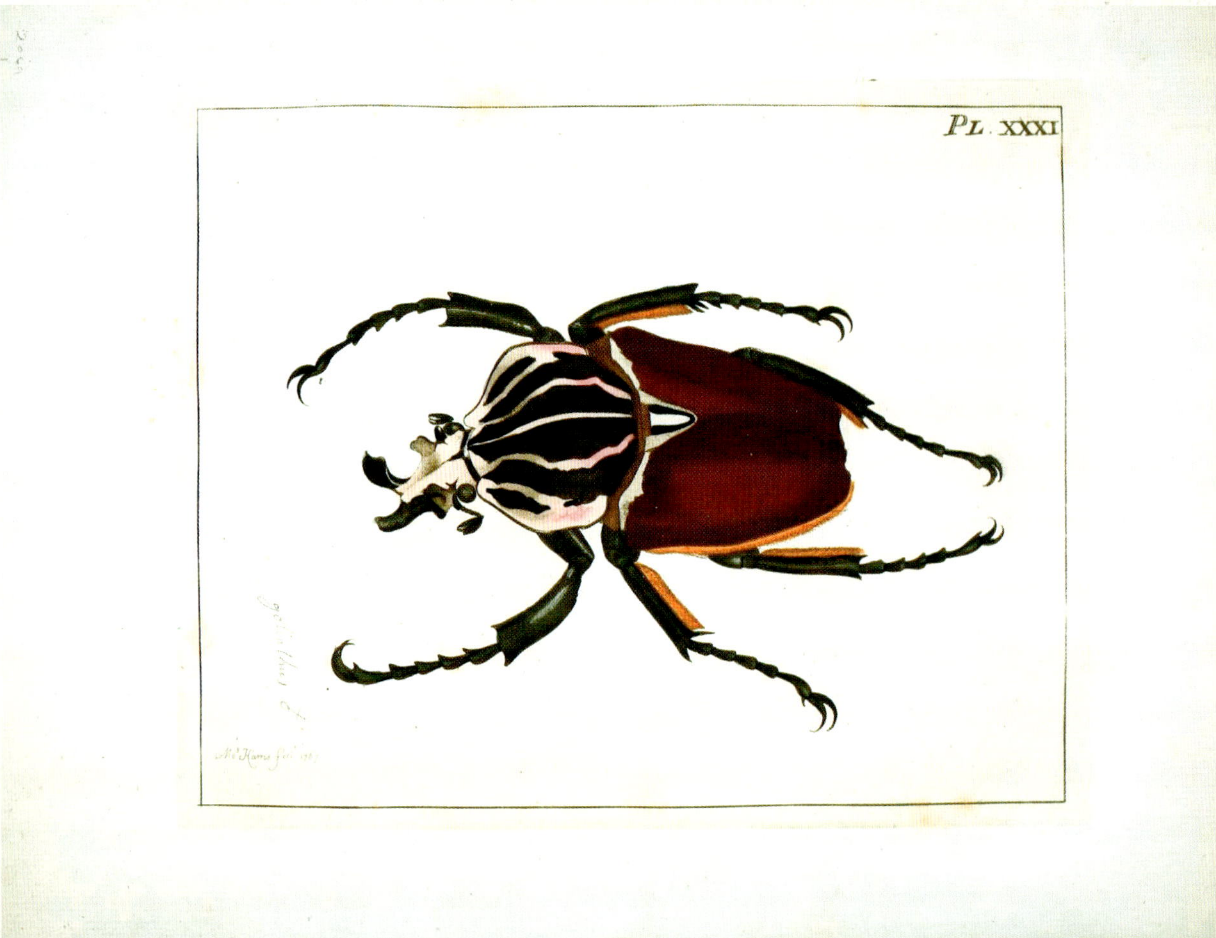

In 1767, the engraver Moses Harris made a stealthy study of the goliath beetle specimen belonging to William Hunter while it was on loan to English naturalist Emanuel Mendez da Costa (1717–1791). Dru Drury bought the engraving from Da Costa while the latter was in debtors' prison and had prints made. He then used the image in his *Illustrations of Natural History* and gave prints to travelers bound for the Gulf of Guinea with notes like the following, addressed to a ship's captain in 1769: "I find your ship will touch at Princess Island. The enclosed print in the box was taken from an insect, a beetle, found in the River Gabon in Africa. I will beg you to show this print to some of the natives both at Callabar and Princess and if it is possible to get such a one I will entreat you to do so."

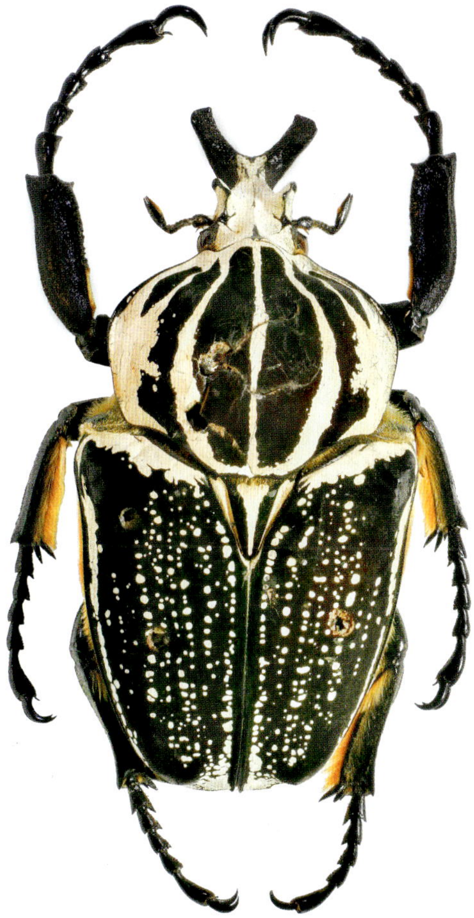

This *Goliathus orientalis* specimen is held by the Natural History Museum in London. It was caught mid-flight in the nineteenth century; there are visible holes in its thoracic shield, and a radiograph (below) shows a piece of lead shot still lodged in its body.
© Conrad Gillett

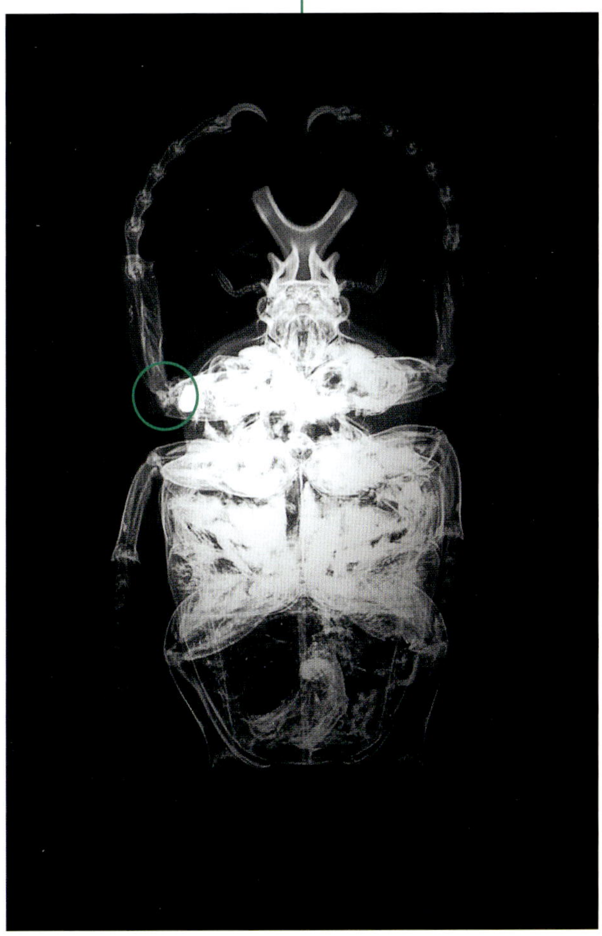

particularly strong and able to carry a load roughly eight hundred times their body weight.

How the larvae develop in the wild is not fully understood—development has only been observed in captive beetles. Females lay thirty to fifty eggs in patches of moist earth, decomposing wood, or forest litter. The larvae feed for several months, until they become the heaviest of all known insects. In fact, the larvae are even bigger than the adults: up to 25 centimeters long and 150 grams! They require protein, so in the wild they likely prey on other beetle larvae that live in the same decomposing organic matter—in stark contrast to other beetle larvae, most of which feed on decaying wood and the fungal organisms that proliferate in it. Metamorphosis takes place inside a protective covering underground. Adults emerge during the wet season, when rainfall softens both the ground and their covering.

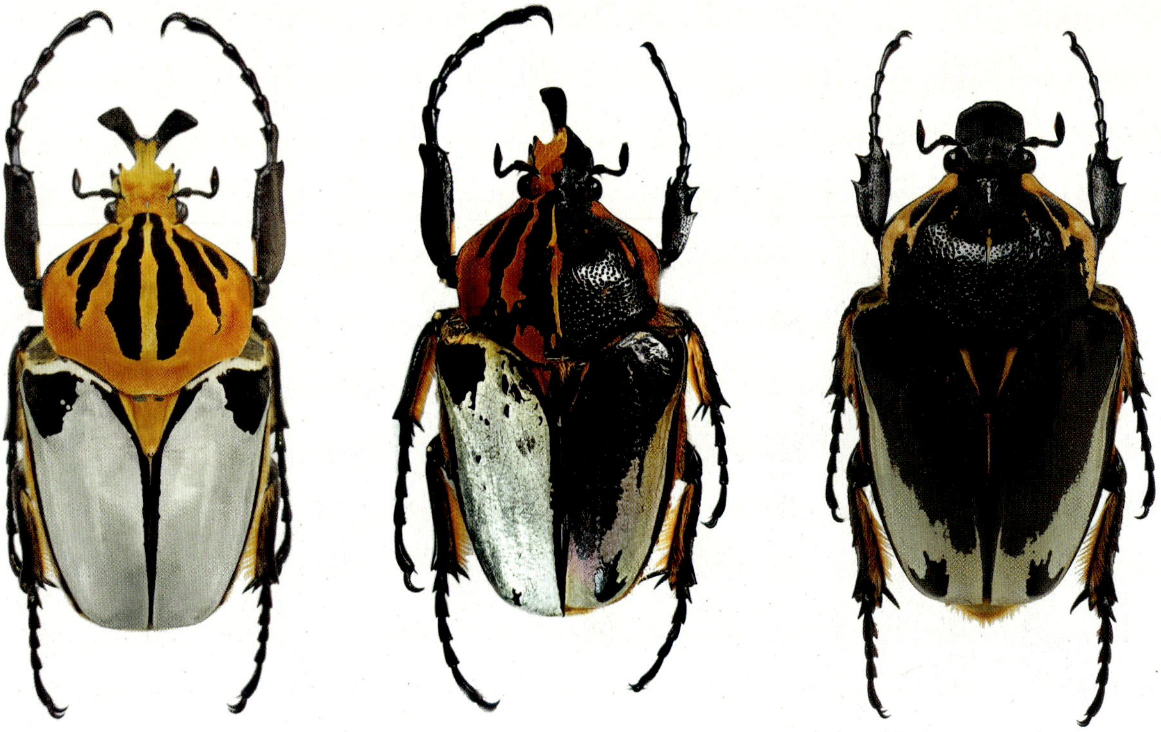

The middle *Goliathus cacicus* specimen is incredibly rare. It is a gynandromorph (its left half is male and its right half is female) caught in Côte d'Ivoire in 1994.

© Mirco Morani

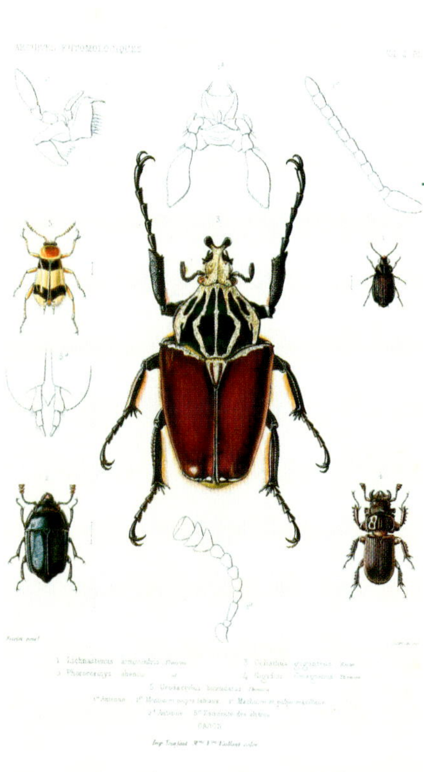

Left: A male *Goliathus goliatus*, native to the forests of Cameroon and Uganda in equatorial Africa. Males measure 50–110 mm long.

© Archives entomologiques, ou, Recueil contenant des illustrations d'insectes nouveaux ou rares, James Thomson, 1858

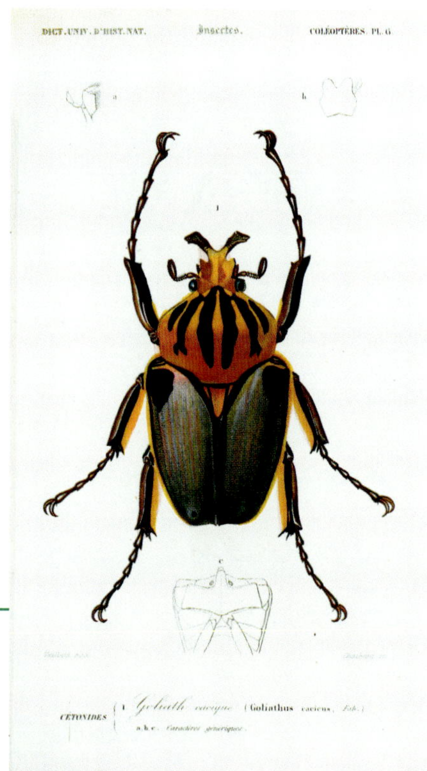

Right: This *Goliathus cacicus*, with its elegant blue and tan markings, lives in the tropical forests of West Africa. The largest males can reach 100 mm long. The species name *cacicus* means "chieftain."

© *Dictionnaire universel d'histoire naturelle*, Charles-Henry d'Orbigny (1806-1876)

During their adult phase, which lasts three to six months, goliath beetles feed on rotten fruit and tree sap. (Their total life cycle lasts nine to twelve months.) They have no particular predators, but may be eaten by some birds and mammals.

These days, hobbyists are able to breed goliath beetles in captivity. Feeding the larvae can be tricky, however, and many die before reaching adulthood. Also, unlike other beetle species raised in captivity, the adults never reach the incredible size of those found in nature. Wild goliath beetles are sadly becoming rare due to deforestation (particularly in Ghana and Côte d'Ivoire) and overhunting. Like titan beetles (see page 13) and members of the genus *Dynastes*, the largest males—measured down to the millimeter—fetch hundreds of dollars on the collectors' market.

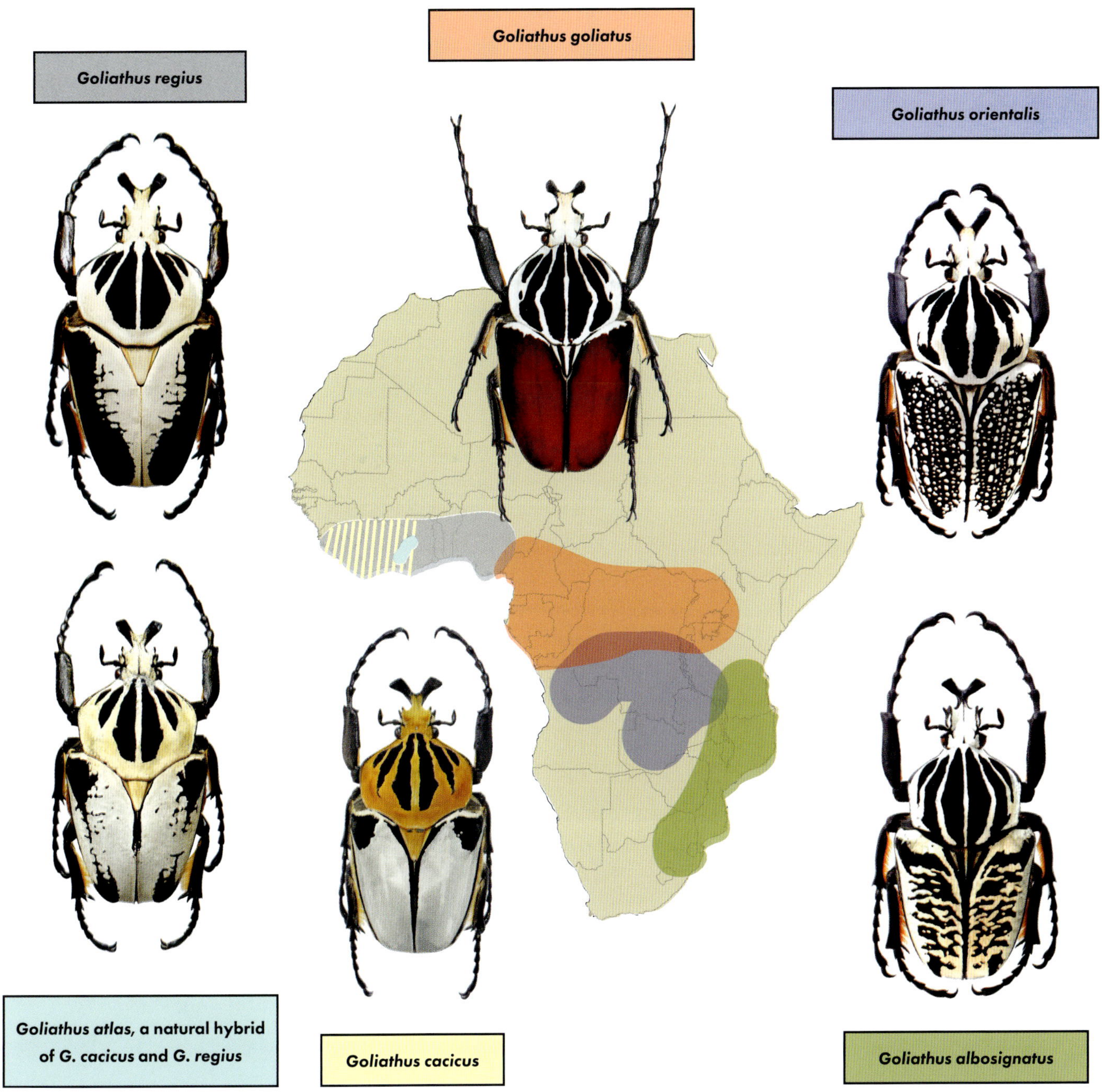

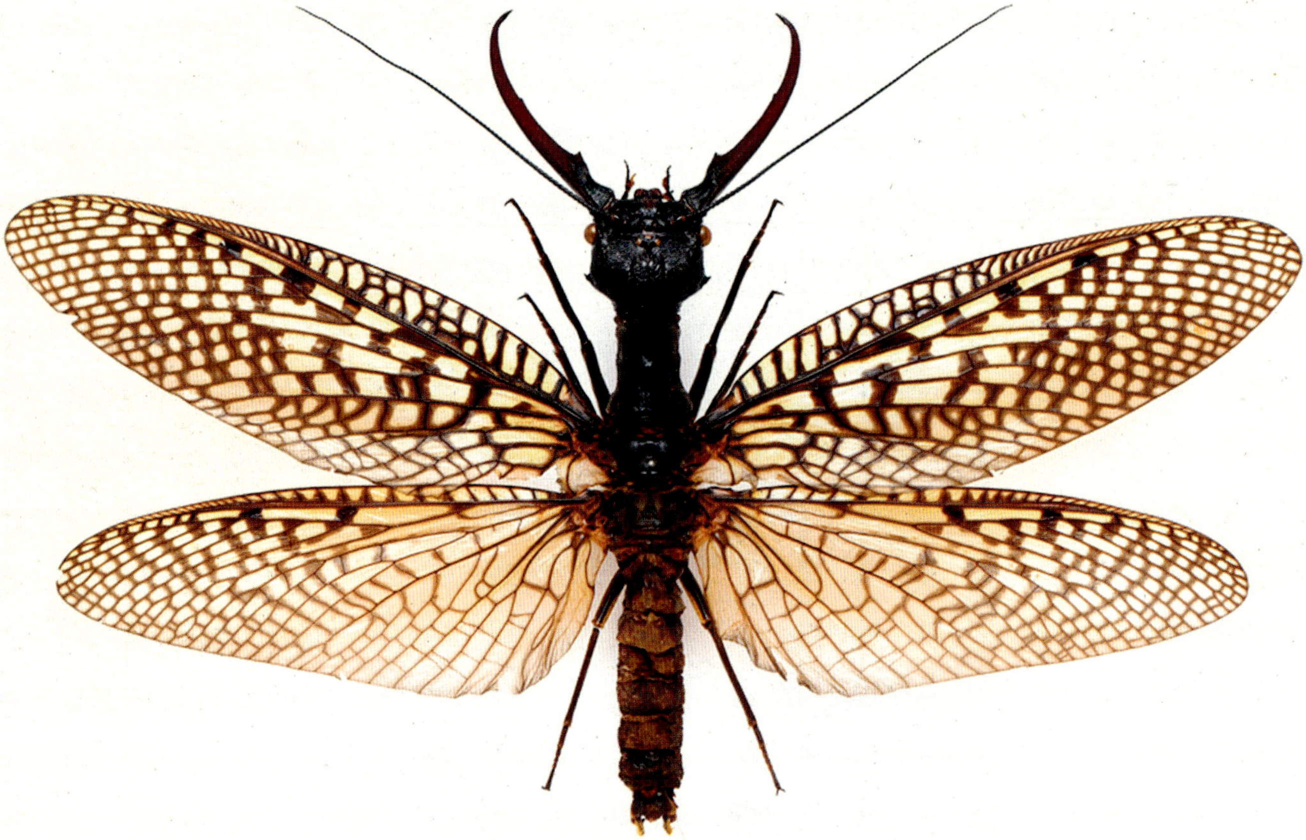

Acanthacorydalis fruhstorferi is as rare as it is impressive,
with a wingspan of over 20 centimeters.

© Seiya Kudo

Males and females look quite different: the male (above) has mandibles that can reach three centimeters long, while the female's (below) are much smaller.

© Insect Museum of West China

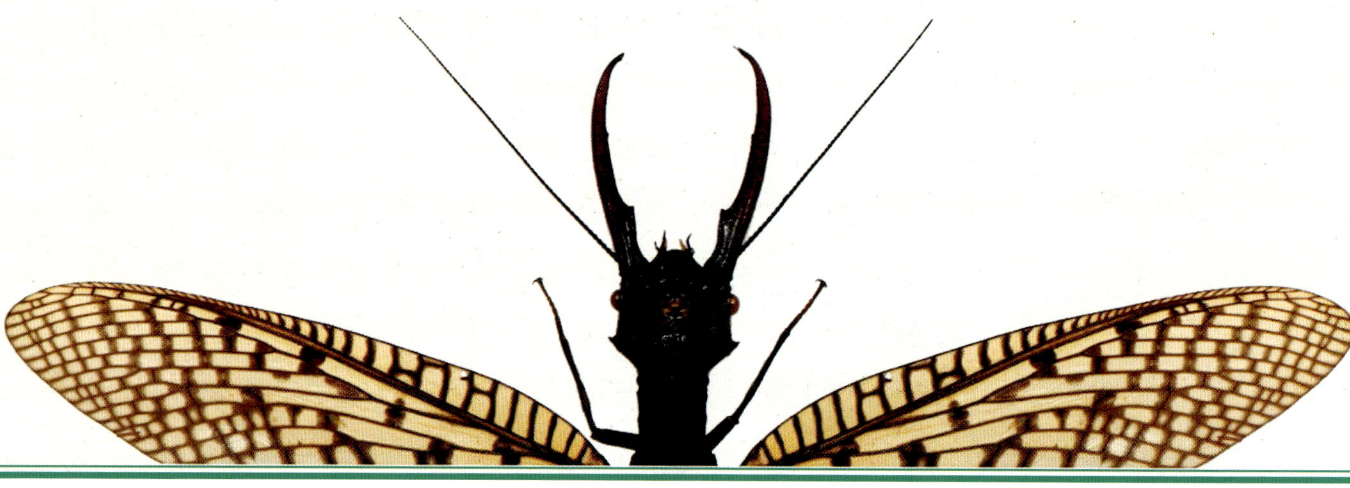

A MONSTER OF THE MICROCOSM

ACANTHACORYDALIS FRUHSTORFERI

(MEGALOPTERA: CORYDALIDAE)

You might find its oversized mandibles unsettling. But while it looks imposing, this "monster" is completely harmless. *Acanthacorydalis fruhstorferi* has the honor of being the largest aquatic insect, with an adult wingspan of nearly 22 centimeters.

This giant species in a small genus—comprising only eight species, all of which live in temperate to chilly continental Asia—was described in 1907 by Dutch entomologist Herman Willem van der Weele (1879–1910) based on a specimen caught in Vietnam. The species' range extends across southern China (Fujian, Guangxi, Guangdong, Guizhou, Jiangxi, Yunnan, and Zhejiang) to northern Vietnam, but it is becoming rarer as the habitat it needs to survive is destroyed.

A. fruhstorferi lays its eggs on rocky mountain streambeds. The larvae can only develop in pristine water that is rich in oxygen, which they absorb using spiracles when on land and gills when underwater. They are highly sensitive to changes in pH levels and are threatened by chemical pollutants in their environment. As larvae, they are voracious predators and feed on other aquatic arthropods, mollusks, small amphibians, and fish larvae. Once

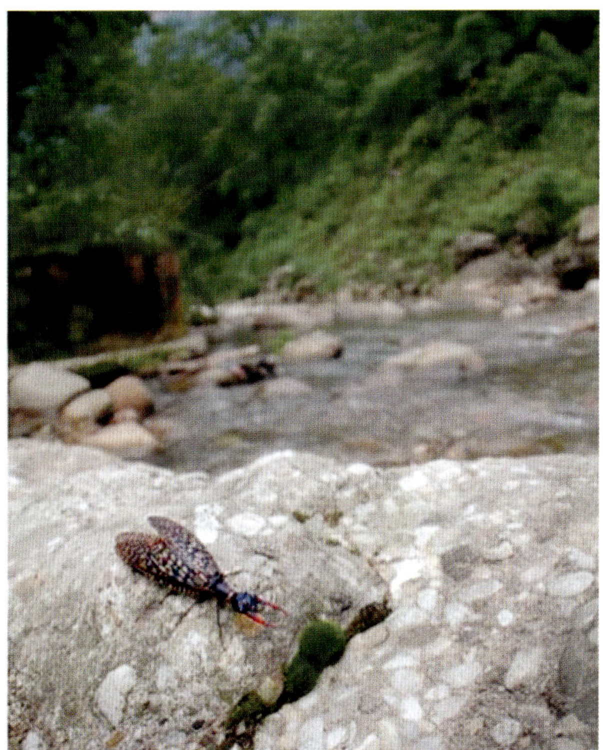

Members of this species never stray far from the streams where they develop as larvae.

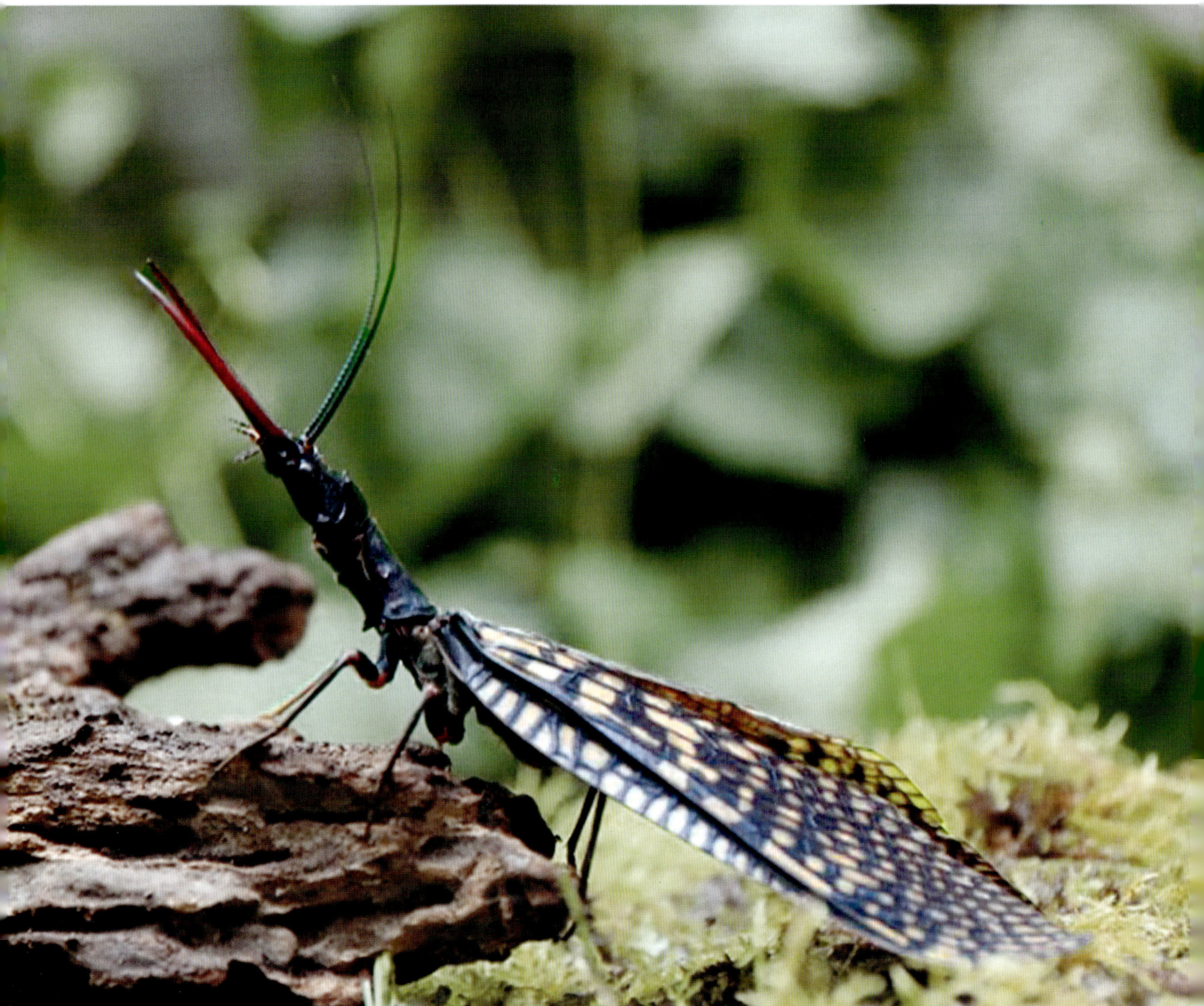

***Acanthacorydalis fruhstorferi* in its natural habitat.**

they become adults, their lives change dramatically. They switch to eating sap from tree wounds but continue to live near running water, and they are sometimes seen flying around lampposts at night. Given the enormous size of this species and its cousins, it is fitting that they belong to the order Megaloptera, which comes from the ancient Greek *mega-* ("large") and *pteryx* ("wing").

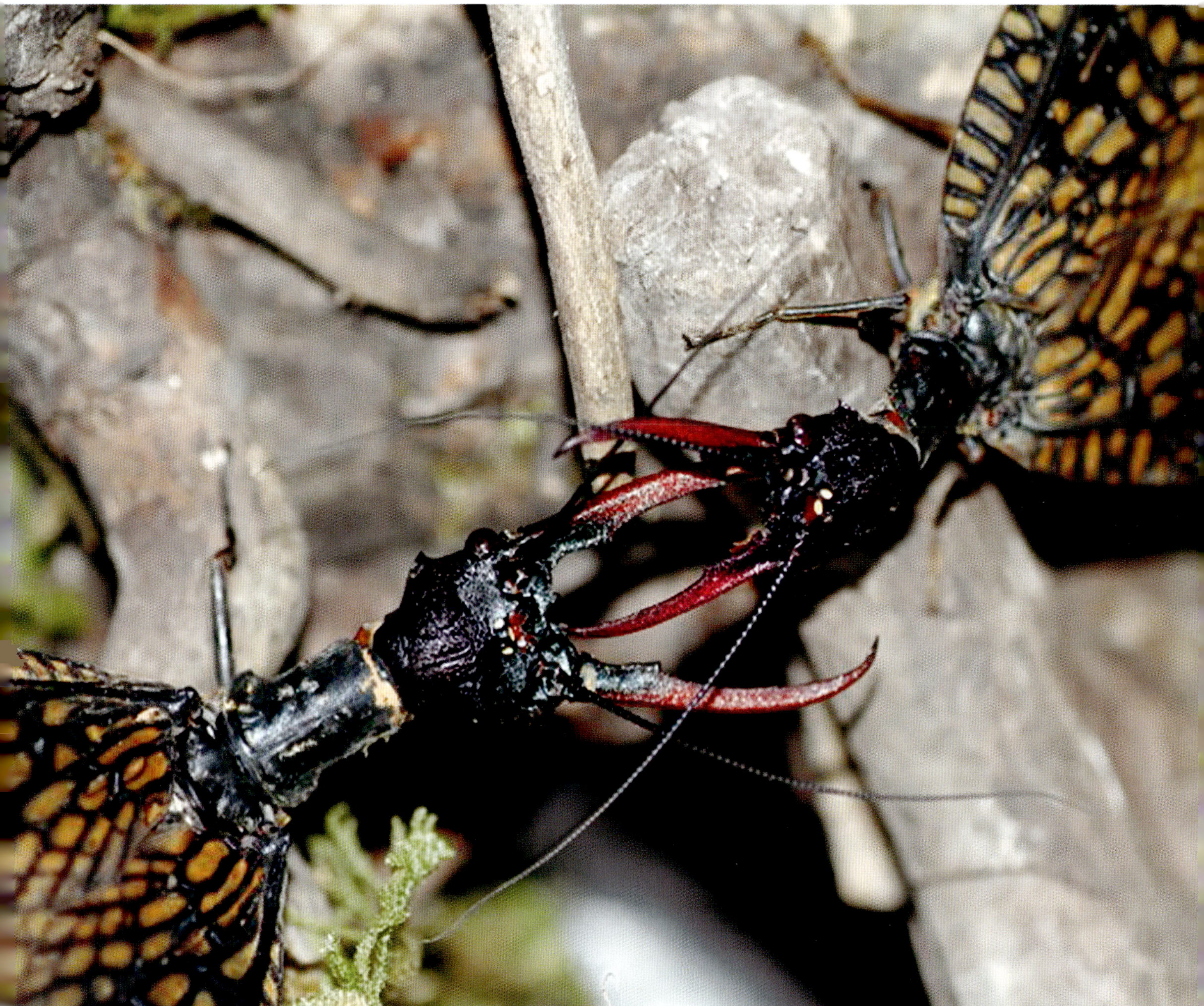

Males compete for the females' attention.

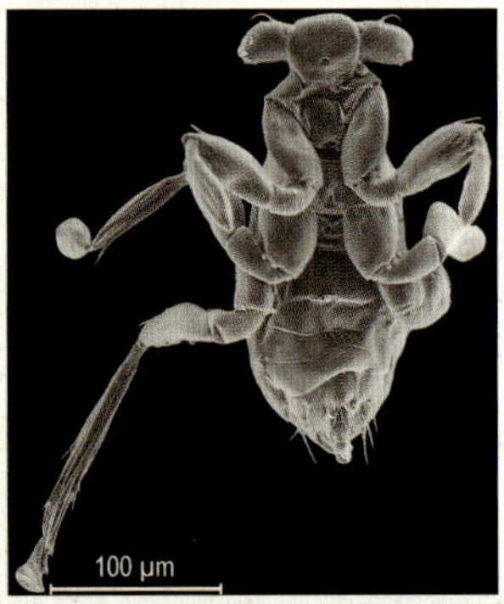

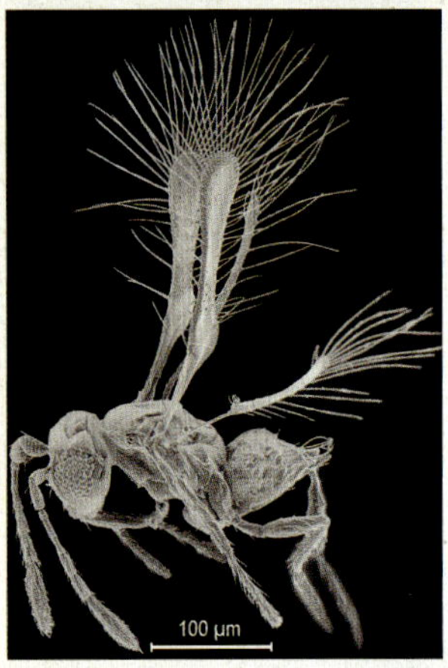

Top: *Dicopomorpha echmepterygis* broke the record previously held by another minuscule wasp, *Megaphragma caribea* (family: Trichogrammatidae), which measures only 170 µm, as does a third near cousin, *Caraphractus cinctus*, a European parasitoid of water beetles in the genus *Dytiscus*.

Center: Have you heard of *Kikiki*? This tiny wasp, also in the family Mymaridae, has been found in Hawaii, Costa Rica, and Trinidad. It was first described in 2000 and, at 190–330 µm, it was the smallest flying insect known to science until 2019. Its name is Hawaiian for "tiny bit," and it is closely related to the 250-µm *Tinkerbella nana* from Costa Rica.

Bottom: This composite image shows the relative size of some of the smallest known insects compared to an amoeba (right) and a paramecium (center bottom).

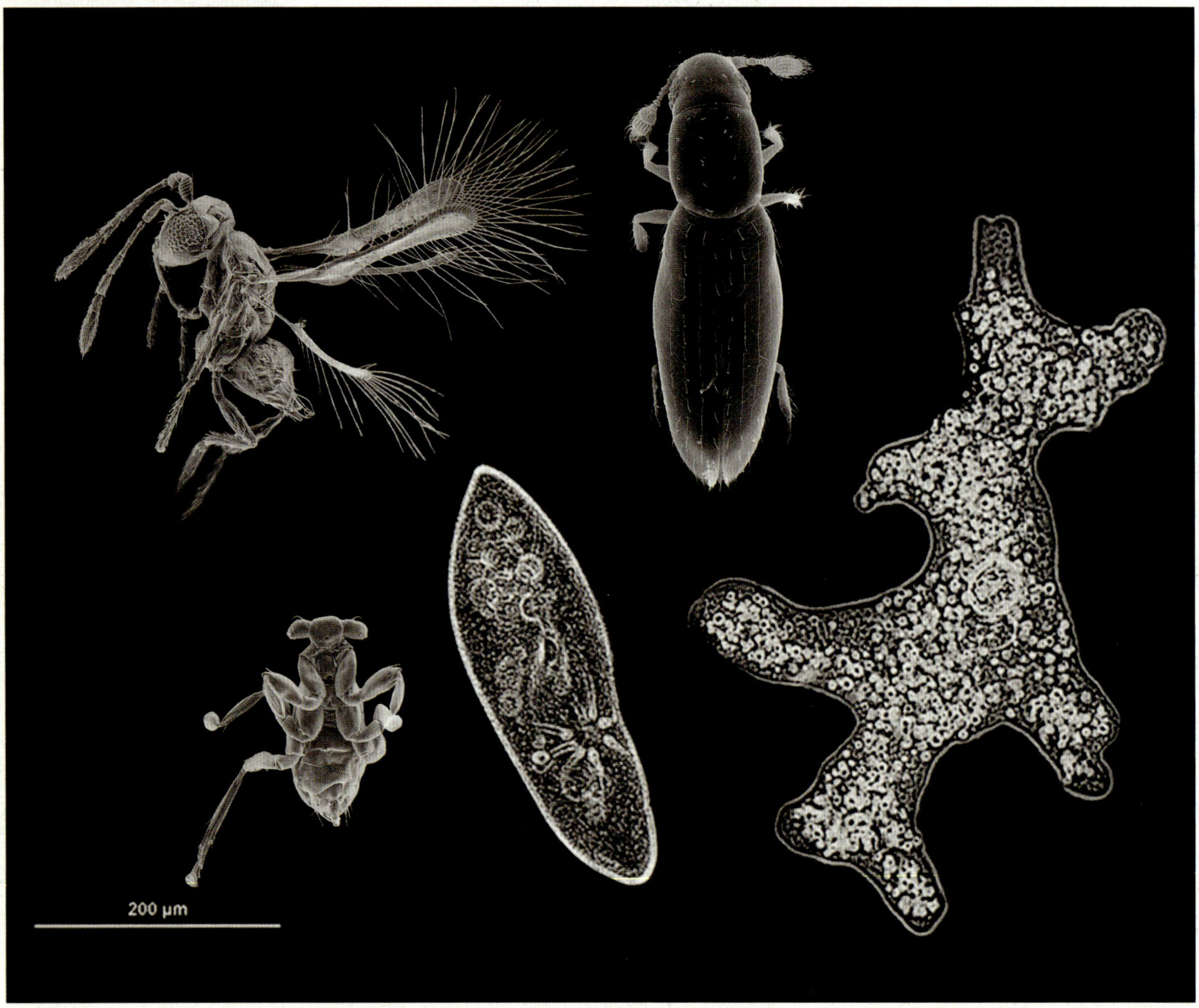

LILLIPUTIAN WASPS

DICOPOMORPHA ECHMEPTERYGIS AND COUSINS

(HYMENOPTERA: MYMARIDAE)

Some insects are seriously tiny: there are probably thousands of species measured in micrometers that are still unknown to science. Despite their minute size, they have the same body structure as their larger cousins, even if it can only be seen through an electron microscope.

The smallest known adult insect is a wasp discovered in Illinois and described by Edward L. Mockford in 1997: *Dicopomorpha echmepterygis*. The smallest male on record measured only 139 micrometers long. Compare that with the width of a human hair (50 to 100 micrometers) or a single-celled organism, the paramecium (120 micrometers). These tiny wasps exhibit strong sexual dimorphism: the males are much smaller (139 to 240 micrometers, compared with 500 to 550 for females), with unsegmented antennae and no compound eyes, mouthparts, articulated tarsi, or wings. They use their long legs to grip onto females when mating, but otherwise can hardly move, let alone disperse to other areas.

These wasps' behavior is as astonishing as their minute size. *D. echmepterygis* are idiobiont parasitoids: the females kill or paralyze their hosts, preventing further development. The host in question is another very small insect, the bark louse (*Echmepteryx hageni*). The mother wasp lays eggs devoid of food reserves directly into bark louse eggs, which her own young use for nutrients. Each louse egg is host to one female and up to three male wasps, one of which mates with the female—its sister—before all the males die without ever leaving the louse egg. Only the female emerges to repeat the cycle. The males' development requires very few nutrients, as their role is limited to fertilizing the female, which is larger and stronger and has eyes and wings that allow her to disperse. This difference between the sexes is due to the limited food available in the host egg. Since the males from species that reproduce through parthenogenesis can also be very small, it is possible that there exist even smaller male insects among the other parasitic wasps that use insect eggs as hosts.

The anatomy of these tiny wasps is not so different from that of larger insects, apart from some pieces of their exoskeletons being fused together. They also lack certain muscles and have differences in some systems. (Simplified or missing eyes, for example: they seek out their hosts by smell.) One notable difference is that, by the time micro-wasps reach sexual maturity, the nuclei have been expulsed from nearly all of their neurons, to save space. The wasps survive their brief adult phase using proteins ingested during their larval phase. Some researchers have theorized that physical, physiological, and structural constraints make it impossible for much smaller insects to exist.

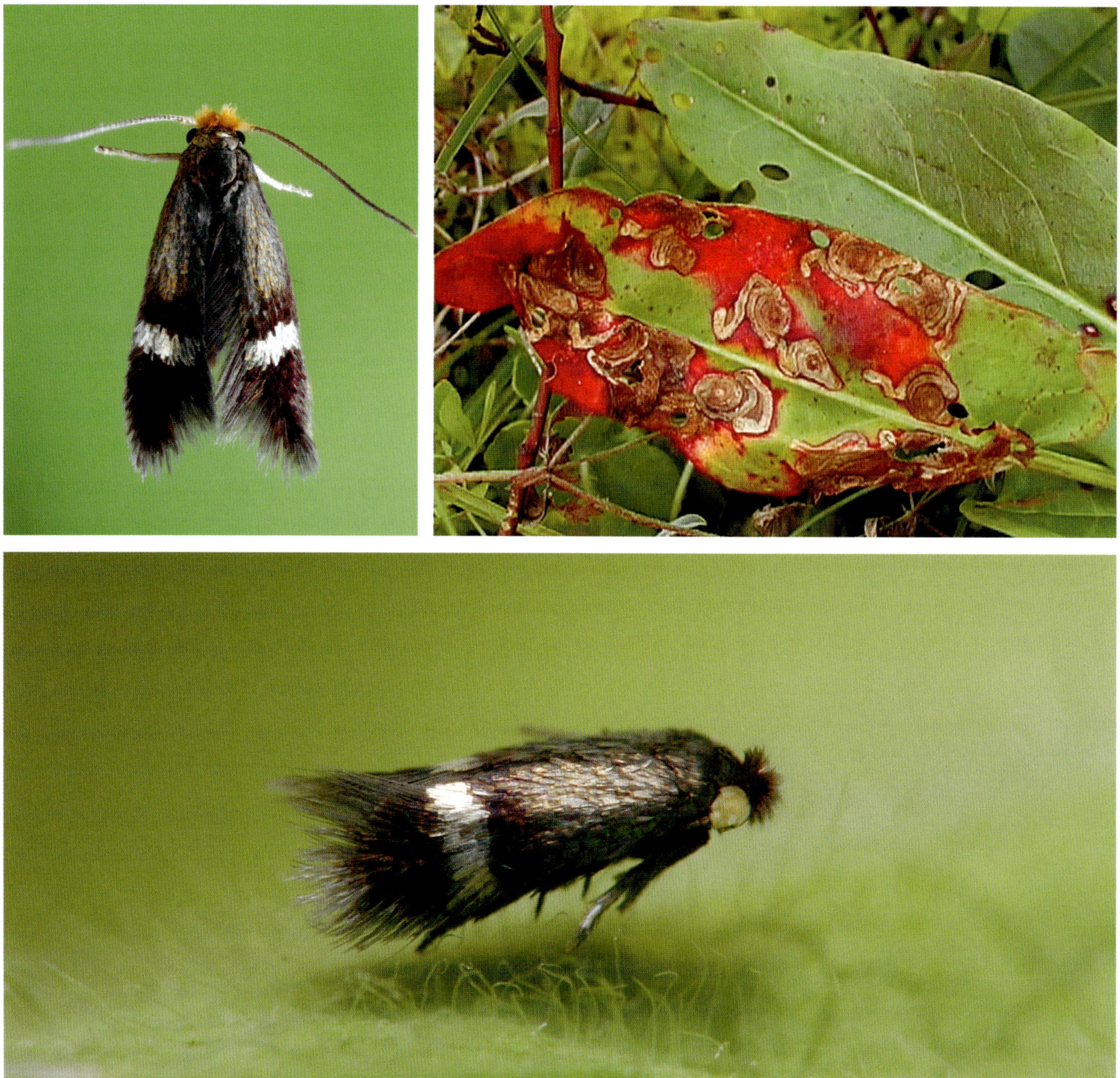

The pygmy sorrel moth (*Enteucha acetosae*, family: Nepticulidae) is the smallest moth in Europe, with a wingspan of only 3 mm. Its caterpillars dig spiral corridors into the tissue of the wild sorrel leaves where they hatch, leaving distinctive red marks. Several caterpillars generally live on a single leaf.

© Janet Graham, © Patrick Clement CC 2.0 (moth)

OTHER INSECTS UNDER THE MICROSCOPE

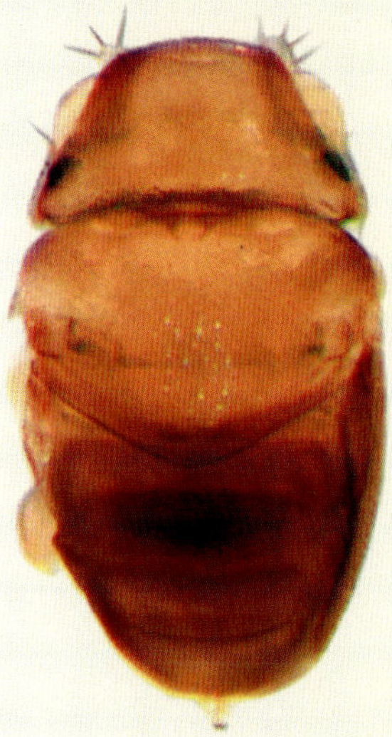

© Brian V. Brown CC 4.0

The tiniest fly in the world (order: Diptera) comes from Southeast Asia. *Euryplatea nanaknihali* is only 0.4 millimeters long but is otherwise anatomically similar to larger flies. It spends its larval phase living inside ants from the genus Crematogaster, themselves only 2 to 6 millimeters long! The female *E. nanaknihali* uses a pointed ovipositor to lay her eggs inside an ant's abdomen. Once they hatch, the larvae dig their way through the ant's organs until they reach its head, where they nibble on muscles and nerve tissue, eventually killing their host. In 2012, Brian Brown, a curator at the Natural History Museum of Los Angeles County, named this minuscule fly after Nanak Nihal Weiss, a boy whose passion for insects he wanted to encourage.

At 325 to 352 micrometers long, *Scydosella musawasensis* (family: Ptiliidae) is the smallest known beetle based on specimens collected in Colombia, although it was first discovered in Nicaragua. It feeds on polypore fungus. Only parasitic wasps that use insect eggs as hosts are smaller. It is probable that the minimum size for ganglia and eggs limits how small insects can be.

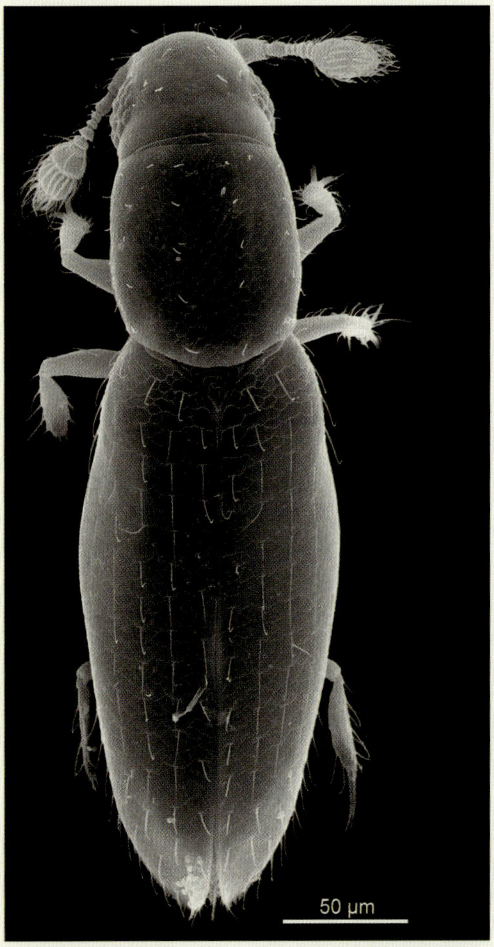

© Alexey Polilov

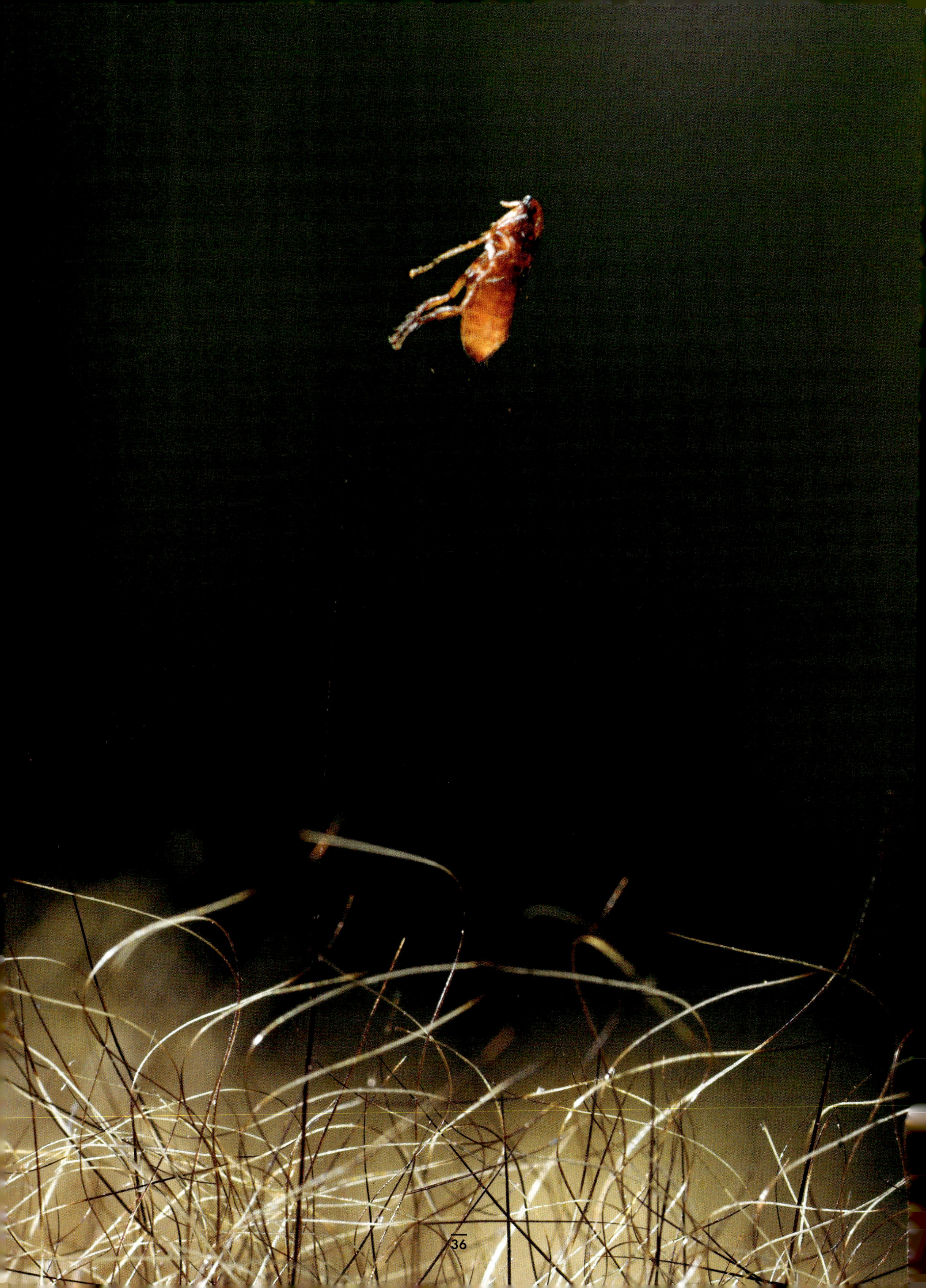

HIGH JUMP RECORD HOLDERS

PULEX IRRITANS

(SIPHONAPTERA: PULICIDAE)

Javier Sotomayor's world record high jump of 2.45 meters is nothing compared to what fleas can do. Sure, they may be only a few millimeters high, but they can jump three hundred times their body height! The flea's anatomy and physiology—like those of other jumping insects—put human capacities to shame.

Fleas are best known for their nasty bite. They are parasites, after all, and feed on the blood of their animal hosts, usually mammals or birds. Because they can easily move from one host to another, they spread diseases in addition to causing allergies. Over 2,500 species have been described, but we humans are most familiar with those that live on our pets: dogs, cats, and—in rarer cases—rats, mice, and ferrets. In the United States, these are usually cat fleas (*Ctenocephalides felis*, which are also found on dogs, rodents, and birds), dog fleas (*Ctenocephalides canis*, a close relative), or human fleas (*Pulex irritans*) also known as house fleas, which—as their name suggests—are the ones that will make you itch and scratch.

Fleas are particularly well adapted to jumping, but their abilities vary greatly by species. The dog flea is only two millimeters long but can jump 25 centimeters (125 times its length) and still land on its feet, which soften the landing like pneumatic shocks. For a long time, exactly how it did this was a mystery. The earliest research dates back to the 1960s, when English zoologist Henry Bennet-Clark showed that fleas store the energy necessary for their incredible jumps using a springlike structure in their thorax. This "spring" is made of resilin, a protein discovered by Danish zoologist Torkel Weis-Fogh (1922–1975), which is the secret ingredient in many insects' astonishing feats (jumping, running, flight, the buzzing sound made by cicadas, and more). Resilin is much more elastic and resistant to wear than polybutadiene (the best synthetic rubber) and has been used to make running shoes and repair damaged arteries.

Left: This 2–3 mm long cat flea can jump distances up to 30 cm and heights of 10–25 cm. Jumping skills vary by flea species.

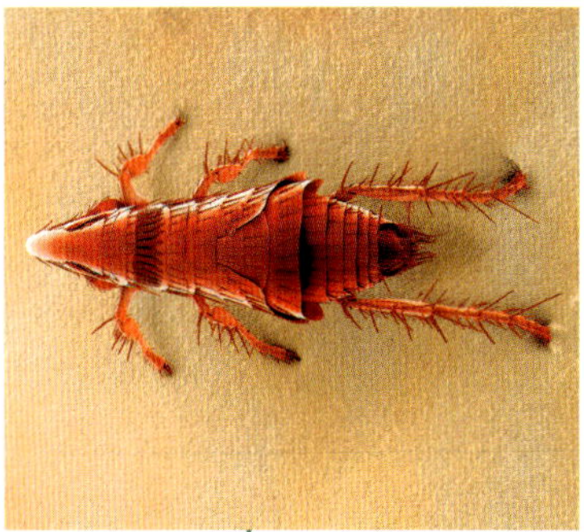

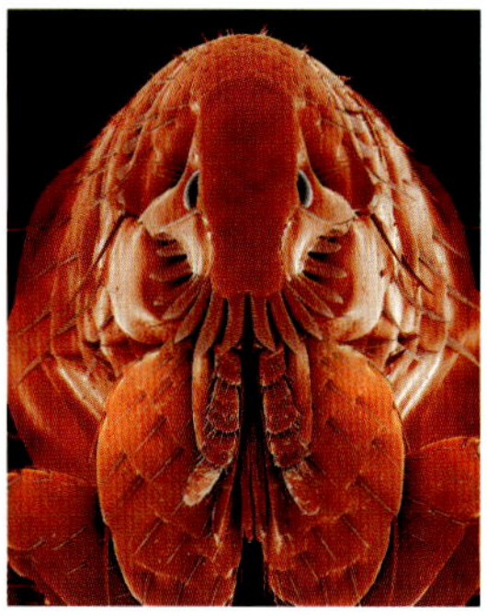

Fleas, like this cat flea, have narrow bodies that make them difficult to crush and allow them to slip through animal hair. The adults have piercing mouthparts (right) specially adapted for sucking blood, which is how all adult fleas feed. They also have ctenidia (or tiny, comblike spines) on their heads and thoraxes, and claws on their feet, which allow them to grip onto the hair of their host.

© David Spears (Last Refuge)/Ardea/Biosphoto

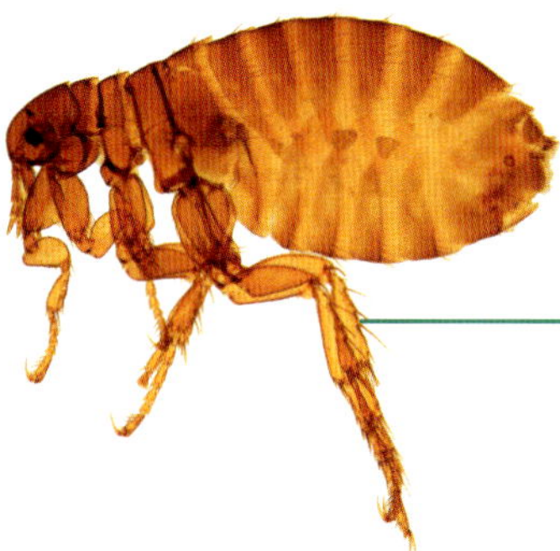

The human flea (*Pulex irritans*) is also known as the house flea. This is a female.

© Katja ZSM

The flea compresses this "spring" by flexing its first leg segment, or coxa, then releases the energy all at once. Scientists once thought fleas might jump using their knees (like crickets) or their tarsi. But in 2011, Gregory P. Sutton and Malcolm Burrows, two biomechanics researchers in Cambridge, England, used a high-speed camera to film fleas jumping. This revealed that fleas transfer power from their resilin "springs" by using their hind legs like a lever and pushing off with their tarsi. When jumping, fleas can reach speeds of 1.3 to 1.9 meters per second, or an acceleration force of 150 g. We humans can "only" survive accelerations of 46 g . . . and only for 0.9 seconds, based on the record set in 1954 by a US Air Force officer in peak physical condition. The average human can only withstand a force of around 18 g! Still, it is impossible to compare the physical performance of insects and vertebrates: apart from special attributes like resilin, fleas owe their impressive jumping skills to their exoskeletons, neuromuscular innervation, and the length-tension ratio of their muscles.

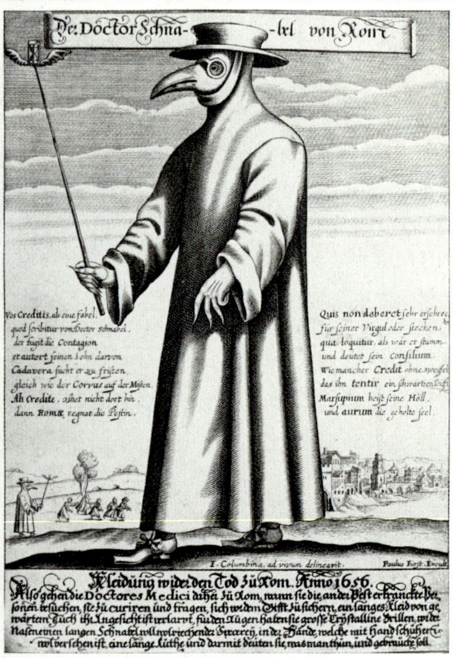

The bacterium that causes plague (*Yersinia pestis*) was discovered in 1894 by Alexandre Yersin (1863–1943). It is spread by many flea species, which pick it up when feeding on their hosts . . . in this case mainly rodents, such as rats. The fleas then regurgitate the bacteria into the blood vessels of their next host, which can cause the plague to spread to vertebrates. More than 80 million people died from plague in Europe between the fourteenth and nineteenth centuries, a time before modern microbiology when protections were ineffective. The famous beaked masks used by seventeenth-century plague doctors contained dried flowers, herbs, camphor, or a sponge soaked in vinegar—all to block the putrid smells that were thought to cause the disease.

© Engraving dated 1656, in Eugen Holländer, *Die Karikatur und Satire in der Medizin*, 1921

EDUCATED FLEAS

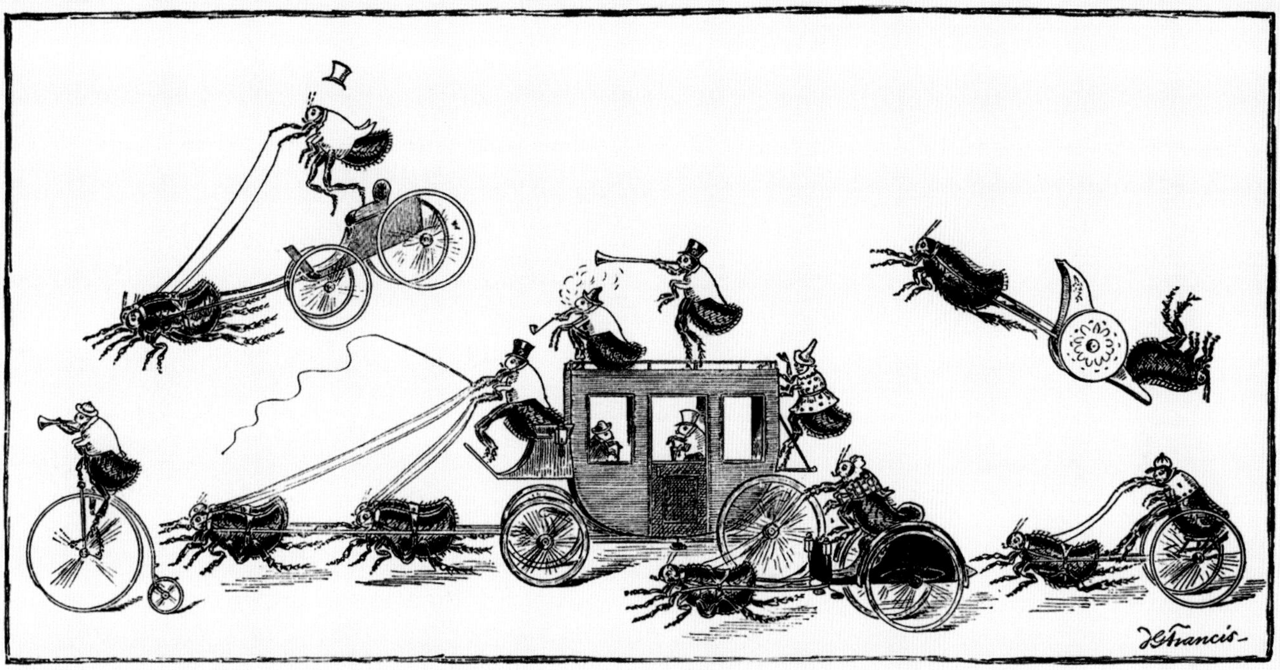

THE "GO-AS-YOU-PLEASE" RACE, AS SEEN THROUGH A MAGNIFYING GLASS.

Flea circuses were once a common sideshow attraction featuring fleas that had been "taught" to pull objects or do tricks . . . although training obviously had nothing to do with it. They first appeared in England in the 1830s, grew in popularity through the nineteenth century, and peaked in the 1930s before disappearing altogether. The astonished public would come to marvel at tiny creatures performing incredible feats of strength for their size. The postwar push for better public hygiene put an end to the "art" of educating fleas.

FASTEST INSECTS

FLIGHT SPEED

The numbers are hard to compare, because of the different methods used: flying insects have been timed both in captivity and in the wild, using cameras, radar, wind tunnels, flight mills, and more. Given the many factors that can influence flight speed (species, weight, anatomy, aerodynamics, type of flight, ambient temperature, humidity, wind, solar radiation, air pressure, etc.), the speed of a single specimen on a single occasion is not a useful measurement.

Robert J. Tillyard (1881–1937) claimed in 1917 that a species of dragonfly (*Austrophlebia costalis*) was the world's fastest insect, at 98 kilometers per hour—which turned out to be a considerable overestimate. One year later, German zoologist Reinhard Demoll (1882–1960) calculated that a hawk moth (see pages 112–115 and 130–135) could reach speeds of 53 kilometers per hour. Sadly, unreproducible one-off measurements like these have no scientific value.

Based on current observations and reliable data, the fastest flying insects are the desert locust (*Schistocerca gregaria*) and the corn earworm moth (*Helicoverpa zea*), which have been measured flying at speeds of 36 and 28 kilometers per hour relative to the ground, respectively. The tobacco hawk moth (*Manduca sexta*) can fly up to 5.3 meters per second (19 kph) and the Urania swallowtail moth (*Urania fulgens*) can reach 3.9 meters per second (14 kph). Many other insects appear to fly faster, but their speed has not been measured using comparable methods. Moreover, whenever insects are not flying in a straight line at a constant altitude, uncertainty remains regarding the difference between absolute speed in the air versus speed relative to the ground.

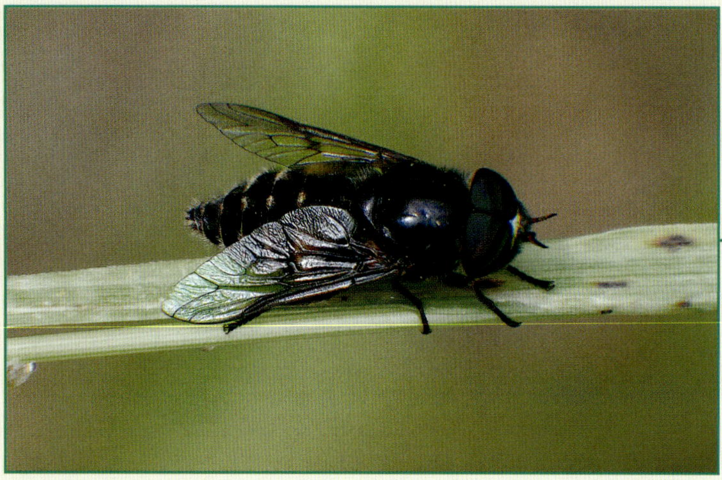

World record? The males of one species of horsefly (*Hybomitra hinei wrighti*) pursue females through the air, catch them mid-flight, then the couple mates as they plummet toward the ground. According to entomologist Jerry F. Butler, a male horsefly managed to catch a piece of plastic (which it took for a female) shot from a rifle at 145 kilometers per hour, as proven by photos from a high-speed camera.

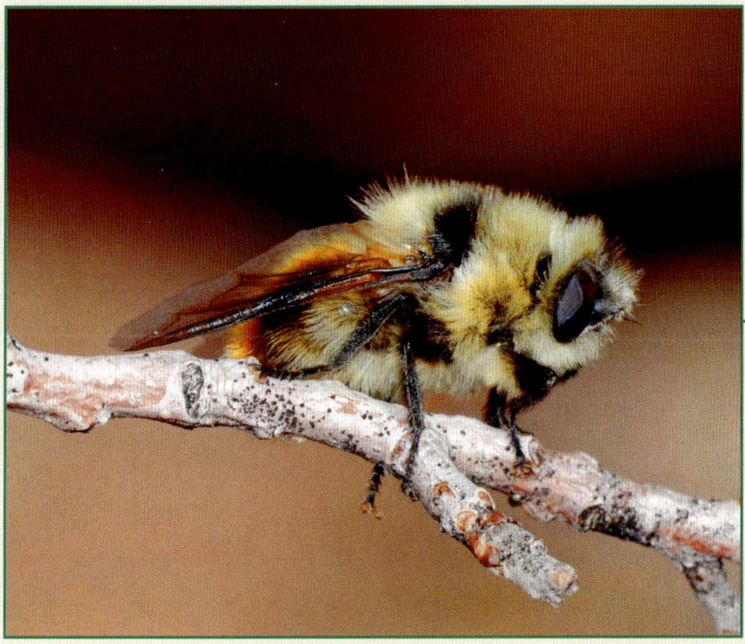

Not so fast!
Estimations of insect flight speeds have changed a lot over the past century. American entomologist Charles Henry Townsend (1863–1944) claimed in 1926, for example, that the botfly pictured here (*Cephenemyia pratti*) could fly at 1,287 kph! Townsend's stunning "observation" was refuted in 1938 by physician and chemist Irving Langmuir 1881–1957, winner of the Nobel Prize in 1932), who showed it was utterly impossible. As it turns out, *C. pratti* can reach speeds of 40 kph at most.

While most insects fly at speeds under 20 kilometers per hour, the wind sometimes blows them much faster. Relative to the ground, the fastest recorded speed was reached by a moth, the ipsilon dart (*Agrotis ipsilon*): between 97 and 113 kilometers per hour, at altitudes of 300 to 600 meters. Ipsilon darts take advantage of the air currents ahead of cold fronts to move that fast; otherwise they barely surpass 13 kilometers per hour.

GROUND SPEED

The world record for the sprint appears to belong to an Australian tiger beetle described in 1997 (*Cicindela hudsoni*). This predatory beetle is two centimeters long and has vestigial wings, so it cannot fly, but it can run at 2.5 meters per second—handy, since tiger beetles have to chase down their prey. Other species can also reach speeds of 1.8 to 2.5 meters per second. *Cicindela eburneola* has the honor of running the fastest relative to its size: 171 times its body length each second, whereas the larger *C. hudsoni* "only" covers 120 body lengths per second.

The American cockroach (*Periplaneta americana*) is also fast—it can run 1.5 meters per second, or 5.4 kilometers per hour. But at three centimeters long, that comes to only 50 body lengths per second.

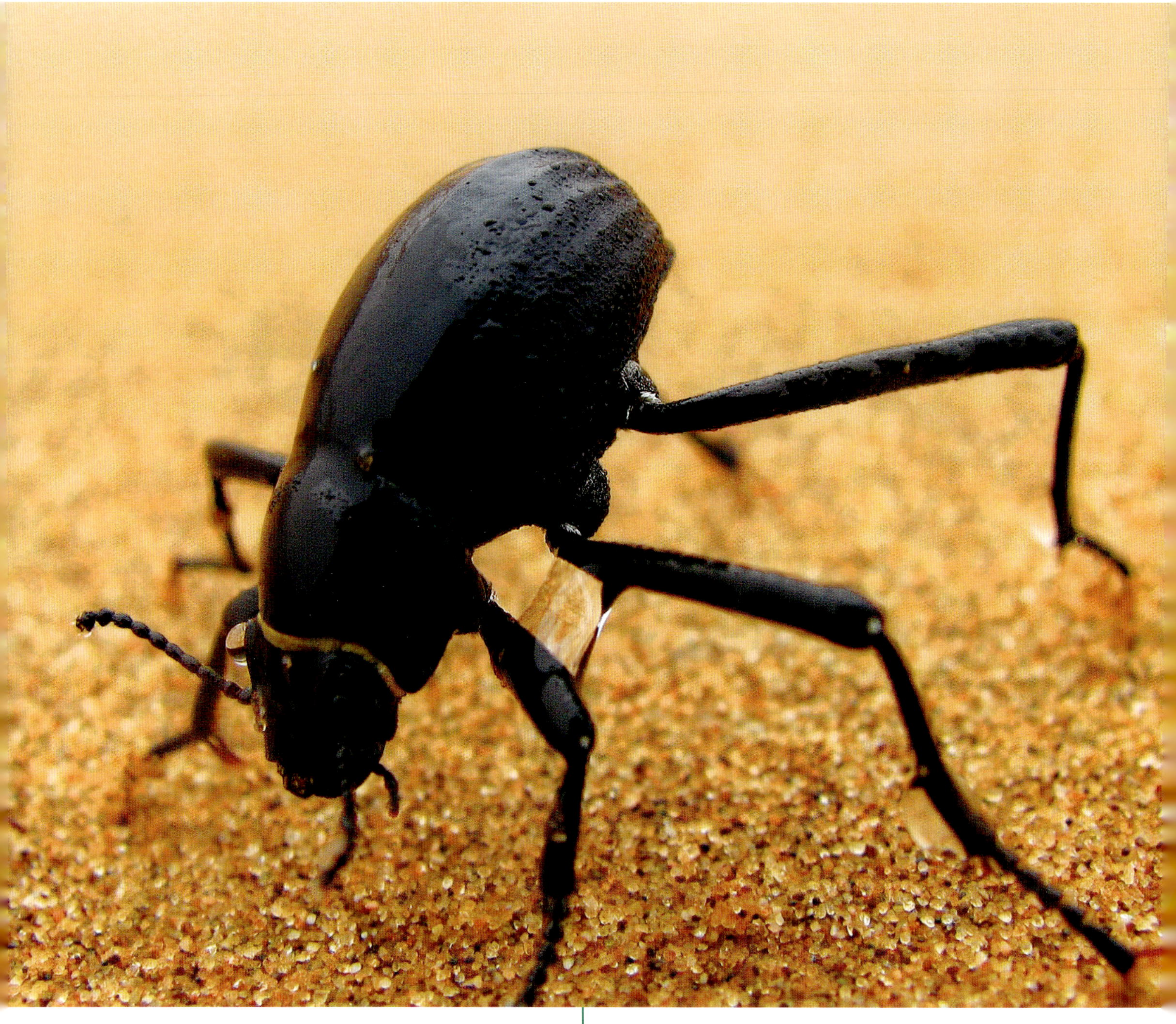

Onymacris unguicularis adopts a characteristic headstand posture to collect condensation from the air, a behavior known as "fog-basking."

SURVIVORS IN THE DESERT

ONYMACRIS UNGUICULARIS

(COLEOPTERA: TENEBRIONIDAE)

Insects live in some of the driest places on the planet, where they are able to survive incredibly harsh conditions: scorching heat during the day, blistering cold at night. They have to make use of what little water is available, and some beetle species in the deserts of southern Africa have come up with an astonishing solution.

"Fog-basking" was originally described in *Onymacris unguicularis* by William J. Hamilton III (1931–2006) and Mary K. Seely in 1976, but it has since been observed in other species.

The technique is used by some desert-dwelling beetles to collect the moisture contained in fog, which drifts up to 100 kilometers inland from the Atlantic Ocean to the Namib Desert for thirty days out of each year and contains about a liter of water per square meter. The beetles spend the night buried in sand, then wake at dawn to climb to the top of a dune, where they hold their elytra up to the moist air with their heads lowered. Water condenses on the ridges of the elytra and forms droplets that roll down into their mouths.

Other beetles employ similarly fascinating strategies. The elytra of *Physosterna cribripes* have a waxy surface that emits infrared rays and a texture that encourages water to condense there. *Lepidochora discoidalis* uses a technique called "fog-trapping": it digs a trench in the sand and waits for water droplets to accumulate along the ridge. And when desert temperatures fall at night, the larvae of *Onymacris marginipennis* and certain other darkling beetles absorb water vapor as it condenses onto their rectal epithelium.

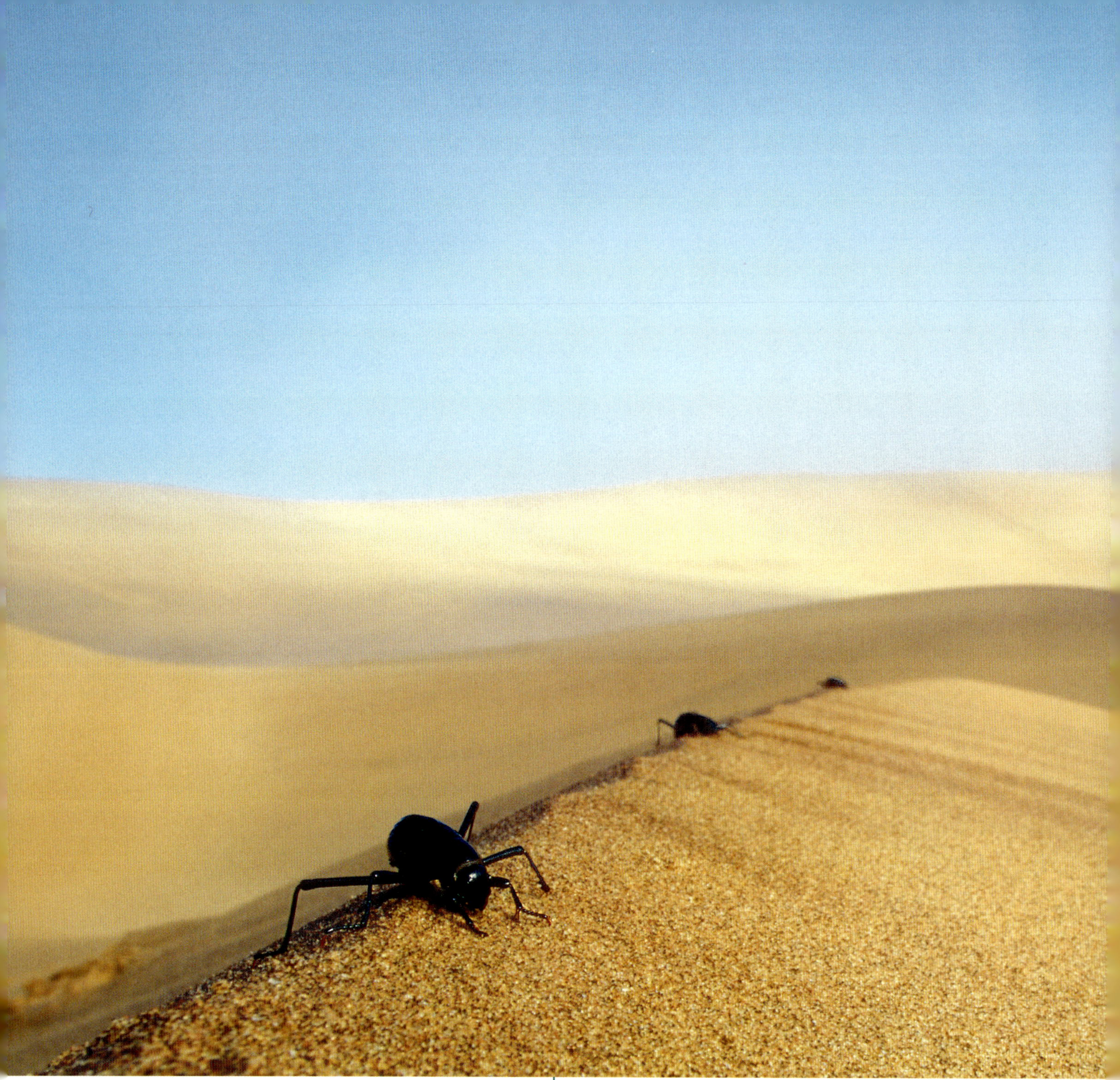

Fog-basking beetles line up on the crests of dunes in the Namib Desert at dawn, facing into the wind. Humidity in the air condenses onto their hydrophobic forewings and flows down into their mouths.

Some darkling beetles can "swim" through the dry, fine sand of the desert using specially adapted hindlegs, like this *Lepidochora discoidalis*. It makes the most of meager water resources in the Namib Desert by "fog-trapping": it digs small trenches atop the dunes at dawn and collects the water that condenses there.

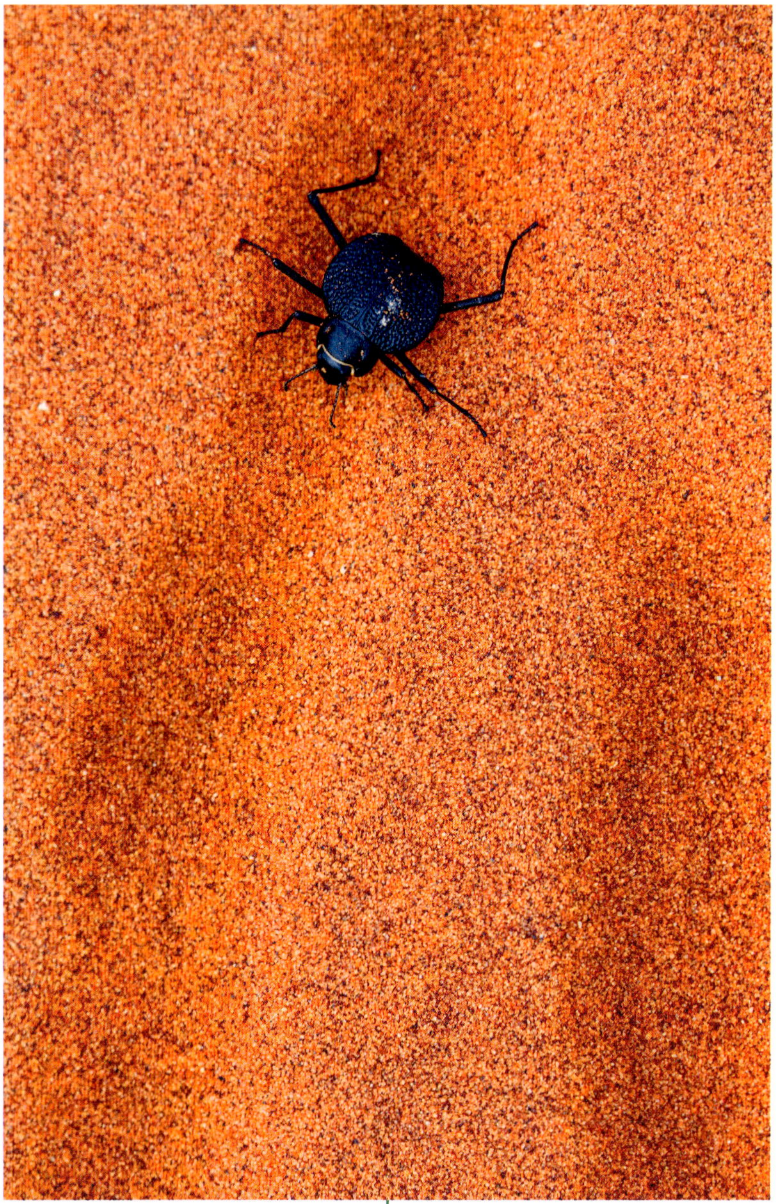

Onymacris plana, a darkling beetle from the Namib Desert that is active during the day, is among the fastest insects on the ground. It can run up to 90 cm per second, or over 3 kph! It dashes between tufts of vegetation on sand dunes to avoid prolonged exposure to the sun.
© Juan-Carlos Muñoz

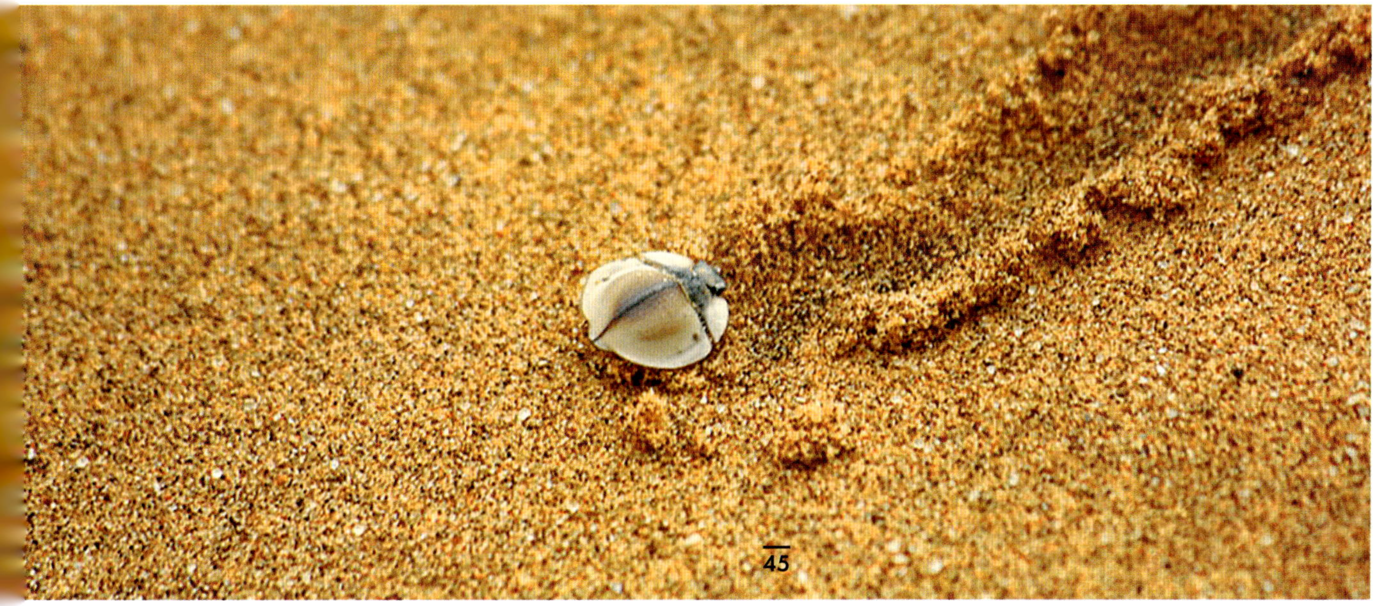

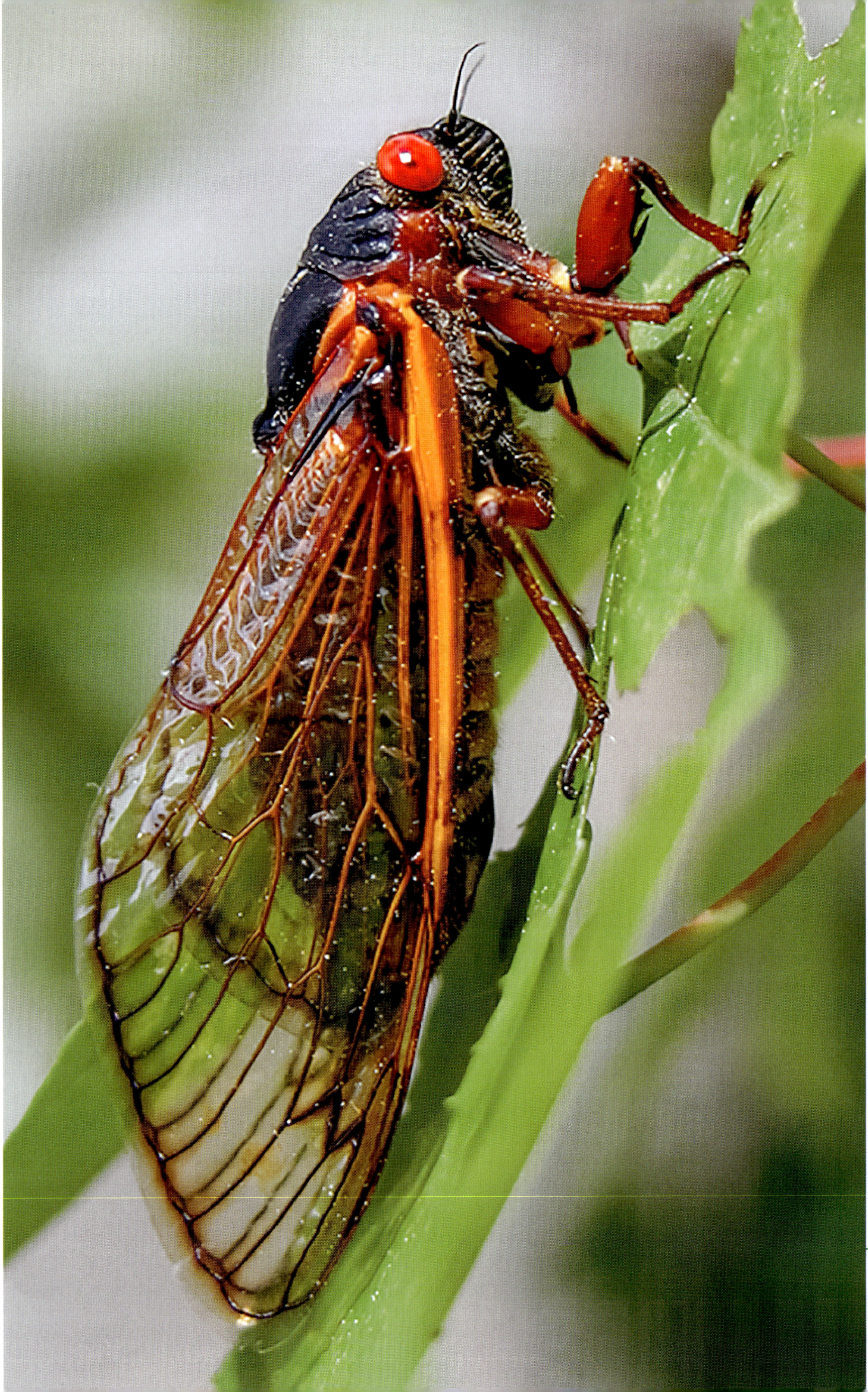

POWER IN (PRIME) NUMBERS

MAGICICADA SEPTENDECIM

(HEMIPTERA: CICADIDAE)

Seventeen years: that is how long it takes for this cicada to develop, making it the longest-living insect. The seventeen-year cicada appears like clockwork from Louisiana to Massachusetts, Georgia to Wisconsin, and belongs to a small group of so-called periodic cicadas.

During all those years, the larvae remain buried underground at a depth of 20 centimeters to one meter, depending on the soil conditions and their level of maturity. They feed by sucking the sap from tree roots and go through five growth stages before making their way to the surface and digging an exit tunnel through which to emerge. At this point, they develop into mobile nymphs. As spring advances and temperatures become warm enough, the nymphs emerge from the ground at dusk and climb onto a raised surface (usually a tree trunk) where they undergo a final transformation into their adult form, which takes six days to complete. The males precede the females by a few days.

When periodic cicadas emerge, they flood the forests in numbers far greater than any other species in their family. It has been estimated that some broods produce over one million individuals per acre. They usually mate in the second half of May, then lay their eggs on tree bark in early summer. When the larvae hatch, they fall to the ground, bury themselves, and a new seventeen-year cycle begins. There are individual insects that can live longer—some beetle larvae have been known to develop in particularly dry, resource-poor wood for over forty years—but such cases are exceptions and occur in species whose life cycles are normally quite short.

The brightly colored seventeen-year cicada, or pharaoh cicada, is 35–45 mm long.

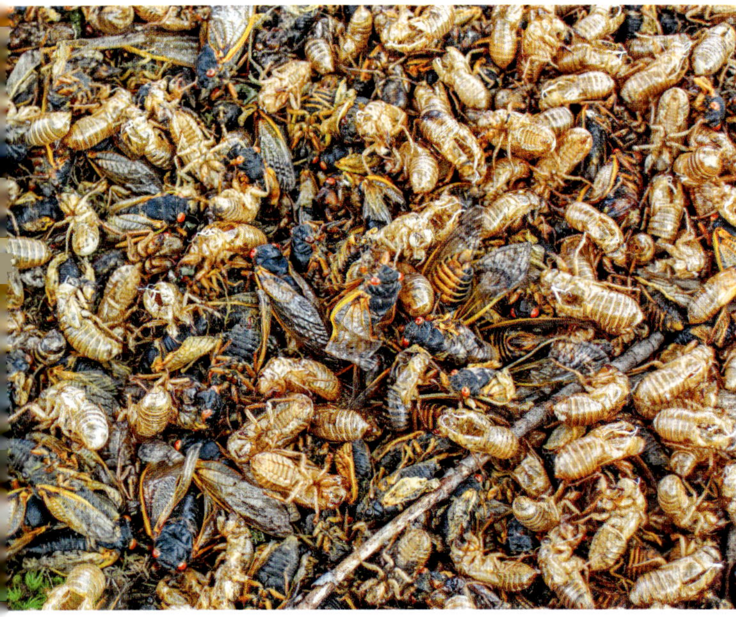

Accumulation of dead seventeen-year cicadas during one of the rare years when the adults emerge.

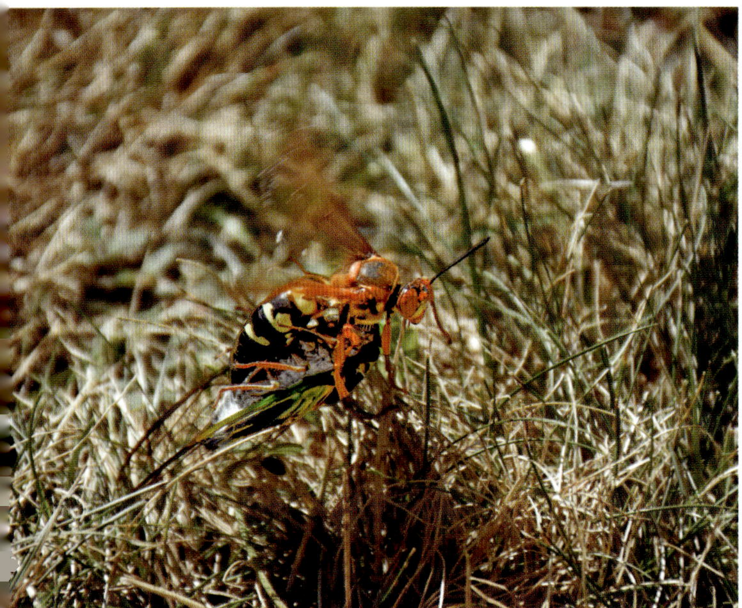

The seventeen-year cicada's life cycle helps it to survive various threats, including cicada killers: wasps that are specialized predators of cicadas, like this *Sphecius speciosus*.

These cicadas, however, pull off their seventeen-year feat as a matter of habit: it is their natural lifespan.

The genus *Magicicada*, to which *M. septendecim* belongs, contains several species of periodic cicadas native to the deciduous forests east of the Great Plains. There are three species of seventeen-year cicada, mostly present in the Northeast, and four species with a thirteen-year cycle, in the South and Midwest. The emergence of periodic cicadas is always big news. There are even smartphone applications designed to alert users when and where mass emergences will take place.

Synchronous emergence paired with a prolonged development phase that lasts a number of years—a prime number, to be precise—is a double protection strategy. Because all the adults emerge at once, there are too many for generalist predators (birds and other animals) to wipe out completely. Tellingly, seventeen-year cicadas are weaker fliers than cicada species that have a shorter life cycle and emerge in smaller numbers. Second, as theorized by American biologist Stephen J. Gould (1941–2002), because prime numbers like thirteen or seventeen are not multiples of any smaller number, a cycle of that length minimizes the chances that their emergence will coincide with a population peak of specialized predators or parasites with a shorter or longer cycle. Most other cicada species have a two- or eight-year cycle, and their emergence is asynchronous: broods of these so-called annual cicadas emerge, as their name suggests, every year.

SUMMERTIME CHORUS

You might say they chirp, buzz, or screech . . . but the most common word is "sing." Males are mostly responsible for the cicada's distinctive chorus, as the females are more discreet. Cicadas sing all day long when the weather is warm enough, sometimes even past dusk. They produce sound using their tymbal, a curved chitinous membrane located at the base of the wings, which is strengthened by a series of ribs. When the cicada flexes special muscles, the tymbal buckles up to one hundred times per second—think of a piece of stiff plastic being bent back and forth with a snap. It has to be warm enough for the tymbal to be flexible: usually at least 22–25 °C (72–77 °F). The cicada's abdominal cavity acts like a sound box, and it has "dampeners," as well as tiny vents between its abdomen and the base of its hindlegs, that allow it to modulate its sound, making each call distinctive enough to tell similar-looking species apart.

Not only are cicadas the longest-lived insect, they are also the loudest. Several American and African species can produce sounds of over 100 decibels at a distance of 50 centimeters. And one species of Australian cicada, *Cyclochila australasiae*, can produce up to 120 decibels, the level at which sound becomes painful and dangerous to human ears.

ANOTHER SOUND RECORD

The lesser water boatman (*Micronecta scholtzi*) holds a special record: it is the loudest insect proportional to its size. Who would guess that the lakes, ponds, and slow-moving streams of Europe were home to a 2-mm-long insect capable of producing 100 decibels? The males make incredibly loud stridulations during the mating season . . . using their penises. Thankfully, the sound is muffled by the water where they live and is barely audible to humans. Exactly how they manage to make such loud sounds is still a mystery.

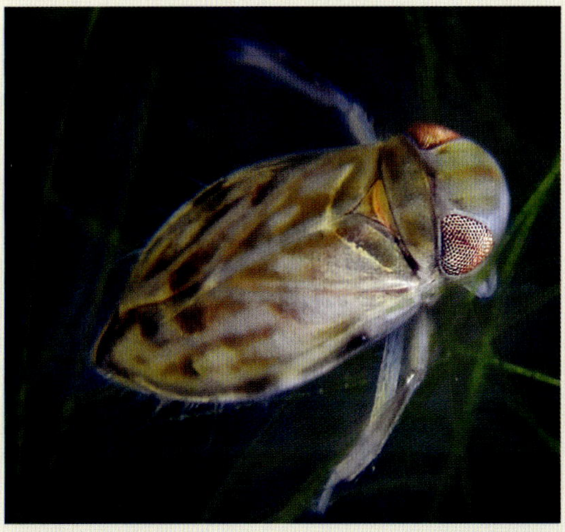

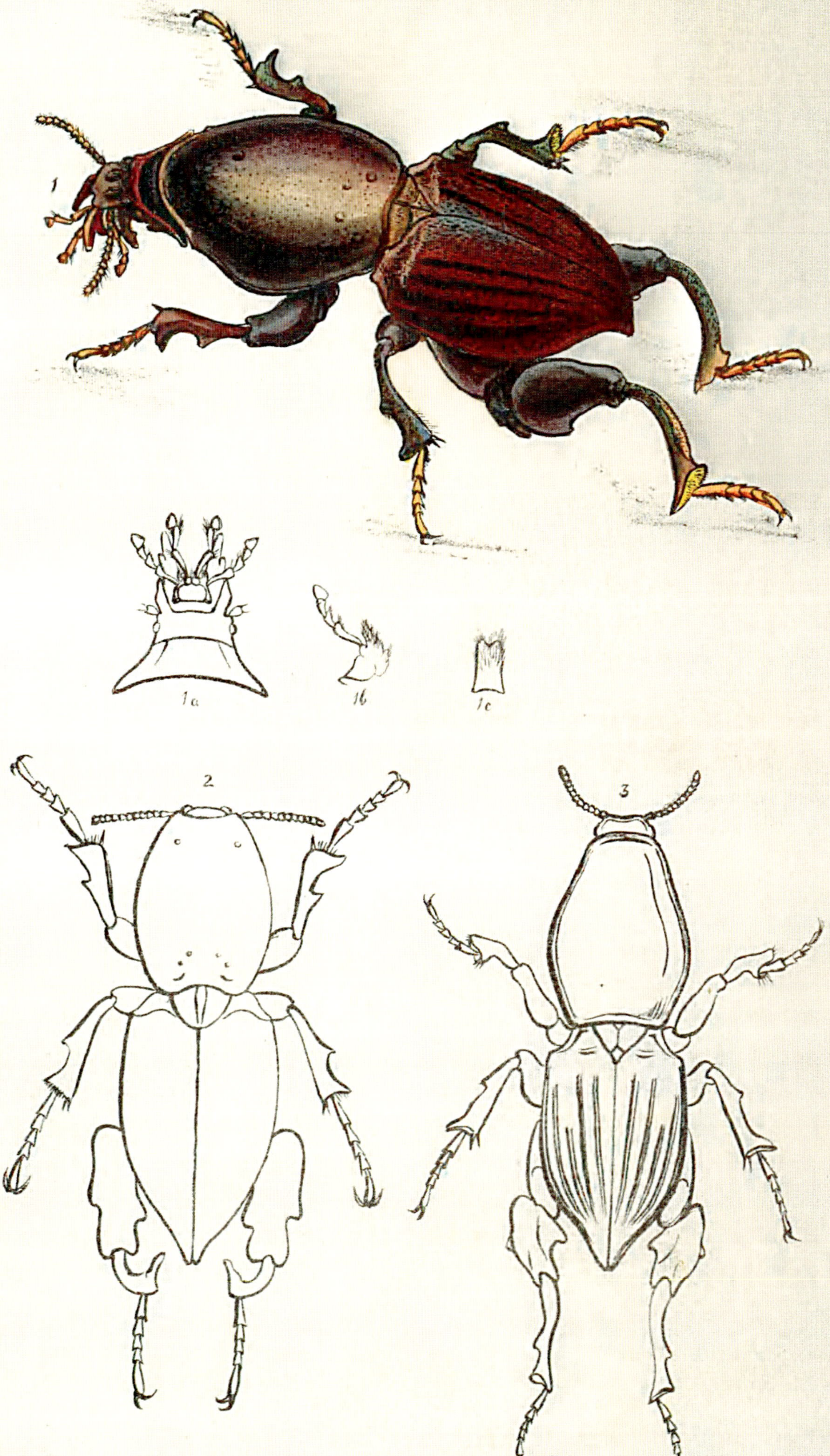
1
1a
1b
1c
2
3

THE MOLE BEETLE OF BRAZIL

HYPOCEPHALUS ARMATUS

(COLEOPTERA: VESPERIDAE)

With its unusual silhouette, this insect looks more like a mole cricket than a beetle. The resemblance comes from both insects having adapted to dig through soil: an example of convergent evolution. The strange appearance of the mole beetle, first described in 1832 by Anselme Desmarest (1784–1838), has long puzzled taxonomists.

This curious-looking creature measures between 45 and 65 millimeters, and its head—which can only move up and down—is placed very low on its body, inspiring the genus name *Hypocephalus*, meaning "low head." Inside its enormous thorax are powerful muscles that move its digging claws. Males differ in appearance from females: their legs, especially the hindlegs, are larger, and their bodies are narrower. Both sexes lack membranous wings and cannot fly. American entomologist Charles W. Leng (1859–1941) called this mishmash of a beetle a monstrosity of nature. We now know that mole beetles are cousins of cerambycids like the titan beetle (page 13) and harlequin beetle (page 97), even if it can be hard to see the family resemblance!

Mole beetles are only found in a small area on the border between the Brazilian states of Minas Gerais, Bahia, and Goiás. They prefer open country with sparse vegetation. While they are usually seen walking over wet earth after the rain, they are actually fossorial and feed on roots. Adult males emerge from their underground galleries when the wet season begins in December. During this period, they can be seen walking overground even during the day, probably in search of females, which remain underground: exactly how the males locate their

Illustration of a mole beetle from *Arcana Entomologica; or Illustrations of New, Rare, and Interesting Insects* (1845) by English entomologist John O. Westwood (1805–1893).

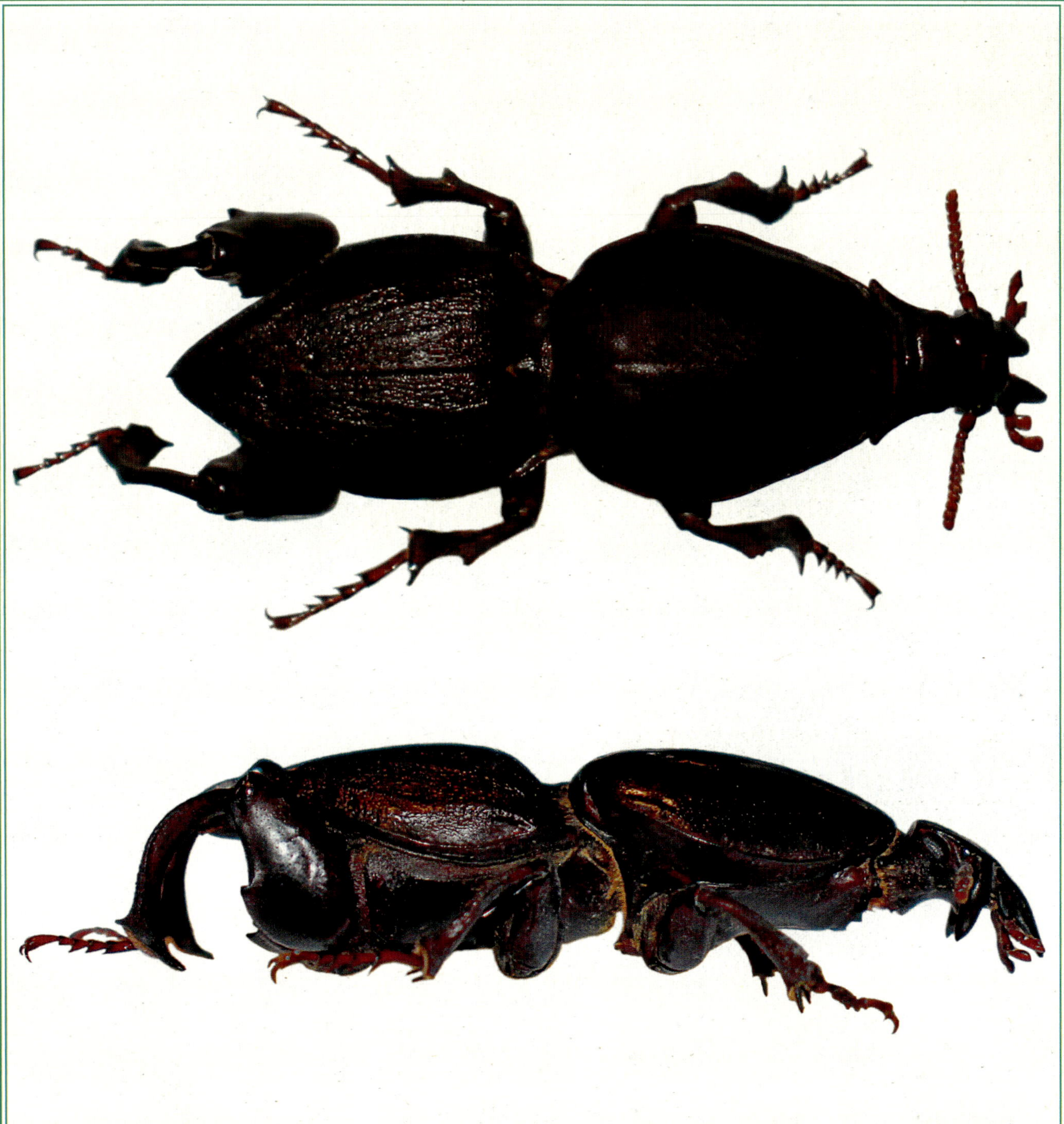

Hypocephalus armatus **is one of the strangest beetles you can imagine, in terms of both habits and anatomy.**

© Pierre-Olivier Maquart

mates is still a mystery. The larvae have never been observed but probably develop underground and feed on roots or decomposing wood, like the larvae of other beetles in the same family.

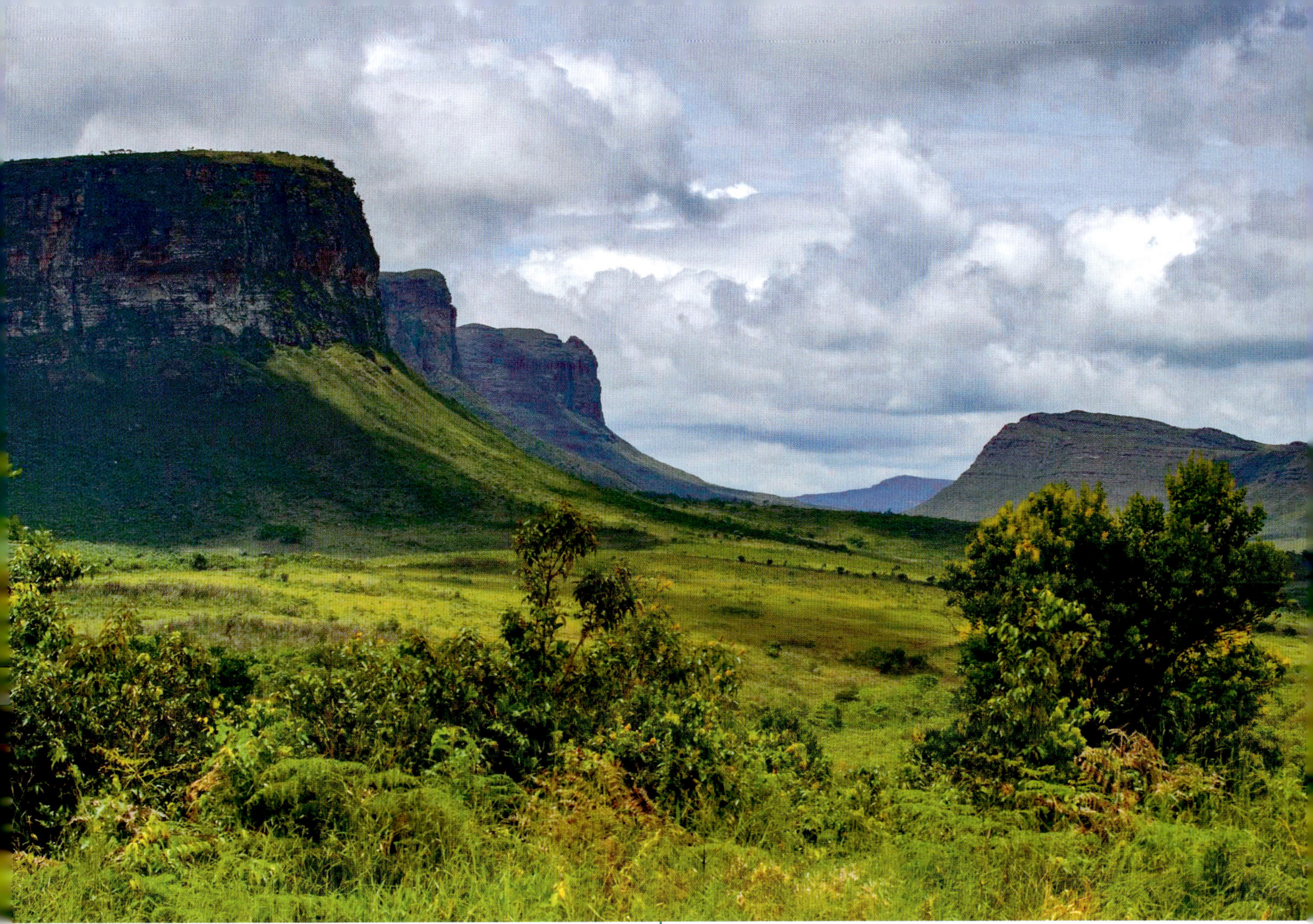

Mole beetles live in the lush landscapes of Chapada Diamantina National Park in Bahia state, Brazil, which looks like something out of Arthur Conan Doyle's *The Lost World* (1912).
© Deltafrut CC2

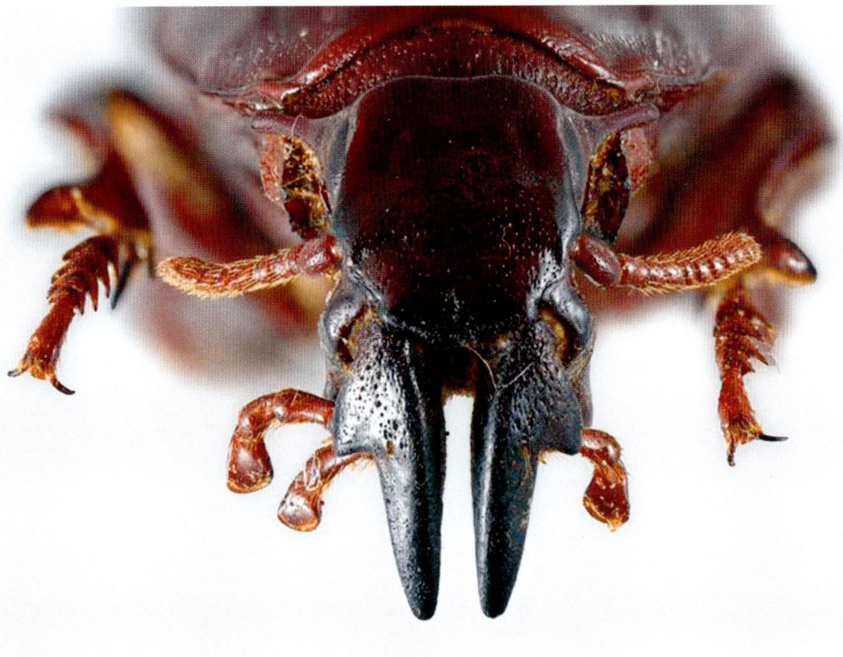

Close-up of a mole beetle head.
© Nathan Lord CC4

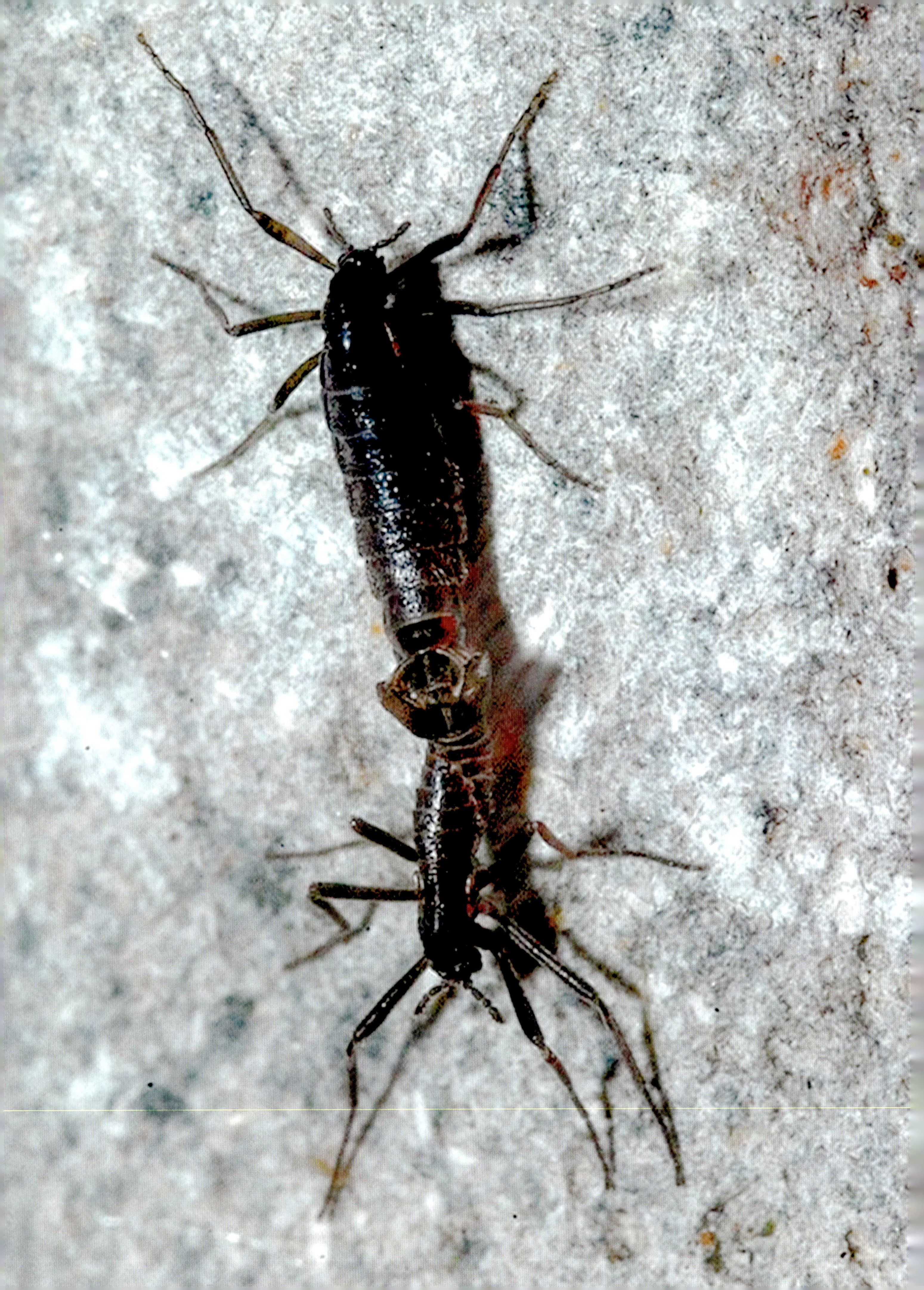

A MIDGE IN THE LAND OF ICE

BELGICA ANTARCTICA

(DIPTERA: CHIRONOMIDAE)

The Antarctic midge is the only insect endemic to Antarctica and the largest purely terrestrial animal native to the continent, despite being barely three millimeters long. It is locally common, sometimes forming groups of over a thousand individuals in scattered sites along the rocky promontories that line the western coast of the Antarctic Peninsula and South Shetland Islands.

Adult Antarctic midges can be observed in relatively protected, humid places where the soil has been enriched with the droppings of penguins and other vertebrates. These midges lack wings, so they cannot be blown away by strong winds. The adults do not feed and only live for about ten days, the time it takes to mate and lay their eggs. This reproductive window takes place during the brief Antarctic summers, from November to February, when temperatures range from −12 to −3 °C (10–27 °F) and sometimes even rise above freezing.

Antarctic midges lay eggs in bunches and cover them with a protein-rich secretion that provides nutrients and thermal insulation and keeps them from drying out. It takes two years for the larvae to ingest enough nutrients to metamorphose into breeding adults. They feed on organic waste, molds, and microorganisms and live under a layer of moss or excrement, or else underground. For two terrible winters, they are iced in and must survive extreme conditions, during which they lose nearly half their body weight. But these larvae are singularly adapted to handle 140 kilometer-per-hour winds, average temperatures of −35 °C (−31 °F), and major variations in salinity. They can survive without oxygen for two to four weeks,

The Antarctic midge looks more like an ant, because it has no wings.

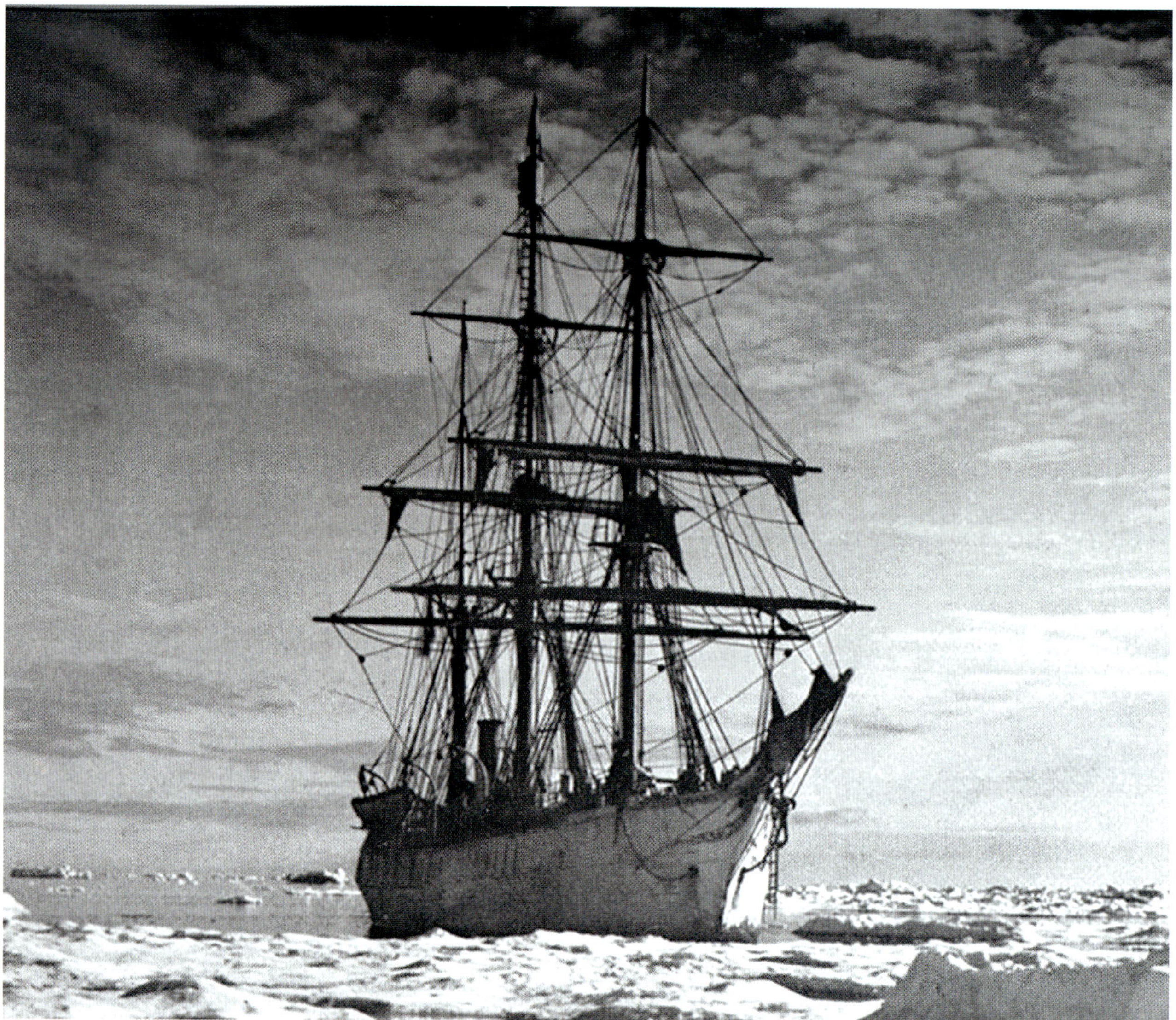

[The genus name *Belgica* was chosen in 1900 by Belgian entomologist Jean-Charles Jacobs (1821–1907), in honor of the (Belgian) ship *Belgica*, which carried the first international expedition ever to spend a winter in the Antarctic, from 1897 to 1899. It was during this expedition that a Romanian naturalist, Emil G. Racoviță (1868–1947), discovered the midge.

withstand intense ultraviolet radiation, and lose up to 70 percent of their body water without dying. (Other insects can only stand to lose about 20 percent, and humans a maximum of 2 percent!) Still, the larvae try to lose as little water as possible by gathering together in tight clumps in winter. Last but not least, their body water can freeze without it hurting them. These adaptations make them what are known as "extremophiles."

Surprisingly, it was discovered in 2013 that the Antarctic midge has the smallest known insect genome, with only 99 million base pairs of nucleotides (the building blocks of DNA) . . . or thirty-two times fewer than humans! Most of the midge's genes are associated with metabolism regulation, and any sequences not related to protein production are kept to a bare minimum—the result of incredible evolutionary pressure to adapt to an extreme habitat.

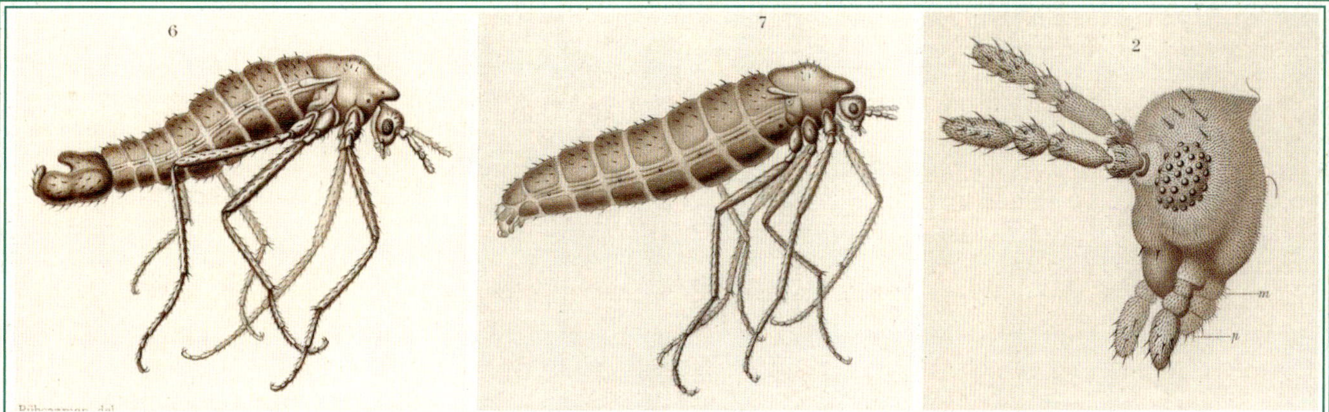

Illustrations of male (left) and female (center) Antarctic midges by Finnish entomologist Ernst Bergroth (1857–1925) in *Résultats du voyage du S.Y. Belgica en 1897-1898-1899 – Zoologie : Insectes.* The detailed engraving of the head (right) shows the high quality and attention to detail in scientific publications of the period.

© Ernst Bergeroth (1906)

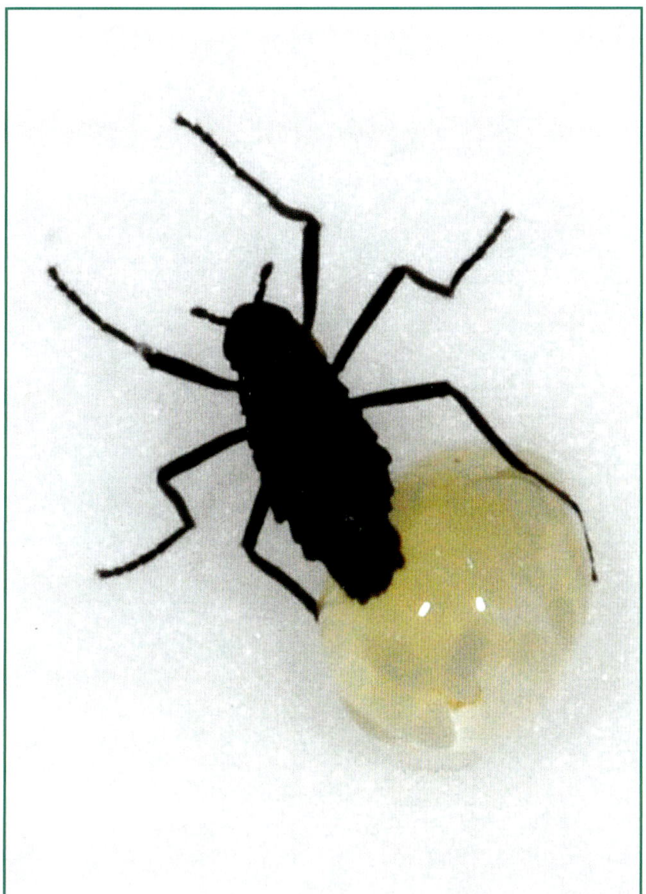

Antarctic midges cover their eggs in a mucus-like substance that protects them from the cold.

© Richard Lee CC4

When dehydrated, the larvae look something like tiny grape seeds. As soon as they encounter water, they reinflate and become active again. Their ability to survive high levels of dehydration is key to surviving extreme cold. Their dark purplish color helps them to absorb as much heat as possible while protecting them from ultraviolet rays.

© Richard Lee CC4

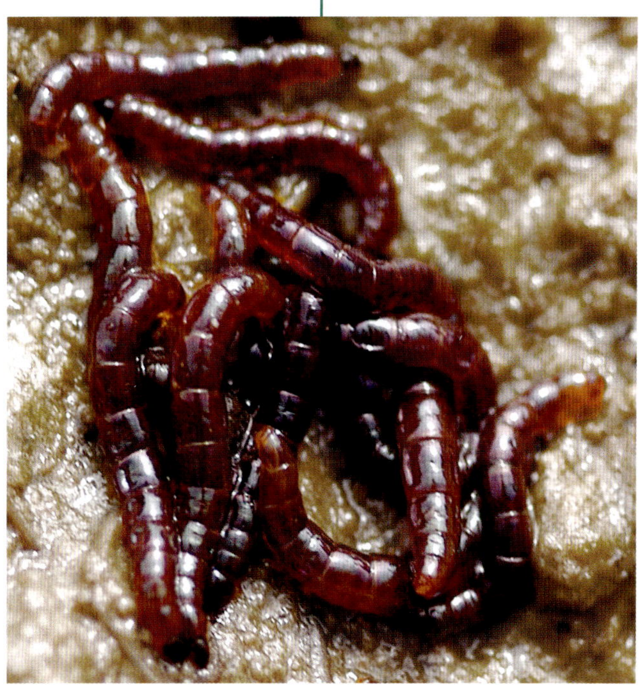

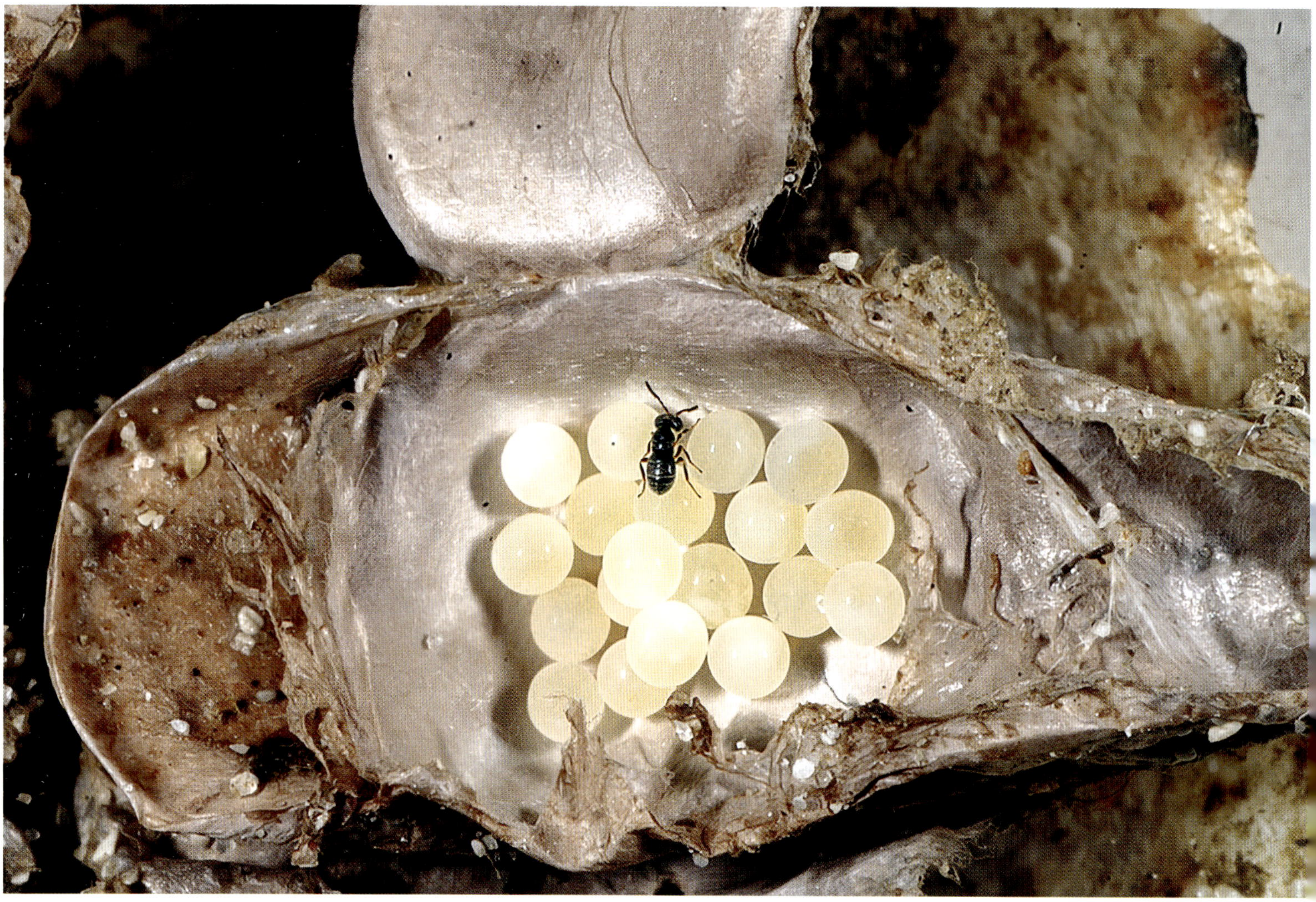

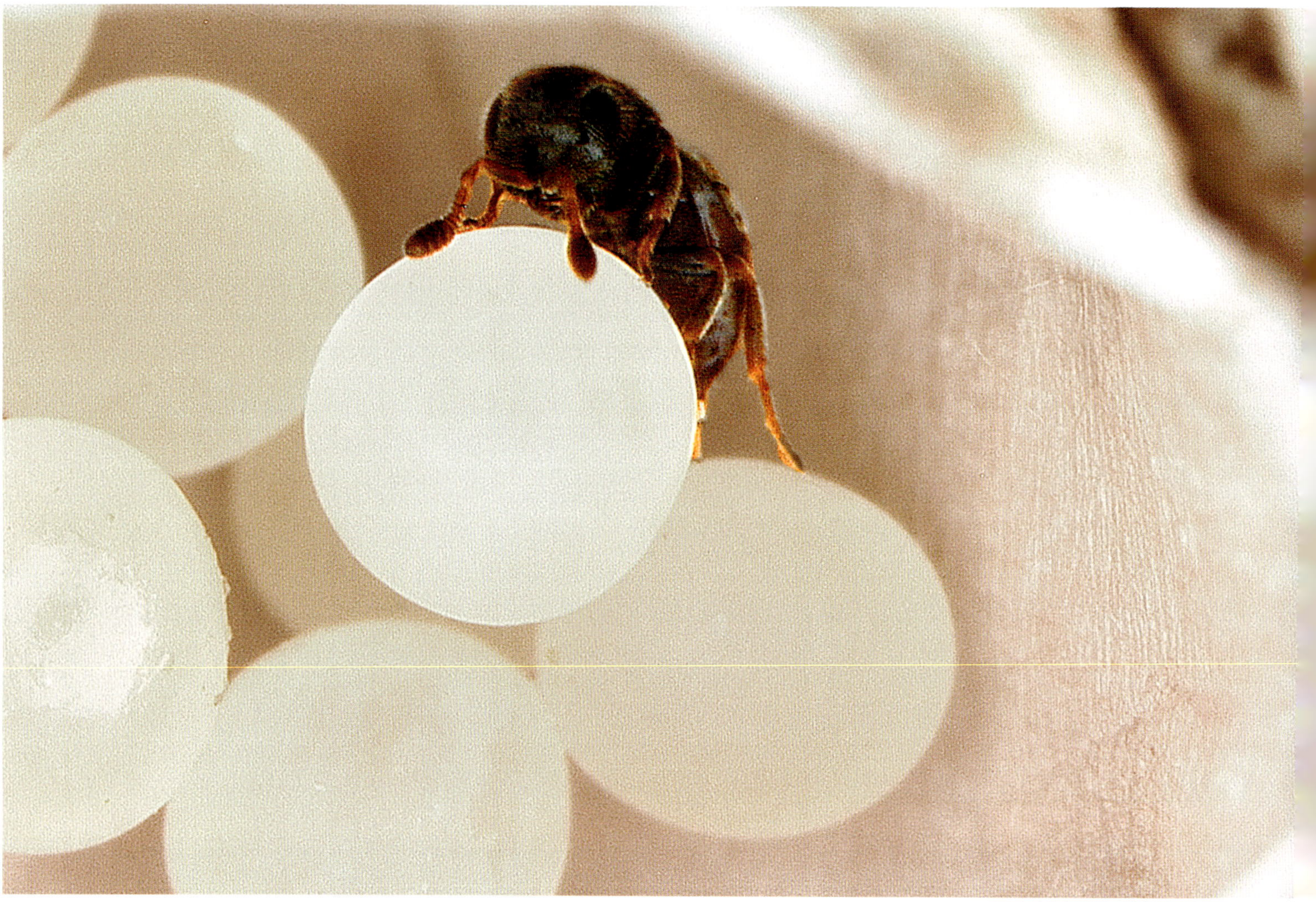

THE WASP OF GOOD HOPE

ECHTHRODESIS LAMORALI

(HYMENOPTERA: SCELIONIDAE)

Some incredible insects can barely be seen with the naked eye. Such is the case for these minuscule wasps, which are only found on an equally minuscule stretch of coastline, where they survive being washed over by the tides. They are parasites that develop inside spider eggs.

Echthrodesis lamorali, a tiny wasp less than a millimeter long, was described in 1968 by Canadian entomologist Lubomír Masner, a specialist in parasitoid micro-wasps that use spider eggs as hosts. The species was first observed not far from the beach town of Kommetjie in Western Cape province, South Africa, in an extremely small area that is believed to be its entire range. The rocky shoreline it calls home is highly saline and submerged by the tide twice a day. The females are completely wingless; the males have tiny wings but are still incapable of flight and only make up about a quarter of the population. In any case, wings would probably be a handicap for these wasps, as they would only make it harder for the adults to emerge from the spider eggs where they spend their larval stage as parasites. Wings would also weigh them down in water or make them easier to blow away in the wind, and they would get in females' way when breaking into spider cocoons to lay their eggs.

The two spider species that the wasps use as hosts both prey on small crustaceans. At high tide, the spiders scurry under the rocks and take shelter inside empty limpet shells that they seal up with silk. They can spend several hours safe and dry in these cocoons. (Both the spiders and the wasps can survive for some time underwater: their bodies are covered in bristle-like setae that trap a film of air

Top: Female *Echthrodesis lamorali* wasp inspecting spider eggs in their silk cocoon.
Bottom: The female lays each of her eggs inside a spider egg.

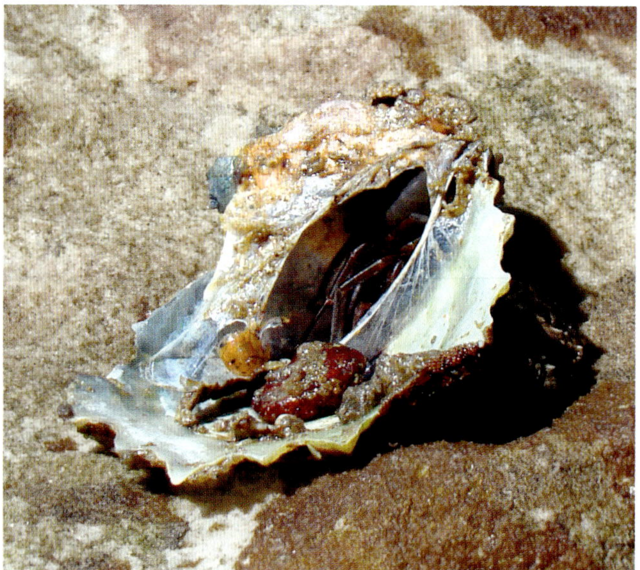

The wasp's host, a spider, spins a silk cocoon inside a seashell.
© Simon van Noort (Iziko Museums of South Africa)

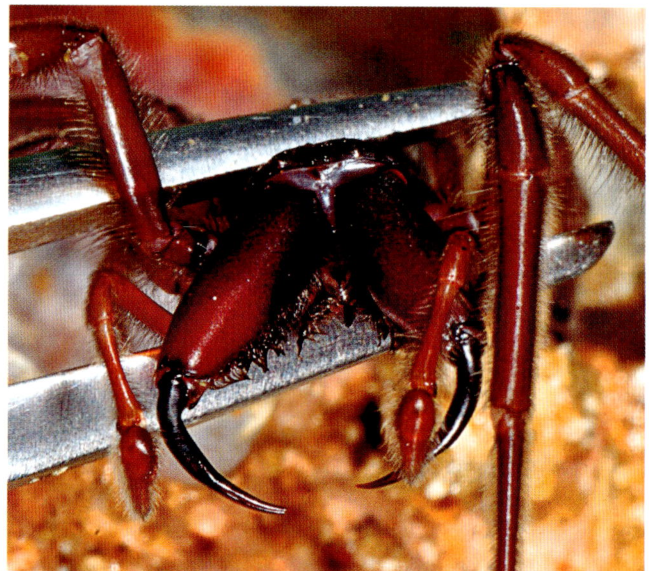

Desis formidabilis, one of the hosts of the parasitoid wasp *Echthrodesis lamorali*, is just as formidable as its name suggests: it has oversized chelicerae for cutting through the exoskeletons of its isopod prey.
© Simon van Noort (Iziko Museums of South Africa)

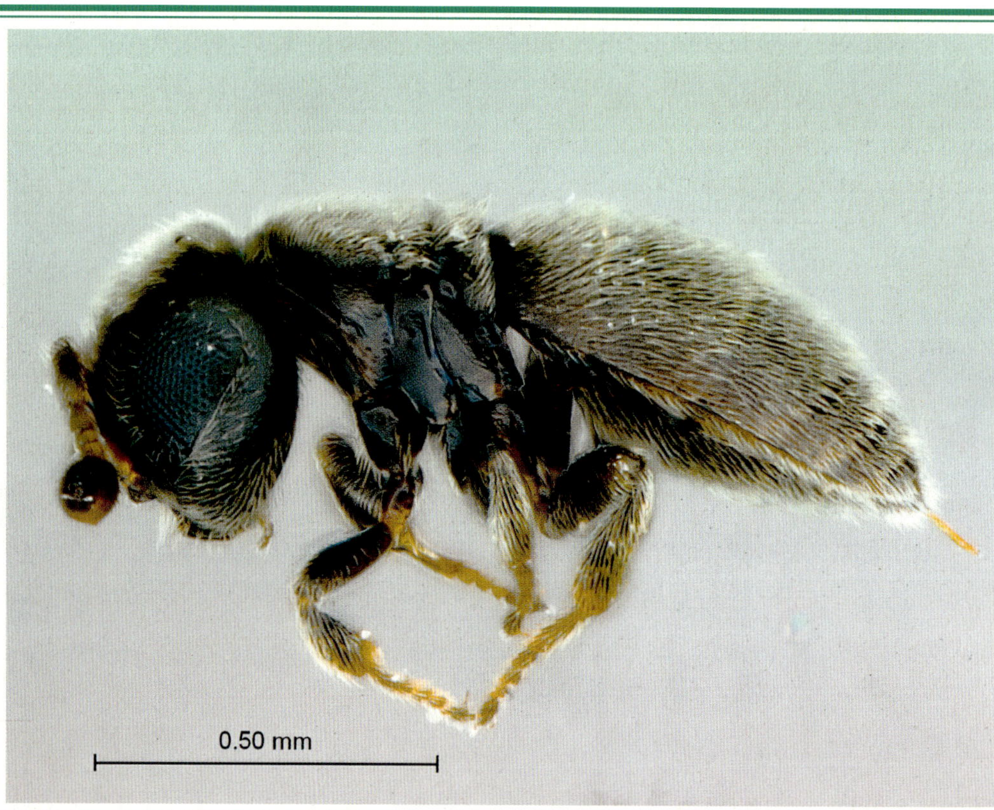

At less than 1 mm long, *Echthrodesis lamorali* is not only wingless but tiny.
© Simon van Noort (Iziko Museums of South Africa)

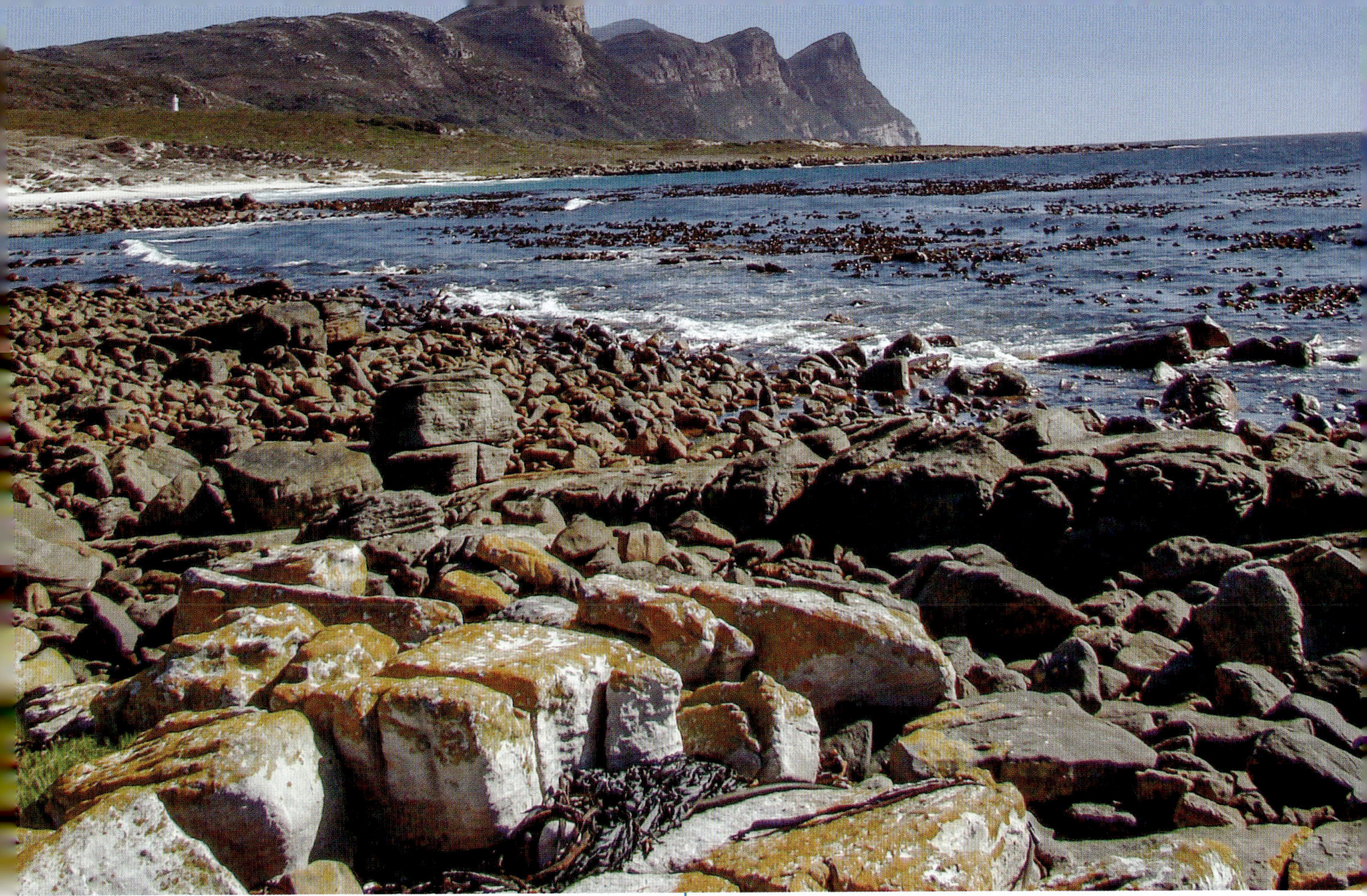

Echthrodesis lamorali's habitat: Kommetjie beach in South Africa.
© Pierre-Olivier Maquart

around them.) During low tide, the female wasp sneaks among the shells in search of spider cocoons. When she finds one, she cuts through the silk with her mandibles, enters the cocoon, and deposits her own eggs into every spider egg she finds. This uses up most of her energy; often a female will only parasitize a single cocoon (which nonetheless contains about a hundred spider eggs).

To defend their eggs, the spiders have developed a ruse. Like the Egyptian pharaohs who built fake treasure chambers into their tombs to trick thieves, the spiders spin empty egg sacs to trick the wasps, which waste energy breaking into them, thus limiting the number of spider eggs infested. As the wasp larvae develop, they eventually kill their hosts. The males emerge first and mate with the females as soon as they emerge. The females then disperse immediately in search of a spider cocoon in which to lay their own eggs.

It is not clear why these wasps have such a small range, as the host spiders have been observed from as far as East London, South Africa, to the coast of Lüderitz, Namibia. While it is true that the wingless females are only capable of dispersing some ten or twenty centimeters on their own, ocean currents, humans, or other animals could easily have spread them farther. No one knows why accidental introductions, despite being statistically probable, have either not occurred or ended in failure.

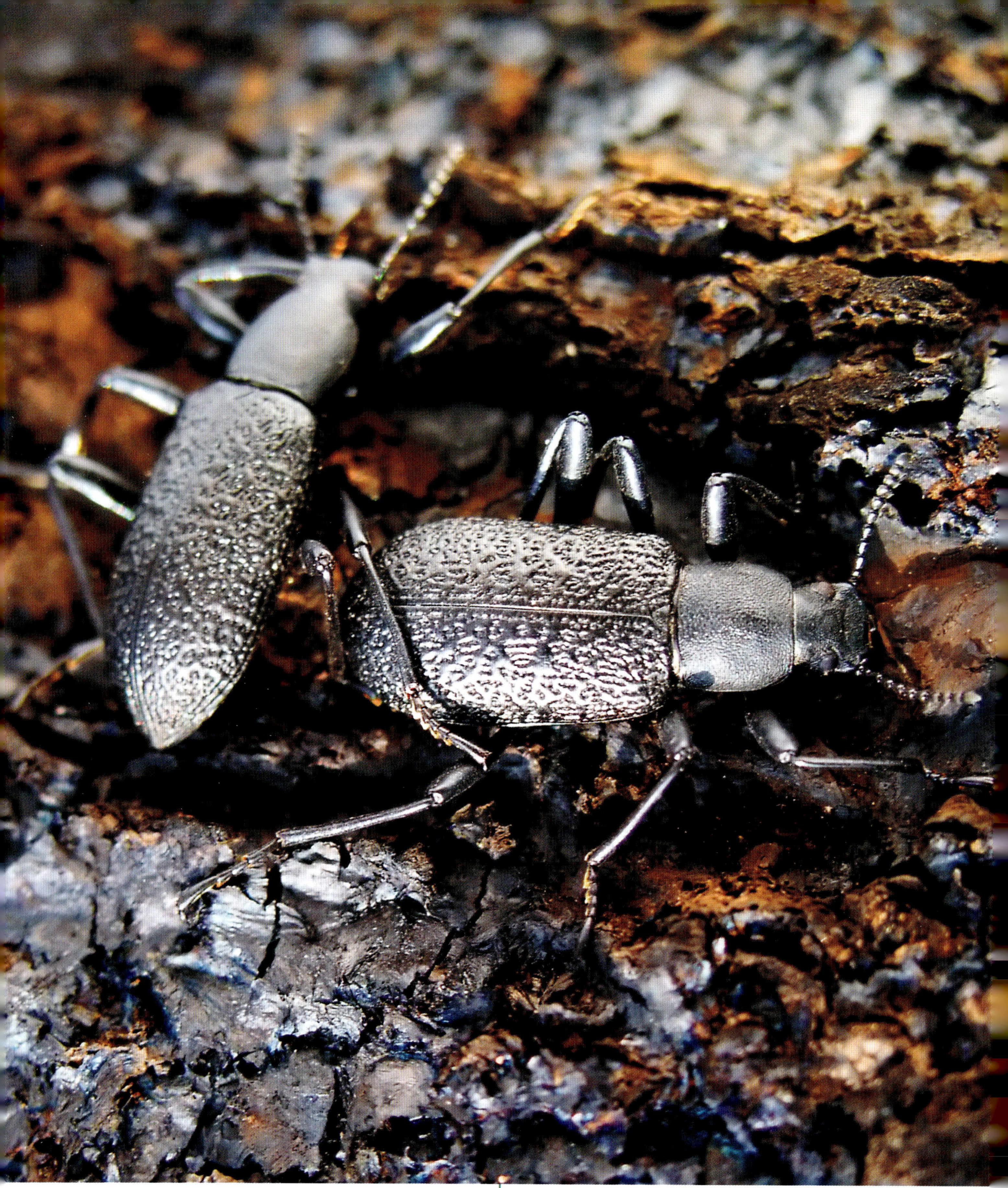

Upis ceramboides can survive even in extreme cold.
© Photowind

FREEZING FOR DEAR LIFE

UPIS CERAMBOIDES

(COLEOPTERA: TENEBRIONIDAE)

Can you imagine insects surviving at −80 °C (−112 °F)? While they are more often found in hot or temperate climates, there are also insects that live in the Arctic and Antarctic, where they are exposed to extreme temperatures and violent winds.

How much cold an insect can tolerate depends on its genetics, stage of development, diet, water retention, the length and intensity of exposure, the amount of daylight, and more. When it comes to surviving cold, insects fall into two categories: freeze-avoiding and freeze-tolerant. Both strategies have been studied mainly in beetles.

Freeze-avoiding insects are more common by far. They cannot survive ice crystals forming within their bodies, so when winter approaches, they produce their own antifreeze (alcohols, sugars, amino acids, etc.) that lowers the temperature at which ice can form.

Freeze-tolerant insects can survive even if their body water freezes. They produce proteins that induce freezing as soon as temperatures get below −10 °C (14 °F), but only in the spaces between their cells. As ice crystals begin to form, their cells expel some of their water to keep the extracellular ion concentrations stable. This keeps the cells themselves from freezing, but it also means that these insects' ability to survive frosty temperatures is directly tied to their tolerance for cellular dehydration. This is the strategy employed by *Upis ceramboides*, a large beetle native to the northern coast of Scandinavia (they were once present in southern Sweden but have since disappeared there), Russia, Canada, and Alaska. They are among the world's most cold-resistant insects, able to withstand temperatures approaching −80 °C/−112 °F—despite freezing at about −8 °C/18 °F—by partially dehydrating their cells. They do this by producing a molecule called xylomannan, which prevents ice crystals from forming within their cells, and a polyol similar to the antifreeze used in cars, which prevents lesions from forming on the cell membranes.

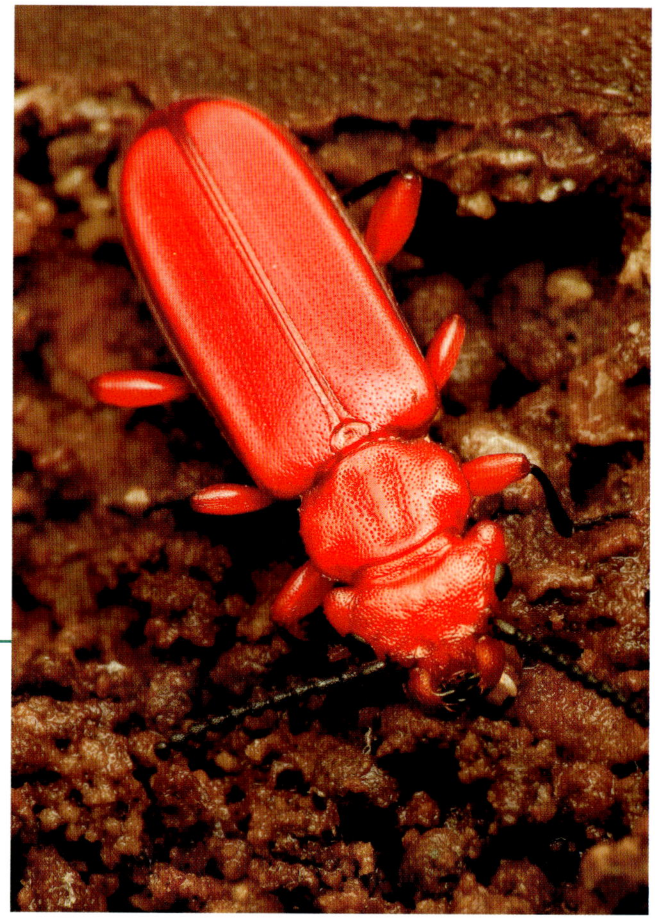

[This bright red beetle, *Cucujus clavipes*, inhabits a wide range in northern Alaska and the Canadian Yukon, where the winters are harsh. It can survive temperatures below −70 °C (−94 °F) and hibernates in the ice that forms under tree bark. Even when exposed to temperatures of −150 °C (−238 °F), the inside of its body still does not freeze! The beetle starts synthesizing and accumulating antifreeze proteins at the end of summer, at which time it stops feeding, desiccates, and purges any potential ice nucleators in its body (including the bacteria in its digestive system).

© Katja Schultz

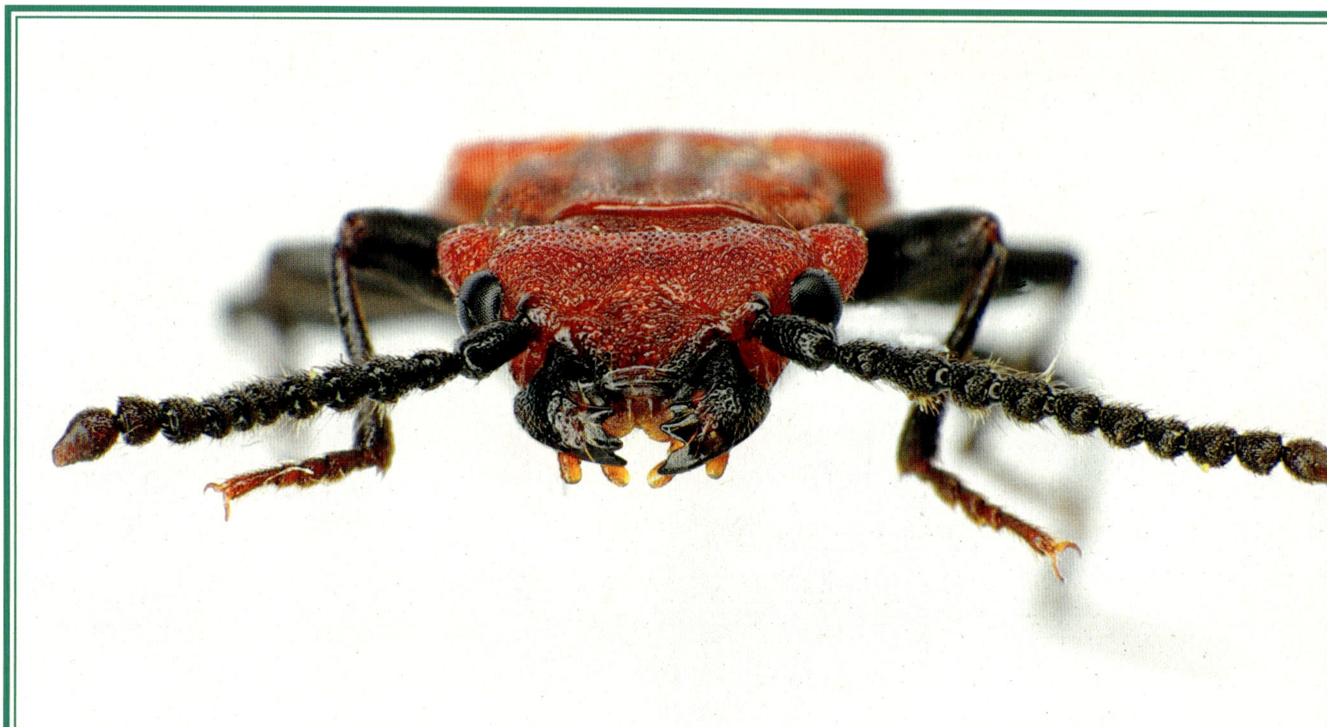

The near-threatened *Cucujus cinnaberinus* has an immense range that extends from Central Europe and the Baltic countries as far as Asia. It is particularly resistant to cold.

© Siga CC 4.0

DESICCATING LARVAE

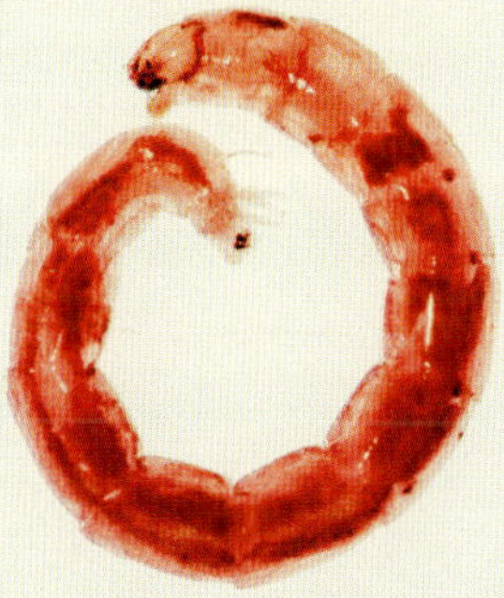

Anhydrobiosis is an adaptation that allows organisms to survive in dry conditions by losing nearly all their body water and more or less suspending vital functions. Creatures able to do this can survive conditions otherwise hostile to life: in a vacuum, extreme heat or cold, strong radiation, etc. Anhydrobiosis also makes it possible to live for a surprisingly long time—some such organisms have survived in their "dry" state for decades . . . or even millennia! The most complex animal capable of anhydrobiosis is the larva of a small fly, the sleeping chironomid (*Polypedilum vanderplanki*), which is native to semiarid regions of Africa where the dry season can last up to eight months. When the puddles under which the larvae live in underground galleries dry up, the larvae gradually lose up to 97 percent of their body water and can survive that way for up to seventeen years! Desiccated larvae are incredibly resilient: they can survive temperatures between –270 °C/–454 °F (five minutes in liquid helium) and +90 °C/+194 °F, not to mention massive doses of gamma radiation and a (near) total vacuum. Their bodies also produce proteins that protect them from osmotic stress. Desiccation damages the larvae's DNA, which needs to be restored through complex biochemical mechanisms after they rehydrate. This cycle of damage and repair is probably conducive to changes in the genome, making anhydrobiosis a driver of new adaptations. The sleeping chironomid can thank an inhospitable habitat, weak flying abilities, and the strong selective pressure of a long dry season for its extraordinary resilience in hostile conditions.

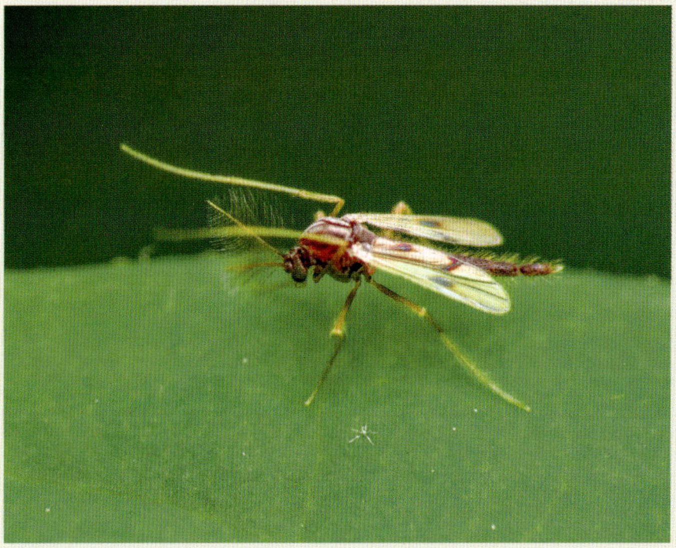

Above: *Polypedilum vanderplanki* larva. © Darrel Mann CC 4.0
Right: A tiny *Polypedilum* adult. © Katja Schulz

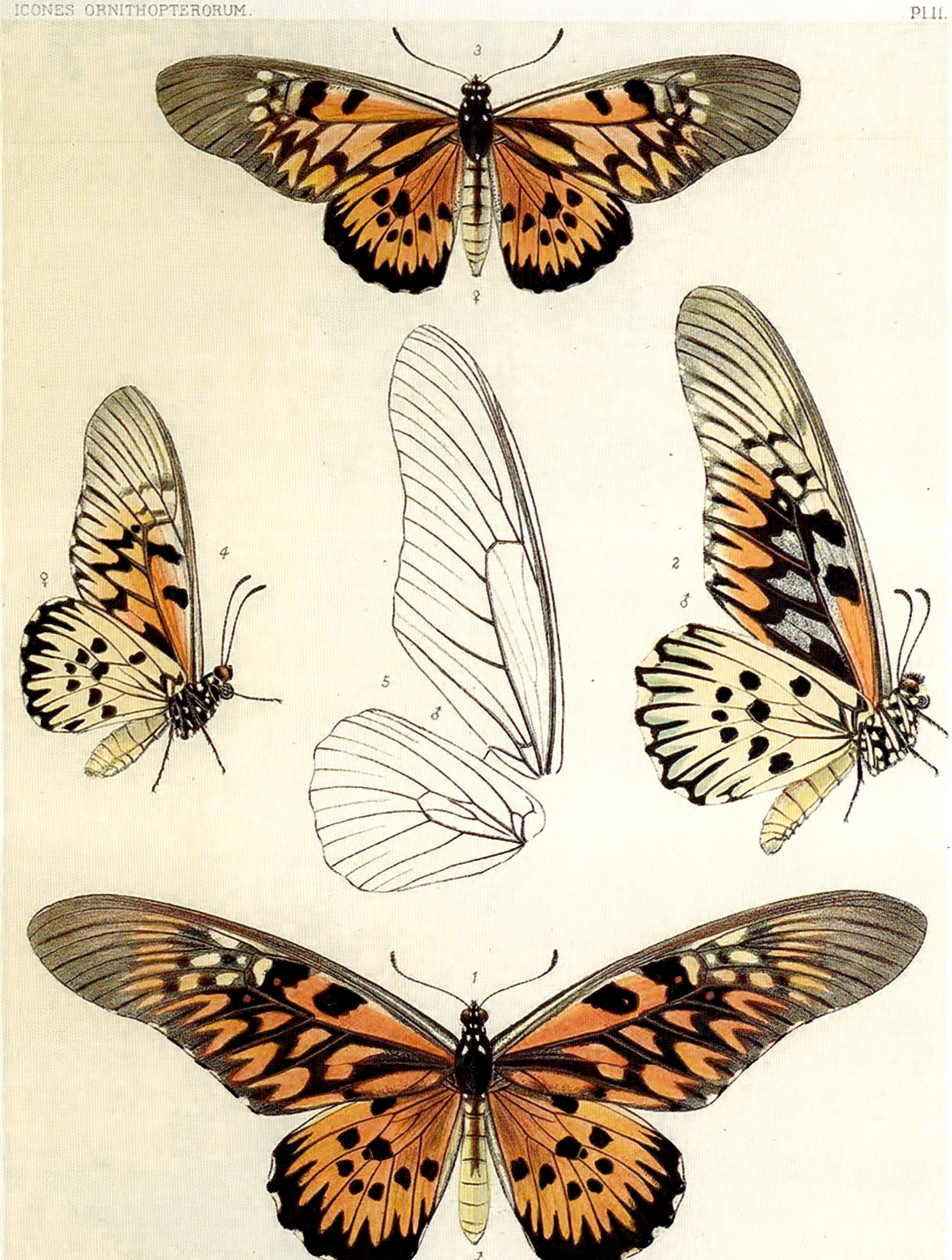

Robt H. F. Rippon. del. et lith. 1894. Hanhart imp.

DRURYIA ANTIMACHUS, *Drury and Auriv.* 1, 2, ♂; 3, 4, ♀.
5, Neuration of ♂.

A MYSTERIOUS GIANT

PAPILIO ANTIMACHUS

(LEPIDOPTERA: PAPILIONIDAE)

Some large insects are hard to miss and yet remain mysterious. Such is the case for the white witch moth (page 100) and this spectacular butterfly, the largest in Africa. While the males are commonly found in collections, the females have rarely been observed, and their life cycle remains largely unknown.

The African giant swallowtail has brown and ochre markings that help it blend into its surroundings despite a wingspan that can reach 24 to 25 centimeters, making it one of the largest butterflies in the world. It was described by English entomologist Dru Drury (1725–1804) and has an immense range that stretches from Guinea and Sierra Leone in the west to Uganda and the African Great Lakes region in the east.

African giant swallowtails can be seen drinking from patches of mud rich in mineral salts. The males are territorial and engage in hill-topping behavior: flying as high as they can and congregating in elevated areas to attract a mate. Once locally common, these butterflies are becoming rarer due to habitat loss and fragmentation of the African rainforests, as well as—on a smaller scale—hunting by local people, either for sale to collectors (who are willing to pay increasingly high prices) or for use in making handicrafts. Sightings are now few and far between in countries such as Guinea and Ghana, or anywhere west of the Dahomey Gap.

Just because females are hard to spot does not necessarily mean that males are more common. The females fly to great heights (over 25 meters) and spend most of their time in the constant sunlight of the treetops, hidden from predators and human observers. The African giant swallowtail's

African giant swallowtail female (top) and male (bottom) in an illustration from *Icones Ornithopterorum: A Monograph of the Papilionine Tribe Troides of Hubner, or Ornithoptera of Boisduval* (1898).

 (see page 85)

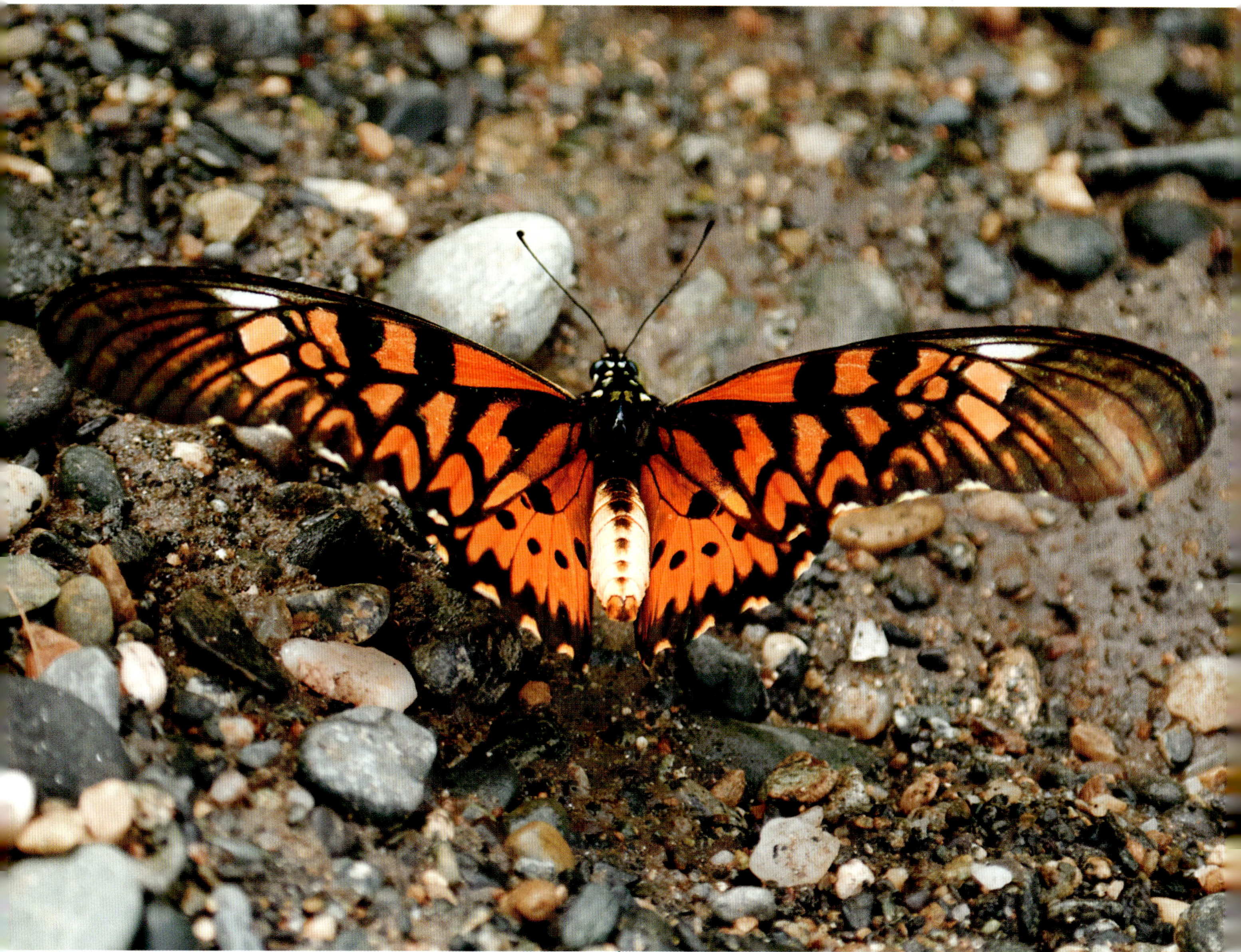

Male African giant swallowtail drinking from mud. The mineral salts in the mud are more important to the butterfly than the water itself.
© Michele Menegon

development is just as mysterious as the lives of its females. Mating has never been observed, and the early life stages remain unknown to science. In 2019, a French expedition scoured the old-growth forest of Lobaye, Central African Republic, where the butterfly population is declining despite the forest remaining well preserved. Three weeks of trekking, climbing trees, and observing the canopy did nothing to solve the mystery.

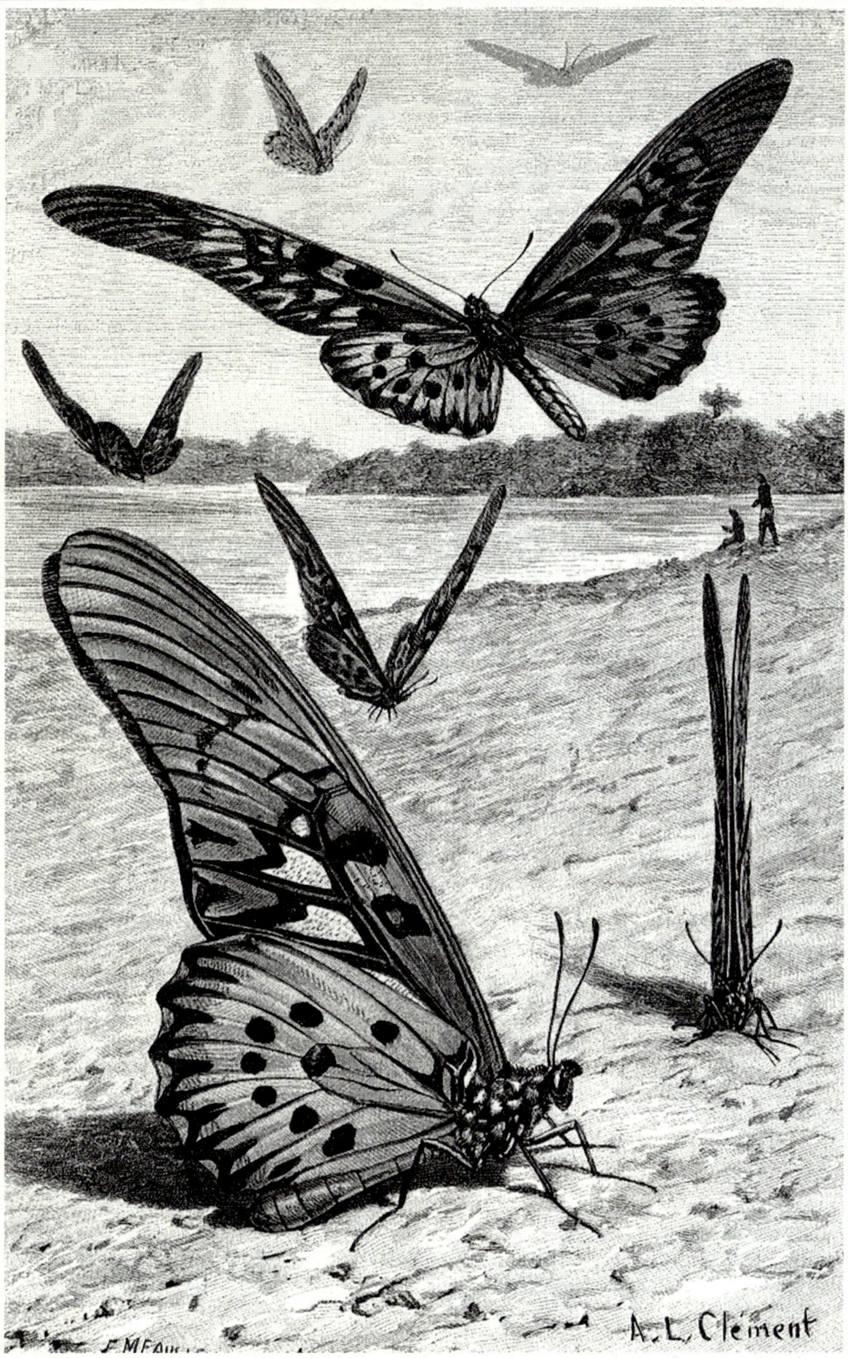

Illustration of male African giant swallowtails by Armand Lucien Clément (1848–1921) in the French science magazine *La Nature*. This illustration accompanied an 1893 article on observations made in the Congo by French explorer Jean Dybowski (1856–1928), who noted: "Until now, [this butterfly] was very rare in collections, and the entomological laboratory of the National Museum of Natural History in Paris had no such specimen until 1891, when it acquired a male, 19 centimeters in breadth, for a high price which only those familiar with entomology could guess at. Another, measuring only 18 centimeters, can be found in the collection left by the late M. de Beaulieu. The butterflies from Bangui will form a highly welcome group of specimens of varying sizes."

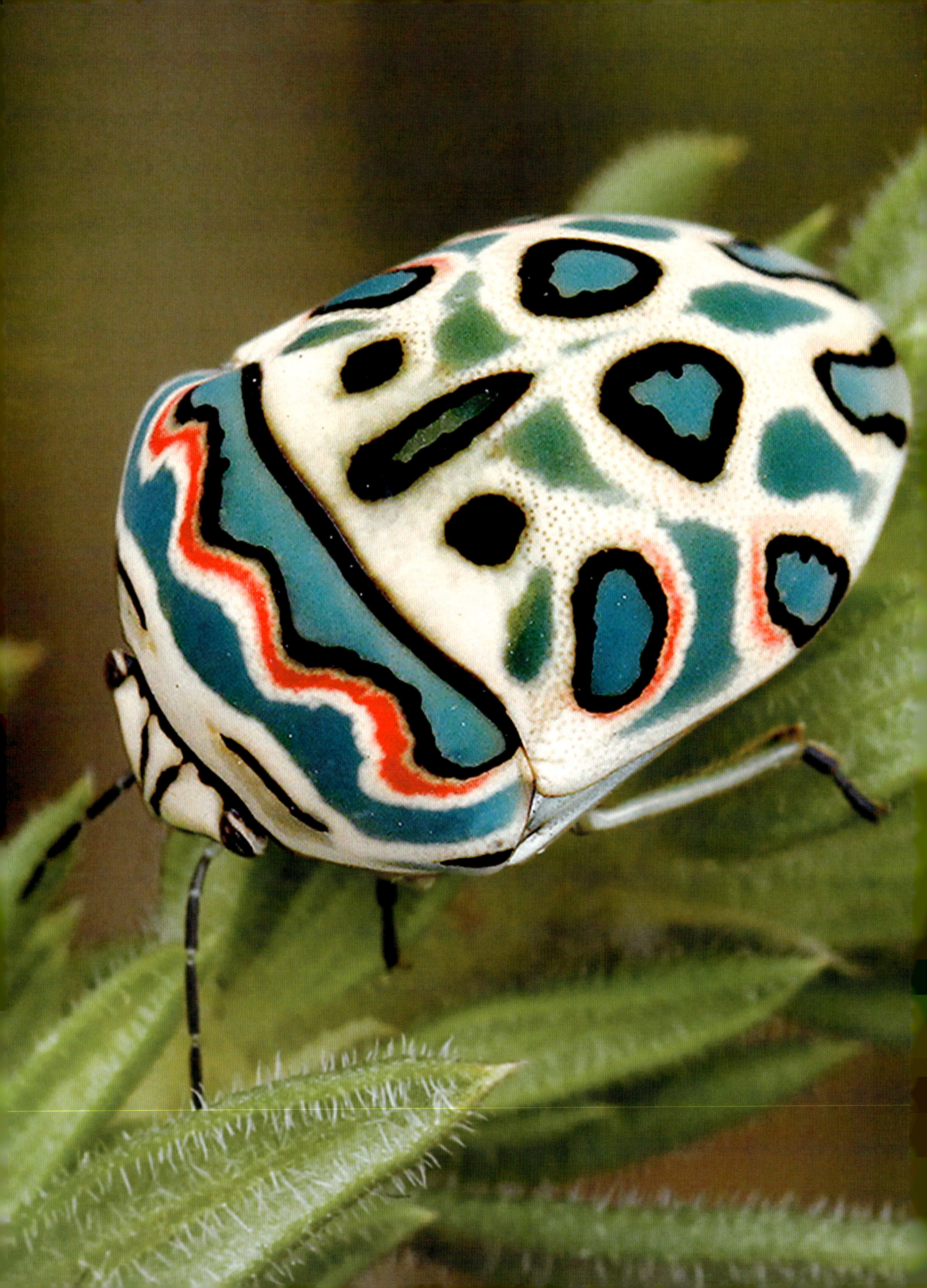

JEWELS AND EMBLEMS

With their flamboyant colors, magnificent markings, metallic sheen, or delicate forms, some insects make a fashion statement. No need for a magnifying glass or an entomologist's keen eye to be dazzled by the electric blue wings of *Morpho cypris* or the elegant silhouette of the paradise birdwing. For millennia, artists all around the world have used particularly beautiful insects to make jewelry and other decorative items. And with the cabinet of curiosities making a comeback in interior design, public interest in insects is also reviving, in an echo of the Enlightenment-era fascination with entomology. Other species, while less visually striking, have held symbolic importance to humanity since the dawn of time: think of the scarab beetle in ancient Egypt, or the death's-head hawkmoth on the poster for *The Silence of the Lambs*.

The Picasso bug (*Sphaerocoris annulus*) from tropical and subtropical Africa is sometimes so abundant that it damages crops, including coffee plantations. It is roughly 1.5 cm long and, like many other insects, has truly spectacular markings.
© Bart Wursten

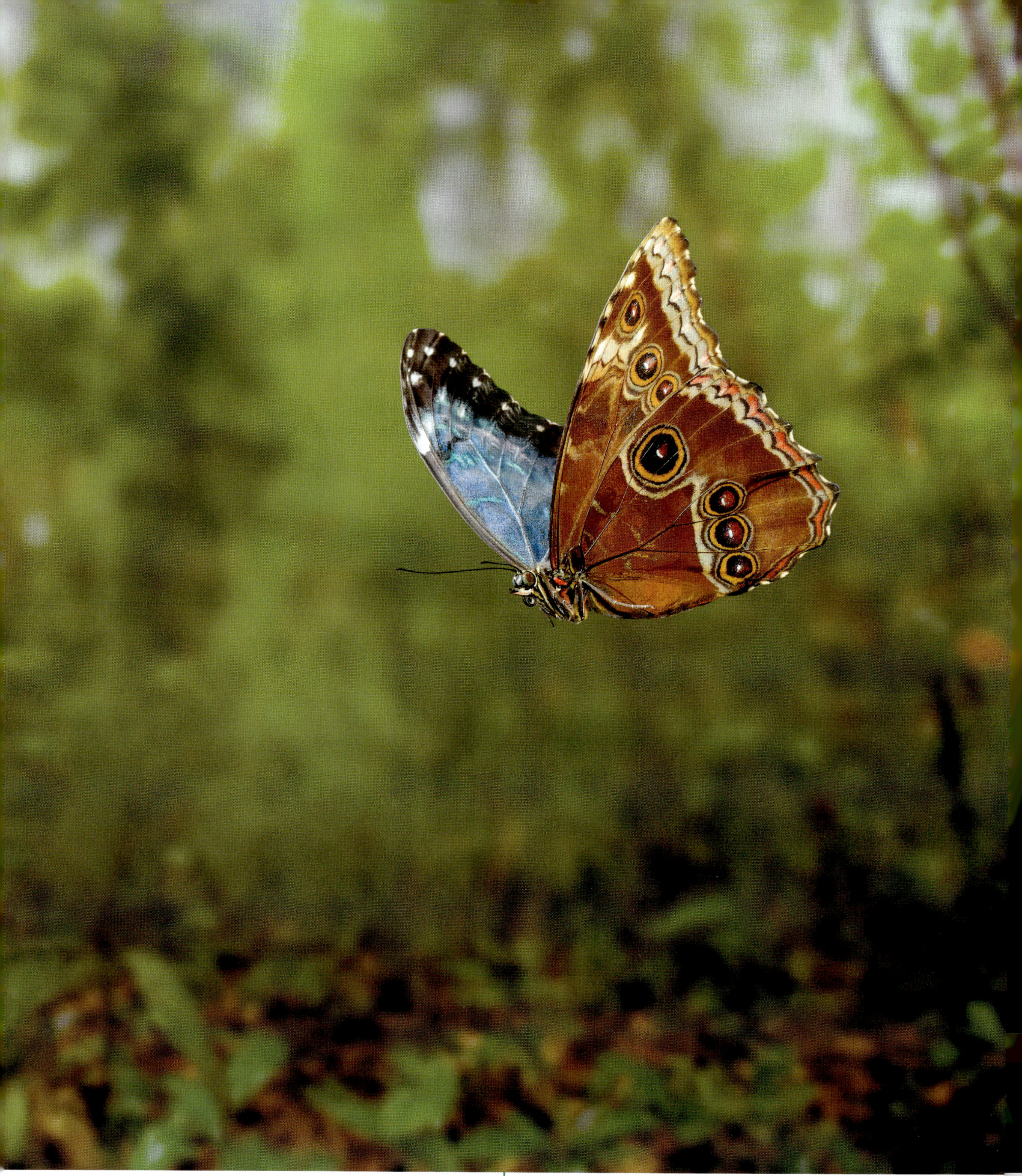

When they are not flying, butterflies in the genus *Morpho* perch on tree trunks, fold up their wings, and blend in with their surroundings. The ocelli (eyespots) on the ventral side of their wings serve to frighten away predators. The markings on this *M. peleides*, found throughout the Neotropical realm, are typical of the genus.
© Stephen Dalton/Photoshot/Biosphoto

A FLASH OF BLUE

GENUS *MORPHO*

(LEPIDOPTERA: NYMPHALIDAE)

The iridescent blue color of male morpho butterflies from South and Central America has fascinated naturalists ever since they were discovered by Europeans. Not only are these butterflies beautiful and diverse, the complex structure of their scaled wings has also attracted interest from researchers in photonics and biotechnology applications.

The genus *Morpho* contains some thirty species of butterflies native to tropical regions of South and Central America, where they inhabit various wooded habitats, from tropical rainforests to dry deciduous woodlands, from sea level to mid-altitude. Most can be seen flying during the day, except for *M. eugenia*, which is only active during a brief period at dawn. They range in size from 8 centimeters (*M. rhodopteron*) to over 20 centimeters (giants like *M. hecuba*).

In many morpho species, the males have an intense, metallic blue sheen on all or parts of the dorsal side of their wings. Subspecies of *M. rhetenor*, such as *M. rhetenor helena*, and *M. cypris* are among the most iridescent. But *M. menelaus*, *M. didius*, and *M. godarti* are also very blue. Others are more of a pearlescent color, such as *M. sulkowskyi*, which can be seen across the northernmost regions of South America. Still others are slate gray to tawny brown without any iridescence at all (*M. hecuba*, *M. telemachus*, etc.). Females usually have black, ochre, and brown markings. Some females are partially iridescent, but much less so than males. And some rare female specimens have been found with blue scales in scattered patches.

In all species and both sexes, the ventral sides of morpho wings are dull brown and marked with eyespots. When their wings are folded up, they are thus hidden from predators, which the eyespots are also intended to deter.

The genus name *Morpho* refers to the dazzling iridescence of these butterflies, and comes from the ancient Greek word *μορφώ* meaning "the Shapely One": an epithet of Aphrodite, goddess of love and beauty.

The dazzling blue is not a pigment—it is the result of structural coloration. Morpho butterfly wings are covered in ridged scales that are actually transparent and colorless. Each ridge is formed from layers of firtree-shaped lamellae whose "branches" diffract light in a network that creates the illusion of color. The lamellae reflect over 70 percent of incident light, including ultraviolet light. This explains why—depending on the angle of observation, wavelength, and refraction index—the resulting color can vary from dark brown to pure blue or turquoise. This particularly vibrant coloring (some species are visible to the naked eye from hundreds of meters away!) is studied as part of photonics, or the science of how light is transmitted in the form of photons.

Male morphos are strong fliers and will chase off any rivals that enter their territory on the forest edge, in clearings, or along rivers and streams. It would therefore seem that their blue coloring is a form of intrasexual communication. Males are attracted to anything blue and easily netted using a blue object to draw them in. Their blue wings may also serve to attract females, which tend to hide in the canopy and fly less often. But the scales also have other purposes, which are becoming clearer with further study. For one thing, they repel water, which helps the butterflies stay clean and protects their wings. The scales also play a role in temperature regulation, changing shape when the chitin overheats so that the lamellae reflect more infrared, thus limiting the wing temperature to around 40 °C (104 °F).

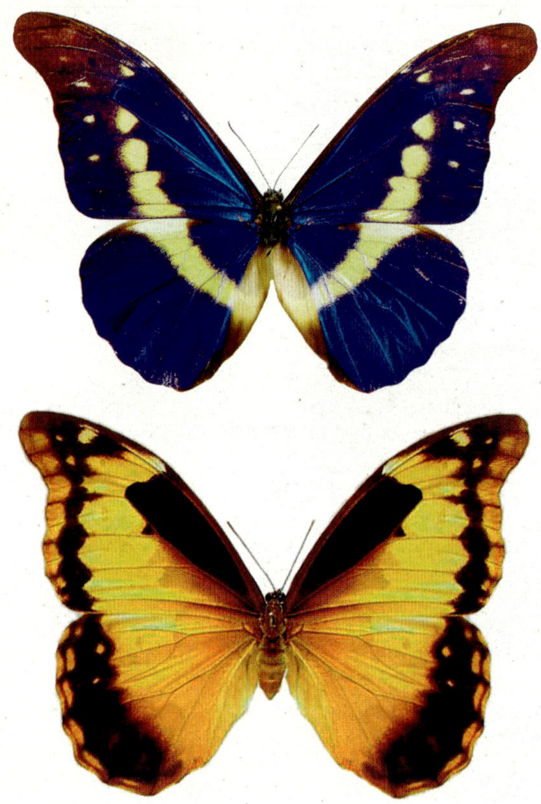

The subspecies *Morpho rhetenor helena* is only found in the Huallaga River valley in Peru. The male (top) measures 120–140 mm, the female (bottom) 140–160 mm. For a long time, this butterfly—the female in particular—was hard to find in collections. As access to the valleys of the Peruvian Amazon has expanded, they are now almost common.

There are various potential biotechnology applications from studying morpho wings (as well as those of other iridescent butterflies and insects in general): dye-free paints, energy-efficient screens, protections for solar panels during heat waves, and more.

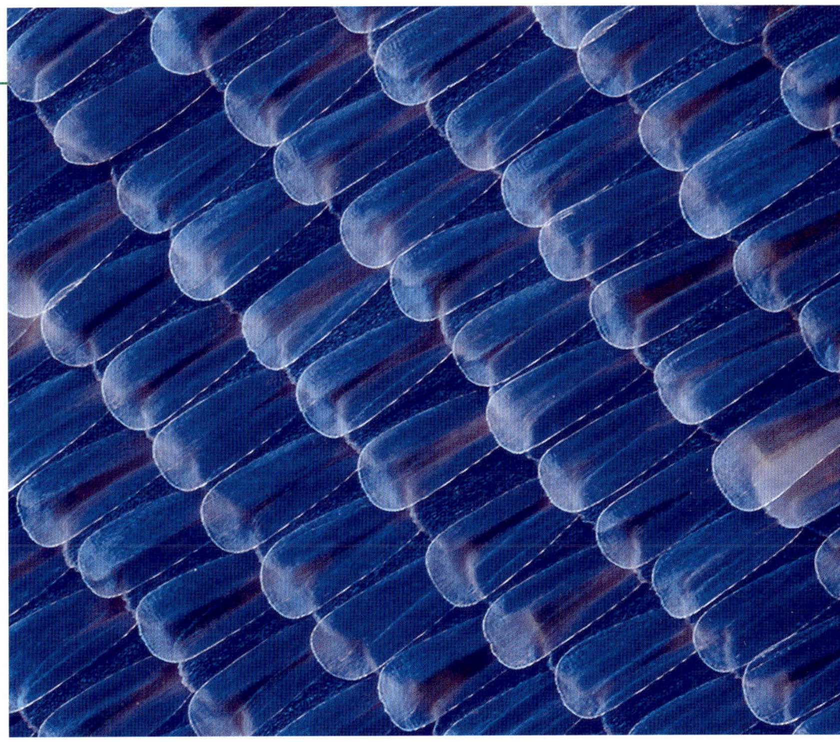

The scales on a morpho wing are only 200–250 μm long and 50 μm wide.
© Linden Gledhill CC 4.0

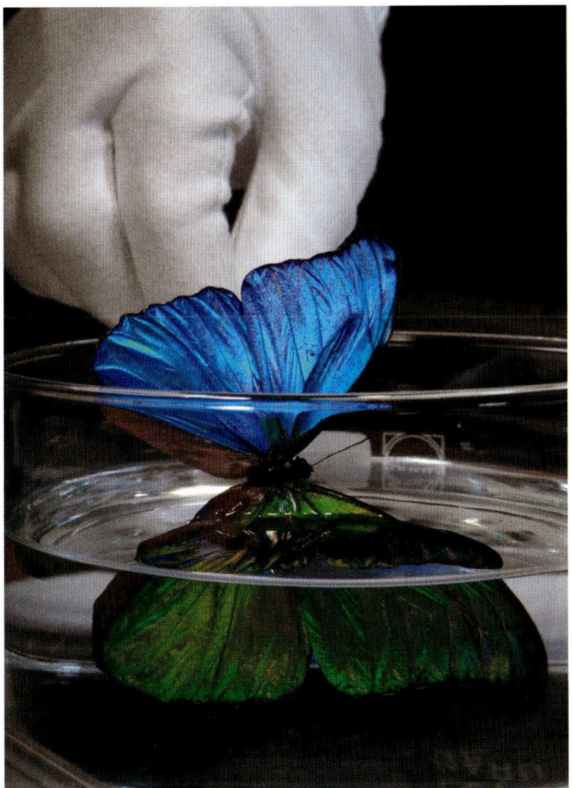

Morpho wings look blue because of physics. Exposure to solvents changes the refraction index of the air trapped in the lamellae on their scales, changing the spectrum that is reflected back. These butterflies thus appear blue in the air but green when dipped in acetone and brown in trichloroethylene.
© Pascal Goetgheluck/Biosphoto

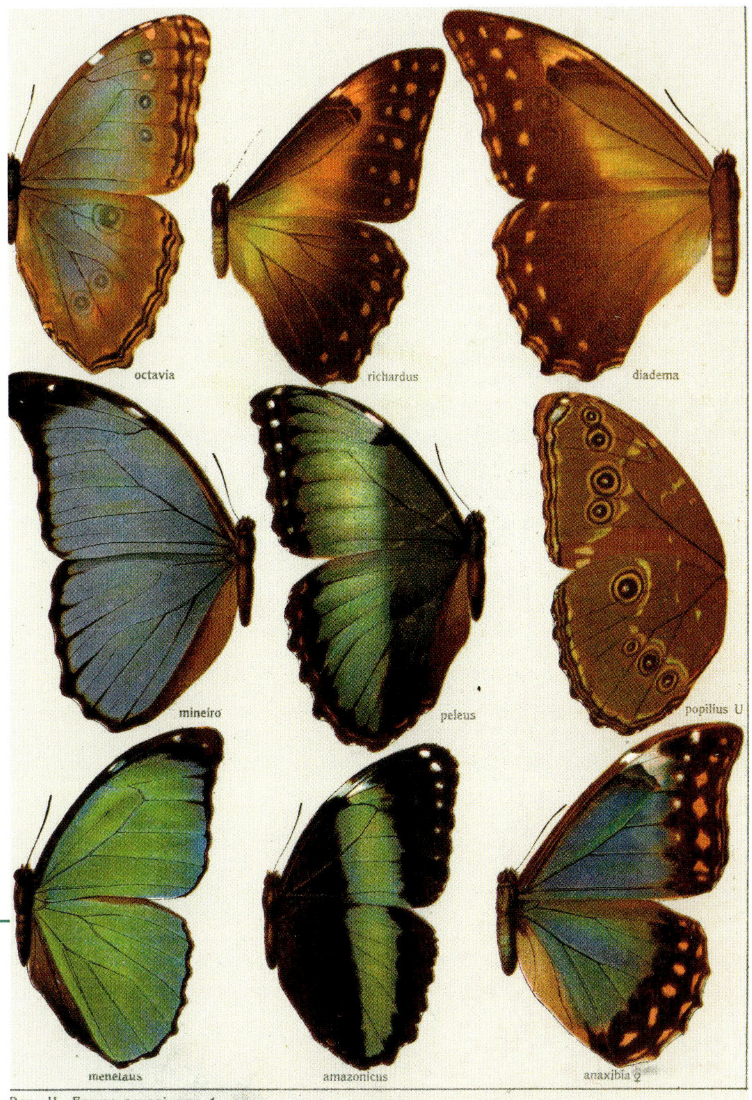

Illustration of morpho butterflies from *Die Gross-Schmetterlinge der Erde* by German entomologist Adalbert Seitz (1860–1938), a twenty-volume treatise on large butterflies and moths that contains 1,364 lithographs. It was originally published in German in the early twentieth century, then later in English and French.

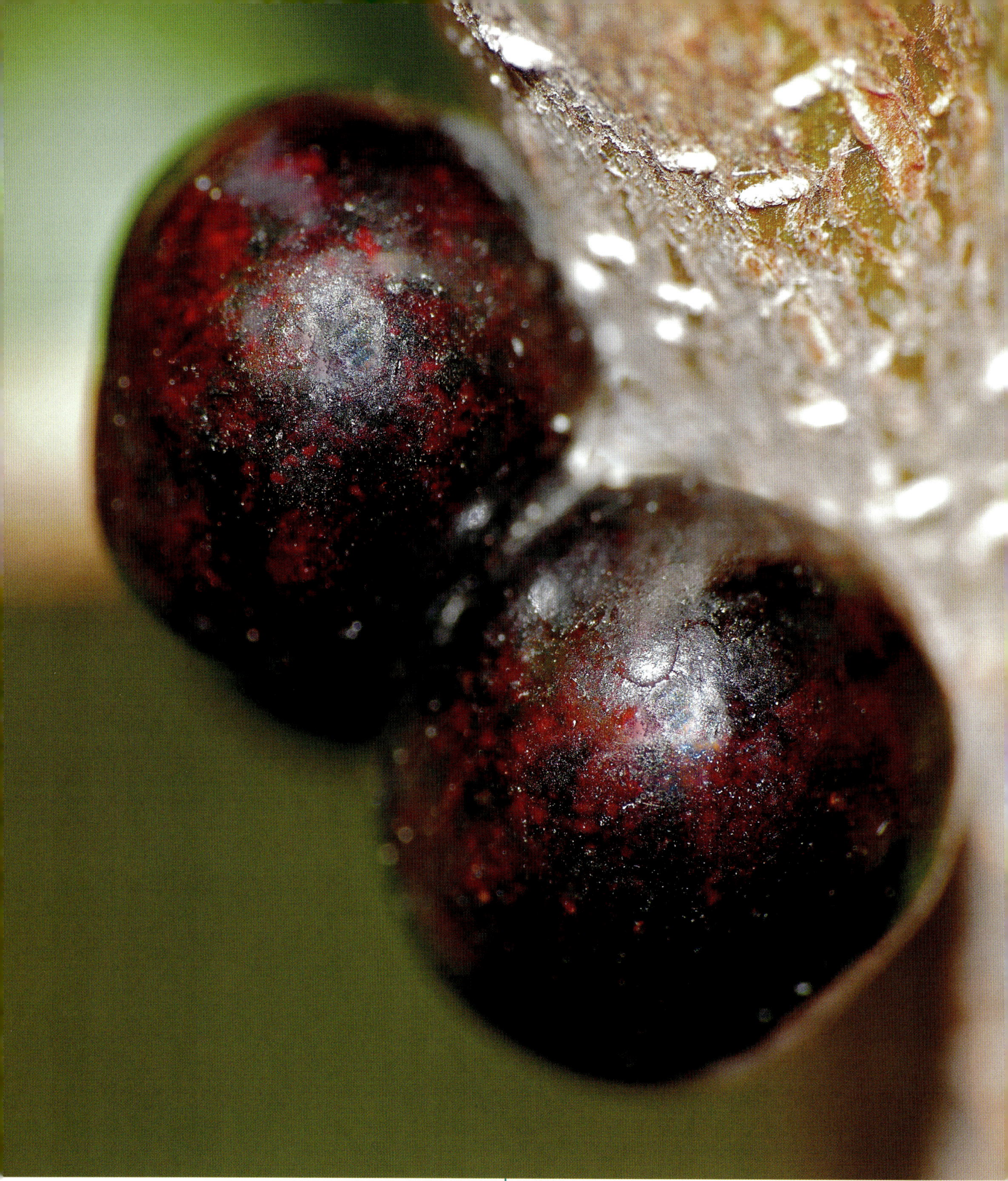

Kermes vermilio are spherical scale insects of 5–6 mm that cling, immobile, to the sturdy twigs and leaves of the kermes oak tree. They have now become rare due to the use of pesticides in vineyards, which are often planted in the open land preferred by the kermes oak.
© Bernard Dupont

TRUE VERMILION

KERMES VERMILIO

(HEMIPTERA: KERMESIDAE)

These "scarlet seeds" are not seeds at all: they are tiny scale insects in the genus *Kermes*, sometimes known as "vermilion." At one time, their eggs were at the center of a brisk artisanal and commercial trade, as they can be used to produce a rich red dye that was a symbol of power for centuries.

Kermes vermilio were once collected by women and children from the branches of the kermes oak in the regions of Languedoc and Provence in the south of France, and Castilla–La Mancha in southeast Spain. The insects were then dried in the sun and crushed to produce a dye that was bright red or, in lower concentrations, pink or slightly purple. The tree's name comes from the Persian *qirmiz* meaning "bloody" (and by extension, "red"), the same origin as the English word "crimson." The species name *vermilio* comes from the fact that this insect was once thought to be a small worm, or *vermiculus* in Latin: the red dye made from its eggs thus came to be called, among other names, vermilion. Harvesting the insect is time-consuming and highly dependent on fickle weather conditions. A kilogram of females full of eggs only yields 10 to 15 grams of pigment, and just how red the pigment will be depends on the level of kermesic acid in each batch.

Kermes dye was used in cave paintings as early as the Neolithic period. Use of the dye spread from the Eastern Mediterranean to Western Europe through ancient history, as it proved easier to produce and less expensive than the red dye extracted from murex sea snails. It brightened the palette of medieval illuminations and brought wealth to the dyers and drapers of Montpellier, France, who invented a way of making it more colorfast using a bath of stannous chloride. Kermes also produced cloth of a brighter scarlet than could be made using plant-based dyes. It took over one million insects to make a single sheet of red cloth, which, in the sixteenth century, cost the equivalent of three years' salary for a master craftsman.

Kermes vermilio was used by dyers until a New World insect, the cochineal (*Dactylopius coccus*), proved to be more profitable. Kermes dye thus became largely obsolete, reserved for royal or papal garments. Artificial dyes eventually put an end to its commercial use.

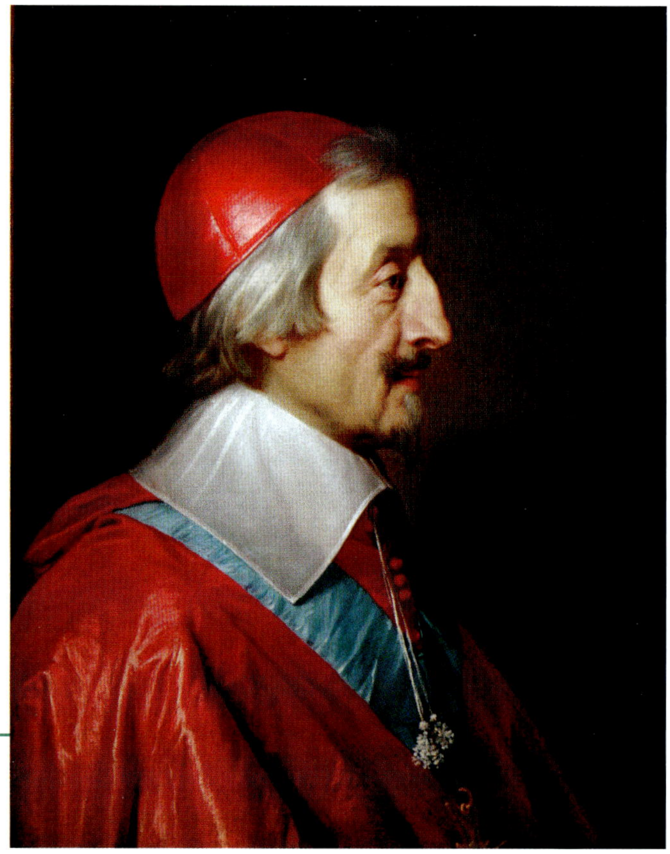

In 1464, Pope Paul II authorized the use of kermes dye for the scarlet garments worn by Catholic cardinals, as seen here on Cardinal Richelieu as painted by Philippe de Champaigne (1642).

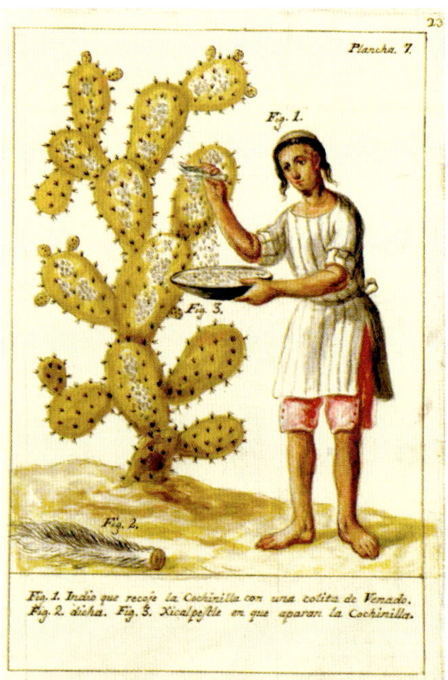

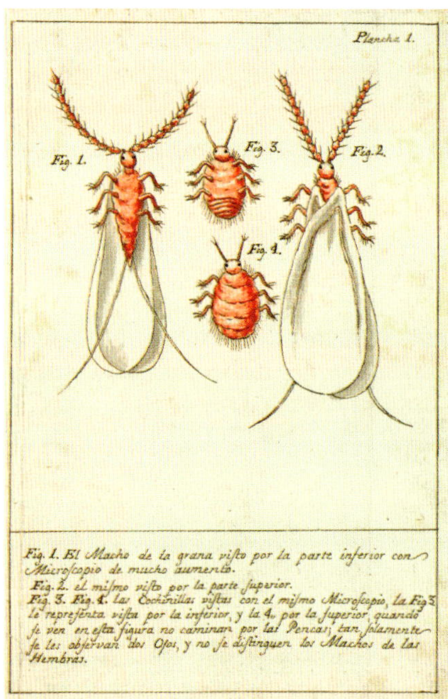

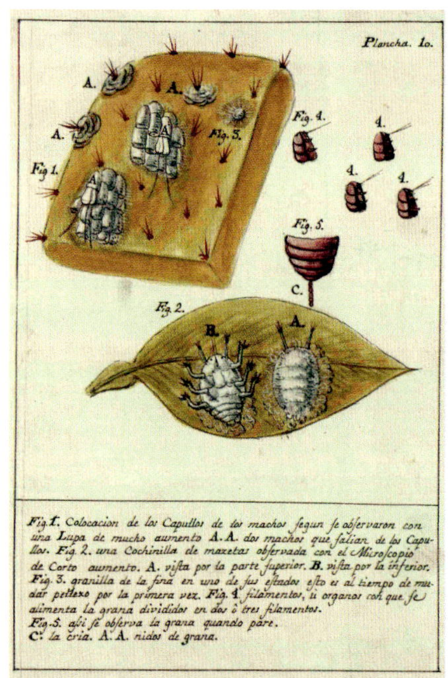

José Antonio de Alzate y Ramírez (1737–1799), a priest in New Spain, published *Memoria sobre la naturaleza, cultivo y beneficio de la grana* in 1777 about the cochineal (*Dactylopius coccus*), a scale insect that lives on the prickly pear (*Opuntia*) cactus. The image on the left shows an Indigenous man harvesting cochineal by brushing them into a basket using a white-tailed deer tail. The middle plate shows the insect itself (males on the right and left, females in the center). The right plate shows the insects feeding on cactus pads.

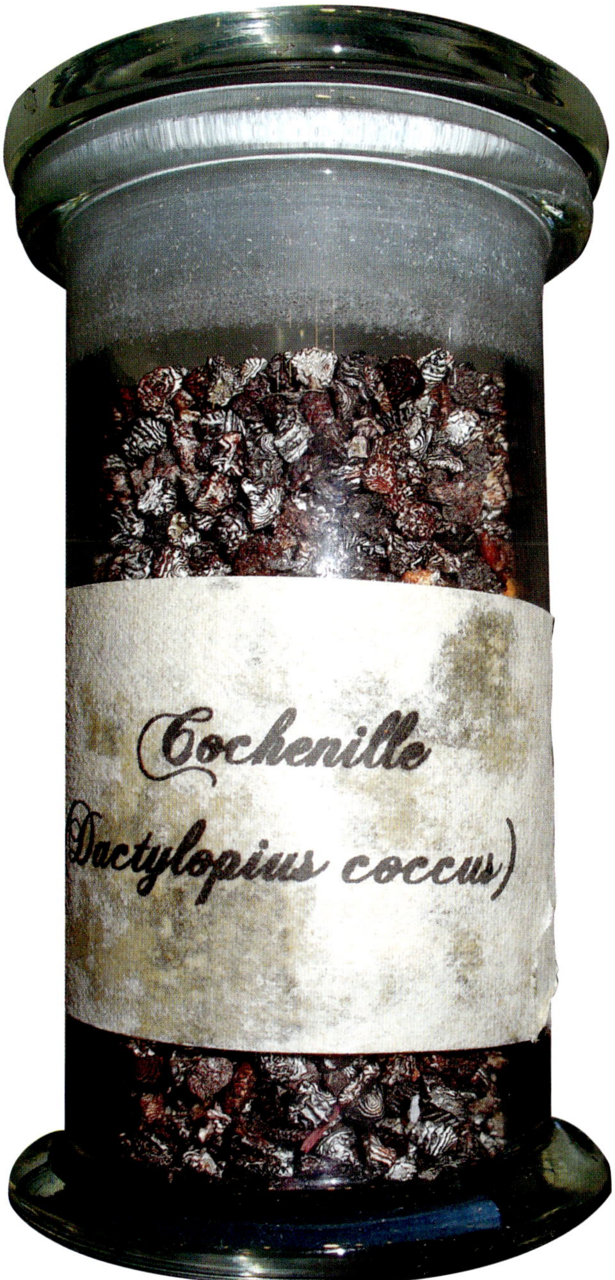

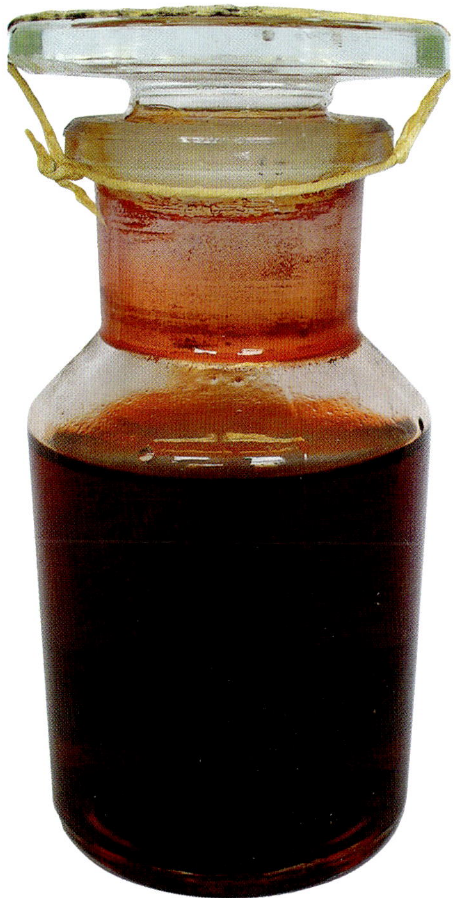

Cochineal extract, or natural carmine dye, is made by grinding up the dried bodies of female scale insects. Once used to color textiles and medieval medicines, it is now used to color foods, pharmaceuticals, and industrial products under the code name Natural Red 4 or E120.

© H. Zell

Carmine or cochineal dye is still produced today using cochineal insects (*Dactylopius coccus*), as it is less expensive to make than kermes dye. The red color in *D. coccus* comes from carminic acid. Peru produces some 80 percent of the world's cochineal, followed by Bolivia, Chile, Mexico, and the Canary Islands. The female insects are harvested by hand, dried in the sun, and sold to dye manufacturers who extract carmine from the precipitate obtained after boiling the powdered insects.

© H. Zell

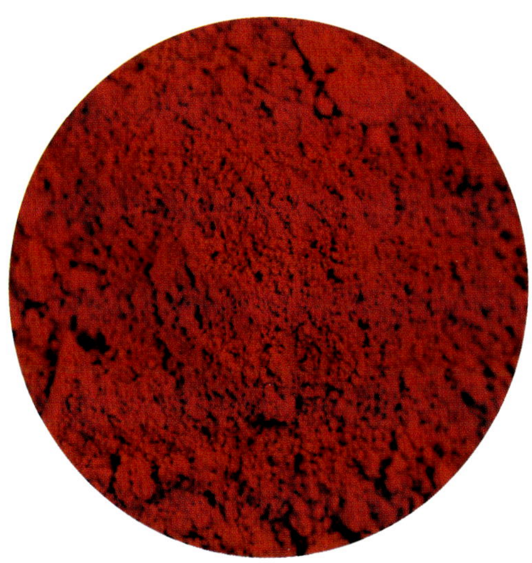

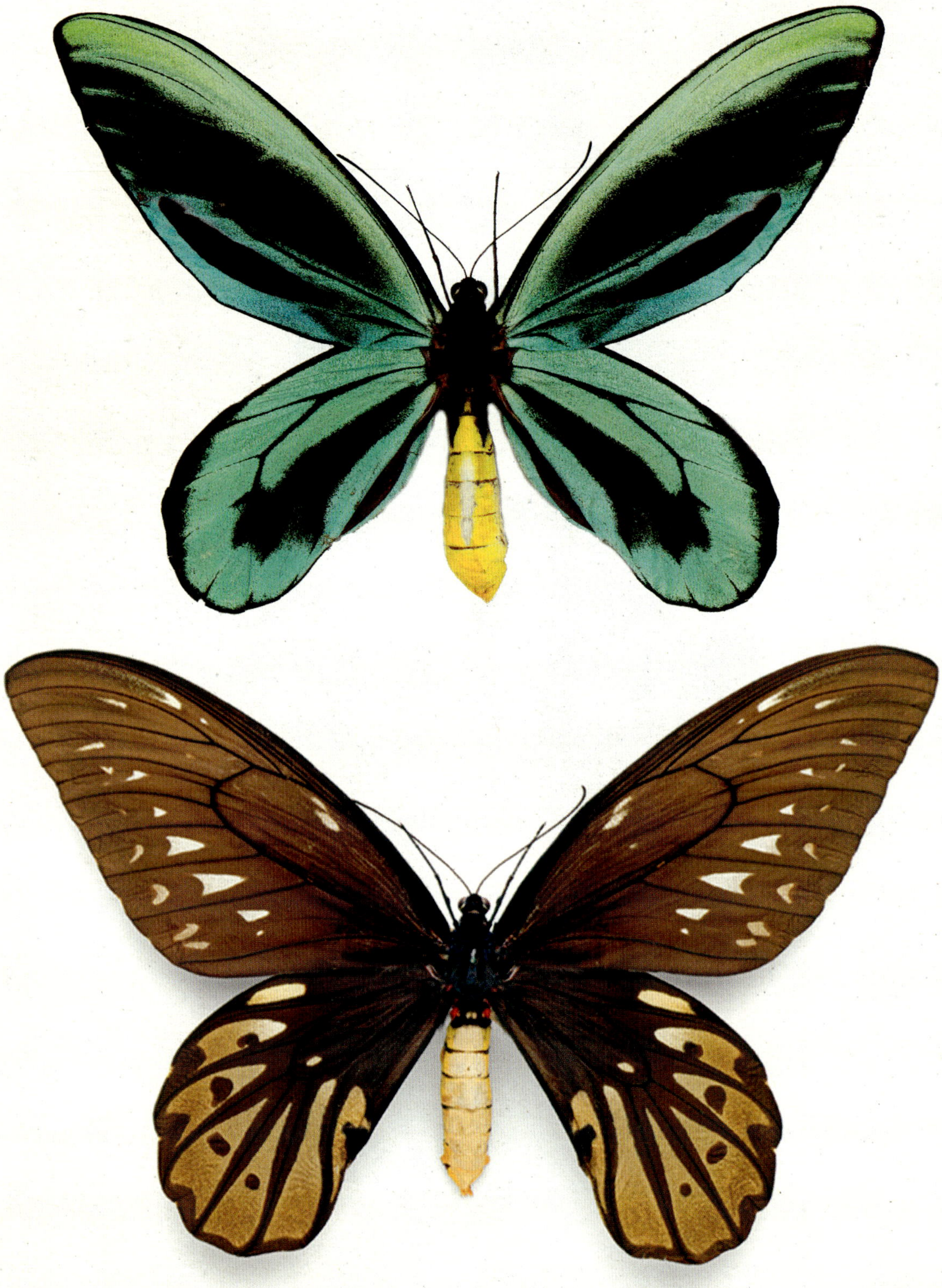

The male (top) and female (bottom) *Ornithoptera alexandrae*, like all birdwing butterflies, look very different. Males have a maximum wingspan of 20 cm, but females range from 18 to 29 cm, making them the world's largest butterflies.

QUEEN ALEXANDRA'S BIRDWING

ORNITHOPTERA ALEXANDRAE

(LEPIDOPTERA: PAPILIONIDAE)

This giant among butterflies is exceptional not just in size but in color. It lives in a restricted range on the island of New Guinea and is endangered—partly due to unscrupulous collectors, but mostly due to habitat fragmentation and deforestation to make room for palm oil plantations.

The Queen Alexandra's birdwing was discovered in January 1906 by Albert Stewart Meek (1871–1943), the employee of a wealthy English banker with a passion for zoology, Lord Walter Rothschild (1868–1937). Rothschild tasked Meek with procuring rare specimens from the Indo-Australian Archipelago, including New Guinea and the surrounding islands, as far as the Solomon Archipelago. The first collected specimen, a female observed at an altitude of roughly 1,500 meters near the Mambare River in what is now Papua New Guinea, was downed with a shotgun. It may seem incredible, but this was a common technique at the time. It was also used by British explorer John MacGillivray (1821–1867) to capture the first specimen of a related species, the Queen Victoria's birdwing, on Guadalcanal in 1854. Meek later captured other specimens using a net, and even managed to discover the butterfly's caterpillar. Rothschild described the species the following year and named it in honor of the queen consort of the United Kingdom, Alexandra of Denmark (1844–1925).

The Queen Alexandra's birdwing is the largest butterfly in the world and found only in Oro province, eastern Papua New Guinea. Four isolated populations survive on a territory of old-growth and second-growth open rainforest less than 100 kilometers square. One population lives at low altitude, on the plain around Popondetta. The other three are found between 500 and 800 meters altitude, including one population in the Managalas Plateau conservation area. The species has since disappeared from the region where it was discovered by Meek over a century ago.

The adults are strong fliers and mostly remain high in the canopy, except when they descend to gather nectar in the early morning and at dusk. The females only lay their eggs on one species of

This male Queen Alexandra's birdwing has just emerged from its pupa and spread its wings for the first time. It is now ready to take flight.
© Angelus Palik

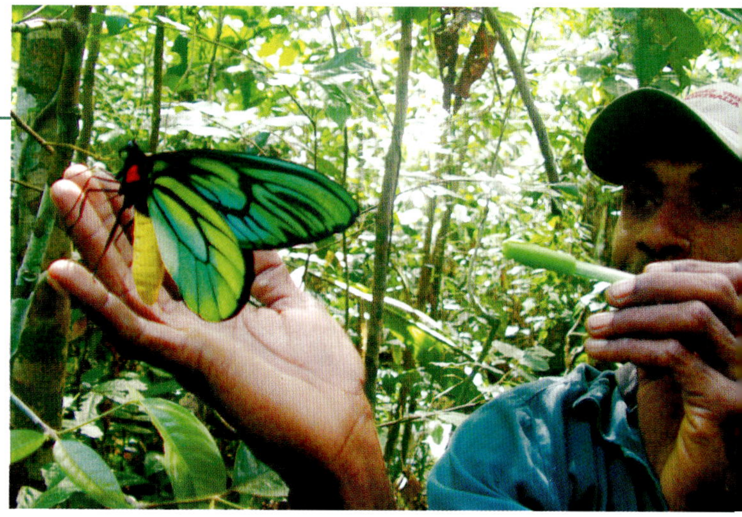

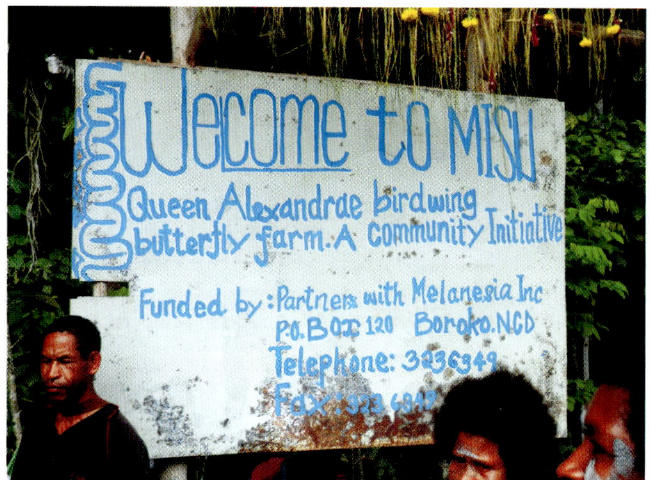

The village of Misu in Papua New Guinea is a hotspot for Queen Alexandra's birdwings. It is located within a protected area run entirely by the local community.
© Camille Cusin

plant, *Aristolochia dielsiana*. The males stake out a territory that they patrol in search of potential mates and which they defend from rival males, other butterfly species, and even small birds. Mating is brief but spectacular: the male flies over the female, releasing sex hormones that increase her receptivity, then fertilizes her over the course of two to three minutes.

The Queen Alexandra's birdwing was studied in detail by Dutch entomologist Raymond Straatman (1917–1987), who moved to Papua New Guinea in 1969. He was put in charge of a project aimed at better understanding and protecting this exceptional butterfly, which was already under threat from deforestation by palm oil producers. The situation was made worse when Mount Lamington erupted in January 1951, destroying a large swath of the birdwing's habitat and fragmenting its range. The eruption is one key reason why it is so rare today.

The species is protected by law in Papua New Guinea since 1966. In 1987, it became one of only a few insects to be listed in Appendix I of the Convention on International Trade in Endangered Species of Wild Fauna and Flora (CITES), meaning all trade is banned. The Queen Alexandra's birdwing was still sold in insect collection catalogues in the 1970s, however. And black market demand has only increased since it was listed as an endangered species, with prices surpassing $10,000. In 2001, a Canadian butterfly expert was fined $31,000 for illegally importing six Queen Alexandra's birdwings hidden inside a fake book that was confiscated by border control agents in Vancouver, B.C. And in 2007, a Japanese trafficker named Hisayoshi Kojima was arrested in California when he tried to sell a pair of Queen Alexandras for $8,500 to a special agent with the US Fish and Wildlife Service who was posing as a collector.

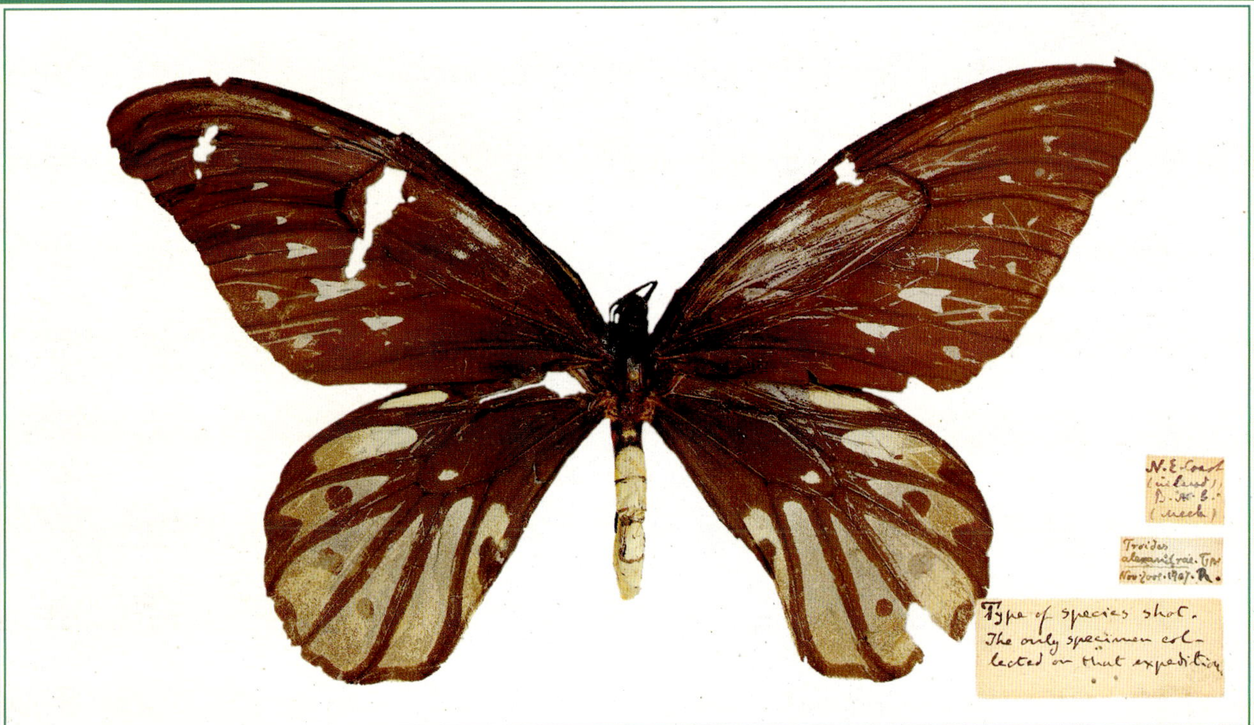

A historic specimen: this is the female *Ornithoptera alexandrae* downed by Albert Meek in 1906 using lead shot, now conserved at the British Museum.

© BMNH

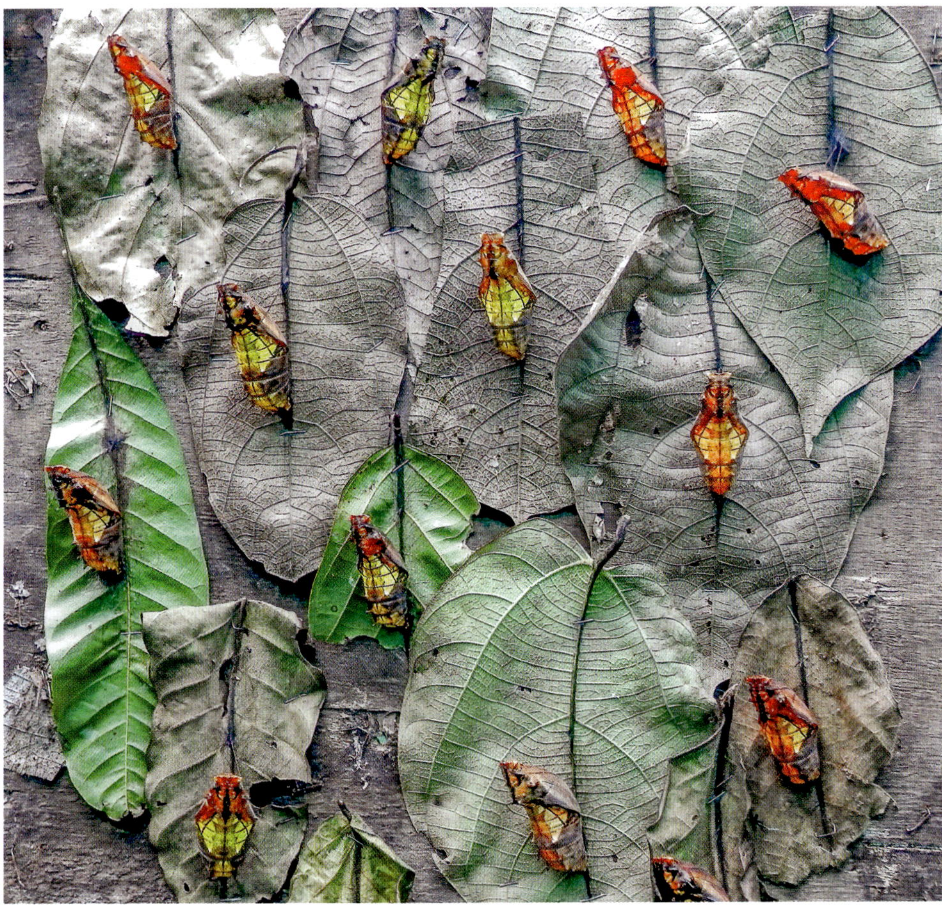

Community members in Misu gather *Ornithoptera alexandrae* chrysalises from the forest so that they are not eaten by rats and spiders. Once the adult butterflies emerge, they are released back into the wild so they can reproduce.

© Camille Cusin

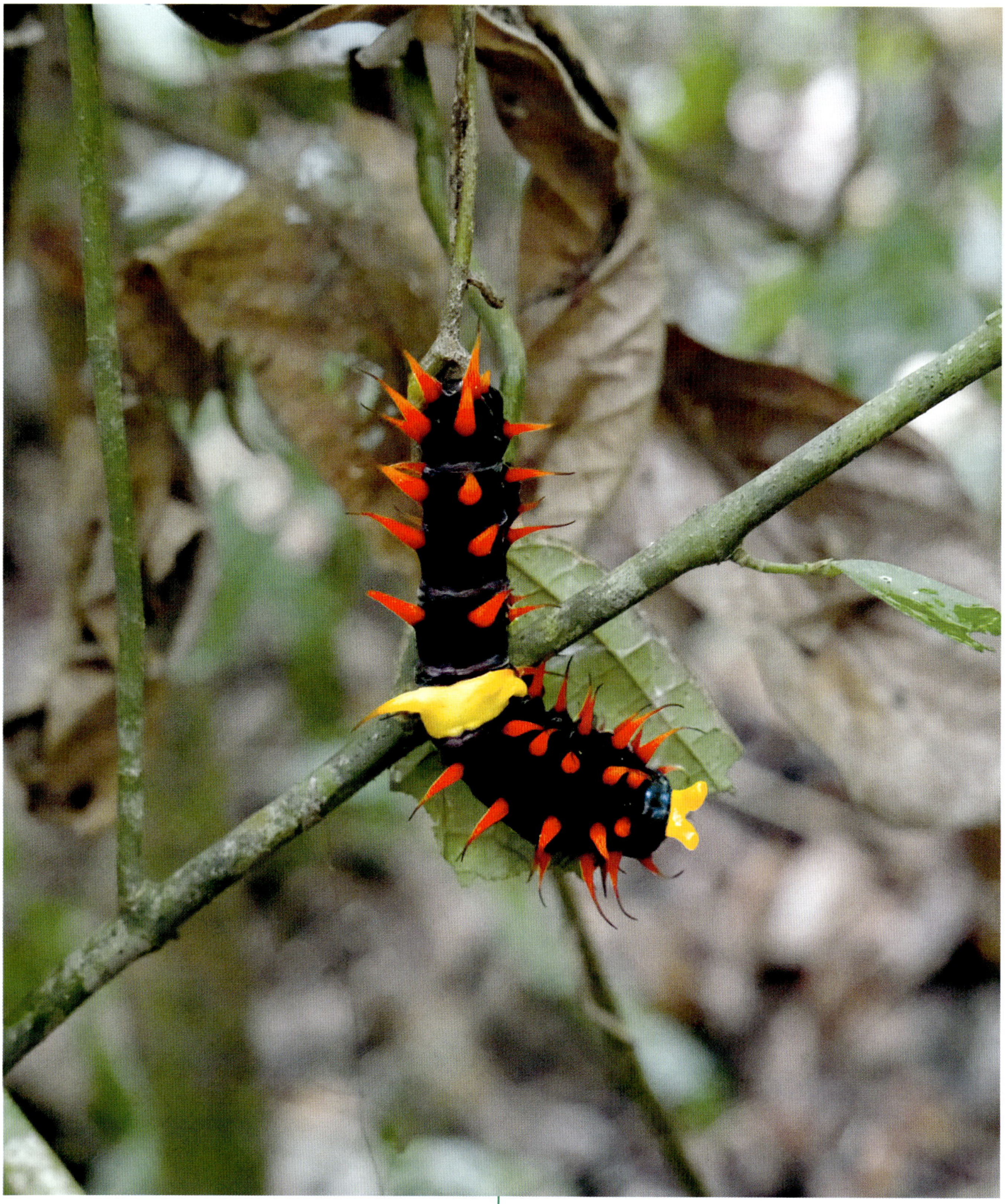

Birdwing caterpillars, like this *Ornithoptera alexandrae*, are tempting prey for lizards and birds and are also vulnerable to parasitoid wasps. Their bright colors warn potential predators that their bodies contain toxins accumulated from the pipevine plants they eat.

© Butterfly Identification

NATURE'S ORNITHOPTERS

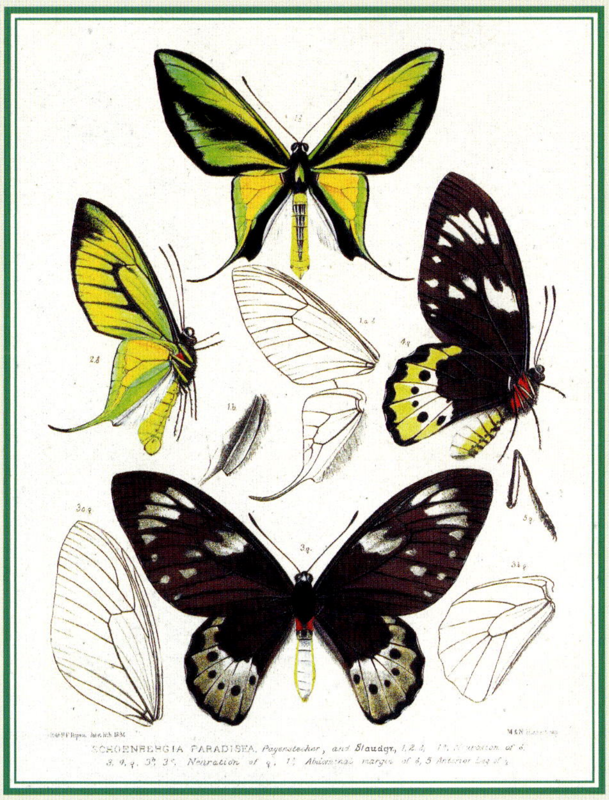

Ornithopters are machines that fly by flapping their wings like birds, with da Vinci's centuries-old design now to be found hovering in the backyards of hobbyists worldwide. But the word has also been used to refer to butterflies in the genus *Ornithoptera*, which are native to Southeast Asia, Melanesia, and northeastern Australia. The name comes from the Greek *órnithos*, meaning "bird," and *pterón*: "wing," as many of these butterflies are the size of small birds. Taken together with *Troides*, another genus of birdwing butterflies, some forty species and numerous subspecies of "ornithopters" can be found in the tropical forests they call home.

The magnificent iridescent colors of male birdwing butterflies have made them highly sought after by collectors, who are sometimes willing to pay hundreds if not thousands of dollars for a rare species or subtle color variant. A number of birdwings are protected by law and are raised in captivity to prevent poaching in the wild. Selling captive specimens can be a source of revenue for local communities and—paradoxically—helps to support conservation. In fact, the greatest danger by far to these beautiful insects is not hunting but deforestation and habitat loss driven by agriculture and other human activities.

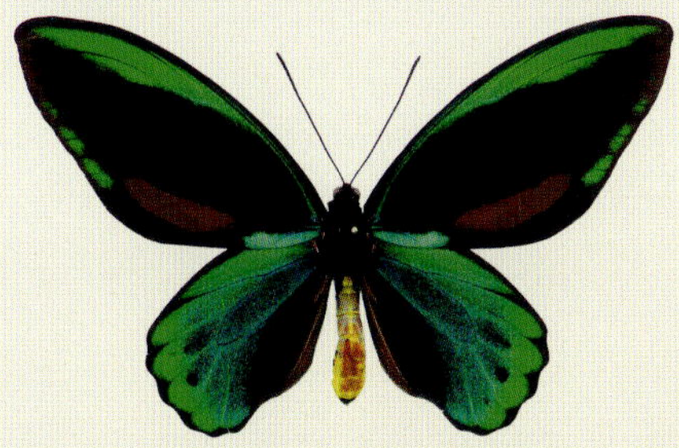

Top left: The male paradise birdwing (O. *paradisea*) from New Guinea has attracted admirers with its striking green-gold color and delicate silhouette. Females are larger but much less colorful. This illustration comes from an extraordinary book, *Icones Ornithopterorum* by English zoologist and illustrator Robert H. F. Rippon (1836–1917). The two-volume set was sold by subscription between 1898 and 1906 and was exceptional in that the author-illustrator colored all 111 lithograph plates in each copy individually and by hand. Rippon spent twenty years filling roughly thirty orders, some of which he finished only a few years before his death. Bottom right: Originally described by Lord Rothschild as *Ornithoptera allotei*, this birdwing was later discovered to be a natural hybrid of O. *priamus urvilleanus* and O. *victoriae*. It is only found on two islands in Oceania, and its rarity and beauty make it one of the most prized butterflies by collectors.

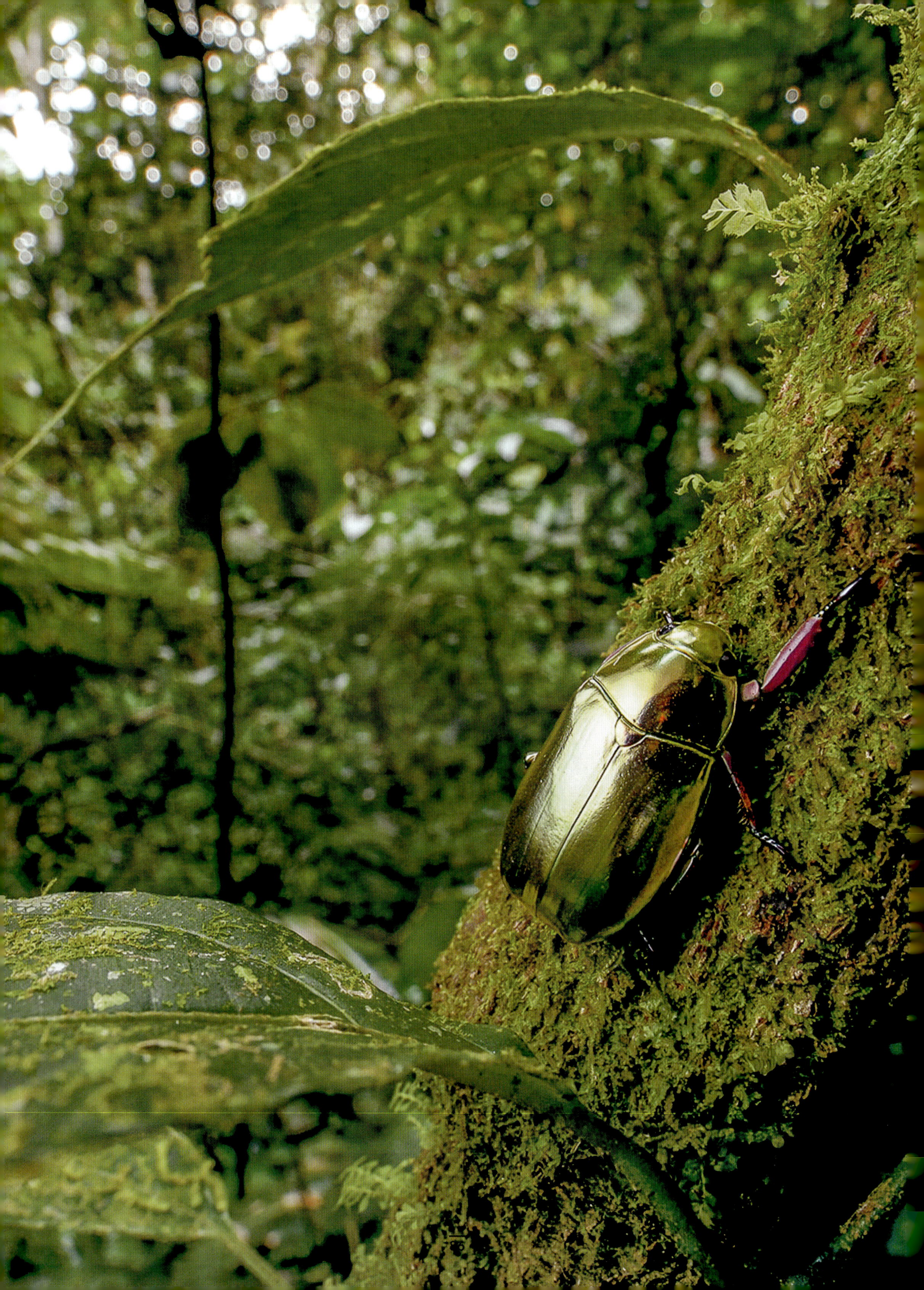

LIVING JEWELS

GENUS *CHRYSINA*

COLEOPTERA: SCARABAEIDAE

Jewel scarabs, as beetles in the genus *Chrysina* are commonly known, stand out for their metallic, iridescent sheen. There are about a hundred species, ranging from the southern United States to northern Ecuador. They are cousins of cockchafers and measure 15 to 35 millimeters long.

Not much is known about the ecology of these luxurious-looking beetles, which are typically found in cloud forests at altitudes of 800 to 1,300 meters. Adults feed on foliage; they are mostly active at night and are attracted to light. The larvae have only been identified for a few species. Those discovered so far live in rotting, semi-buried logs or roots and take two years to develop.

Jewel scarabs are known for their intense colors. Many are green, but they can also be red, gold, or silver in any combination imaginable. No wonder they are prized by collectors: rare color variants can sell for hundreds of dollars.

As in many other iridescent insects, the metallic color is the result of structural coloration, not pigment. The effect is created by structures in the top few micrometers of their outer covering, which are only visible through an electron microscope. Specifically, their iridescence is produced by chitin molecules organized as liquid crystals and made up of helicoid structures that reflect and polarize light. The reflected color depends on the pitch of these microscopic spirals: the tighter the coils, the more the reflected color will tend toward blue or even ultraviolet; the widest coils will make the insect appear red, or even reflect back infrared, and so on

A jewel scarab (*Chrysina argenteola*) in Panama. Its silvery-green metallic sheen plays tricks on the eyes of predators.

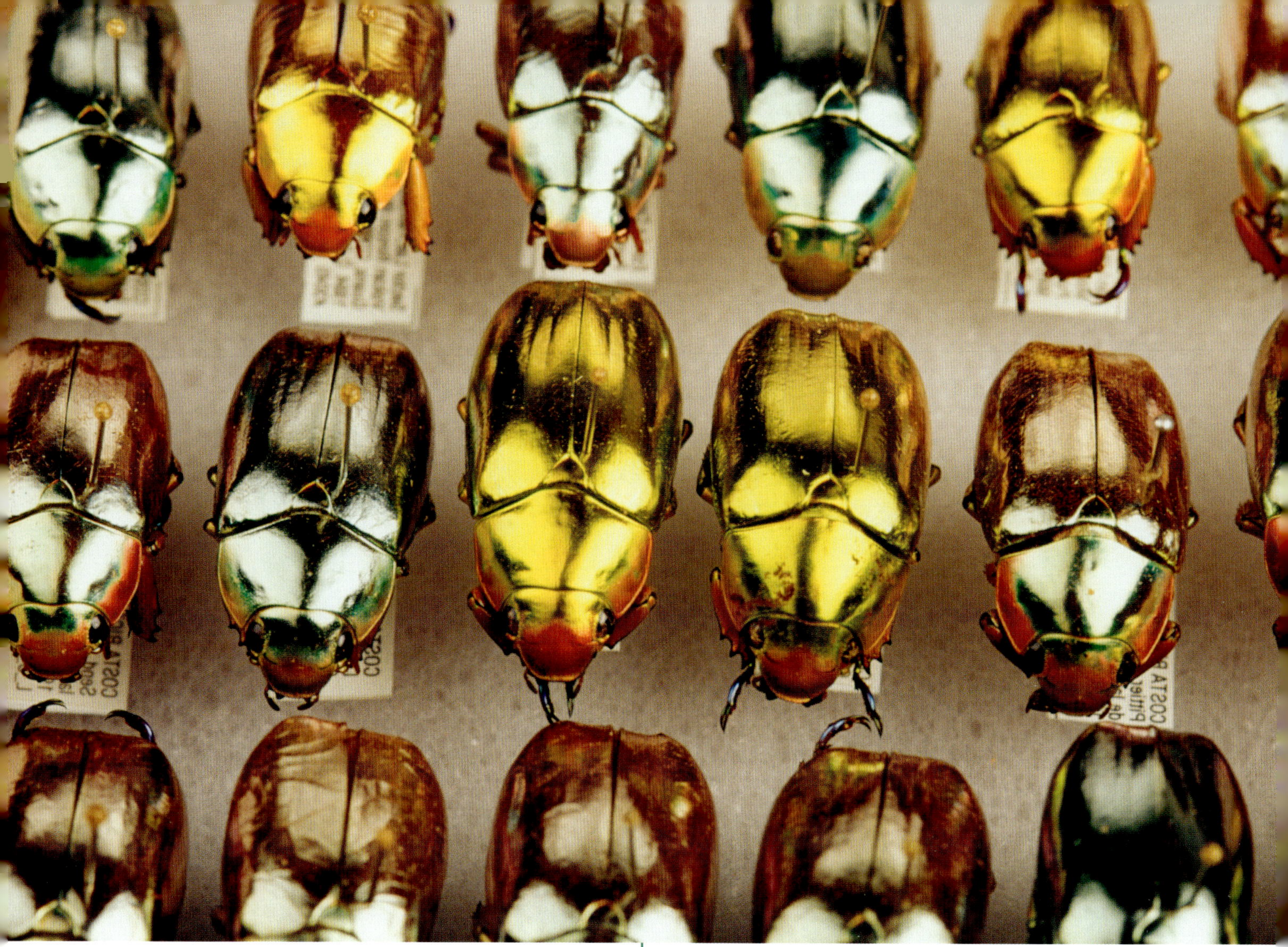

Jewel scarabs are particularly diverse in Central America. Some parts of Guatemala, for example, are home to some fifteen different species.
© Frans Lanting/Mint Images/Biosphoto

for every color in between. A silvery effect means the surface acts like a mirror, reflecting a broad range of the visible spectrum and beyond.

These dazzling colors help members of different sexes identify each other. They also play a protective role as camouflage: many diurnal predators have difficulty judging the distance and position of shiny objects, or might mistake them for water droplets. Structural coloration may also have nonvisual functions, such as regulating temperature, repelling water, or improving aerodynamics. Jewel scarabs have inspired a number of cutting-edge technologies: bendable mirrors used in adaptive optics, microlens arrays, and chiral optic devices, to name just a few.

Because of their beauty, size, and ease of collecting, these beetles have played an important role in various Central American societies. In Ecuador and Peru, for example, Indigenous peoples create pendants and headpieces from the elytra or whole bodies of the all-green shining leaf chafer (*Chrysophora chrysochlora*). In Guatemala, traditional craft workers sell items decorated using similar species to tourists. And contemporary creators like Christopher Marley, an American artist and designer, have also used jewel scarabs in their work.

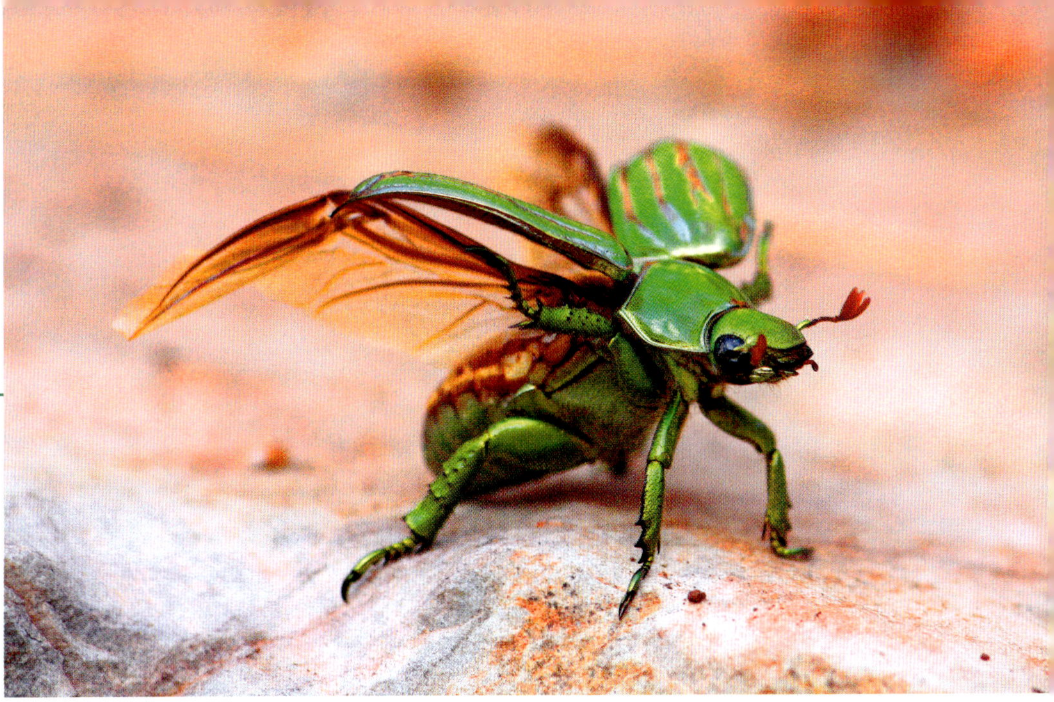

The glorious scarab (*Chrysina gloriosa*) is common in the Madrean Region, a biodiversity hotspot covering parts of Mexico, Arizona, and New Mexico. These semiarid mountains and prairies are sandwiched between two climate zones (temperate and subtropical), two mountain ranges (the Rockies and the Sierra Madre Occidental), and two deserts (Sonora and Chihuahua).
© Carla Kishinami

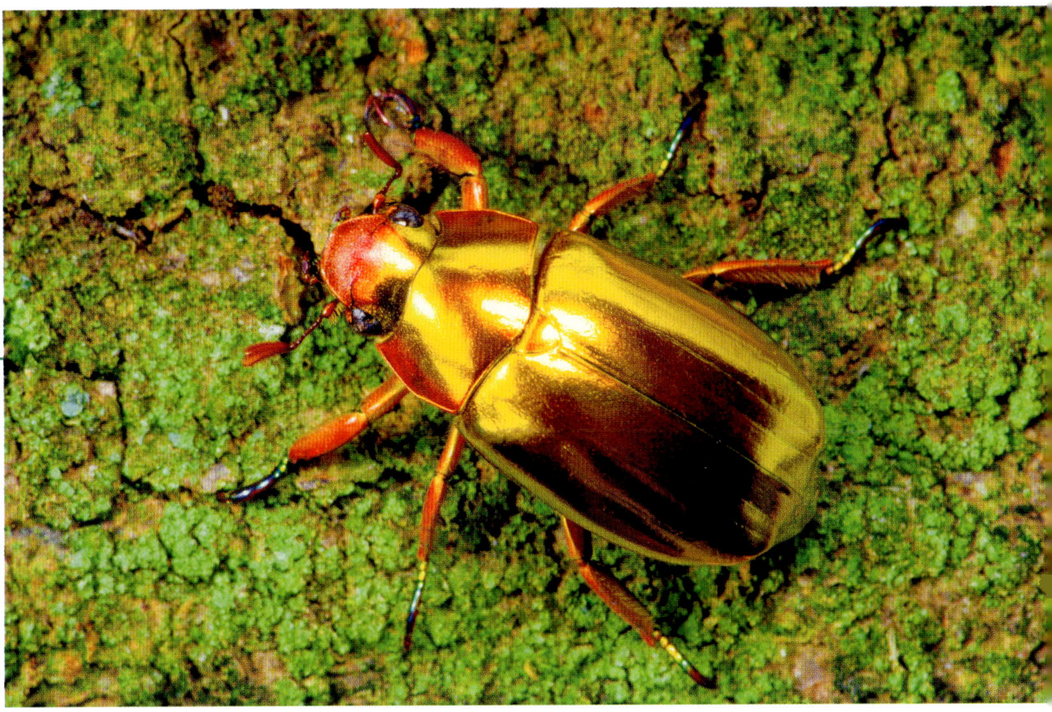

An object is considered iridescent if it changes color depending on the angle of light or observation. The light reflected off the backs of jewel scarabs sends a powerful color signal, especially at dusk, when many iridescent insects are active. This *Chrysina beyeri* was spotted in Costa Rica.
© Michael Turco/Biosphoto

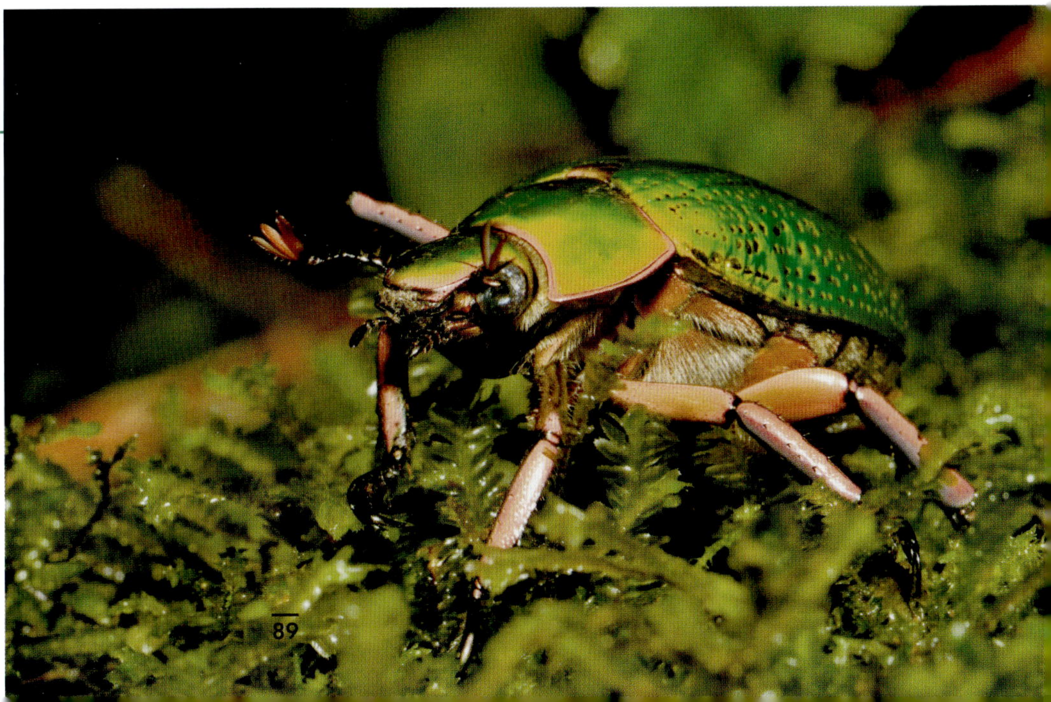

Chrysina spectabilis lives in high-altitude Central American forests.
© Andrew Snyder CC 2.0

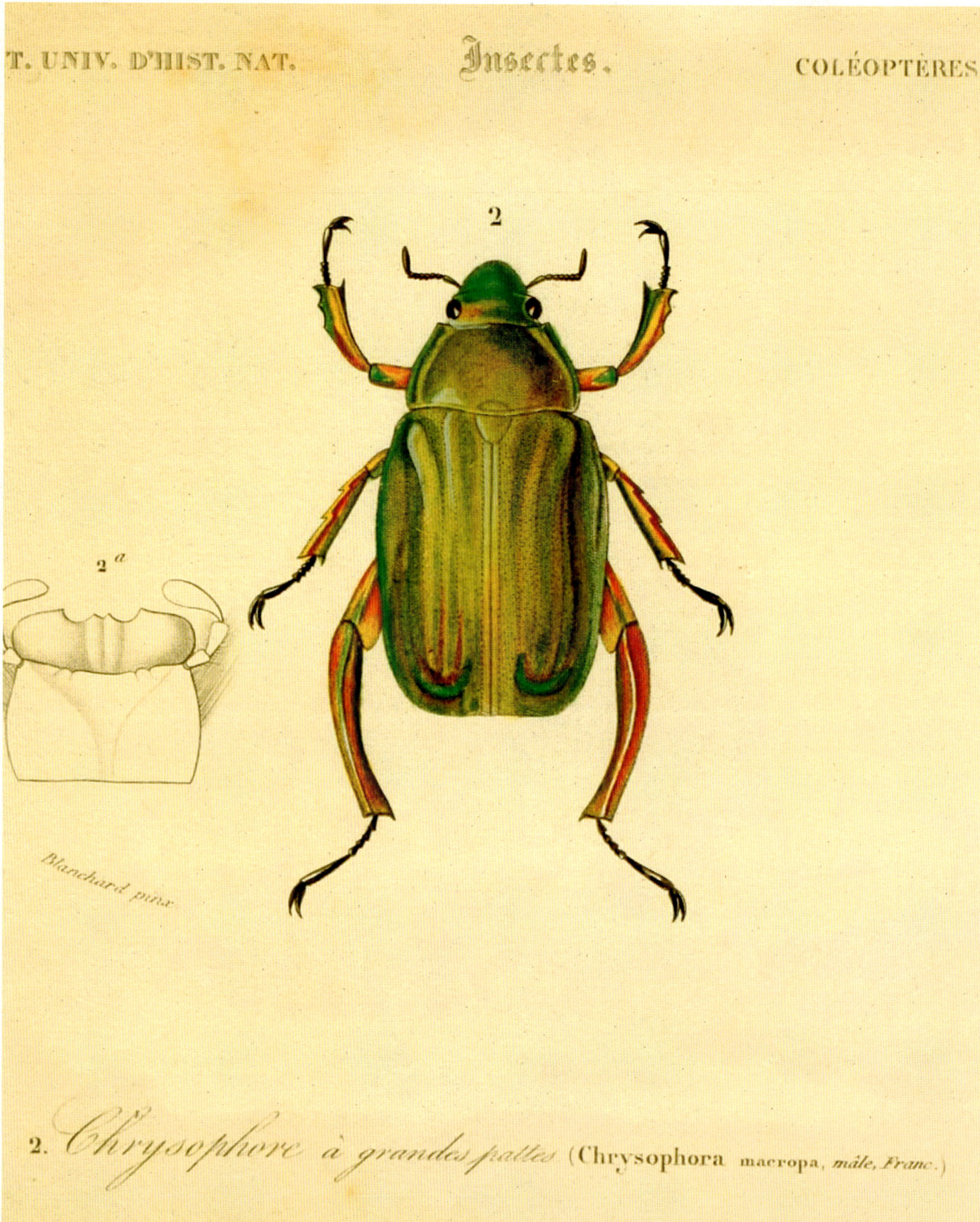

Illustration of *Chrysina macropus* in the *Dictionnaire universel d'histoire naturelle* edited by Charles-Henry d'Orbigny (1806–1876), which is considered one of the best natural history reference works of the nineteenth century. It is composed of sixteen volumes published between 1841 and 1849.

POE'S GOLD BUG: PURE FICTION!

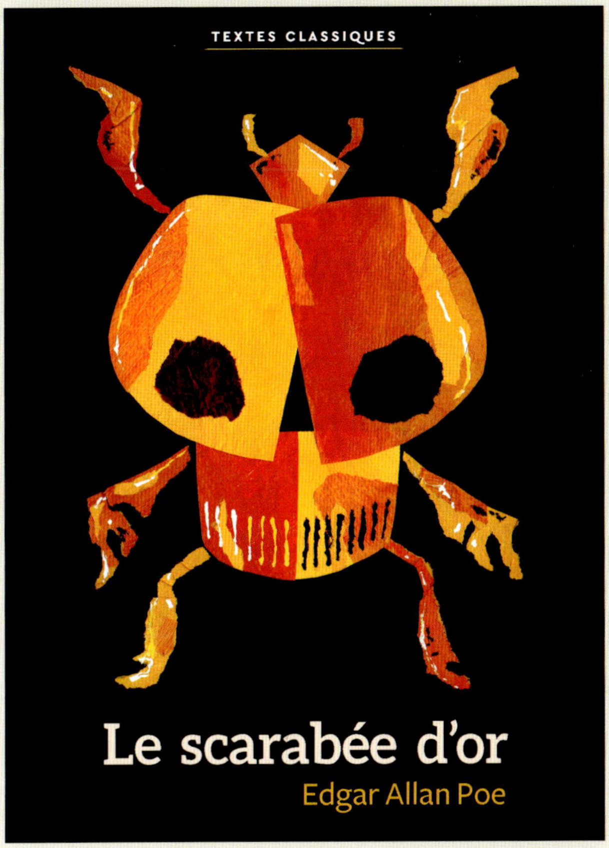

Ellison A. Smyth, Jr. (1863–1941), in addition to being the first football coach at Virginia Tech, was also a celebrated entomologist. In 1910, he attempted to identify the mysterious beetle at the heart of a story by Edgar Allan Poe (1809–1849). Upon entering the army, Poe was stationed from 1827 to 1829 on Sullivan's Island, South Carolina, which he used as the setting for "The Gold-Bug," published in 1843. Smyth was an expert on insects of the region, and he gave Poe credit for his keen observations of Sullivan's Island and its fauna. Smyth deemed the bug in the story to be a mix of several local species. It is described as "oval," "the size of a hickory-nut," and "a brilliant gold color." That made it roughly the size and shape of *Callichroma splendidum*, a longhorn beetle known to live in the area.

Smyth hypothesized that Poe added features from *Phanaeus carnifex*, a common dung beetle, and *Alaus oculatus*, a darkling beetle. And so, despite its name, Poe's gold bug probably had no connection to jewel scarabs.

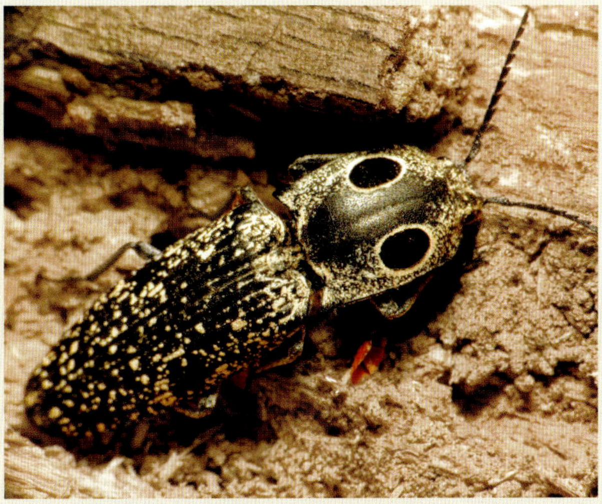

Top left: The beetle on the cover of a French edition of "The Gold-Bug" by Edgar Allan Poe resembles a jewel scarab. © Gallimard

Bottom right: The eyed elater (*Alaus oculatus*) is among the species that may have inspired the bug in Poe's story. The black eyespots match Poe's description of a beetle with markings like a skull. © Katja Schulz CC 4.0

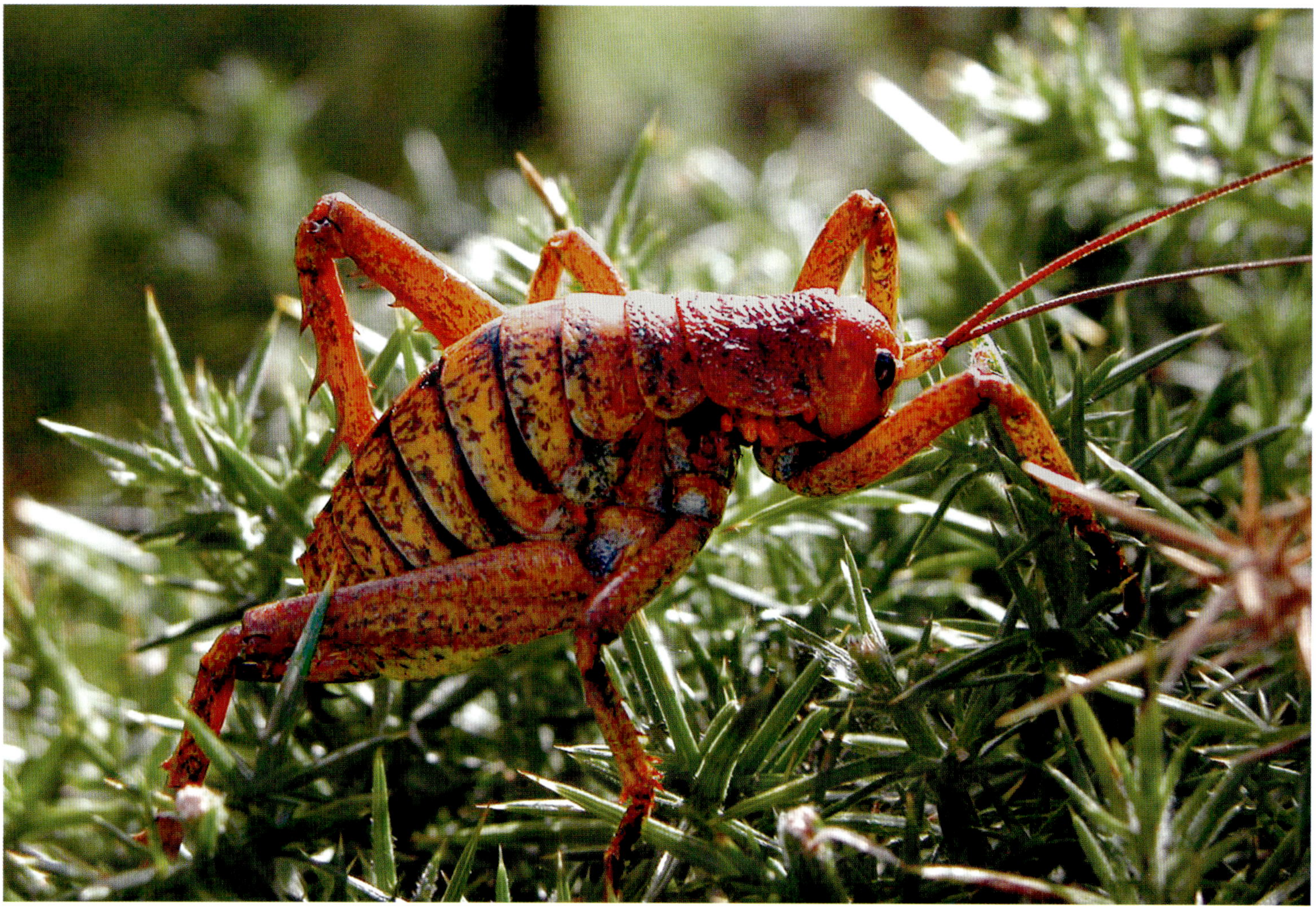

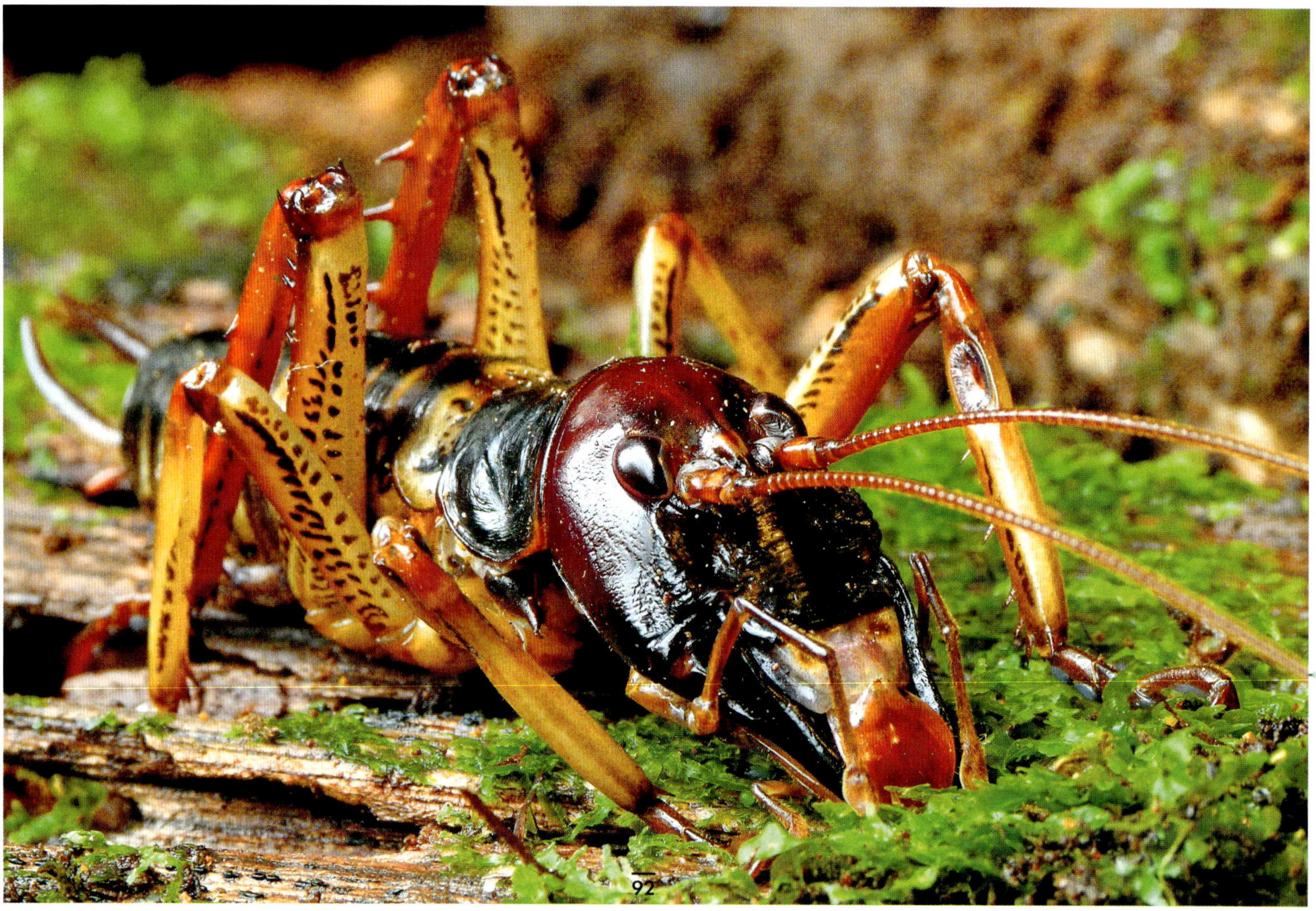

THE GOD OF UGLY THINGS

DEINACRIDA HETERACANTHA

(ORTHOPTERA: ANOSTOSTOMATIDAE)

This insect from New Zealand gets its common name from the Māori word *wētāpunga*, meaning "god of ugly things." Despite its intimidating size, weight, and appearance, it is highly vulnerable. A protection program now exists to preserve the wētāpunga and other wētā species.

Wētā are related to grasshoppers, crickets, and locusts and belong to a family mainly present in Australia, South Africa, and India that emerged during the Cretaceous period, 65 to 80 million years ago. New Zealand is home to nearly sixty species, eighteen of which are considered giant wētā (genera *Hemideina* and *Deinacrida*). They can reach 7–8 centimeters long, not counting the legs and antennae, and weigh over 30 grams. The largest wētā species is the wētāpunga or Little Island giant wētā: females can reach over eight centimeters long and weigh up to 40 grams—the equivalent of two mice! One female raised in captivity weighed a whopping 71 grams. (Males are smaller, only 17–18 grams.) Wētāpunga are considered one of the heaviest insects in the world and are an example of island gigantism (see pages 146 and 174).

New Zealand offers a diverse range of habitats and microhabitats, all of which were once home to at least one species of wētā, which occupied a niche

Top: *Deinacrida mahoenui* is a giant wētā that can still be found in a small area on New Zealand's North Island. Its habitat has been invaded by a nonnative plant, common gorse (*Ulex europaeus*), which nonetheless provides the wētā with food and protection—a rare example of an invasive plant contributing to the preservation of a threatened native species.

© Amanda Haigh, New Zealand Department of Conservation

Bottom: The genus *Hemideina* contains some of the most common giant wētā species, which continue to thrive despite the impacts on their habitat. They can be seen even in areas where the landscape has been transformed by humans.

© Steeve Reekie

similar to that of small rodents. Some wētā species had a larger range than others, and some ranges overlapped or connected. Because the fauna of New Zealand evolved in isolation from the mainland, in an ecosystem without mammals or competition, some wētā were able to grow into giants, having no need to move quickly or flee from predators. When Polynesian peoples arrived on the islands around a thousand years ago, however, the Pacific rat (*Rattus exulans*) came with them. Later, European colonists would introduce other rat species, along with cats and mustelids. These new predators devastated the endemic bird, reptile, and insect populations. Now, most wētā species have dwindled to the point that they can only be found over a few acres. Giant wētā have all but disappeared from the two main islands of New Zealand and are only found on smaller islands nearby.

D. fallai lives on the Poor Knights Islands, where it is still common. *D. mahoenui* was thought to be extinct until 1962, when it was found still to exist in a small area on the North Island.

D. heteracantha, the wētāpunga, was once known on the North Island, Great Barrier Island, and Little Barrier Island. Due to predation by rats, it now survives only on Little Barrier Island, where rats were eradicated in 1980. Wētāpunga live in temperate, subalpine forests at altitudes

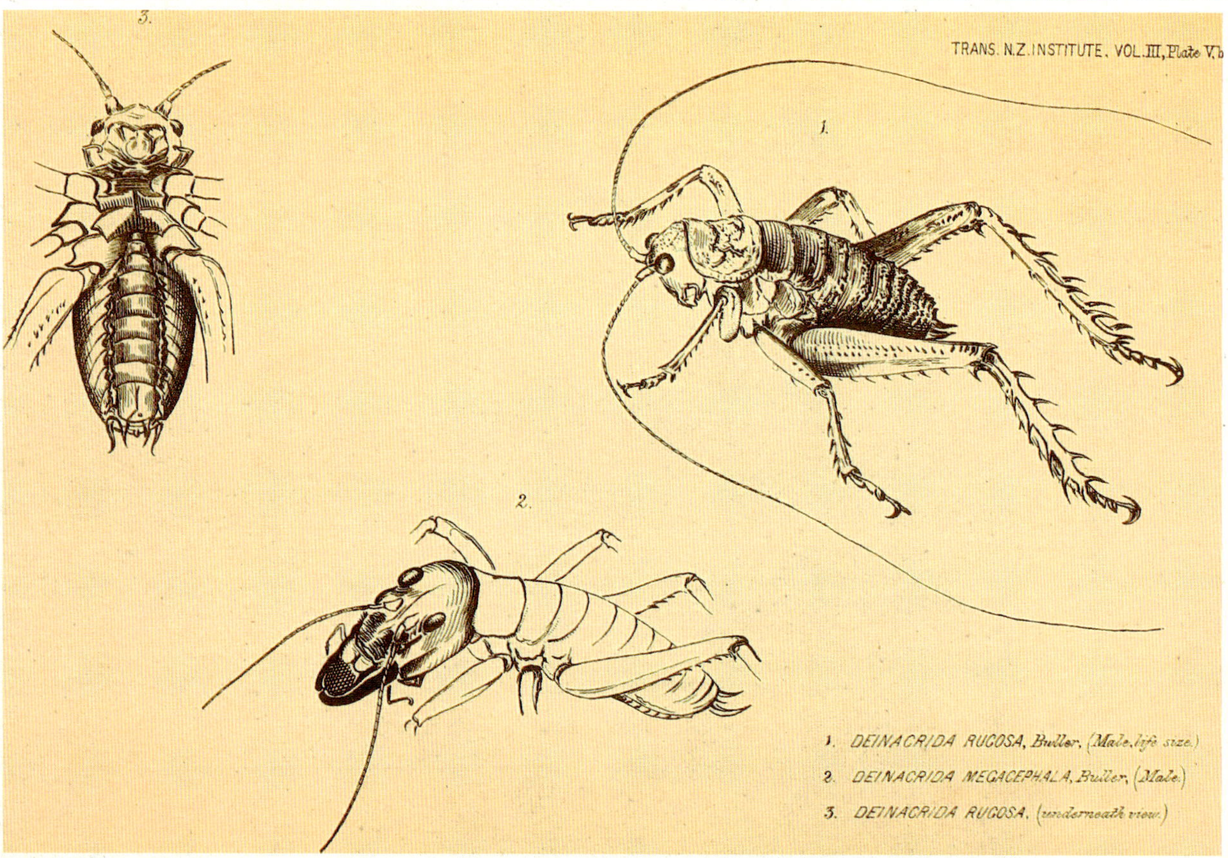

Like other members of their family, wētā are wingless and have defensive spines on their legs. The males have fearsome-looking mandibles.

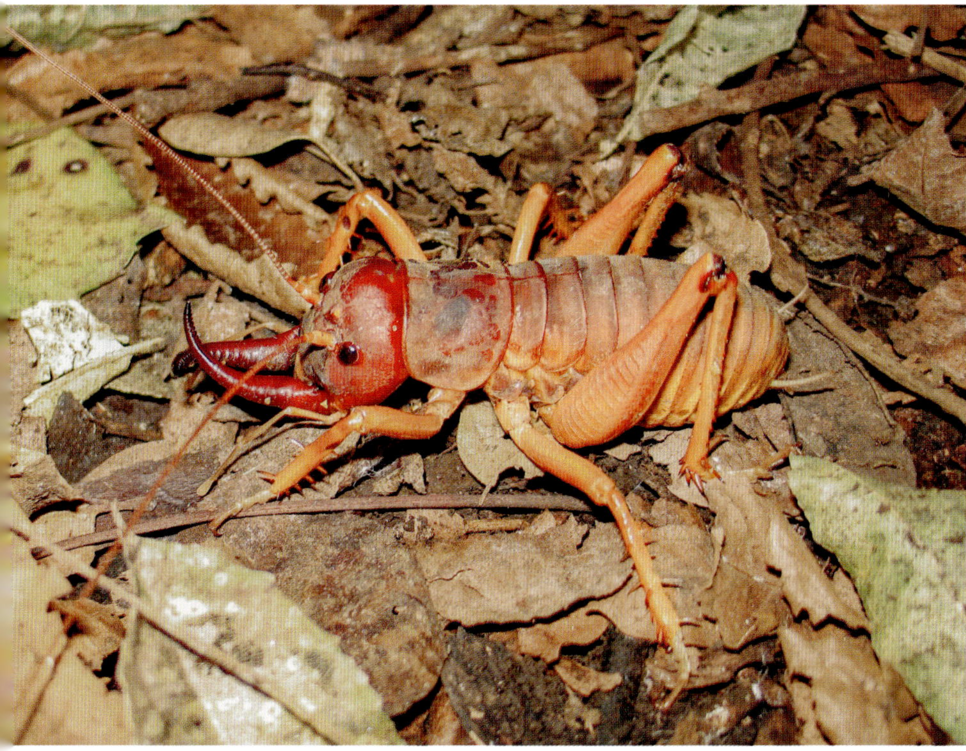

Male tusked wētā, like this *Motuweta isolata*, have large mandibles shaped like the tusks of an elephant, which they use to fight over females during the mating season.

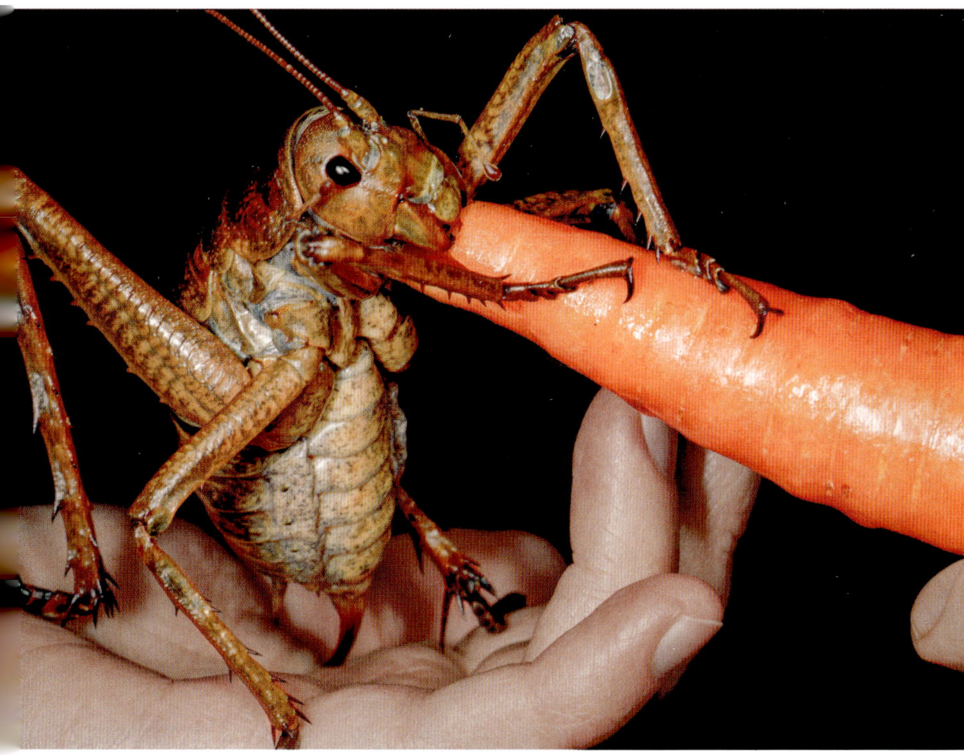

Deinacrida heteracantha, the largest wētā species, eating a carrot. These insects are now found only on Little Barrier Island, off the north coast of New Zealand.

of 900 to 1,300 meters. They are a tree-dwelling species (only the females descend to ground level to lay their eggs) and feed at night on the shrubs and epiphytes that they use for shelter during the day. Adults are wingless, but they can walk over 30 meters in a night, especially males in search of a mate. The larvae develop over approximately two years, molting eleven times before entering their adult stage, which lasts about six months. Larvae and adults can cohabitate, but the larvae are more often found in groups.

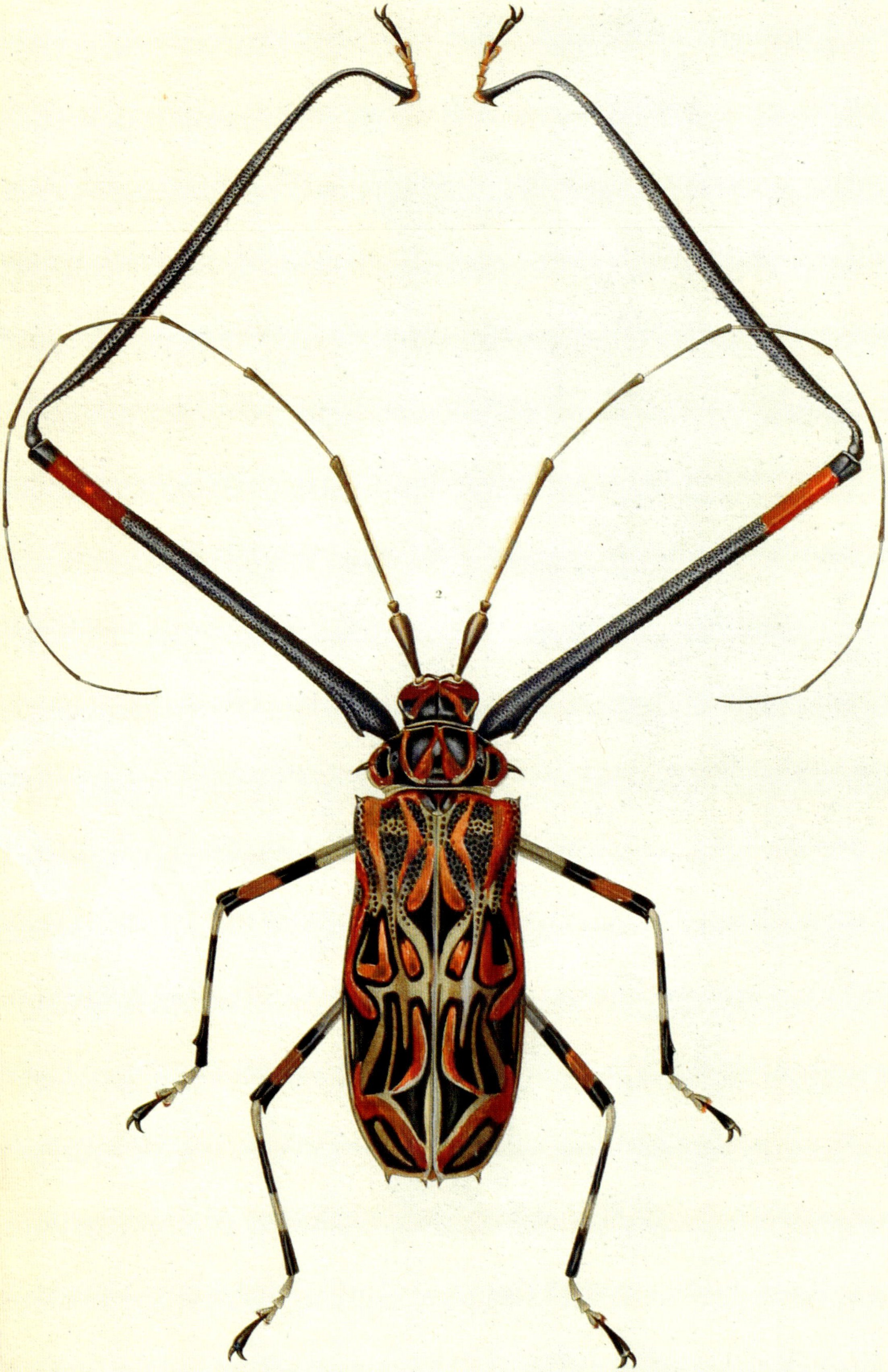

2. *ACROCINE LONGIMANE* (Acrocinus longimanus *Lin.*)

A FOREST HARLEQUIN

ACROCINUS LONGIMANUS
(COLEOPTERA: CERAMBYCIDAE)

The harlequin beetle, a colorful giant longhorn beetle, has an enormous range covering much of the American tropics, from southern Mexico to Paraguay and northern Argentina. It is found in tropical and subtropical forests at up to 2,000 meters altitude.

Harlequin beetles are sexually dimorphic: the males can have curved, hooklike forelegs that can be up to 15 centimeters long, twice the length of females'. These powerful weapons are used in combat over mates, which takes place on tree trunks and branches and usually ends with one of the rivals being driven off the tree, often causing injuries.

Like titan beetles (page 12), harlequin beetles are attracted to light, despite being mainly diurnal. They are often found on dying or recently fallen trees in the genera *Ficus* and *Eucalyptus*, among others. The adults feed on sap released from the trunks, while the larvae feed on the wood itself. The larval stage lasts at least eight months out of a total life cycle of about one year. Harlequin beetle larvae play an important role in speeding up the decomposition of wood, making it easier for other invertebrates to access.

Harlequin beetles are also used as transportation by several species of pseudoscorpions (especially *Cordylochermes scorpioides*). These tiny cousins of spiders, which are only a few millimeters long, live in decomposing wood and feed on termites and the larvae of small insects. When harlequin beetles reach adulthood and emerge from the trees they inhabited as larvae, they give off pheromones that attract pseudoscorpions. The tiny hitchhikers nibble on the joints between the beetle's abdominal

Illustration of a male harlequin beetle from volume III of *Le Règne animal*, a treatise on zoology and comparative anatomy published in 1817 by Georges Cuvier (1769–1832).

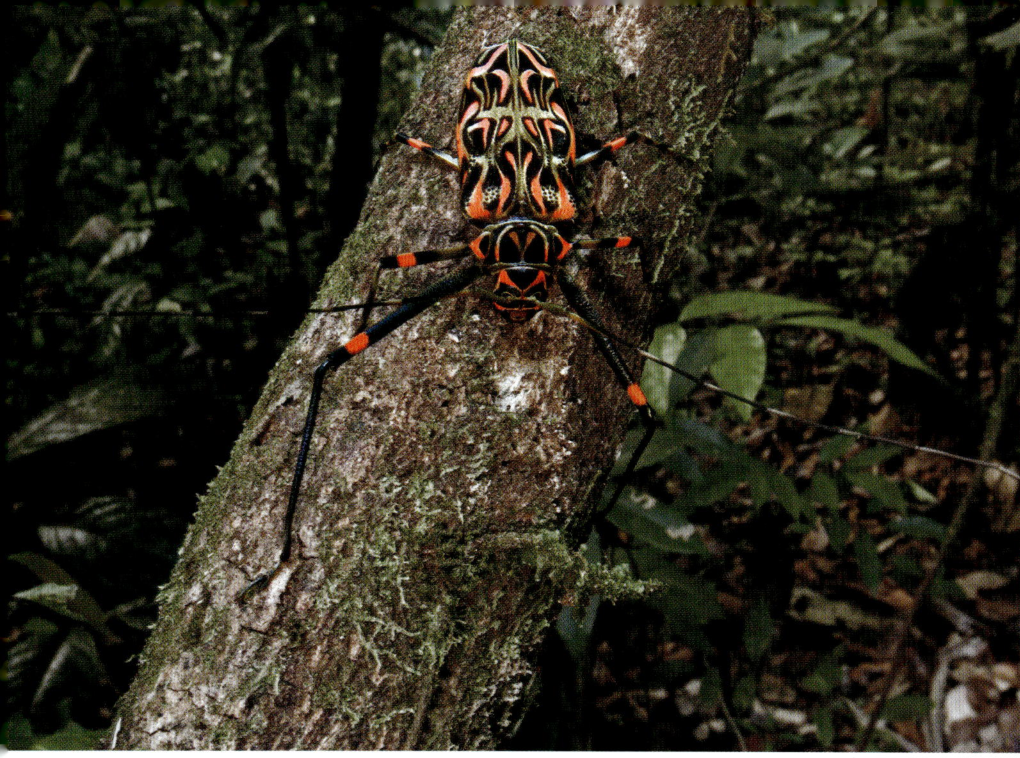

The harlequin beetle is a massive longhorn beetle with a body length of 4.5–7.5 cm. Its name comes from the characteristic red, gray, and black markings that resemble the costume of the eponymous commedia dell'arte character.
© Piotr Naskrecki/Minden Pictures/Biosphoto

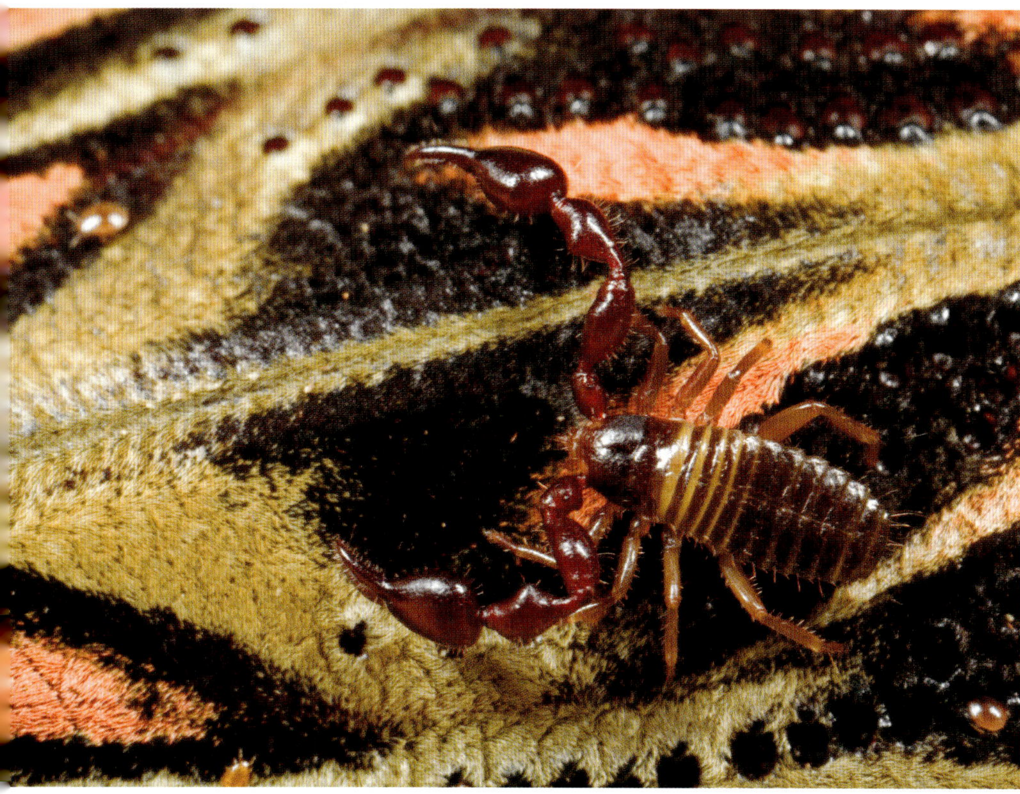

Cordylochermes scorpioides, which looks like a tiny scorpion without a tail, is a commensal of the harlequin beetle: it is not a parasite, because it does not feed on the beetle or even bother it much. It simply hitches a ride so it can disperse to new territory.
© Piotr Naskrecki/Minden Pictures/Biosphoto

This painting by Jan Brueghel the Elder (1568–1625) features a live harlequin beetle in the bottom left. Where the painter could have acquired it is a mystery.

segments, triggering a reflex that causes the beetle to partially open its elytra. The pseudoscorpions then slip under the elytra and cling to the beetle's abdomen using their claws and silken strands. The males fight for prime placement, because this is where the pseudoscorpions mate. The weaker males must either remain on their log or hitch a much more dangerous ride on the beetle's legs. When the harlequin beetle flies to a new fallen tree to mate and lay its eggs, it brings its tiny passengers along, allowing them to disperse and conquer new territory.

Like other tropical and subtropical xylophagic insects, harlequin beetles are threatened by deforestation. Their numbers are dwindling in many places where they were once abundant.

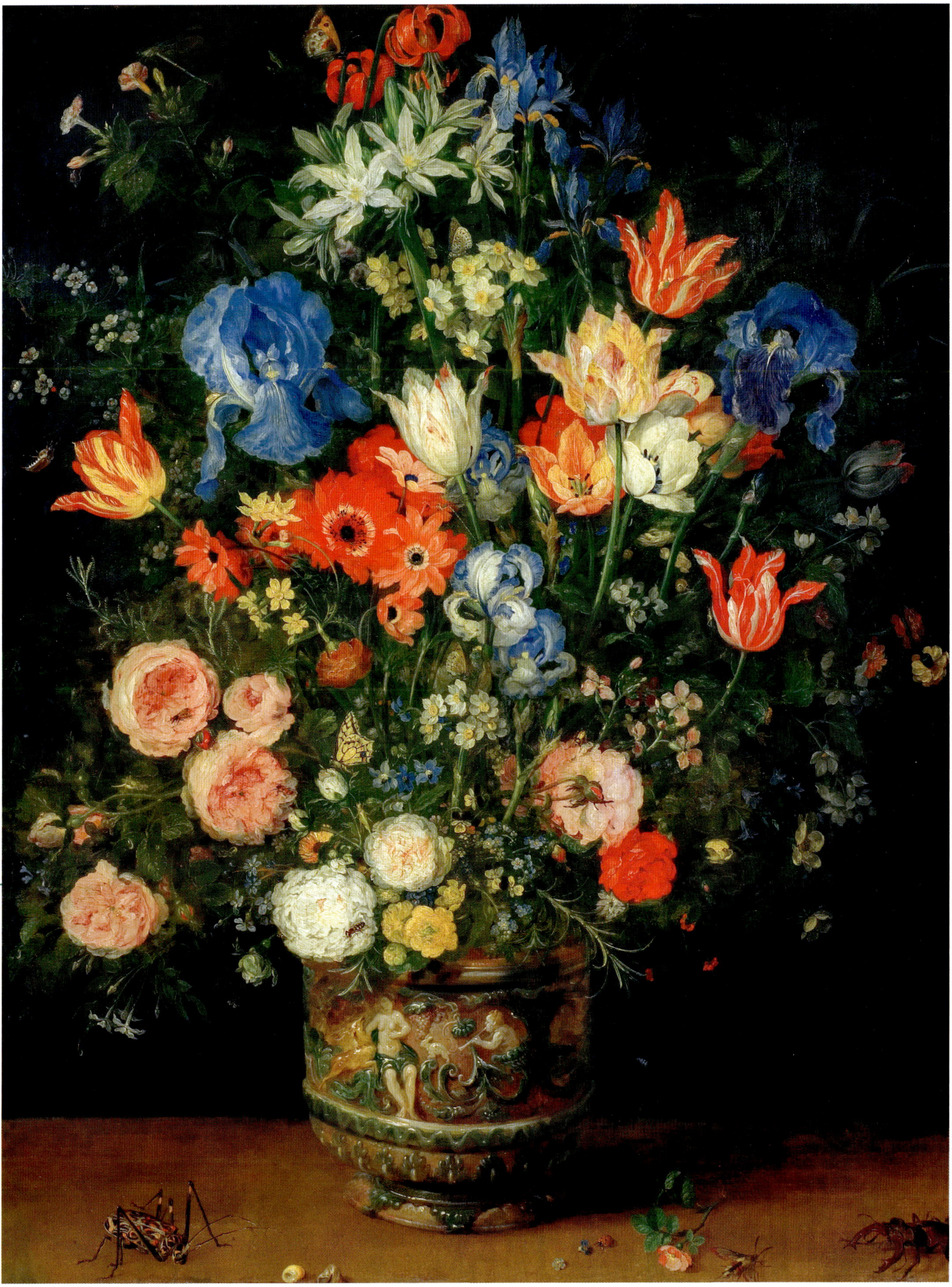

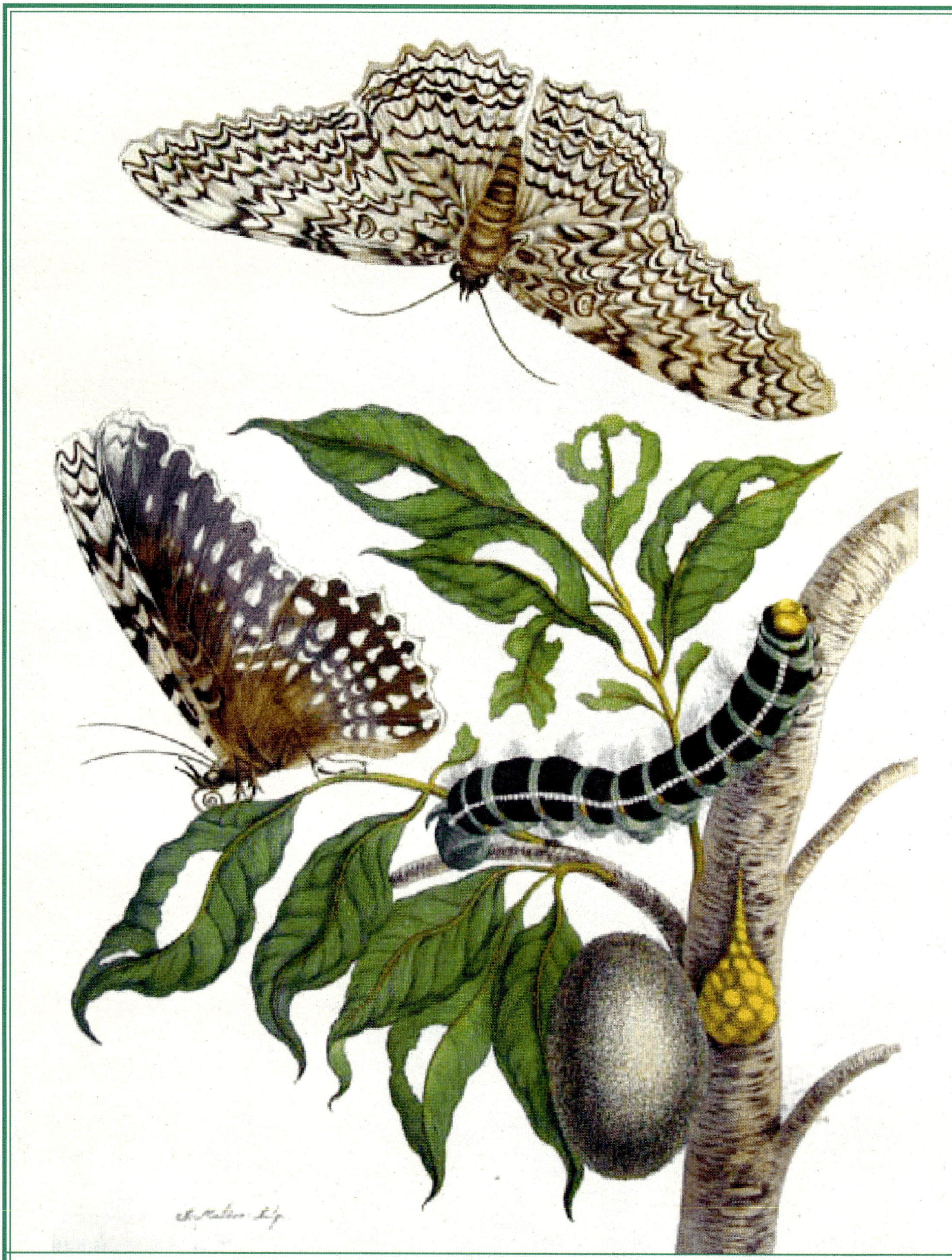

Thysania agrippina as represented in 1705 by Maria Sibylla Merian (1647–1717). The caterpillar that appears here is actually that of a different moth, probably a hawkmoth.

WITCH OF ILL OMEN

THYSANIA AGRIPPINA
(LEPIDOPTERA: EREBIDAE)

A pale specter emerges from the dark, then disappears in a flash —a ghostly vision in the tropical night. It is hardly surprising that this eerie moth haunted the imaginations of the first entomologists to explore Latin America. Despite its remarkable size, the moth commonly known as the white witch has not yet revealed all its secrets.

Thysania agrippina, commonly known as the white witch or ghost moth, was described by Pieter Cramer (1721–1776) based on a specimen brought to Europe from Suriname. Its vast range covers every part of South America north of Uruguay, through Central America to Texas. One stray individual was even observed in Guadeloupe in late 2020, having probably reached the island aboard a cargo ship.

The white witch might be the largest of the lepidopterans (butterflies and moths), with a wingspan of up to 29 centimeters. Other contenders include the Atlas moth (*Attacus atlas*), which can reach 27 centimeters, or the Queen Alexandra's birdwing (page 81). The white witch is known in Spanish as *la bruja blanca* and in French Guiana as *le meunier* or "miller."

This relatively common moth is a fast flier and often mistaken for a nocturnal bird. Seeing one has been considered an ill omen, perhaps because of its spectral appearance, or because it is so large it evokes another spooky winged creature—the bat. White witches are attracted to rotting fruit and drawn to light. They land on walls, tree trunks, and bushes near windows and lampposts, where they remain immobile during the day. Astonishing as it may seem, the immature life stages were completely unknown until 2014, when a white witch caterpillar was observed for the first time near Belém, Brazil.

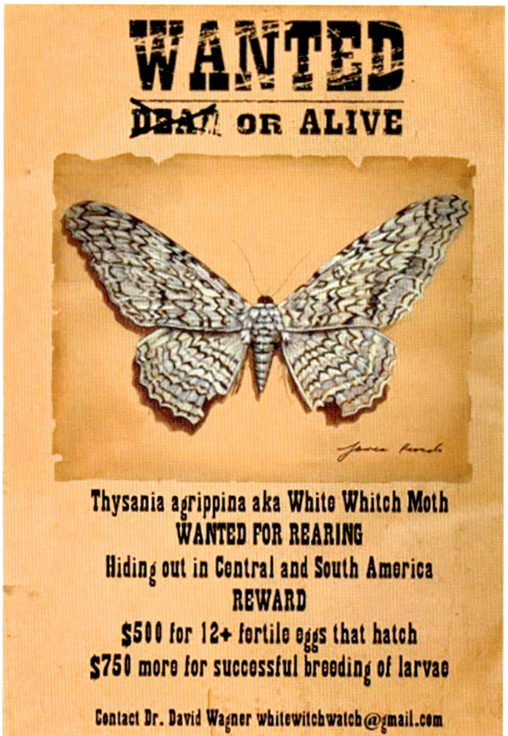

A citizen science project was organized throughout South America and on social media to identify the eggs and larvae of the white witch.

© White Witch Watch, CC 4.0

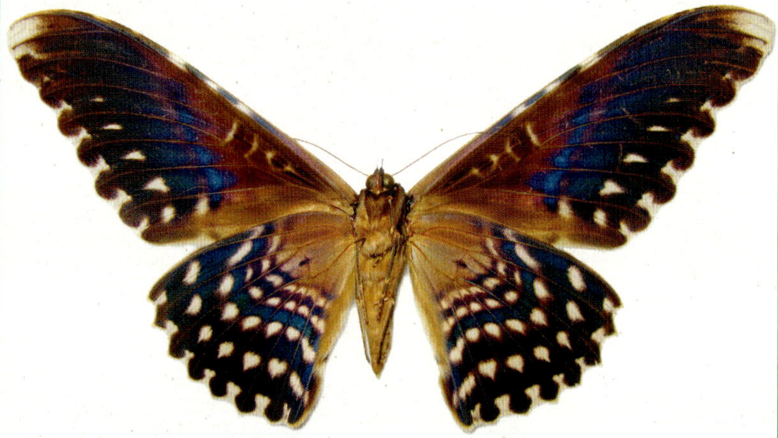

The shimmering, reflective underside of the white witch's wings is a sumptuous contrast to the pale dorsal side.

© Anaxibia CC 4.0

The white witch's common name refers to its pale color, which makes it appear ghostly in the night. It may also refer to the fact that early hunters found the moths almost impossible to shoot down. Their bodies are so small relative to their wing area that they can keep flying even when peppered with lead shot, surviving as if by magic.

© White Witch Watch

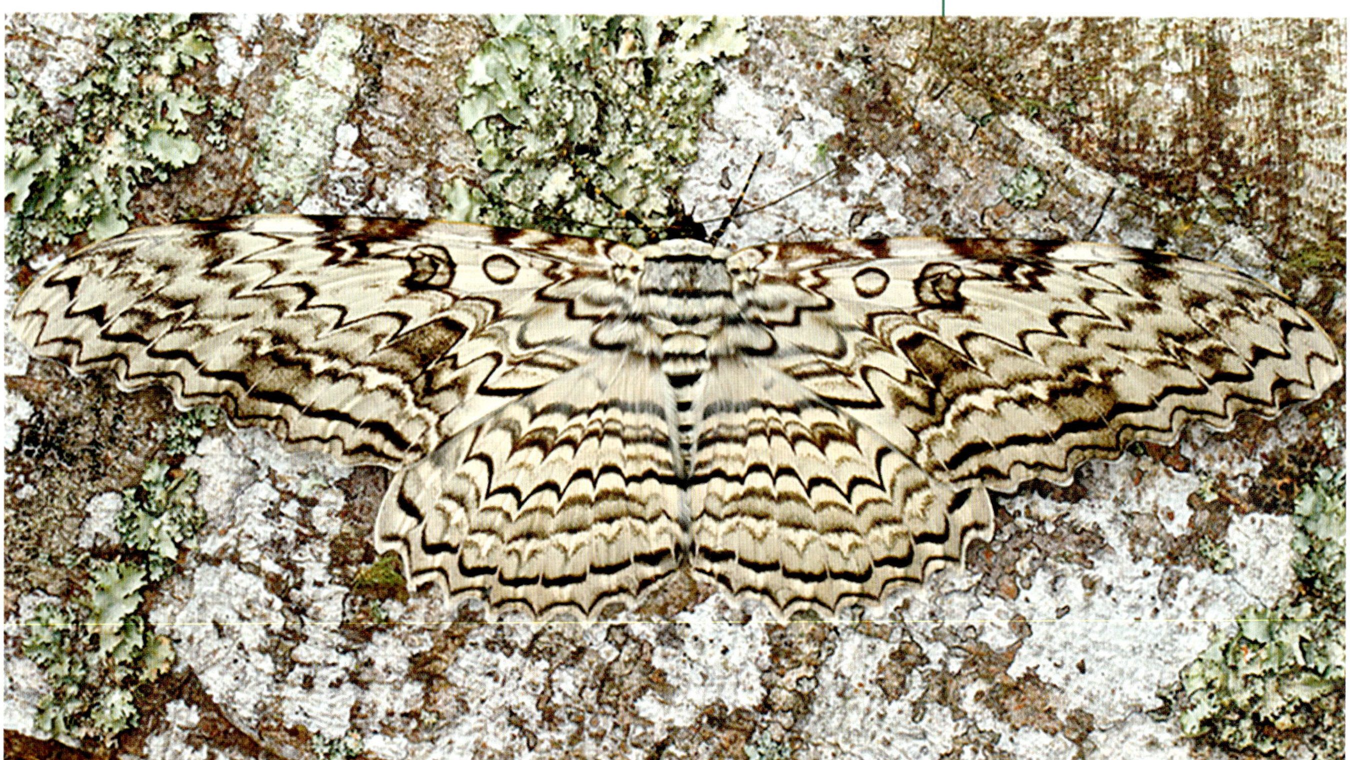

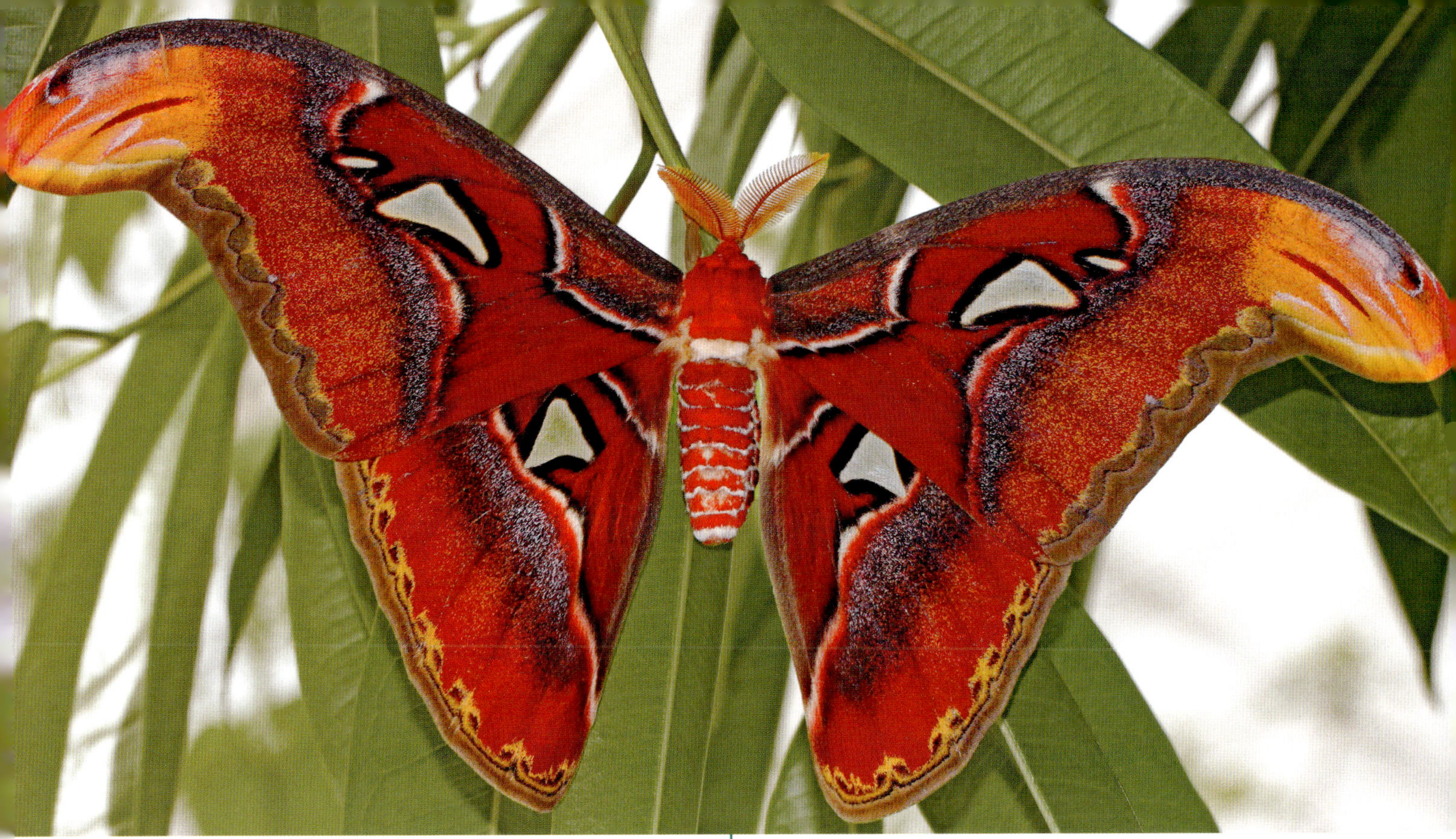

While the white witch may be the largest lepidopteran in terms of wingspan, others have a larger wing area. For example, some saturniids can reach impressive sizes, including several Asian moths in the genus *Attacus*. The mighty Atlas moth (*Attacus atlas*), which ranges across tropical and temperate Asian forests, has a wingspan of up to 27 cm and a wing surface area of over 160 cm ^{2}.

The giant peacock moth (*Saturnia pyri*) is the largest moth in Europe, with a wingspan of up to 15 centimeters. Like the death's-head hawkmoth (page 113), it still cuts an impressive figure.

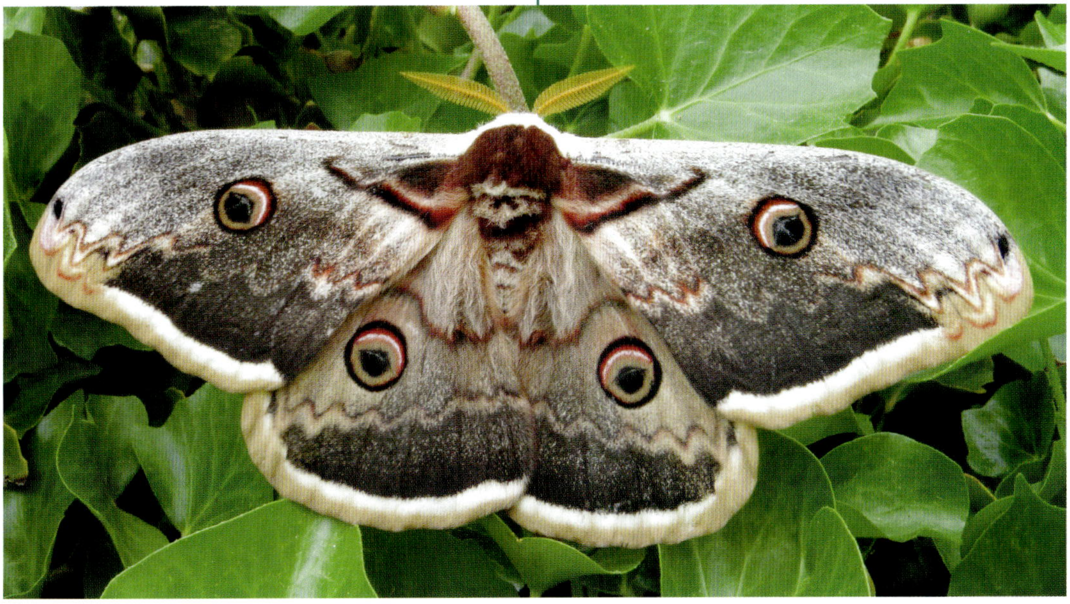

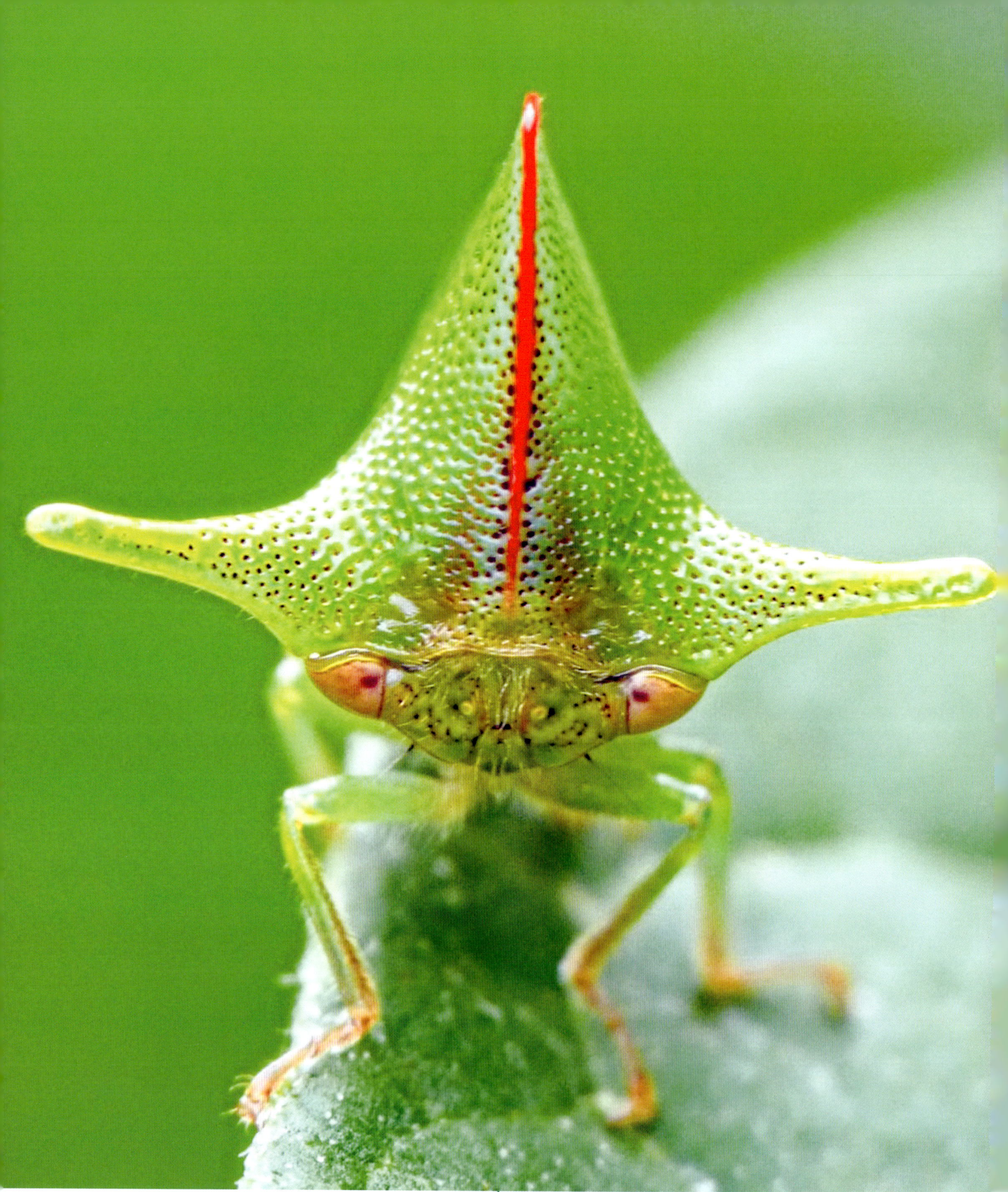

Frontal view of *Alchisme grossa*, a treehopper from Ecuador.

© Andreas Kay

FLAMBOYANT TREEHOPPERS

(HEMIPTERA: MEMBRACIDAE)

Insects in the family Membracidae, commonly known as treehoppers, are related to aphids, cicadas, and leafhoppers. Some 3,300 species have been described around the world. The most ornate come from Central and South America, which is where their morphology and behavior have been most often studied.

Adult treehoppers feed on sap by piercing plant stems with their tube-shaped mouthparts. The sap is then filtered inside a special intestinal sac, and—like aphids—they excrete the undigested excess as honeydew: a nutrient-rich substance that is consumed by gregarious insects like ants, wasps, and bees. Treehopper larvae feed on plant matter. Depending on the species, they may have a single host plant (in temperate regions), a few, or even many (in tropical regions). This is true at all life stages.

How treehoppers mate is not well understood. The females may be fertilized by one or many males, depending on the species. Some species deposit their eggs within the host plant by cutting slits with their saw-like ovipositors; others simply lay their eggs on the plant's surface. In both cases, females cover their eggs with a waxy substance that protects them from desiccation, predators, parasites, mold, and chemical substances secreted by the plant as a defense mechanism, such as resin or latex. Larval development usually happens in five stages. The larvae look much like the adults and do not undergo complete metamorphosis like flies, butterflies, or beetles. Treehopper species from temperate climates produce one generation per year and spend the winter as eggs; those from tropical climates go through several generations each year.

Social behavior also varies across different types of treehoppers. Most species are solitary. Others live in groups composed of larvae of different ages from the same mother, or larvae of the same age from different mothers. Some groups include members at all life stages of one or more species. Group living has advantages in terms of protection, food gathering, and attracting ants, with which some treehoppers have a symbiotic relationship. Other species are subsocial, as was suggested in the late nineteenth century by American entomologist

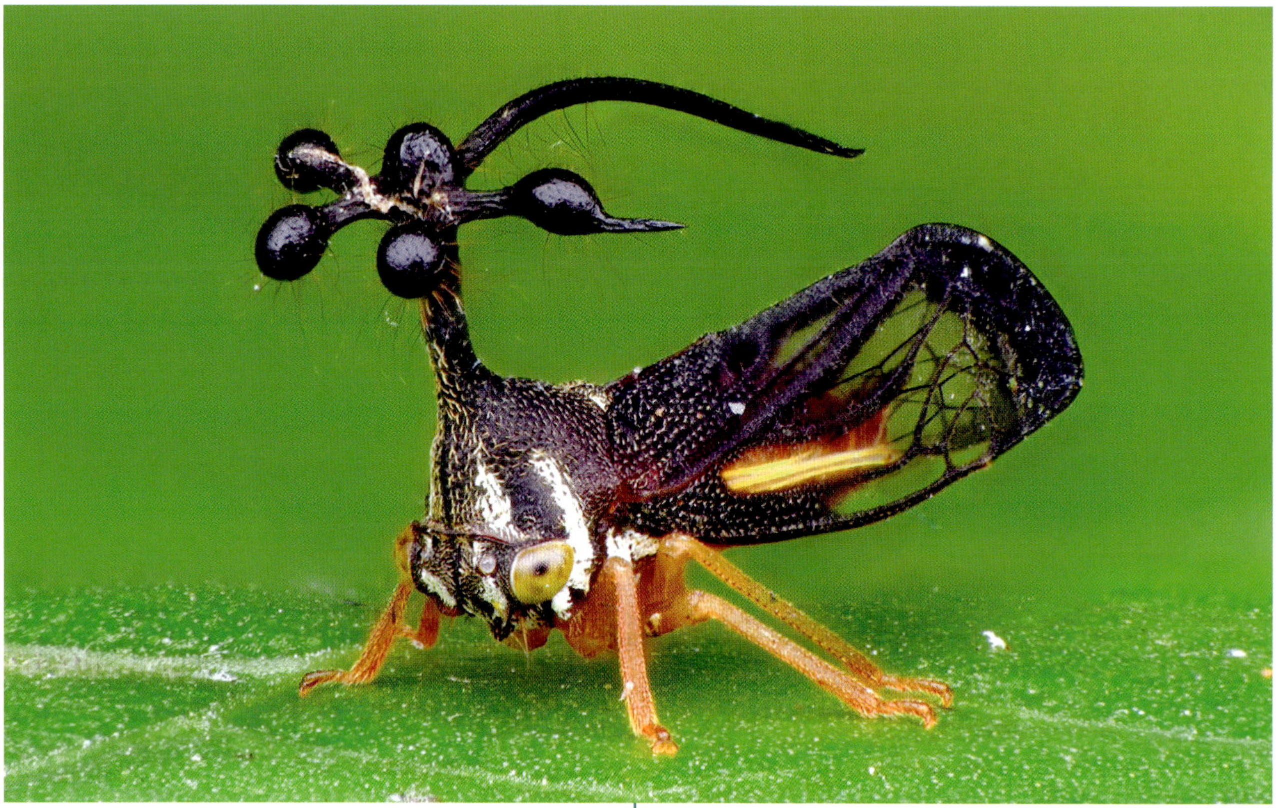

The 7-mm-long Brazilian treehopper (*Bocydium globulare*), found mainly between Costa Rica and Brazil, looks like something from another planet. The globular pronotum protruding from its thorax is covered in sensitive spines that it uses to detect vibrations, wind direction, and chemical substances in the air (particularly sex hormones).

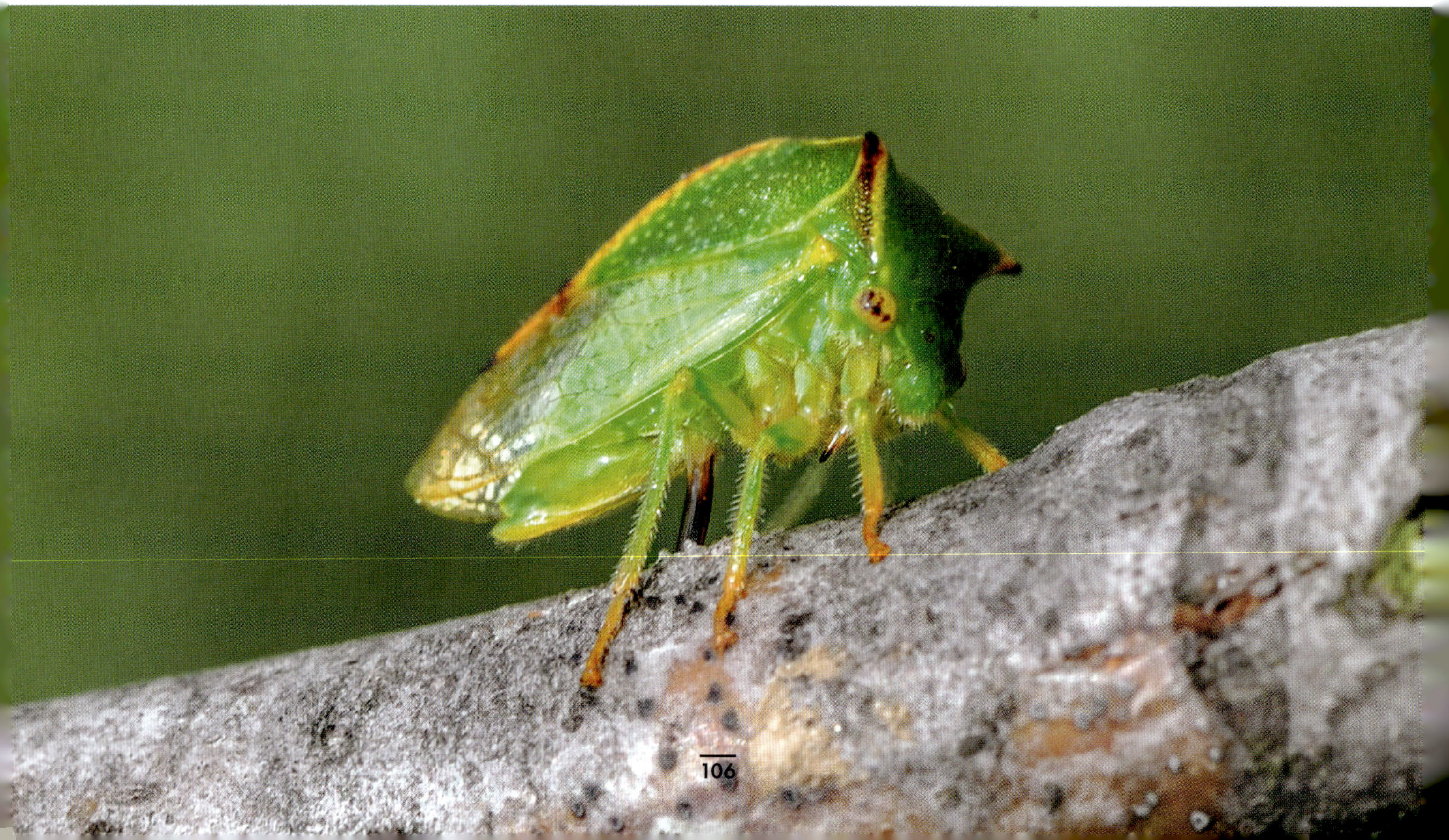

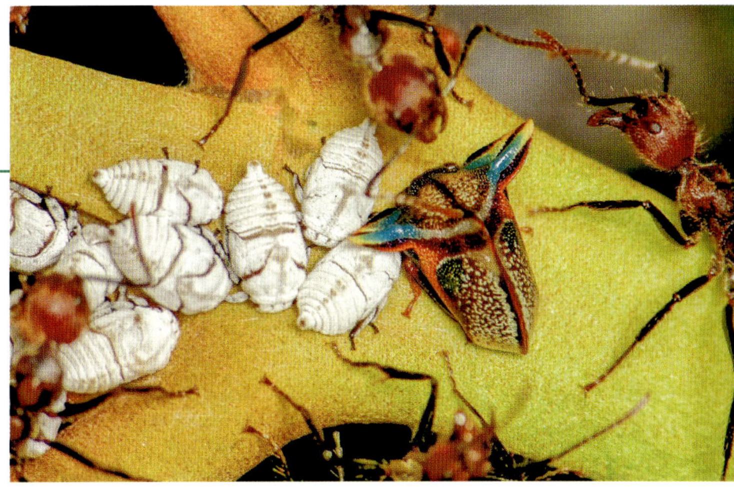

Many treehoppers have a mutually beneficial relationship with ants. The ants pictured here are watching over nymphs and one adult *Tropidolomia auriculata*, a 3-mm-long treehopper species from Central America.
© Andreas Kay

Mary E. Murtfeldt (1848–1913) but not proven until 1970. Subsocial treehoppers protect their eggs and/or larvae from predators and parasites for a period that varies by species but can last until the offspring reach adulthood. A single female may even care for the eggs of different mothers.

Some treehoppers take parenting even more seriously: females help their young feed by sawing into plant tissue with their ovipositors if the larvae are unable to pierce it with their mouthparts. Others create "wells" where nutritious sap accumulates for easy feeding. And females from various species will demonstrate aggressive behavior at the approach of predators (shield bugs, ladybugs, hoverfly larvae, etc.) or when alerted by their offspring. They will kick, spread their wings while making a buzzing sound, make darting movements that cause the plant to move, or emit chemical substances to alert their young.

Many treehopper species have a facultative mutualistic relationship with ants, which protect the treehoppers from predators in exchange for the

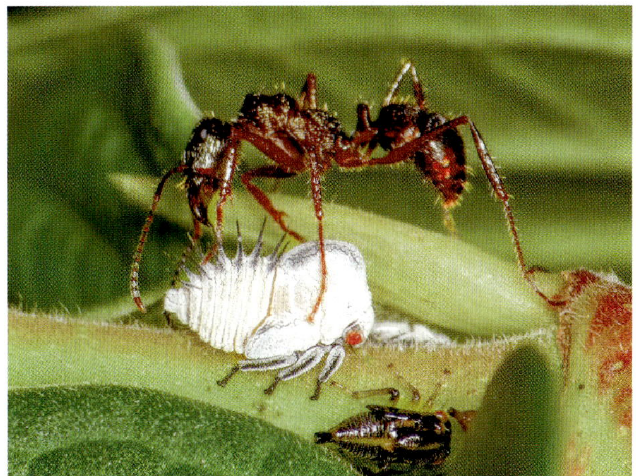

An ant looking for honeydew from a *Membracis dorsata* larva.
© Andreas Kay

nutrient-rich honeydew they produce. This quid pro quo probably led to more social behavior in treehoppers, as living in groups attracts more ants. Some ant species even build "shelters" for treehopper larvae and/or adults out of soil and plant fibers, where

Despite being associated with tropical climates, some treehopper species are found in the United States and Europe. The buffalo treehopper (*Stictocephala bisonia*, left) is native to North America, and the thorn-hopper (*Centrotus cornutus*) is present in most of Europe. *Gargara genistae* and *Centrotus chloroticus* are rarer. All are less flamboyant than their Neotropical cousins.
© Quartl CC 3.0

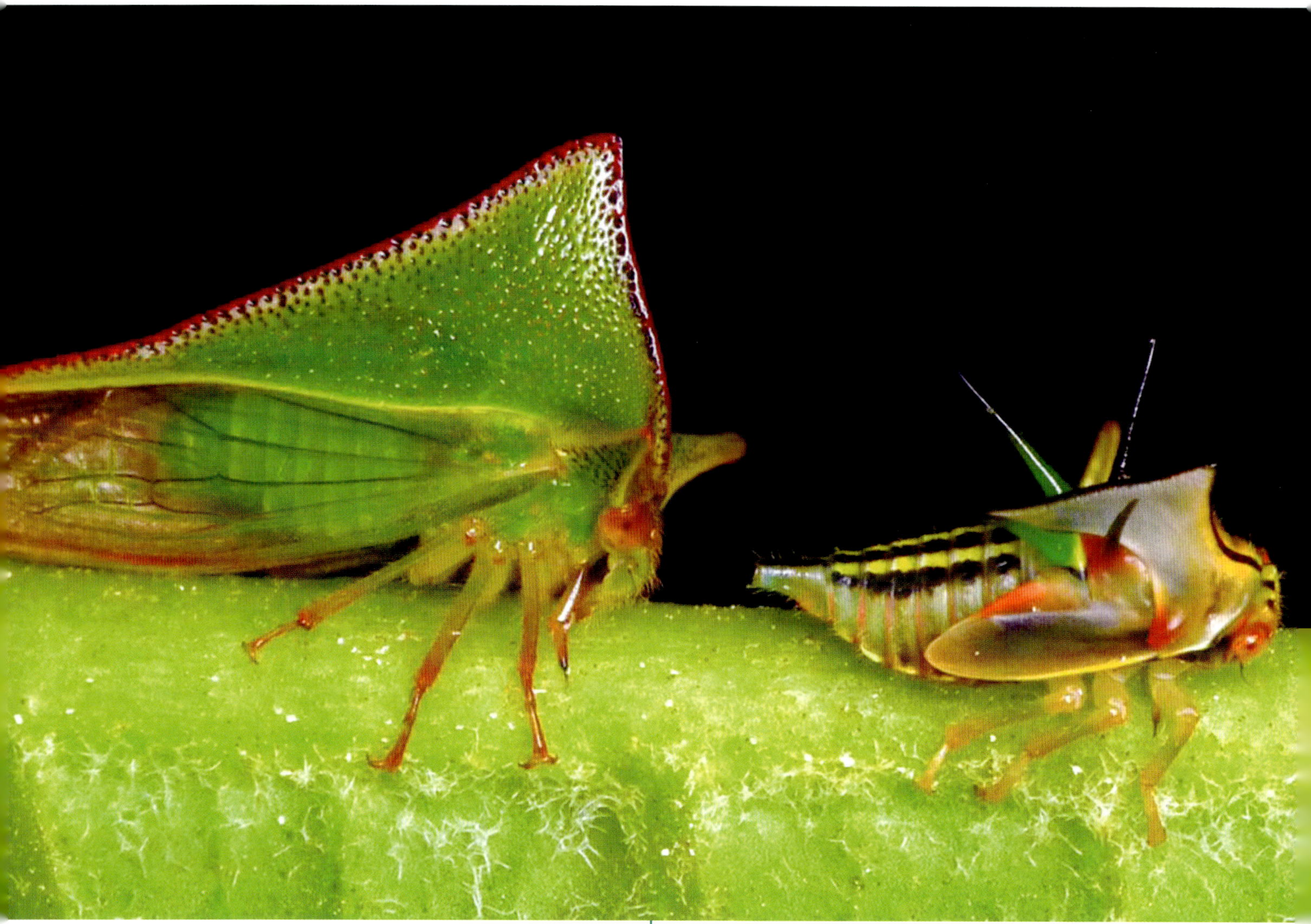

Alchisme grossa, seen here as an adult and a larva, is found in Central and South America. While some treehoppers are aposematic (meaning they have bright, colorful markings to warn predators that they contain toxins), others mimic the color and texture of the plants on which they live. In some species, the larvae are a completely different color from the adults.

© Andreas Kay

several species may live together. The shape and size of these shelters vary by ant species. They are more of a bonus than a necessity, however, as treehoppers can be observed both inside and outside the shelters.

When threatened, treehoppers can escape by flying or using another particularly effective mechanism: their incredible jump. The "hop" in treehopper is an understatement: they can reach a peak speed of 5 or 6 meters per second within milliseconds, an acceleration of 550–700 g! They can do this thanks to powerful thoracic muscles that contain resilin, an elastic protein like a natural rubber that can store large amounts of energy and release it in a fraction of a second (see page 37). The aerodynamic shape of many treehoppers adds to their incredible jumping skills.

OVER-THE-TOP GLAMOUR

The dorsal and/or lateral sides of the treehopper's thorax extend over its head and body to form a hollow pronotum or "helmet" of varying shape, color, and size depending on the species. The evolutionary origin of this adaptation is still disputed. One hypothesis is that it evolved from a third pair of wings that treehoppers may have had some 250 million years ago. Such wings would not have been necessary for flight, so they could have been modified into the helmets seen on many species today. Such major changes to an insect's body structure are extremely rare, however. Another hypothesis is that the helmet is merely an extension of the thorax.

The helmet's exact function is also up for debate. It might be used for crypsis: to mimic plants or other insects (ants, for example). Or it might be used to frighten off predators or warn them of the treehopper's venomous properties, a phenomenon known as aposematism. Some researchers think the helmet might also act like a sound box for exchanging signals in the form of vibrations sent through plant tissues. These vibratory signals (made prior to mating, or among members of a group, between larvae and their mothers/guardians, etc.) might be picked up using sensitive strands on the underside of the helmet. Treehoppers do appear capable of detecting and locating the source of sounds, but the pronotum has not been proven to play a role: some treehopper species have no helmet but can still pick up vibrations.

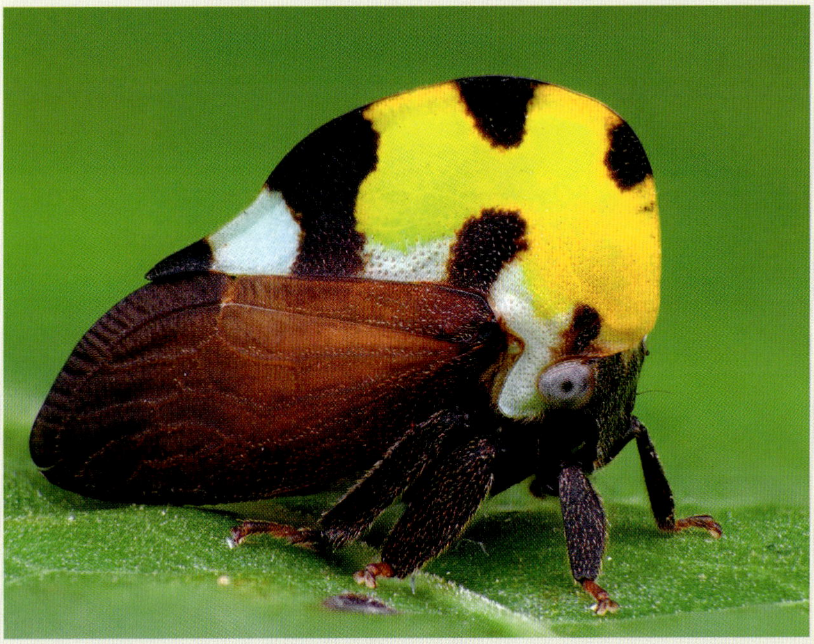

The large, flattened pronotum of this *Membracis mexicana* mimics leafcutter ants of the genus *Atta*, which carry pieces of leaves over their heads.

© Andreas Kay

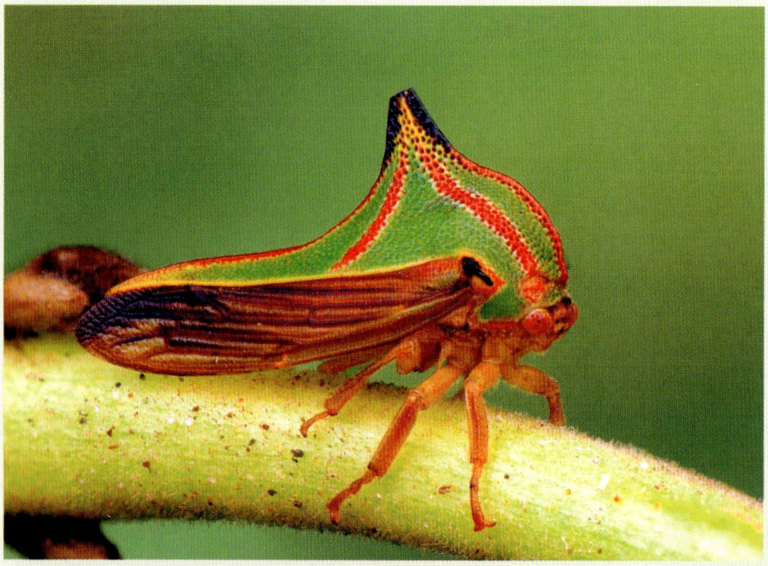

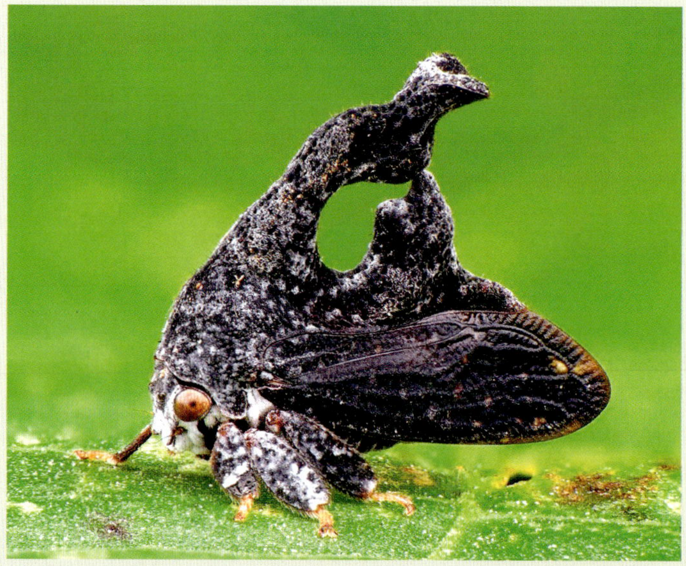

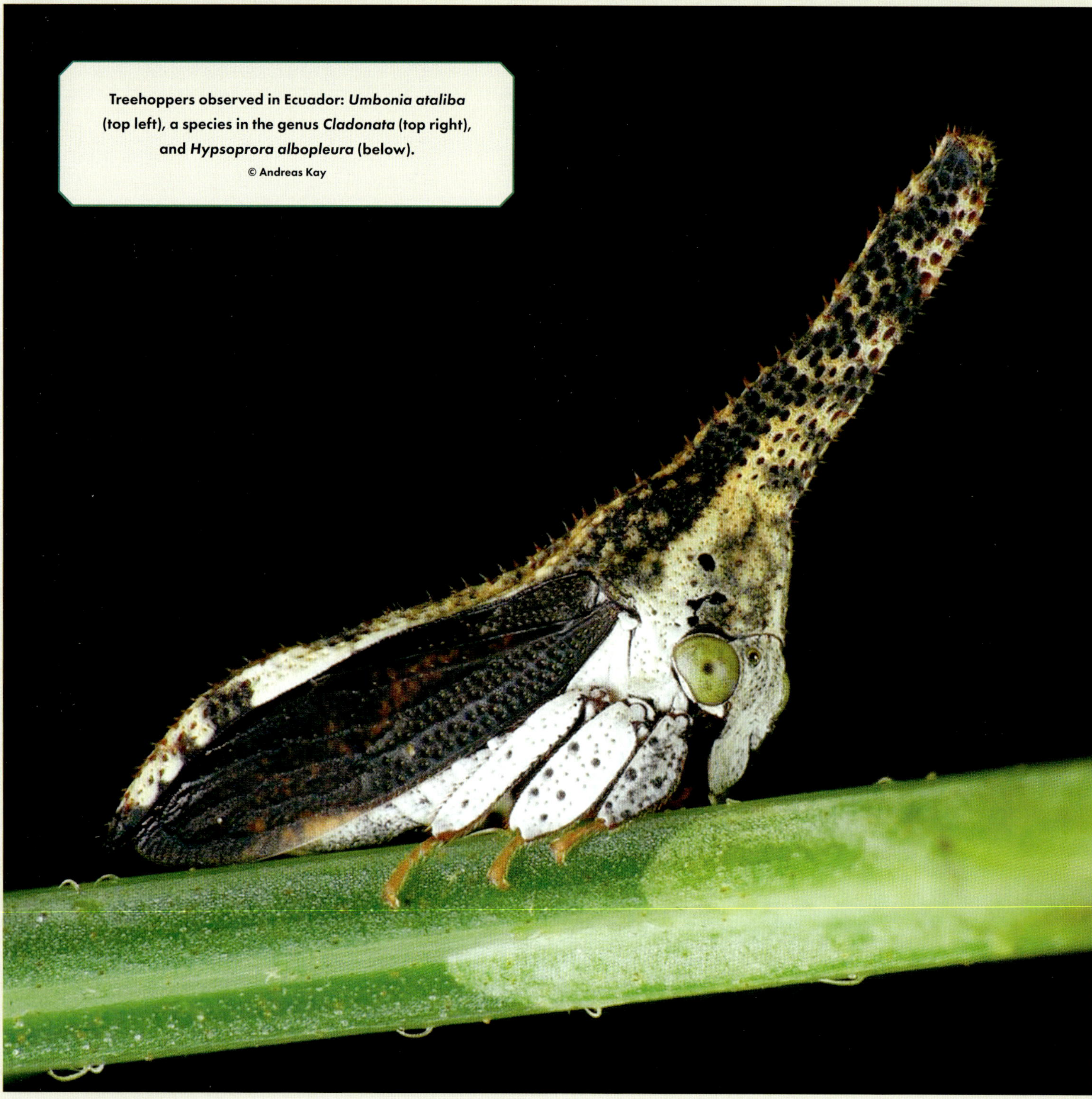

Treehoppers observed in Ecuador: ***Umbonia ataliba*** **(top left), a species in the genus** ***Cladonata*** **(top right), and** ***Hypsoprora albopleura*** **(below).**

© Andreas Kay

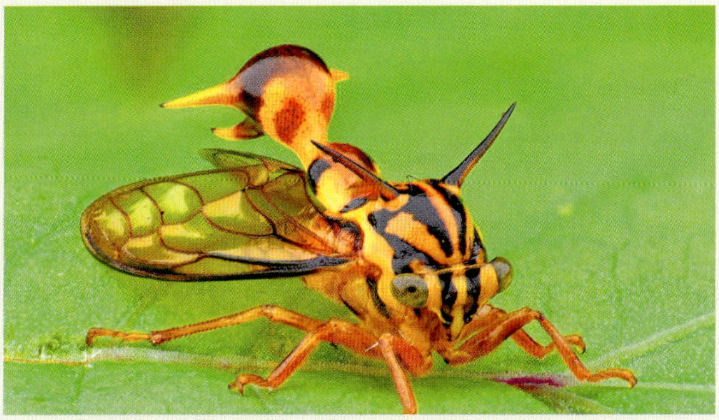
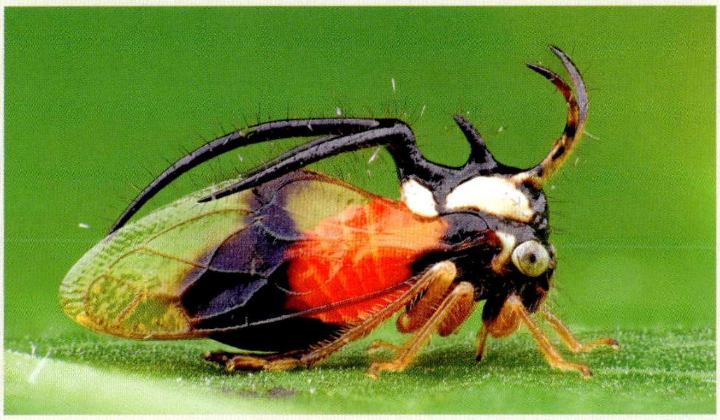
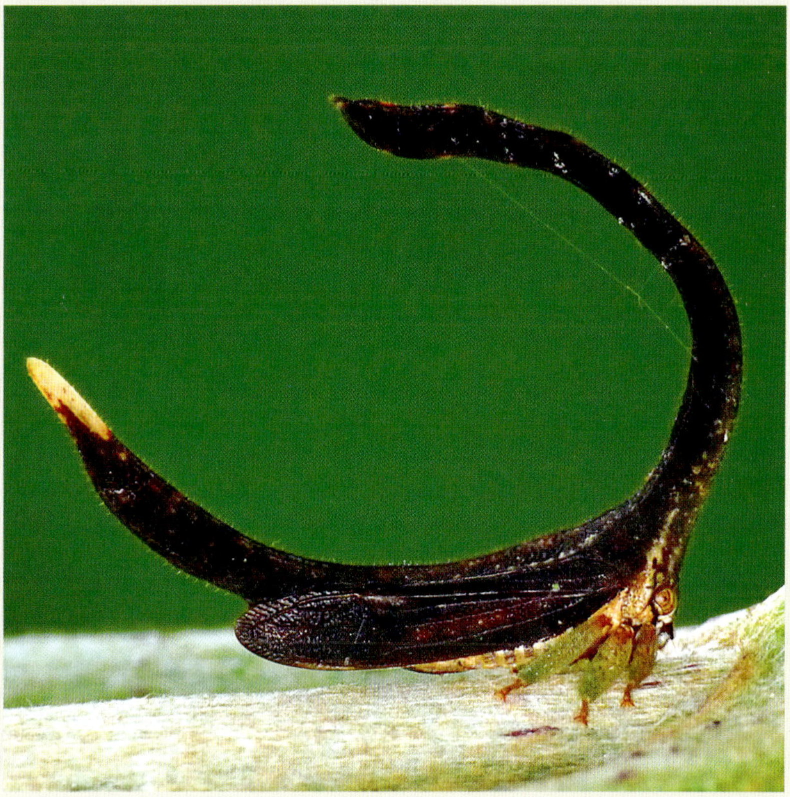
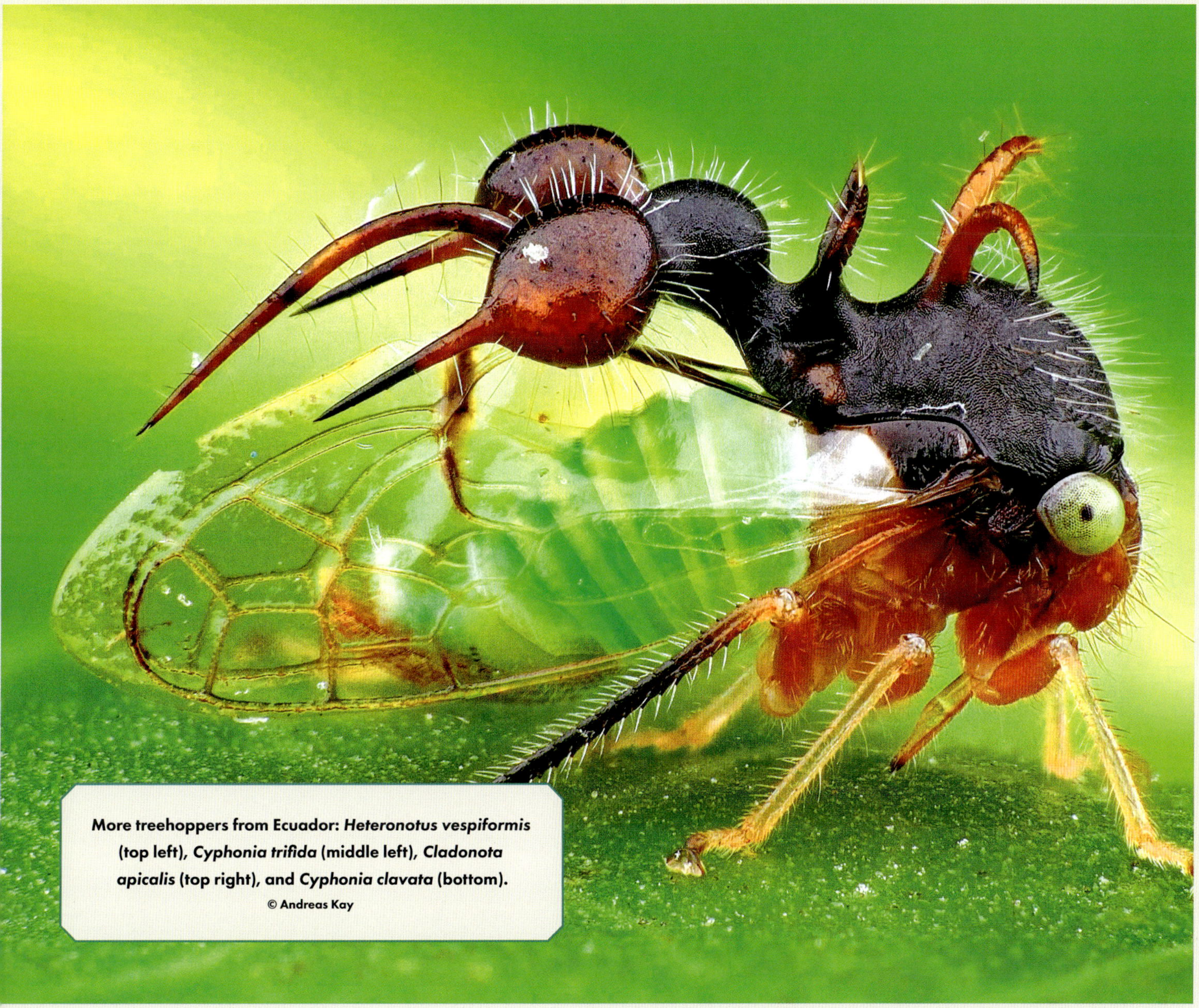

More treehoppers from Ecuador: *Heteronotus vespiformis* (top left), *Cyphonia trifida* (middle left), *Cladonota apicalis* (top right), and *Cyphonia clavata* (bottom).

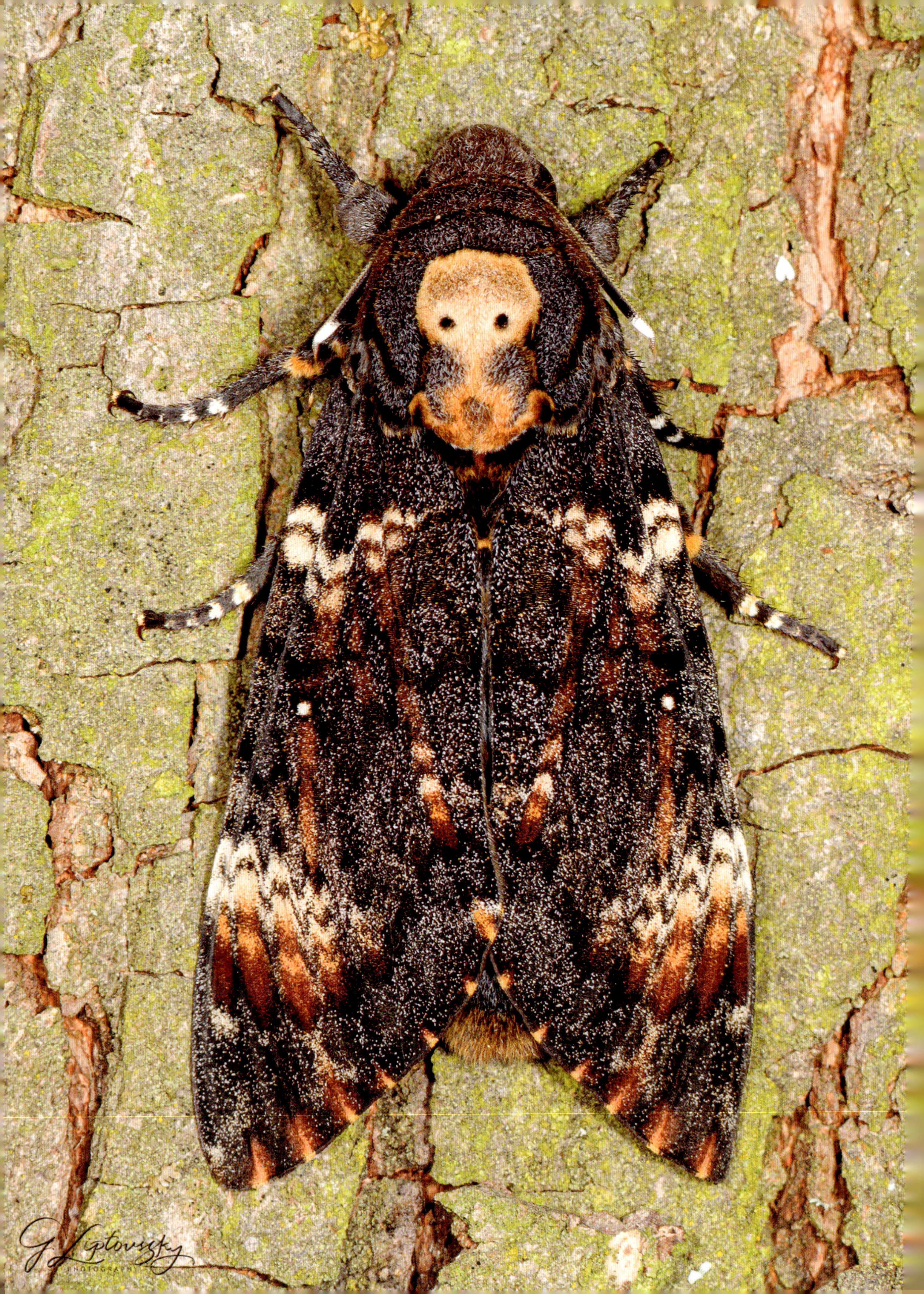
G Liptovszky
PHOTOGRAPHY

THE DEATH'S-HEAD HAWK MOTH

ACHERONTIA ATROPOS

(LEPIDOPTERA: SPHINGIDAE)

In addition to its gothic flair, the African death's-head hawkmoth is also impressively large: 13 to 14 centimeters across. It owes both its scientific and its common name to the pattern resembling a human skull on its thorax. But that is not the only reason it has long inspired irrational fears. When threatened, it also produces an eerie sound like a shriek.

No wonder this moth with a skull on its back used to strike fear into people's hearts when it emerged from the night to flutter in the light of their windows. Its appearance was so frightening that, in the eighteenth century, it was thought to be an omen of tragic events to come. As English entomologist Moses Harris (1730–1787) wrote: "It is regarded not as the creation of a benevolent being, but the device of evil spirits [. . .] conceived and fabricated in the dark, and the very shining of its eyes is thought to represent the fiery element whence it is supposed to have proceeded. Flying into their apartments in the evening it at times extinguishes the light; foretelling war, pestilence, hunger, death to man and beast." Military authorities in Brest, France, went so far as to consult naturalist René-Antoine Ferchault de Réaumur (1683–1757) about a panic spreading among the peasants; Réaumur explained that the uproar was due to an abundance of death's-head moths, which had the locals convinced that a

Many insects have ocelli, also known as eyespots, or other markings to scare off predators. The skull on the death's-head hawkmoth does not fall into this category, however . . . because it is only frightening to humans! The plaintive "shriek" made by these moths has also been considered an evil omen. They make the sound by inhaling air, which vibrates the epipharynx (a flap between the mouth and throat), then exhaling with the flap open, causing a variation in the sound. The sequence is repeated roughly every five seconds. It was Réaumur who first demonstrated that this "plaintive and macabre" cry was of natural origin and not a warning of divine anger.

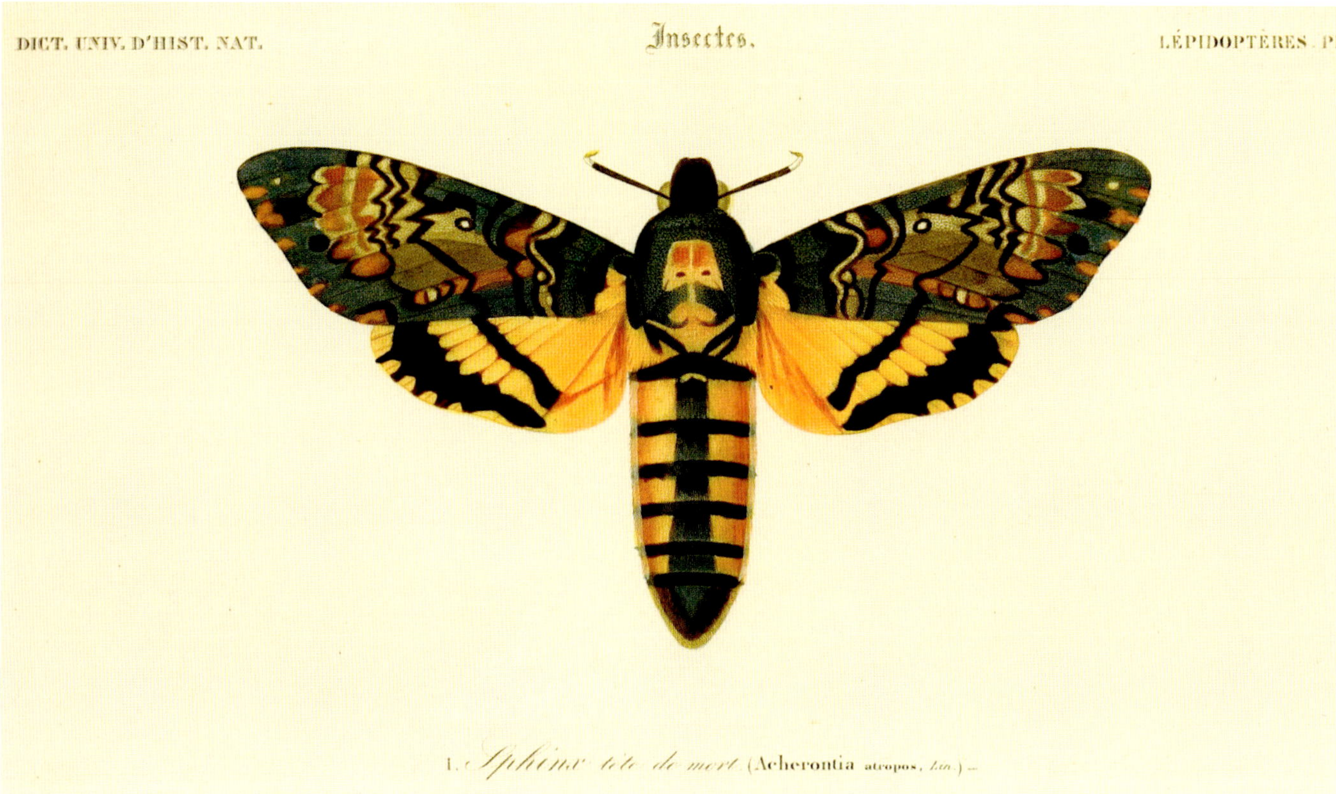

When threatened, the African death's-head hawkmoth spreads its wings to show off its size and reveal its yellow lower wings and striped abdomen, which imitate the markings of stinging insects like wasps and hornets.

© Charles d'Orbigny, *Dictionnaire universel d'histoire naturelle*, 1849

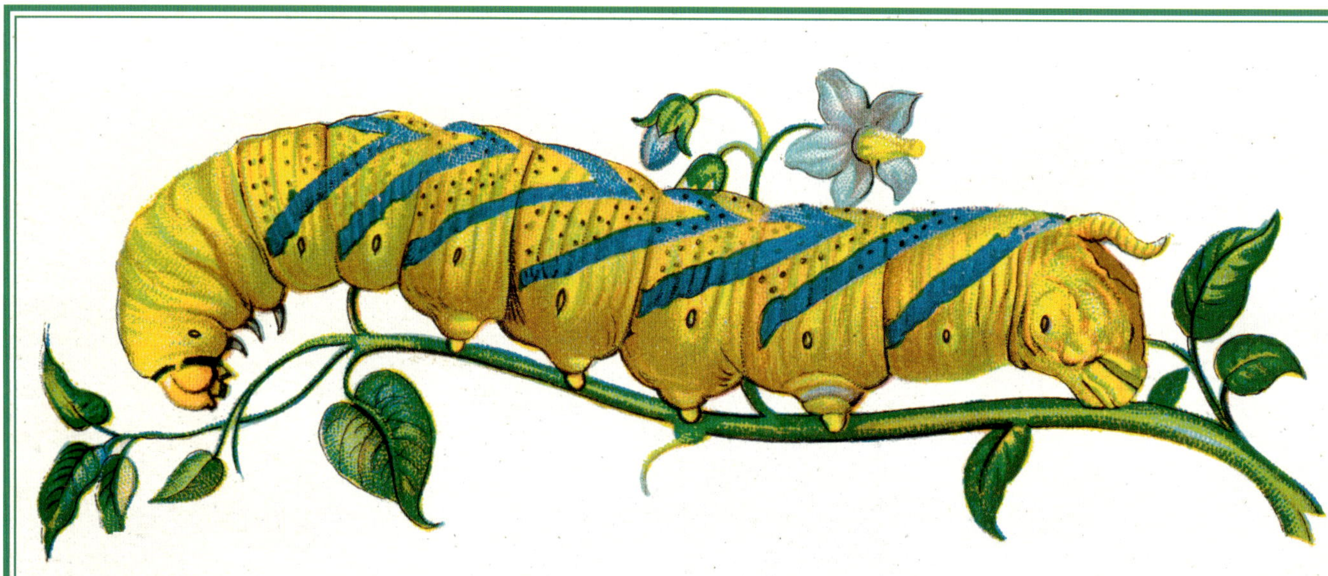

The caterpillar of the African death's-head hawkmoth can grow up to 12 cm long and is observed mainly on potato plants and other nightshades. Once it has grown to full size, it burrows underground to metamorphose into a moth (if it survives the pesticides and mechanized harvesters now used in potato fields, that is).

© Dr. F. Nemos, 1895

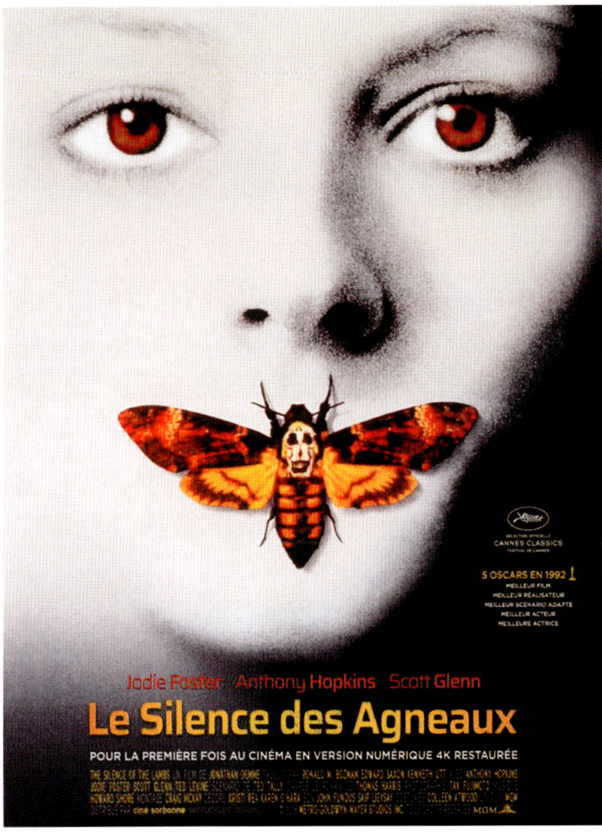

The 1988 novel *The Silence of the Lambs* by Thomas Harris features another species of death's-head hawkmoth, *Acherontia styx* from Asia: the serial killer in the novel places the moth's pupa in the throat of his victims as a calling card. But it was *A. atropos* that appeared on the poster for the movie adaptation three years later.

© Orion Pictures Corporation, CC 4.0

plague was imminent. In Africa, some people still believe the moth has a deadly stinger (actually its proboscis, or in some cases the "horn" on the posterior of the caterpillar, which is typical in hawkmoth larvae). Inhabitants of the island of Mauritius once believed—and some may still—that if the moth collides with a wall, the scales shed from its wings like dust can blind you if they touch your eyes.

The scientific name chosen by Carl Linnaeus, *Acherontia atropos*, is no less sinister than the common name and likely contributed to the moth's fearsome reputation. The genus *Acherontia*, which comprises three species with the "death's head" marking, is a reference to the Acheron, the river across which souls were ferried to the underworld in early Greek mythology. And Atropos was one of the three Fates who cut short the thread of mortal lives. Given its associations with evil, it comes as no surprise that the death's-head hawkmoth has featured in a number of literary works. It is the subject of a horror story by Edgar Allan Poe, "The Sphinx," published in 1846. Count Dracula, in the original 1897 novel by Bram Stoker, gives a death's-head moth to his servant Renfield. The moth also appears as a symbol of death in Thomas Hardy's *The Return of the Native* (1878) and in John Keats's poem "Ode on Melancholy" (1819).

Death's-head hawkmoths can fly at speeds of up to 45 kilometers per hour. They are native to tropical Africa but migrate to the Near and Middle East, Macaronesia, and Europe, which they reach by crossing the Mediterranean Sea from northern Africa. They can range as far north as Great Britain and even Scandinavia. While they sometimes winter in southern Europe, where the winters are mild, it is rare for their caterpillars and pupae to survive there.

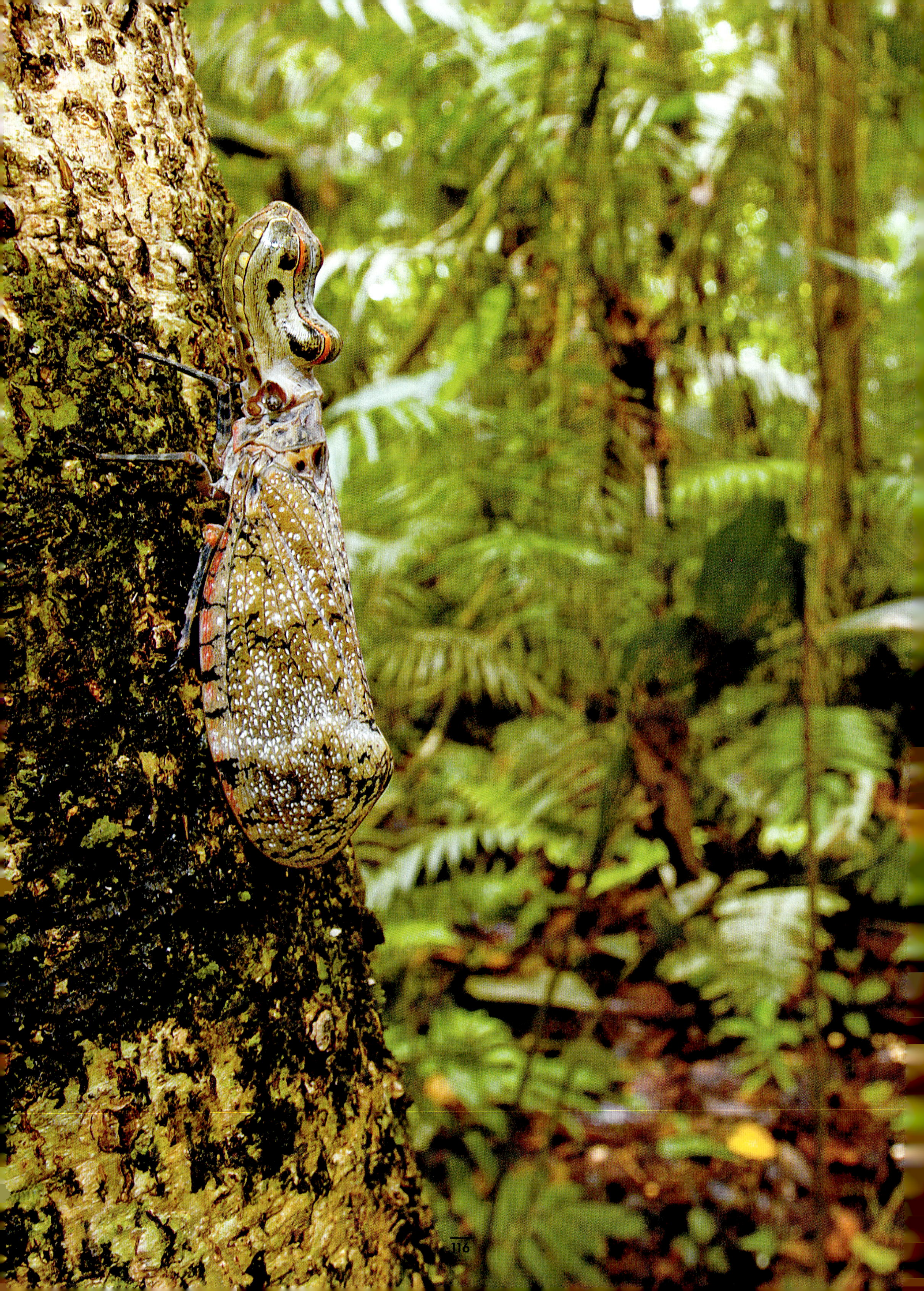

A LANTERN IN THE DARK?

FULGORA LATERNARIA

(HEMIPTERA: FULGORIDAE)

Lanternflies owe their trademark look to a hollow protuberance on their heads that can be nearly as large as their bodies. Their heads were long believed to be luminescent: it was German entomologist Maria Sibylla Merian (1647–1717) who originated the false idea that they glowed in the dark.

Insects in the family Fulgoridae, commonly known as lanternflies, are diverse and mainly found in the tropics. They are of moderate to large size and feed on plant sap, which they collect using piercing and sucking mouthparts. Some bear a passing resemblance to butterflies because of their bright colors and patterned wings. Their enlarged heads are just for looks, however—they do not emit any light whatsoever. False though it proved to be, the idea nonetheless inspired several species names chosen by Carl Linnaeus, including *laternaria*, *phosphorea*, and *candelaria*.

Fulgora laternaria is known by many names: the *machaca* in Spanish and the peanut-headed lanternfly in some other languages. It is native to the tropical forests of Central and South America and can reach lengths of 8.5 to 10 centimeters, with a wingspan of 10 to 15 centimeters. It uses camouflage to blend in with tree bark, and the 10- to 15-millimeter protuberance on its head mimics a lizard head. When attacked, it flashes yellow eyespots on its wings to startle its aggressor and releases a foul-smelling substance. It feeds on the sap of trees such as courbaril, white mahogany, *Simarouba amara*, and *Zanthoxylum*

The outgrowth or "process" on some lanternfly heads is shaped, patterned, and placed to mimic the snout of a lizard, complete with eyes, teeth, and nostrils. Can you see it?

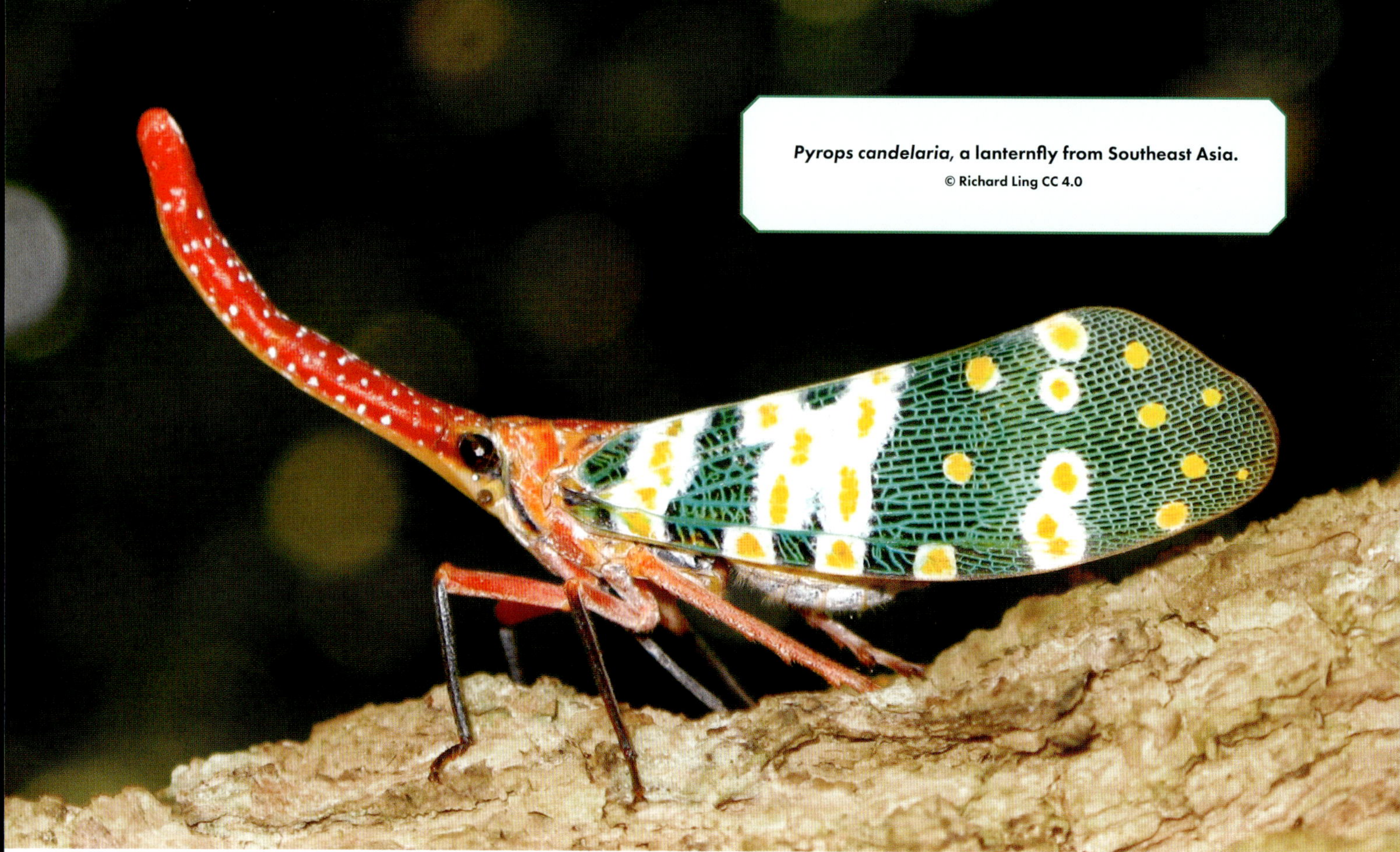

Pyrops candelaria, a lanternfly from Southeast Asia.

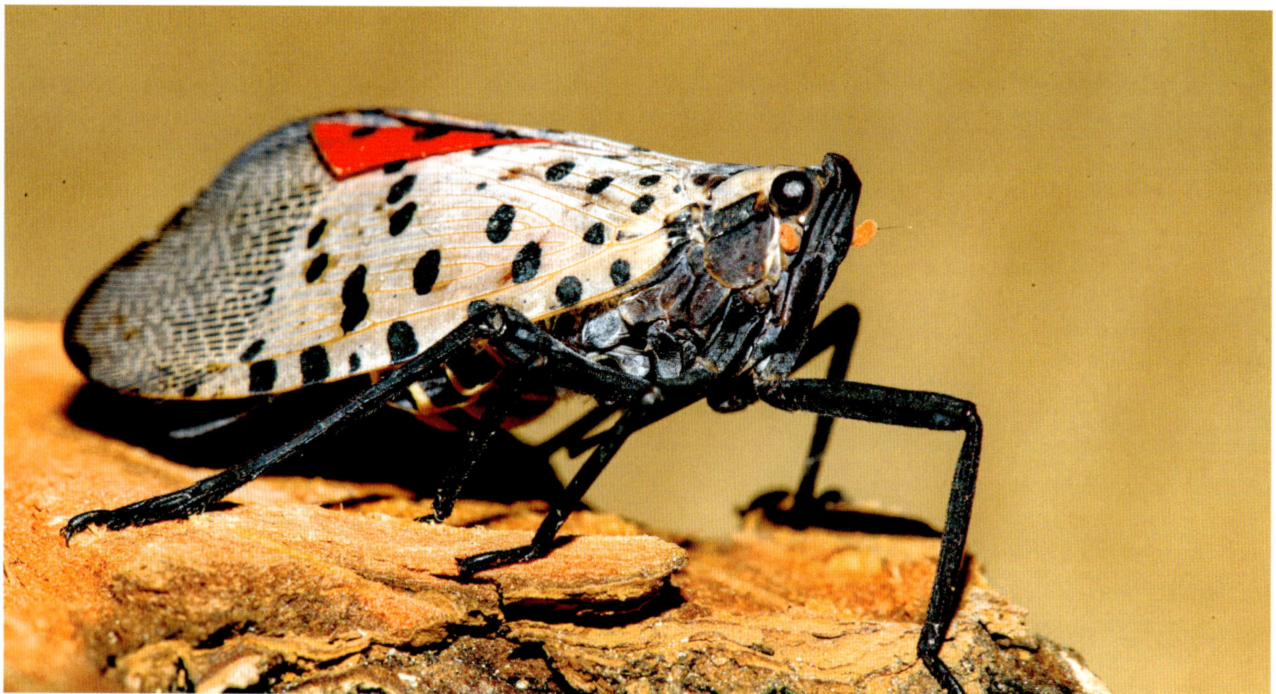

The spotted lanternfly (*Lycorma delicatula*) is roughly 25 mm long and native to southern China and parts of Vietnam. Although it has two pairs of wings, it jumps more often than it flies. While it can live on vines, fruit trees, and various woody plants, its preferred host is the Chinese sumac (*Ailanthus altissima*). Spotted lanternflies have been accidentally introduced to the United States, where they were first observed in 2014 and have become an invasive species, causing damage to various trees and ornamental plants.

species. Adults generally hide inside tree trunks during the day. According to a South American legend, the bite of these insects (which neither bite nor sting!) is fatal; British entomologist Henry Walter Bates reported being told that a lanternfly once flew onto a boat and killed eight of the crew. A certain sex act can supposedly prevent death by lanternfly bite, if practiced quick enough. . . .

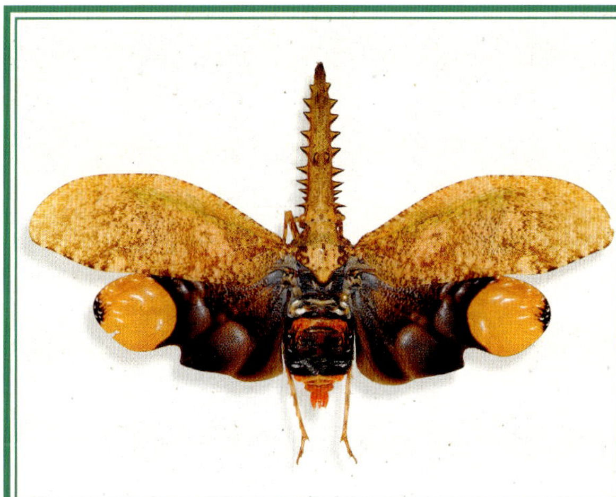

***Cathedra serrata*, which has an astonishing, saw-like head process, lives in South America. Little else is known about it.**

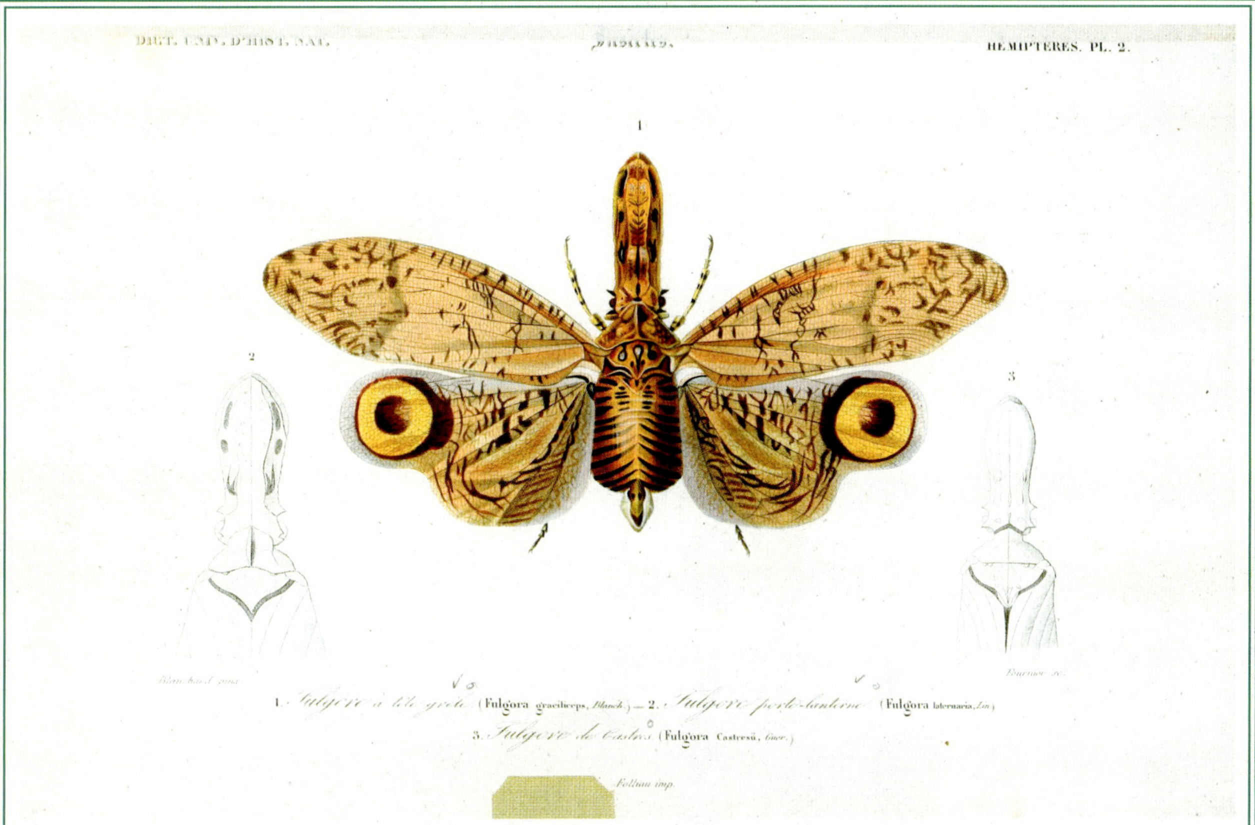

The peanut-headed lanternfly or alligator bug (*Fulgora laternaria*) as pictured in *Le Dictionnaire universel d'histoire naturelle* by Charles d'Orbigny (1849).

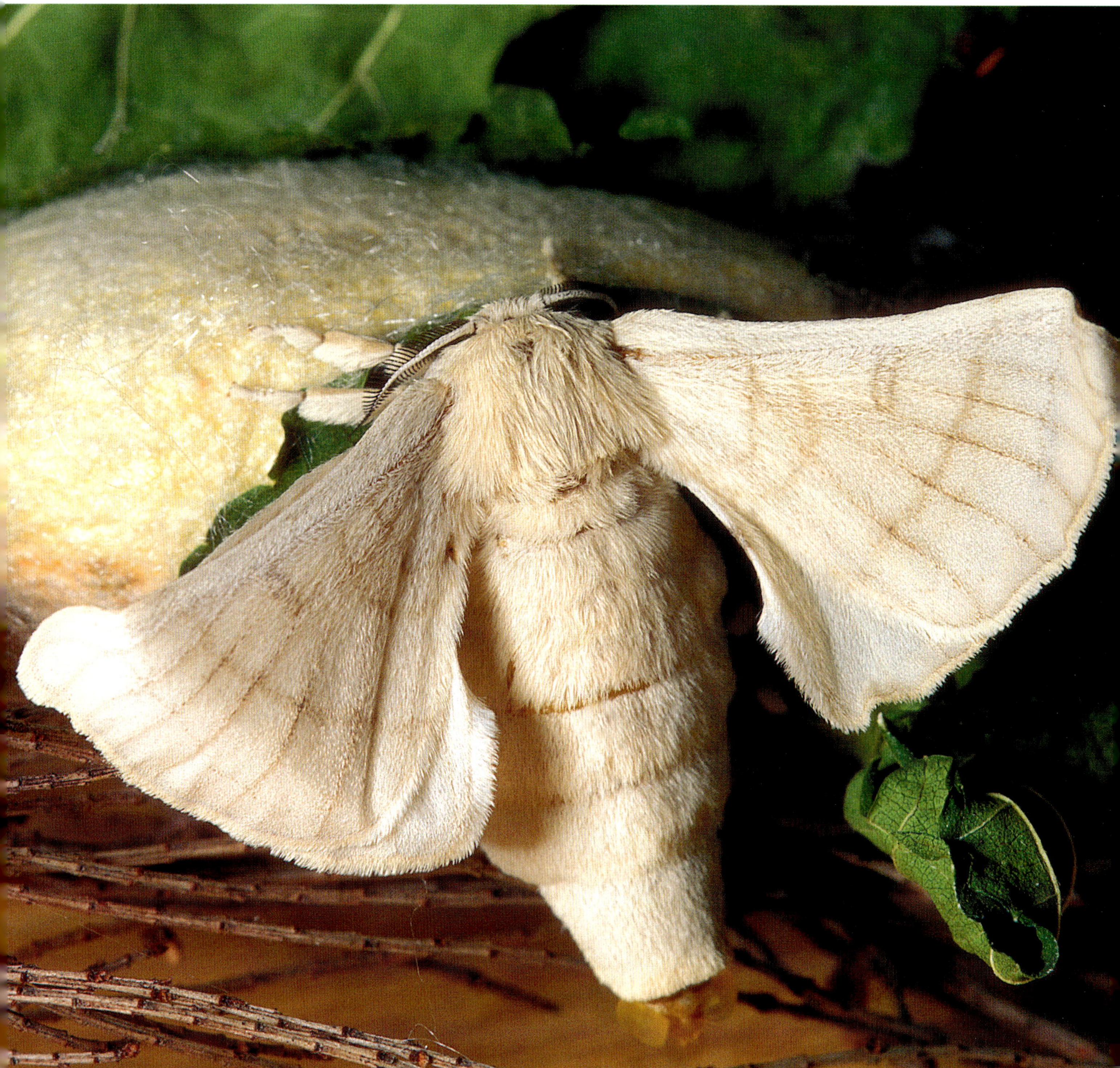

The domestic silk moth is colorless, clumsy, and incapable of flying or feeding. Its short adult life is entirely dedicated to mating and—for the female—laying around five hundred eggs, which silk farmers call "seed."

© Alain Carrara/Biosphoto

SPINNERS OF SILK

BOMBYX MORI

(LEPIDOPTERA: BOMBYCIDAE)

Did you know that silk comes from insects? Specifically, the caterpillar of the domestic silk moth. The art of silk-making was born in China over five thousand years ago and remained a closely guarded secret for centuries, during which time the precious cloth was traded without any other country knowing how it was made.

Over time, knowledge of silk-making spread to India, Japan, and the Middle East as trade expanded along the famous Silk Road, eventually reaching the Eastern Mediterranean around the sixth century. Arab civilizations introduced silk farming to Spain and Italy, and the practice reached France in the thirteenth century. Starting in the sixteenth century, silk-making flourished in France thanks to the efforts of agronomist Olivier de Serres (1539–1619) and King Henri IV. Jean-Baptiste Colbert, a minister to Louis XIV, later promoted the trade in the countryside around Lyon, where farms and workers specialized in making silk began to multiply. Silk production was industrialized in the nineteenth century: in France alone, a record 26,000 tons of silk cocoons were produced in the Rhone valley, Provence, Cévennes, and Vivarais in 1853. This boom had a downside, however. With so many silkworms being raised in dense concentration, epidemics of viral, bacterial, and fungal infections soon broke out. Silkworm diseases such as grasserie, flacherie, and muscardine were rampant. And in the mid-nineteenth century, a devastating outbreak of pébrine (a parasitic disease) was only contained when the authorities rallied biologists, including Louis Pasteur (the inventor of pasteurization), to the cause. The European silk industry never recovered. Persistent pockets of disease, the high cost of producing European silk, low profit margins from raising mulberry trees compared with fruit trees, and declining demand for silk all spelled its downfall. The opening of the Suez Canal in 1869 also made it easier to import goods from China and Japan, both of which were industrializing their own silk production and starting to export some

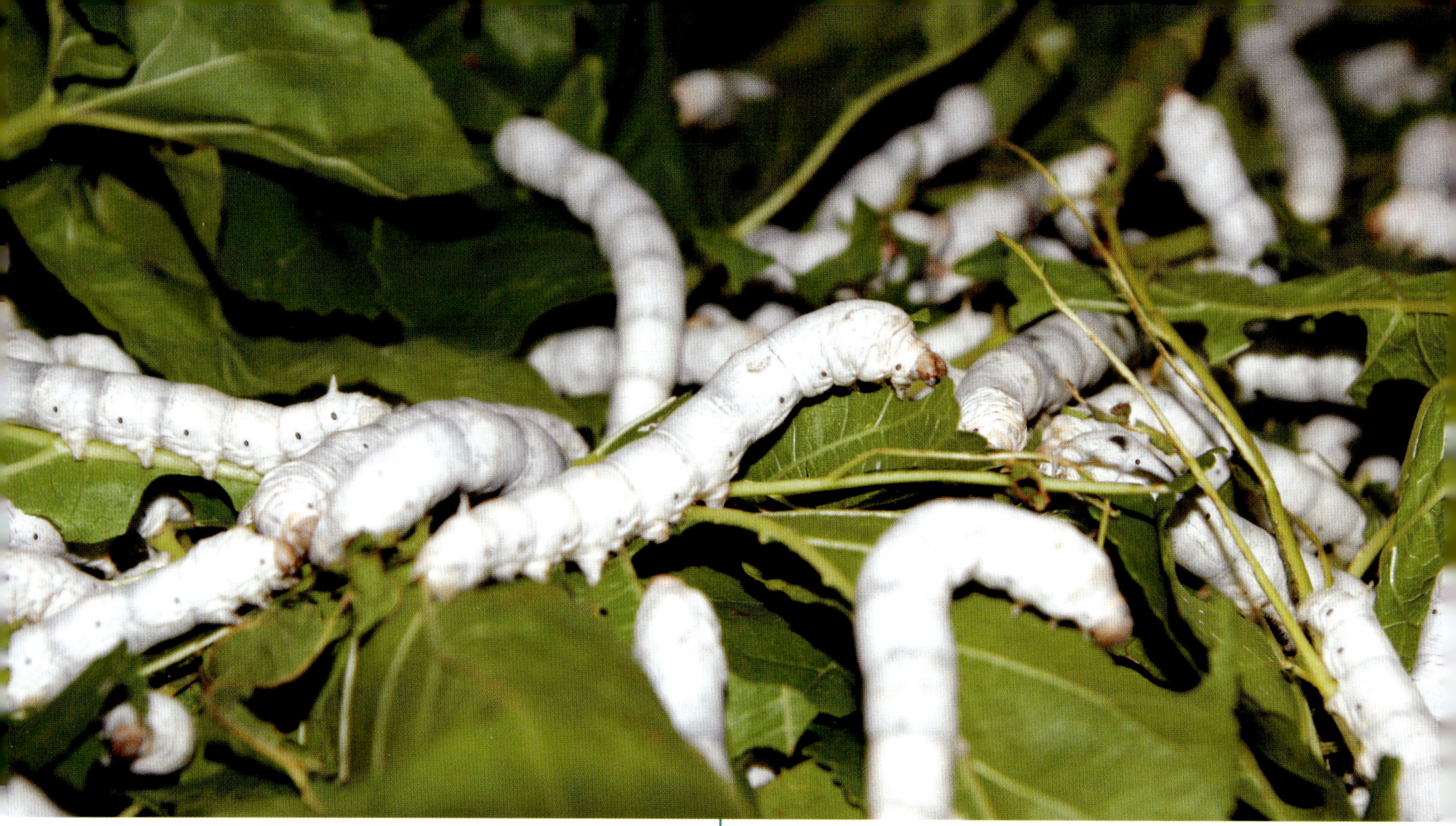

Silkworms are not worms but caterpillars—the larvae of the domestic silk moth. Over the course of six weeks, they consume impressive quantities of mulberry leaves before metamorphosing inside a protective cocoon made up of a single, 800- to 1,500-m-long filament produced from their salivary glands.
© Armin Kübelbeck CC 4.0 (larvae, top); © Kerstin Hinze/Biosphoto (cocoon, below)

of the first synthetic textiles made from nitrocellulose. Silk farming has now become economically insignificant in Europe.

Producing silk requires pesticides and fertilizers to produce food for the silkworms and prevent disease. And most silk is produced in Asia, where environmental regulations are often weak—heavy metals and PCBs have both been detected in silk. You should take the environmental impacts into consideration before buying silk—and if you do, choose certified organic suppliers.

Raw silk is produced in the silkworm's salivary glands and consists mainly of two proteins: fibroin and sericin. Its shine comes from the structure of the fiber, which refracts light differently at different angles. It is essentially a waste product that

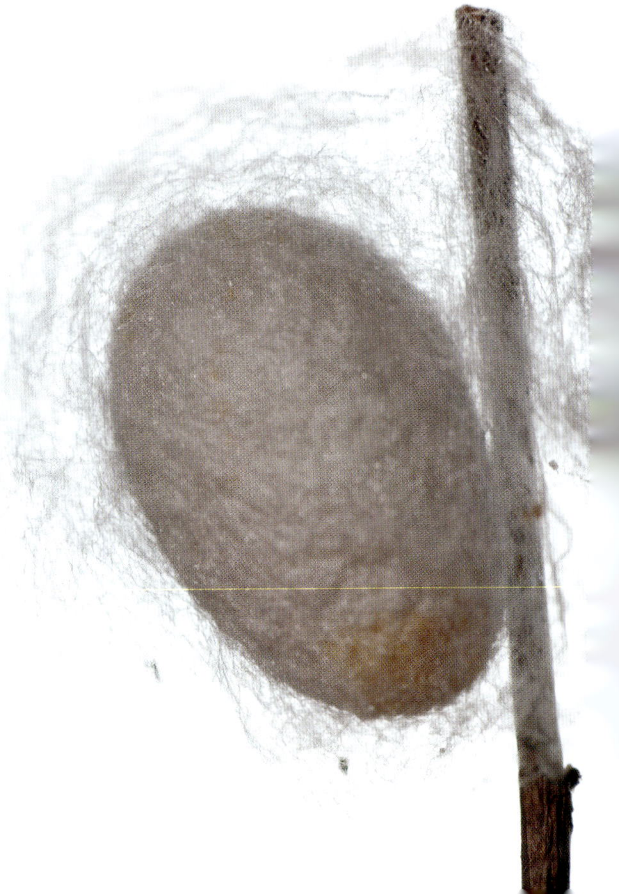

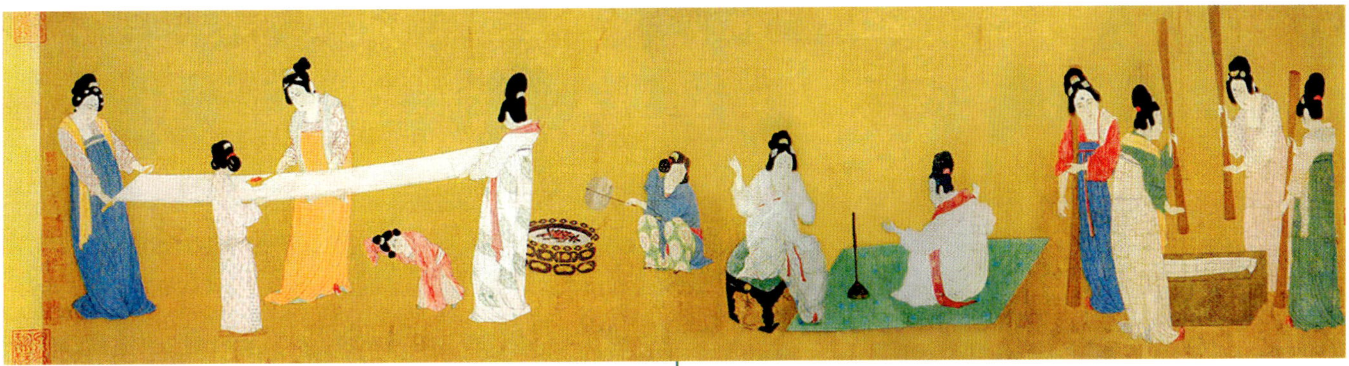

According to a Chinese legend, Leizu, the wife of Emperor Huangdi, discovered silk by accident over five thousand years ago. She was drinking tea under a mulberry tree when a cocoon fell in her teacup. She pulled on one end of the thread, which unraveled into a long, delicate filament that she wove into a cloth so fine that she ordered silkworms to be raised to produce more. This painting on silk from the early twelfth century shows the creation of silk at Emperor Huizong's court.

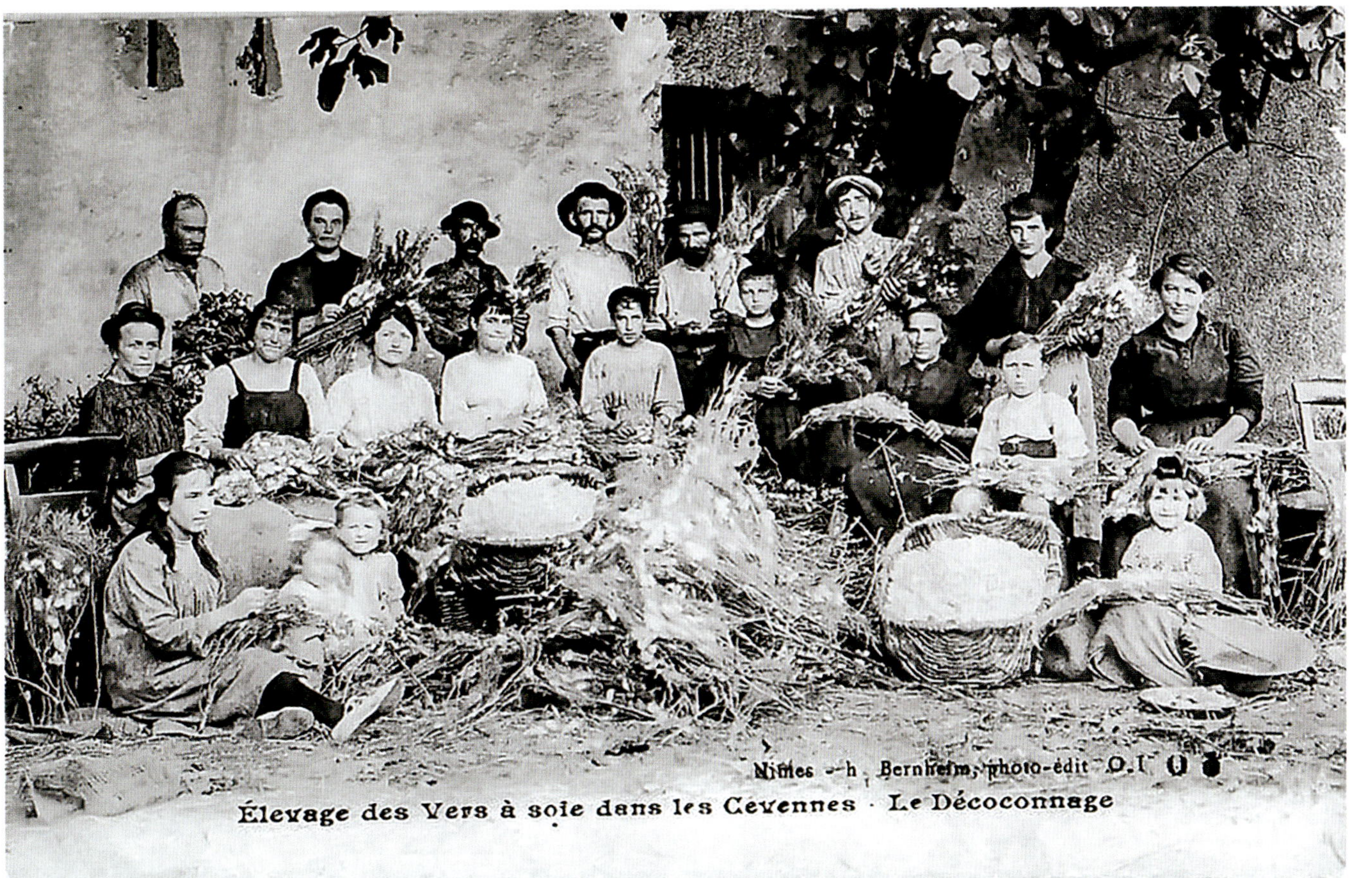

In turn-of-the-century France, families and neighbors gathered silkworm cocoons by hand from tree branches. This photograph was taken in Cévennes, circa 1900.

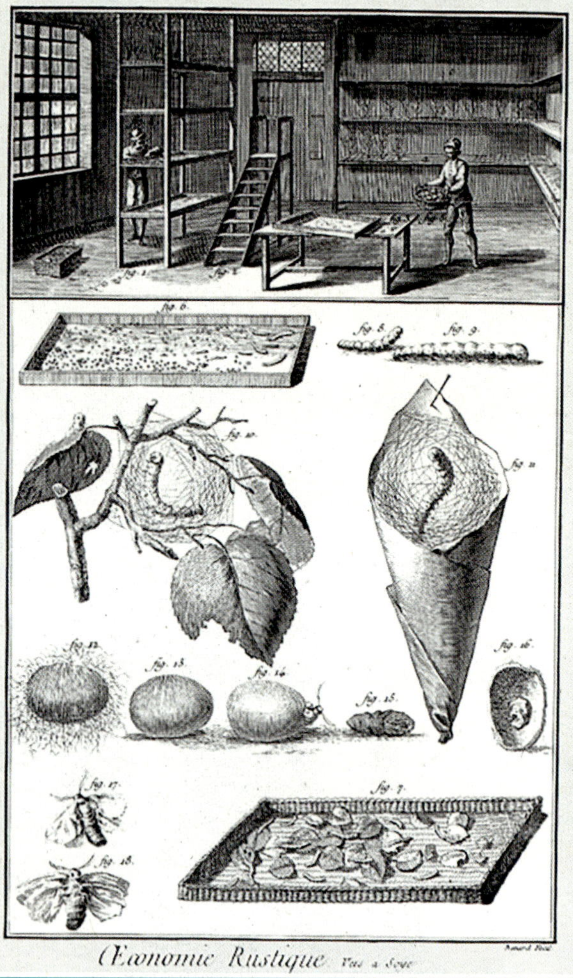

Silk, a luxury product, is actually a metabolic by-product from moth larvae. Producing 1 kg of silk using domestic silk moths requires raising some five thousand larvae, which consume 200 kg of mulberry leaves. This engraving from Diderot and d'Alembert's *Encyclopédie* (1761) shows the stages of silk farming.

silkworms excrete in the form of filaments that they wrap around themselves to form their cocoons. The silk itself does not play an essential role, since pupae can develop without cocoons, and many butterflies and moths do not make them.

Researchers are now trying to use *Bombyx* caterpillars to produce silk with properties similar to spider silk. To do so, they have taken genes responsible for silk production in spiders and inserted them into the caterpillar's genome, creating a genetically modified organism. The modified caterpillar's sericin glands produce silk that is stronger and more elastic despite containing only 2 to 5 percent spider silk. This research could have a number of technological applications.

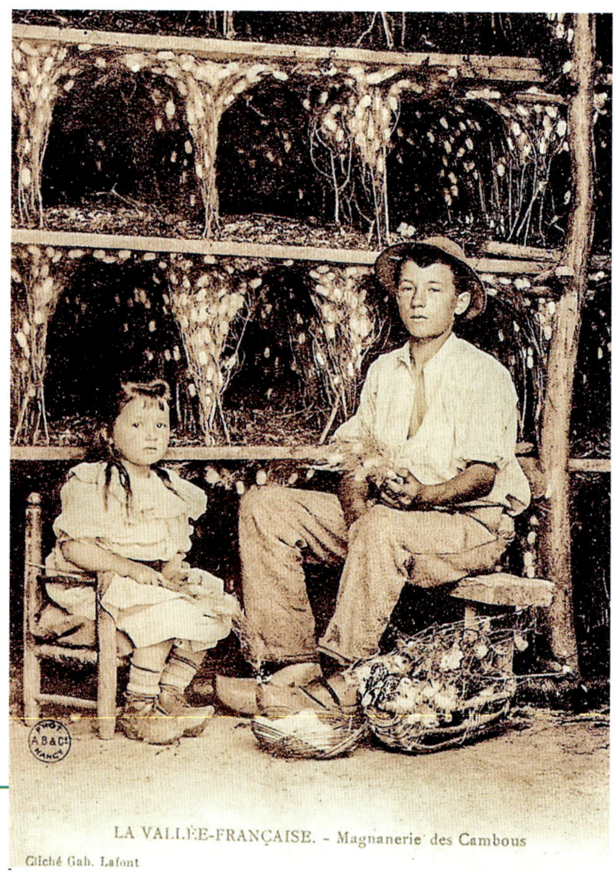

Young silk farmers posing with silkworm cocoons in Cévennes, circa 1900.

OTHER SILK MOTHS

Many arthropods, including spiders, produce some form of silk, but only silk from the caterpillars of certain moths is suitable for weaving into cloth. Domestic silk moths (*Bombyx mori*) are used to made conventional silk, but other types of silk can be made using other species. For example, eri silk comes from the eri silkworm (*Samia ricini*), and tussar silk from the muga silkworm (*Antheraea assamensis*). Several such varieties of so-called wild silk are available, mostly produced in Asia and on a lesser scale than conventional silk. Wild silks have a different color and less uniform texture. The filament from wild-harvested cocoons also tends to be shorter, because the larvae tear their cocoons when they emerge. Carding wild silk is therefore more difficult and time-consuming.

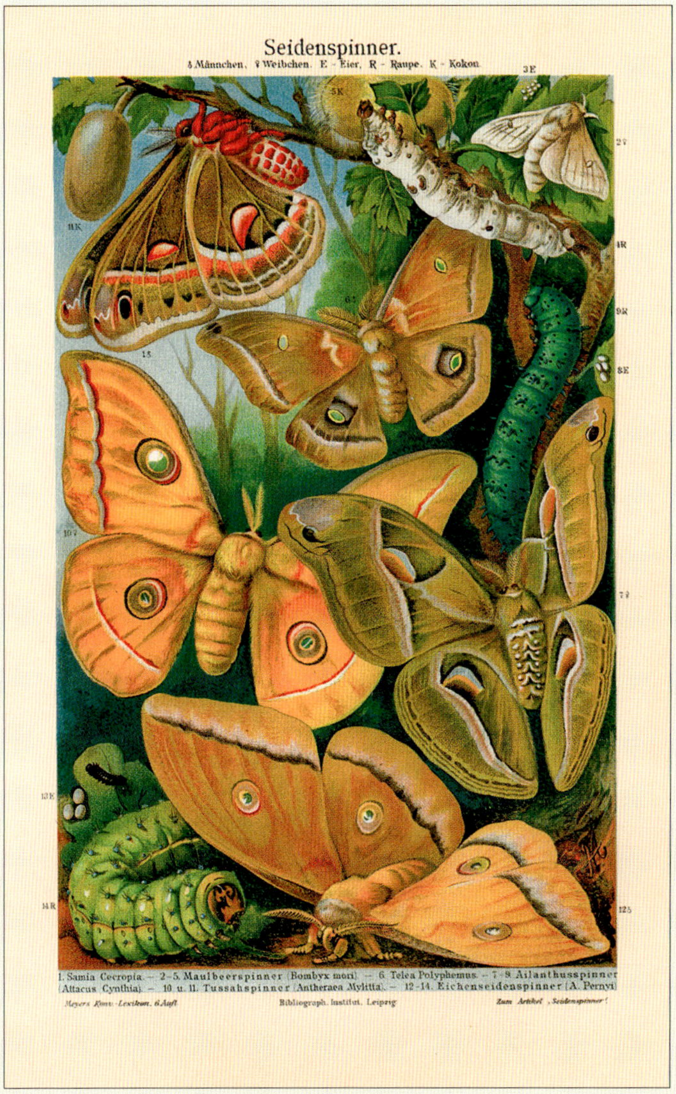

Illustration of silk-producing moths (including *B. mori* and its caterpillar, top right) from the sixth edition (1906) of *Meyers Großes Konversationslexikon*, a German encyclopedia first published in the late nineteenth century.

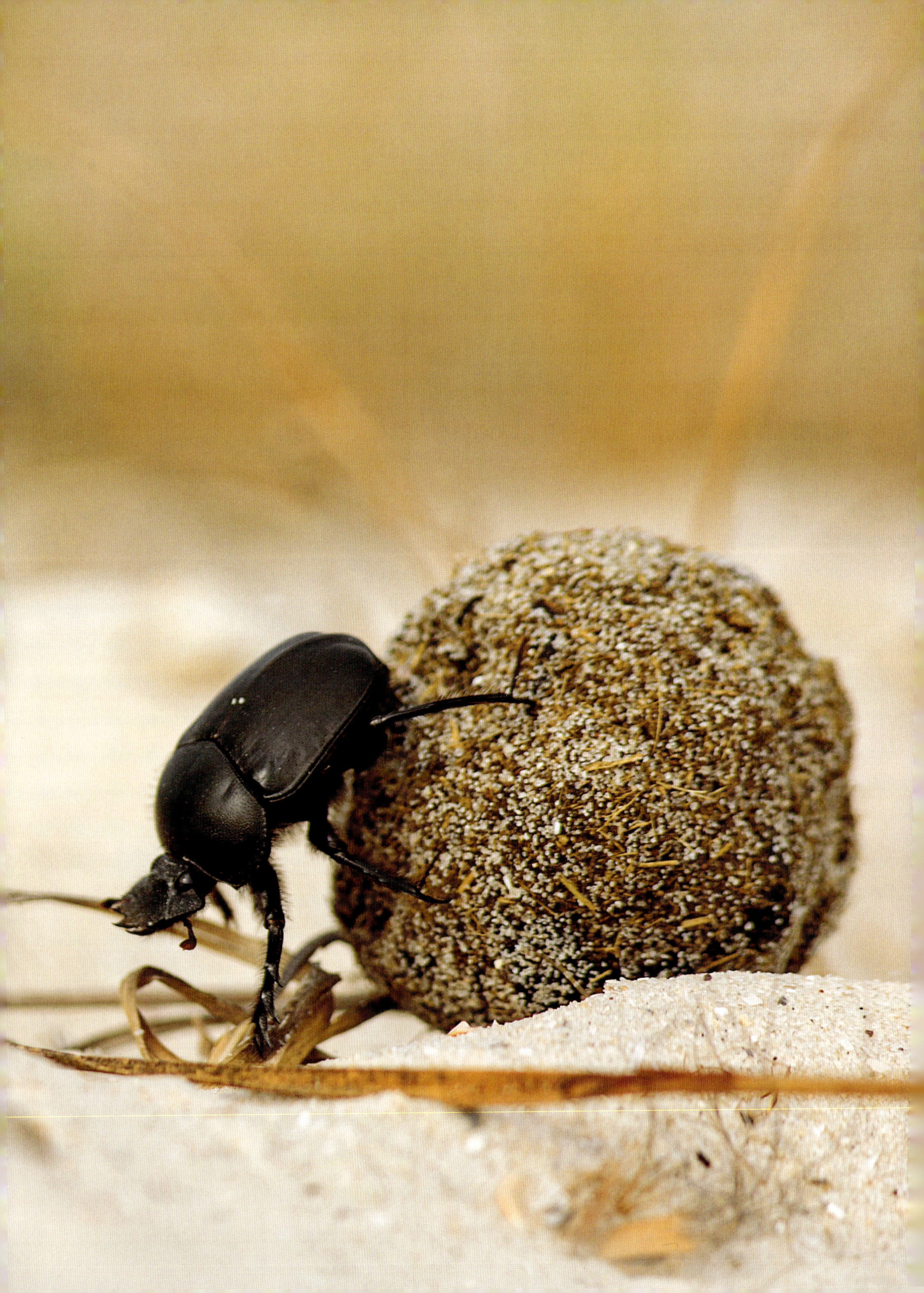

HOLY DUNG BEETLE

SCARABAEUS SACER

COLEOPTERA: SCARABAEIDAE

How did this beetle from the Mediterranean Basin come to be known as the sacred scarab? The ancient Egyptians were able to look past its coprophagic habits and considered it a symbol of the sun and eternal life. Hardly surprising, then, that scarabs appear on countless Egyptian artifacts and have played a central role in the relationship between humans and insects for millennia.

In ancient Egypt, the sacred scarab was a symbol of the sun god Ra, creator of the universe. The projections on its head look a little like sunrays, and the Egyptians saw a parallel between the sun's course across the sky and the ball of dung that the beetle rolls across the ground using its hindlegs (before burying it in the ground to serve as food for its young). The Egyptians believed that the sun was created each morning at dawn by a deity called Khepri, who was one form or aspect of Ra. Khepri was represented as a scarab-faced man or a scarab beetle holding aloft the sun, and his name meant "to come into existence" or "to be born." After traveling across the sky, the sun was drawn into the underworld, where Khepri would cause it to be reborn in triumph the next morning.

The Egyptians saw a reflection of this solar cycle in the scarab's life cycle, as explained by the ancient Greek philosopher Plutarch: "The race of [scarab] beetles has no female, but all the males eject their sperm into a round pellet of material which they roll up by pushing it from the opposite side, just as the sun seems to turn the heavens in the direction opposite to its own course, which is from west to east." Because the young beetles emerged from buried dung balls, the Egyptians thought they were

Sacred scarab rolling a ball of dung.

© Bogomaz Mykhailo CC 4.0

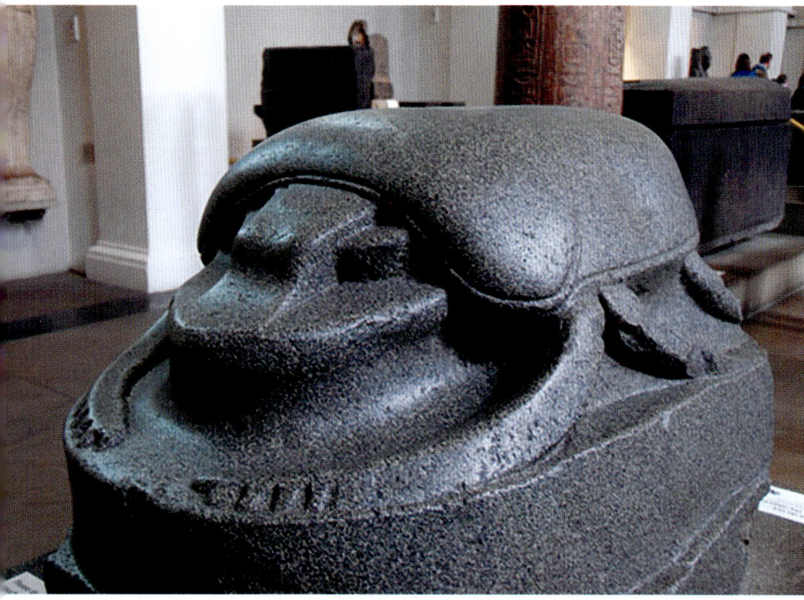

This 2,200-year-old sculpture depicts a coprophagic scarab beetle, most likely a stylized *Heliocopris* gigas, sculpted from a single, 1.5-m block of granite, and comes from a temple in Heliopolis. It is among the most famous Egyptian antiquities held by the British Museum in London.

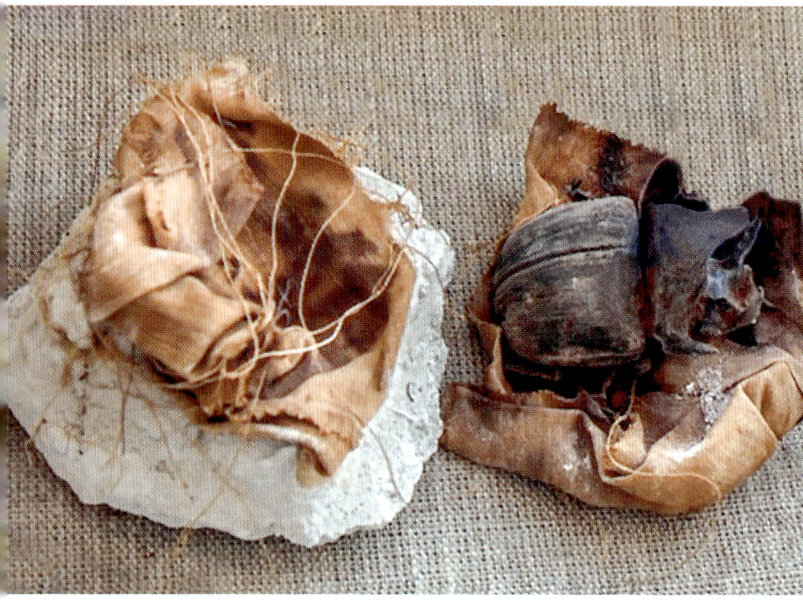

In 2018, Egyptologists working in Saqqara discovered a number of mummified scarab beetles in a chest decorated with a beetle motif. Among the mummies were a pair of *Heliocopris gigas*—a giant nocturnal species that may have symbolized the Moon in the ancient Egyptian pantheon. The scarabs were mummified in the Fifth Dynasty, some 4,500 years ago. In a sense, they could be considered the world's oldest insect collection. *H. gigas* feed on the dung of pachyderms and other large mammals and lived in Egypt at a time when wild elephants and hippos could still be found there.

born from the earth itself, having returned from the underworld. They even looked like tiny mummies!

In addition to their religious significance, sacred scarabs were also symbols of good luck. They were clearly an important part of Egyptians' everyday lives during the First Dynasty, as they were represented on rings, pendants, chest ornaments, amulets, and other objects. These items sometimes featured another of the three large dung beetle species found in the region, *Kheper aegyptiorum*, which has a more greenish, metallic sheen. *K. aegyptiorum* also had highly positive associations and was a symbol of fertility, joy, and youth. A particularly famous example is the "heart scarab": an amulet in the shape of a sacred scarab that was placed on the chest of a mummified body. The heart scarab was supposed to prevent the heart from testifying against the deceased during interrogation by an assembly of underworld deities. Led by Osiris, these gods determined the nature of the deceased's conduct while on Earth and whether he or she should be accorded eternal life. Each heart scarab bears an inscription from the Book of the Dead that is intended to pacify a heart capable of lying to the gods sitting in judgment.

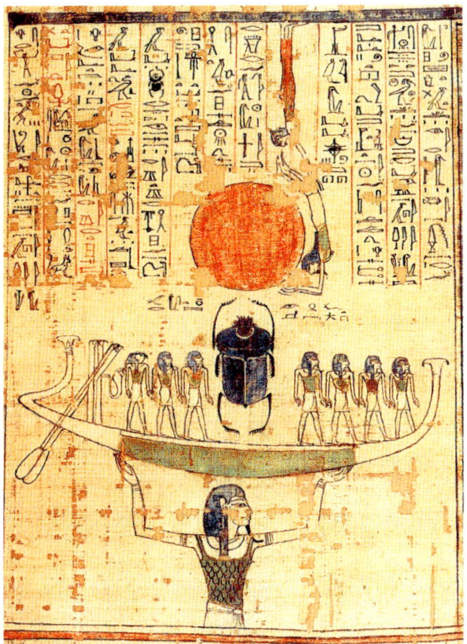

Nun—the ancient Egyptian god of the primordial waters—lifts the solar barque containing the new-born Sun (pictured as a scarab holding the solar disc) from the waters of creation.

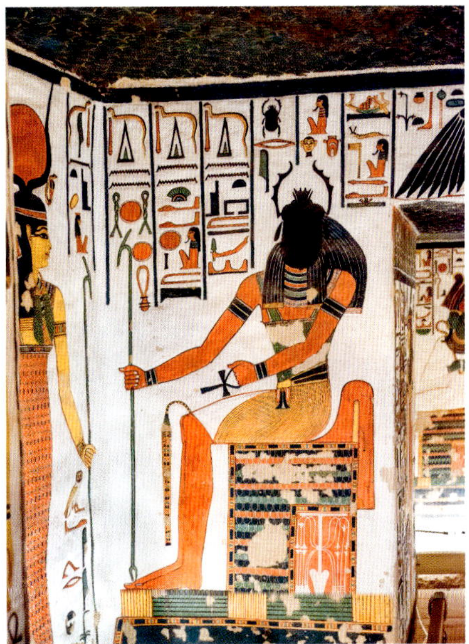

Khepri, the scarab-headed god, watches over the sarcophagus of Nefertiti (fourteenth century BCE).

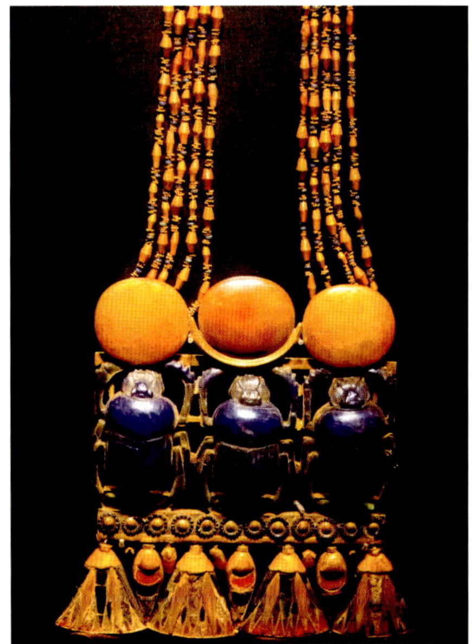

Chest ornament from Tutankhamun's tomb featuring three sacred scarabs.

The projections on the sacred scarab's head are used to dig and shape balls of dung. For the ancient Egyptians, they symbolized the rays of the rising sun.

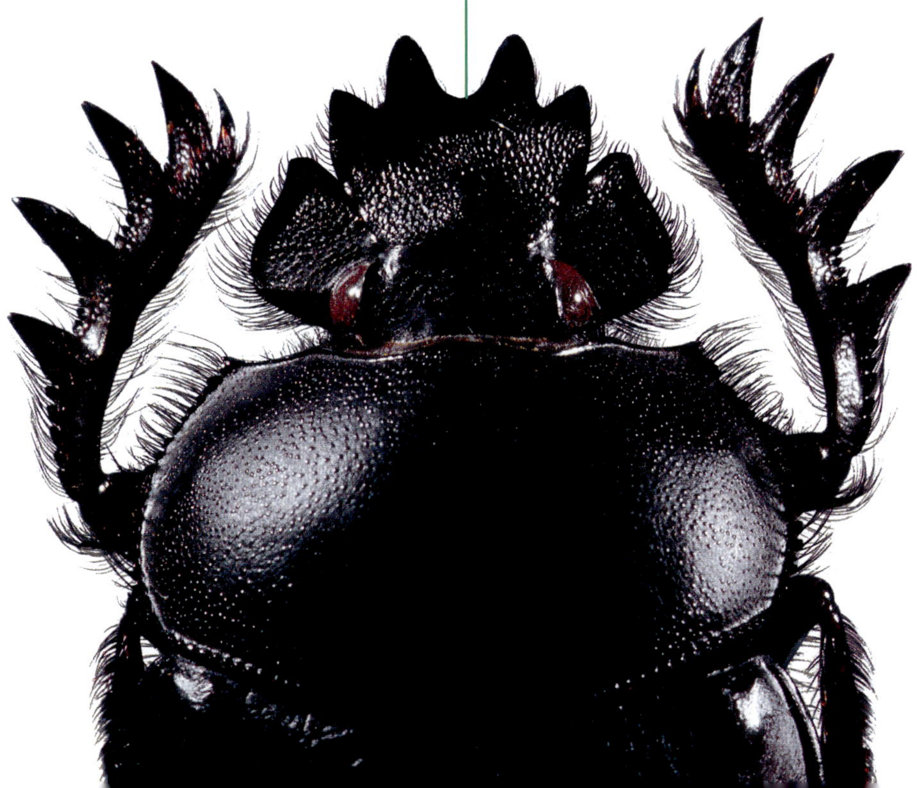

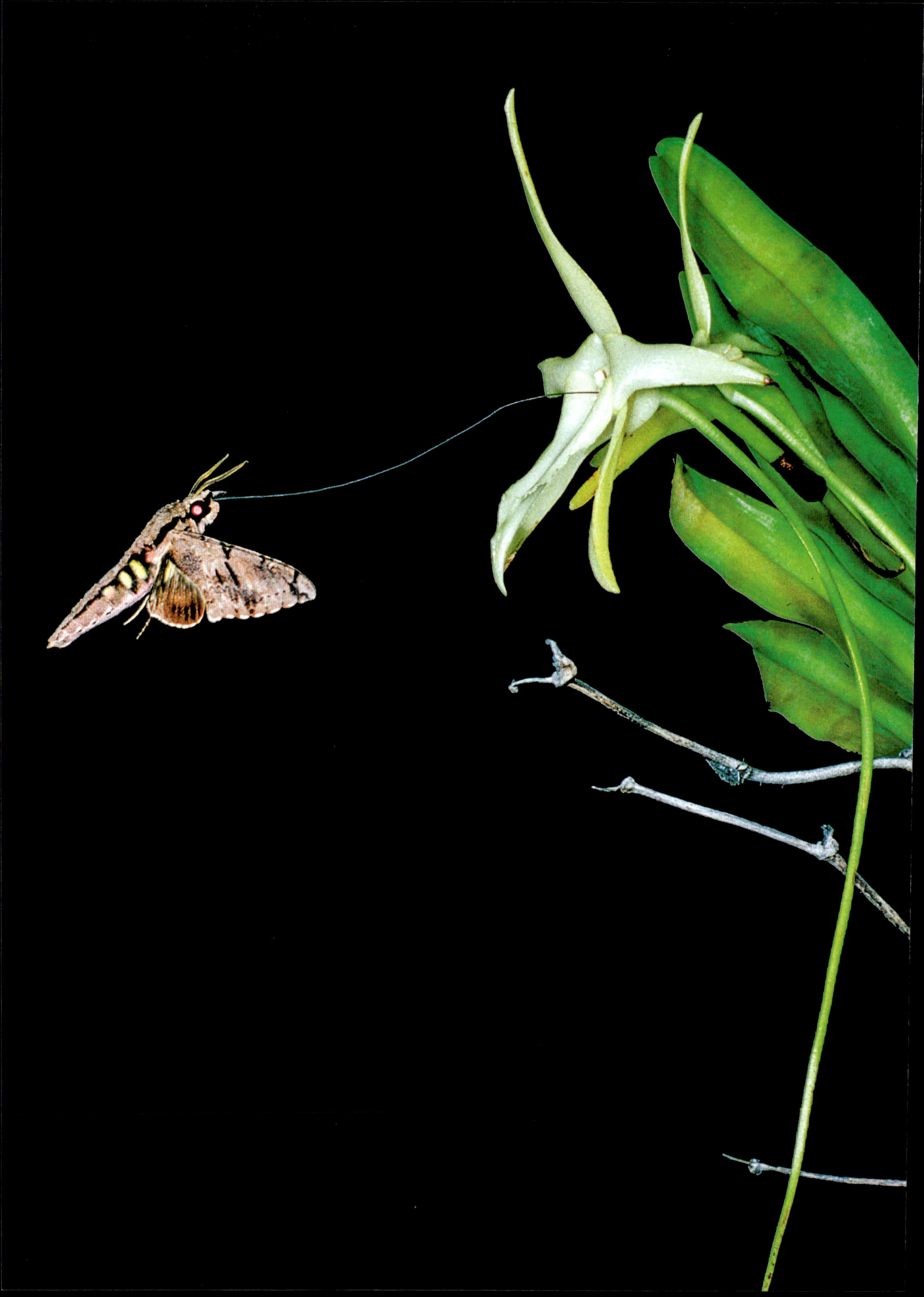

DARWIN'S MALAGASY SPHINX

XANTHOPAN MORGANII PRAEDICTA

LEPIDOPTERA: SPHINGIDAE

English naturalist Charles Darwin (1809–1882), author of the seminal scientific text *On the Origin of Species* (1859), dedicated his life to understanding the evolution of living things. In an 1862 article about a unique orchid, he predicted the existence of a moth capable of pollinating it . . . even though such a moth had not yet been observed.

The spectacular *Angraecum sesquipedale*—an epiphytic orchid from Madagascar commonly known as the Star of Bethlehem orchid or Darwin's orchid—has white, star-shaped flowers and an incredibly long nectary, or nectar spur: a 30-centimeter-long tube with nectar at its bottom to attract pollinating insects. Tiny balls of pollen on the flower's corolla stick to the insect's head while it dips its proboscis into the spur to drink the nectar; when it goes to feed on other flowers, the pollen rubs off, fertilizing the plant. Darwin thus inferred that there must be an insect capable of drinking nectar from *A. sesquipedale*—probably a large butterfly or moth with a very long proboscis. At the time, most naturalists did not take the idea seriously, although some of Darwin's colleagues agreed with him. One of them was Alfred Russel Wallace (1823–1913), who published an article in 1867 expressing support for Darwin's hypothesis and pointing out that the Morgan's sphinx moth (*Xanthopan morganii*) from tropical Africa had a proboscis over 17 centimeters long, and that a similar moth with an even longer proboscis might exist in Madagascar.

The existence of a moth with a particularly long proboscis was hypothesized as early as the 1870s. Alfred R. Wallace pointed out that the Morgan's sphinx moth from tropical Africa, with its 17-cm-long proboscis, might be capable of pollinating orchids with very long nectar spurs.

© Wasserthal, L. T. Bot. Acta. 110 (1997), 343-359

IN DARWIN'S WORDS

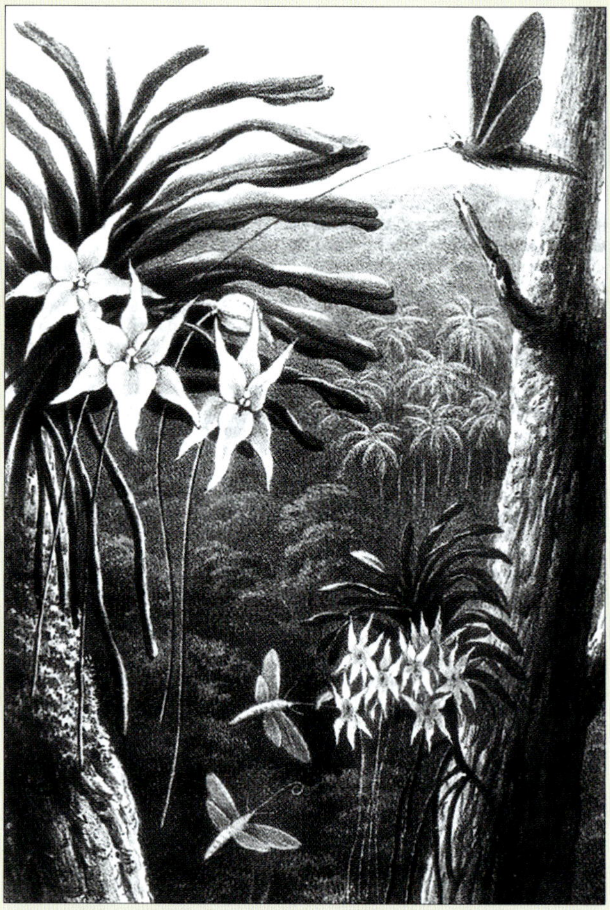

"I fear that the reader will be wearied, but I must say a few words on the *Angraecum sesquipedale*, of which the large six-rayed flowers, like stars formed of snow-white wax, have excited the admiration of travelers in Madagascar. A whip-like green nectary of astonishing length hangs down beneath the labellum. In several flowers sent me by Mr. Bateman I found the nectaries eleven and a half inches long, with only the lower inch and a half filled with very sweet nectar. What can be the use, it may be asked, of a nectary of such disproportional length? We shall, I think, see that the fertilization of the plant depends on this length and on nectar being contained only within the lower and attenuated extremity. It is, however, surprising that any insect should be able to reach the nectar: our English sphinxes have probosces as long as their bodies: but in Madagascar there must be moths with probosces capable of extension to a length of between ten and eleven inches!"

Darwin conducted experiments on the flower specimen in his possession to test how it might be pollinated. He concluded:

If the *Angraecum* in its native forests secretes more nectar than did the vigorous plants sent me by Mr. Bateman, so that the nectary becomes filled, small moths might obtain their share, but they would not benefit the plant. The pollinia would not be withdrawn until some huge moth, with a wonderfully long proboscis, tried to drain the last drop. If such great moths were to become extinct in Madagascar, assuredly the *Angraecum* would become extinct. On the other hand, as the nectar, at least in the lower part of the nectary, is stored safe from depredation by other insects, the extinction of the *Angraecum* would probably be a serious loss to these moths. We can thus partially understand how the astonishing length of the nectary may have been acquired by

successive modifications. As certain moths of Madagascar became larger through natural selection in relation to their general conditions of life, either in the larval or mature state, or as the proboscis alone was lengthened to obtain honey from the *Angraecum* and other deep tubular flowers, those individual plants of the *Angraecum* which had the longest nectaries (and the nectary varies much in length in some Orchids), and which, consequently, compelled the moths to insert their probosces up to the very base, would be fertilized. These plants would yield most seed, and the seedlings would generally inherit longer nectaries; and so it would be in successive generations of the plant and moth. Thus it would appear that there has been a race in gaining length between the nectary of the *Angraecum* and the proboscis of certain moths; but the *Angraecum* has triumphed, for it flourishes and abounds in the forests of Madagascar, and still troubles each moth to insert its proboscis as far as possible in order to drain the last drop of nectar.

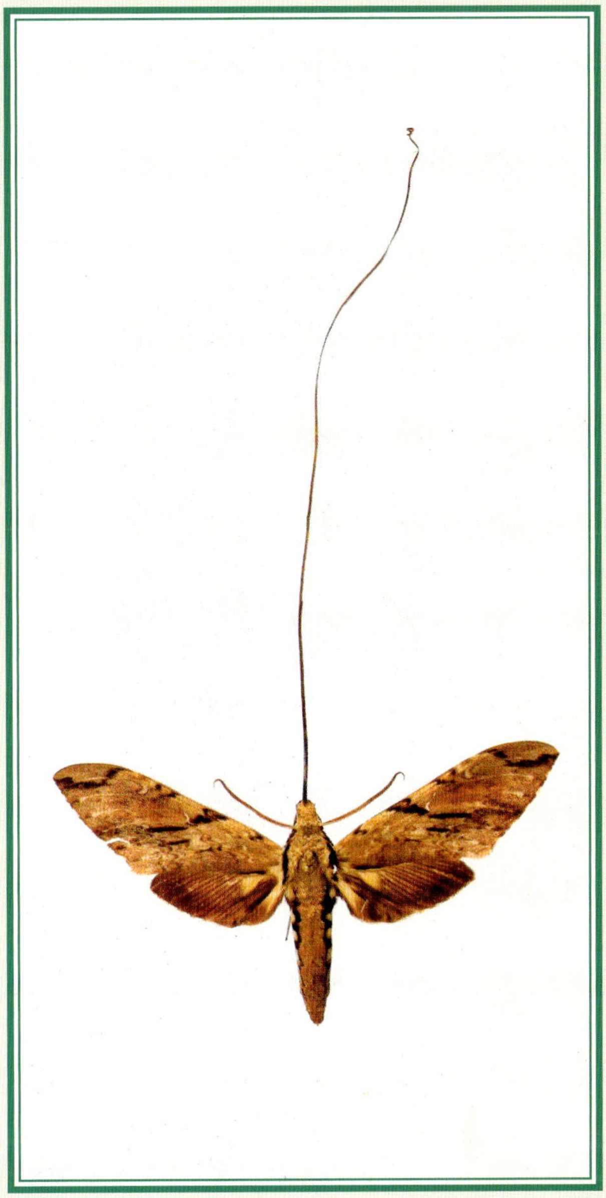

Excerpt from *On the Various Contrivances by which British and Foreign Orchids are Fertilised by Insects, and on the Good Effects of Intercrossing*, London: John Murray, 1862.

Opposite page: *Xanthopan morganii praedicta* and *Angraecum sesquipedale* are a remarkable example of coevolution. The orchid has a nectar spur over 30 cm, and the moth's proboscis is almost as long, allowing it to access nectar that other insects cannot reach.

Above: In Madagascar, there are over seventy species of orchids with nectar spurs over 18 cm long that are pollinated by sphinx moths with very long probosces, of which five species are currently known on the main island. But such a specific pairing of plant and insect is rare, since most pollinating insects feed from a number of different flowering plants.

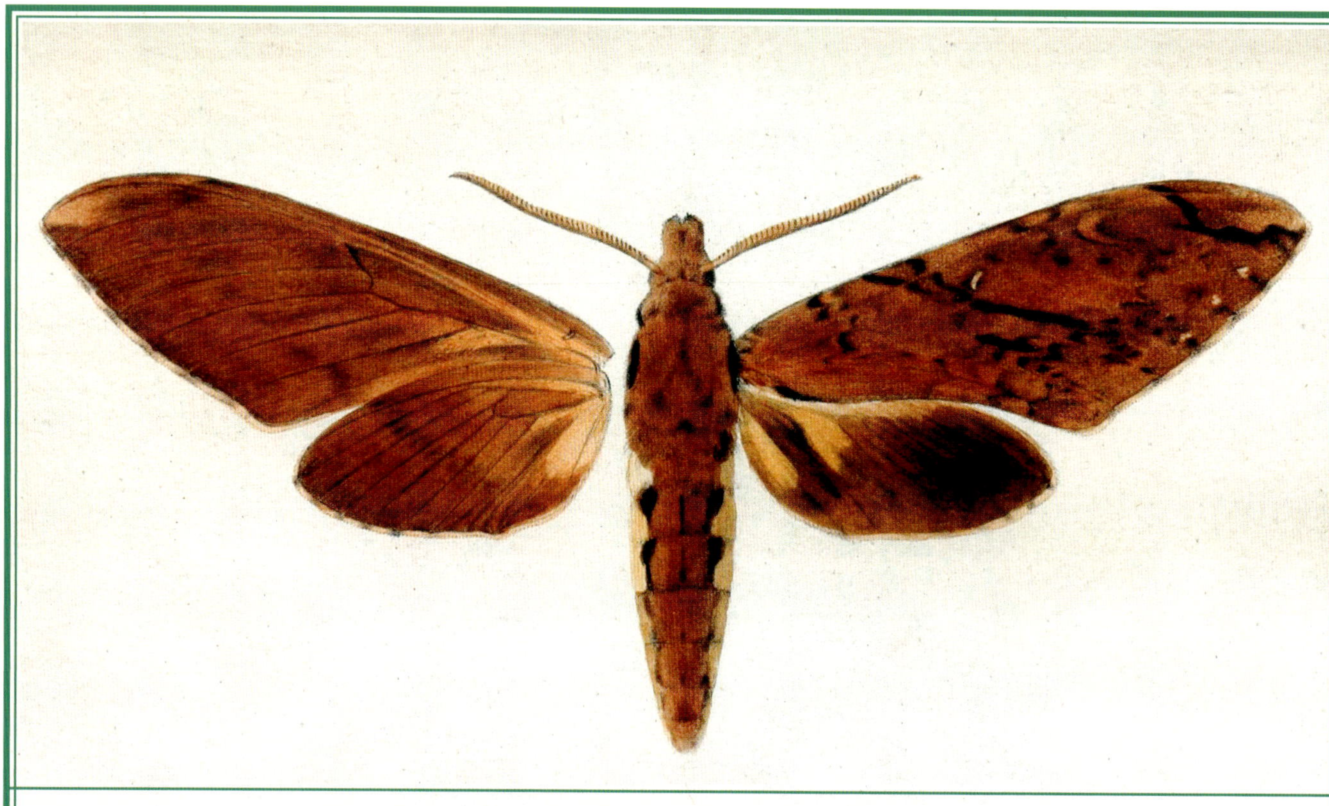

Xanthopan morganii praedicta **pictured in** ***Études de lépidoptérologie comparée*** **(1904) by French entomologist Charles Oberthür (1845–1924).**

Darwin was not proved right until 1903—years after his death—when English entomologists Walter Rothschild (1868–1937) and Karl Jordan (1861–1959) described a subspecies of *X. morganii* that had been captured in Madagascar by Paul Mabille (1835–1923). This new moth's proboscis was an incredible 27 centimeters long and had to be rolled up into twenty coils when retracted under the moth's head. The subspecies name *praedicta* ("predicted," "foretold") is an homage to Wallace, not Darwin. Rothschild and Jordan did not actually observe the moth pollinating the orchids, however. The mystery was only solved for good in 1997, when German zoologist Thilo Wasserthal filmed a Malagasy sphinx moth feeding from *A. sesquipedale*, putting an end to 130 years of speculation.

TWO MODELS OF COEVOLUTION

In the model hypothesized by Darwin, formalized by Wallace, and accepted by many naturalists who came after them, these moths and orchids adapted to each other through a mutual process of natural selection. Orchids with longer spurs had a selective advantage because they increased their pollinators' contact with their pollen, while the insects benefited from an exclusive food source by feeding on nectar that only they could reach. The arrangement was thus mutually beneficial. According to this hypothesis, their coevolution was a back-and-forth, like a race.

In 2007, however, American zoologists Justen B. Whittall and Scott A. Hodges proposed applying a different model: based on a phylogenetic analysis of buttercups (family: Ranunculaceae), they concluded that the lengthening of the orchid's spur likely occurred in response to the moth's morphology with no reciprocal evolution by the moth.

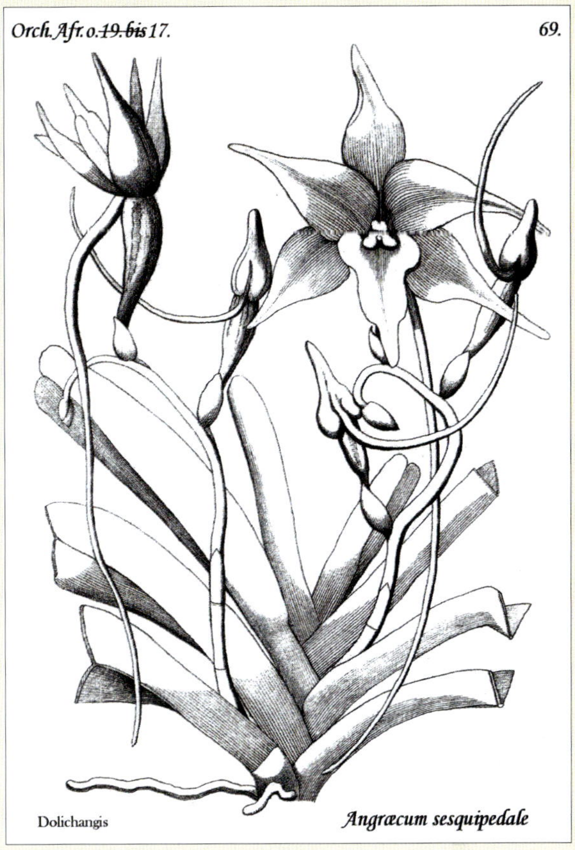

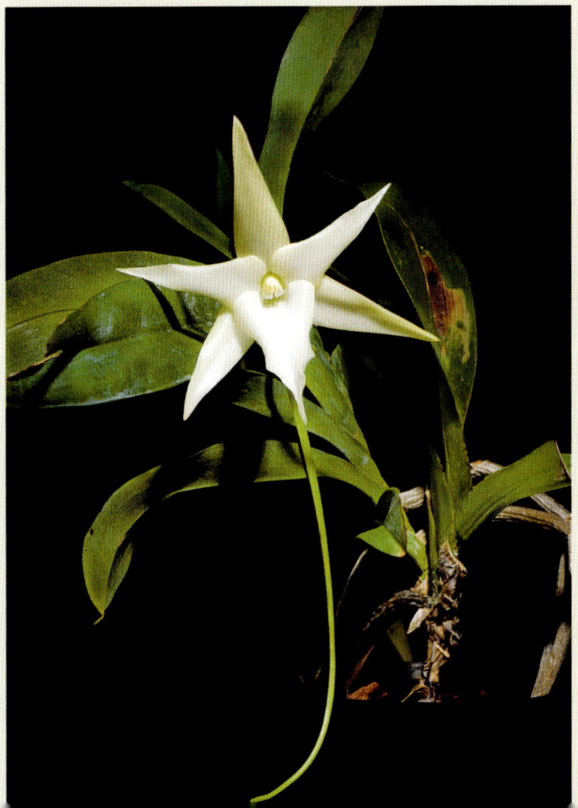

Top: Illustration of *Angraecum sesquipedale* in *Histoire particulière des plantes orchidées recueillies sur les trois isles australes d'Afrique, de France, de Bourbon et de Madagascar* (1822) by Louis-Marie Aubert du Petit-Thouars. Bottom: Darwin predicted the existence of an insect that could pollinate *Angraecum sesquipedale* orchids before anyone had seen it.

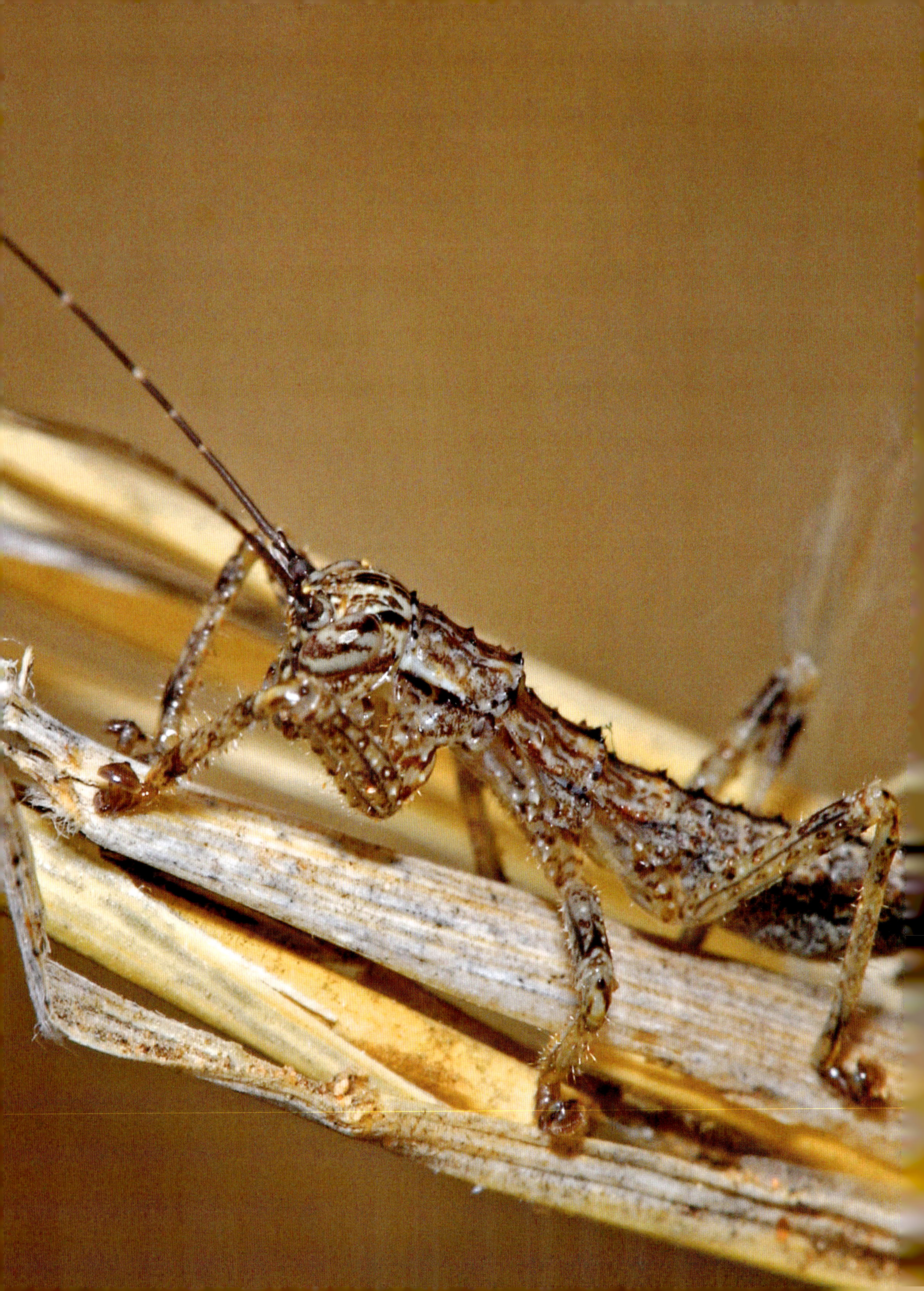

RELICS AND REDISCOVERIES

Naturalists are always hoping that plants and animals once thought to be extinct will reappear after going undetected for years—through a stroke of luck, or thanks to new research techniques. In fact, insect species have been rediscovered fairly often, including some of the most iconic. In this chapter, we will share a few rare pieces of good news from a planet devastated by human irresponsibility and greed. Despite these happy examples, the global collapse of insect populations—especially those sensitive to changes in habitat— unfortunately remains very real, as does the destruction of biodiversity around the world.

Similarly fascinating are plant and animal species that strongly resemble distant ancestors that disappeared long ago. These evolutionary relics are sometimes referred to as "living fossils." Coelacanths, nautiluses, and cycas plants are relatively well-known examples. Insects in this category do not always get the same attention, despite their considerable interest to science. They fully deserve what little notoriety the following pages can offer.

Tyrannophasma gladiator, from Namibia, is a carnivorous, wingless insect that looks like a cross between a stick insect and a praying mantis. It is part of the order Mantophasmatodea, which comprises less than twenty described species, all of which live in Namibia and South Africa. But similar insects were once much more widespread: fossils dating back to the Jurassic period (180 million years ago) have been found as far away as China, making today's *Tyrannophasma gladiator* what is known as a relict species.

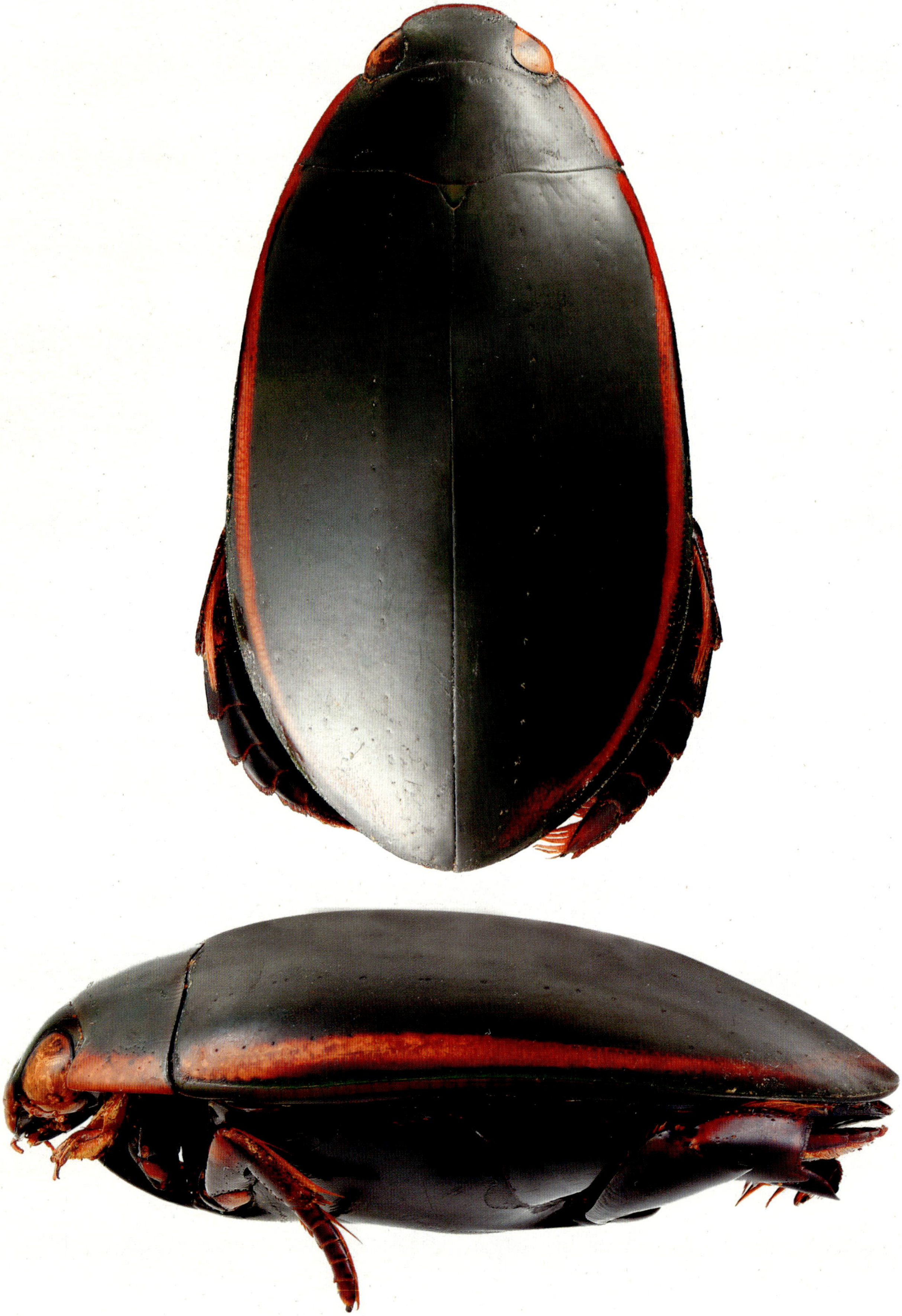

The only collected specimens of *Megadytes ducalis*, the largest known diving beetle, are from the 1800s.

A BEETLE FROM ANOTHER AGE

MEGADYTES DUCALIS
(COLEOPTERA: DYTISCIDAE)

Until 2018, *Megadytes ducalis* was only known from a single specimen: a male collected in Brazil in the nineteenth century. Rumor had it that this unique diving beetle—the world's largest—was caught in a puddle at the bottom of a canoe on the Amazon River.

The species was described in 1882 by English entomologist David Sharp (1840–1922) based on the lone specimen now held at the London Natural History Museum. It was considered a top candidate for rarest insect in the world until 2018, when a German specialist examining the historical collections of the French National Museum of Natural History in Paris discovered no fewer than ten specimens, all females. Some had labels indicating they were captured in the late nineteenth century, in the savannahs of the Cerrado in eastern Brazil (specifically, in Santo Antônio da Barra, now called Condeúba). In other words, nowhere near the Amazon! At the time, inhabitants of the Cerrado would sell insects, including mole beetles (pages 50-53), to middlemen who would pass them on to European collectors. From 1884 to 1914, French entomologist Pierre-Émile Gounelle (1850–1914) captured a large number of insects in the Cerrado, and this was probably when the *Megadytes* specimens were collected. Gounelle likely gave some of his finds to colleagues such as Maurice Régimbart, Ernst Wehncke, and Charles Oberthür, whose collections were later acquired by the Paris museum.

The species certainly lives up to its name, *ducalis*, which comes from the Latin word for "leader": the largest female specimens are five centimeters long. They must have adapted to survive contrasting wet and dry seasons, with variable amounts of water available. Their closest relatives (smaller species in the genus *Megadytes*) live in water with dense aquatic vegetation. All diving beetles are strong swimmers (including *Dytiscus latissimus*, page 141) and extremely hard to trap.

The International Union for Conservation of Nature (IUCN) considers *M. ducalis* to be extinct. Since the 1990s, the Cerrado has been devastated by soy farming and charcoal production. Dams have disrupted the rivers, and the wetlands have been drained. Still, little is known about the biology and range of these giant diving beetles, and no research has been conducted in the waters of the Cerrado . . . leaving a ray of hope for adventuresome entomologists!

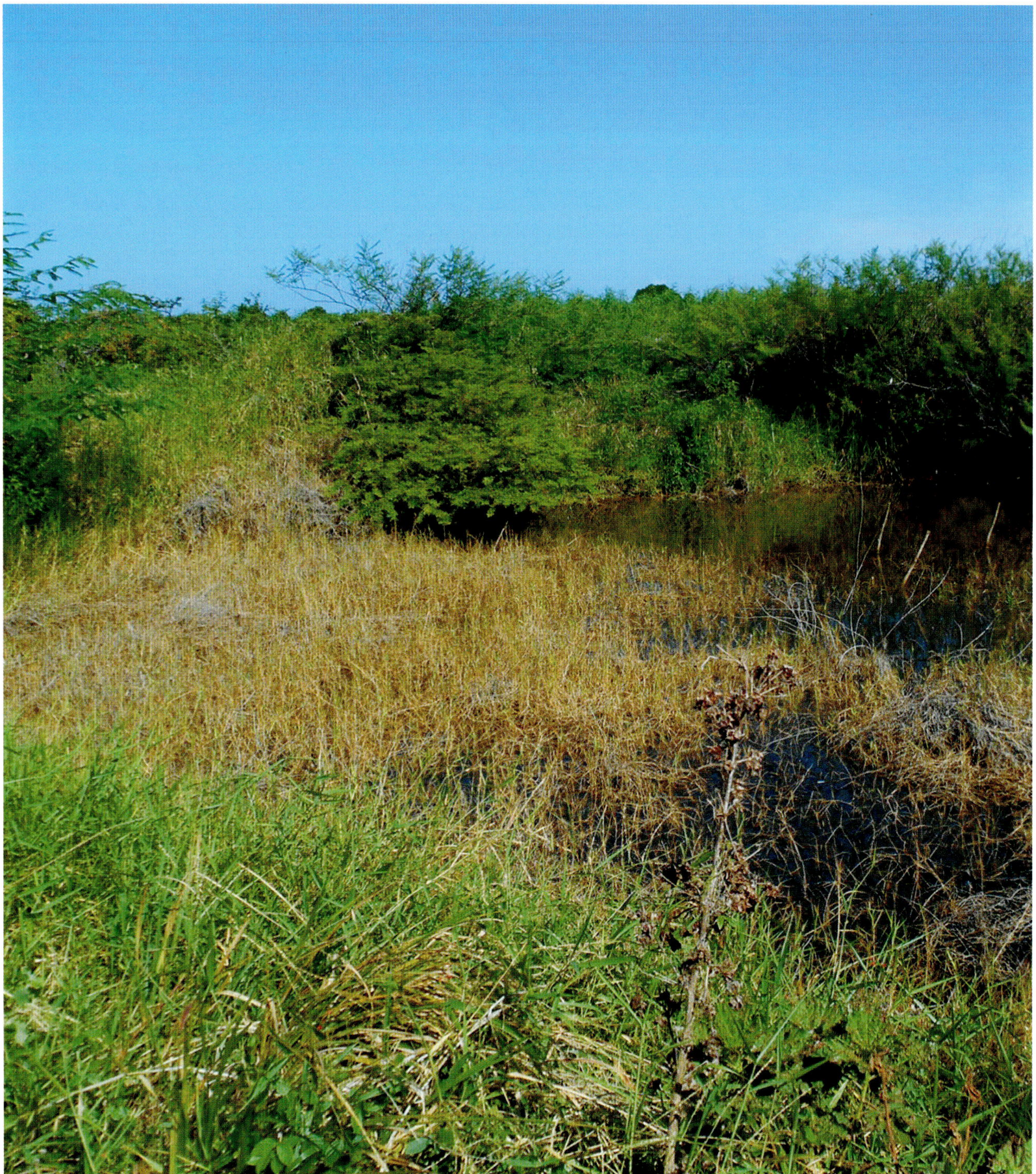

Close relatives of *Megadytes ducalis* survive in habitats like this one in Savane Desroières, Guadeloupe.

THE EUROPEAN DIVING BEETLE

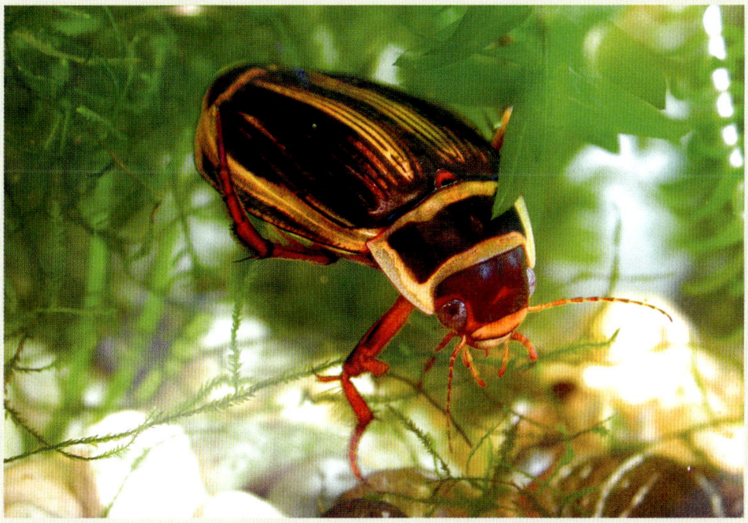

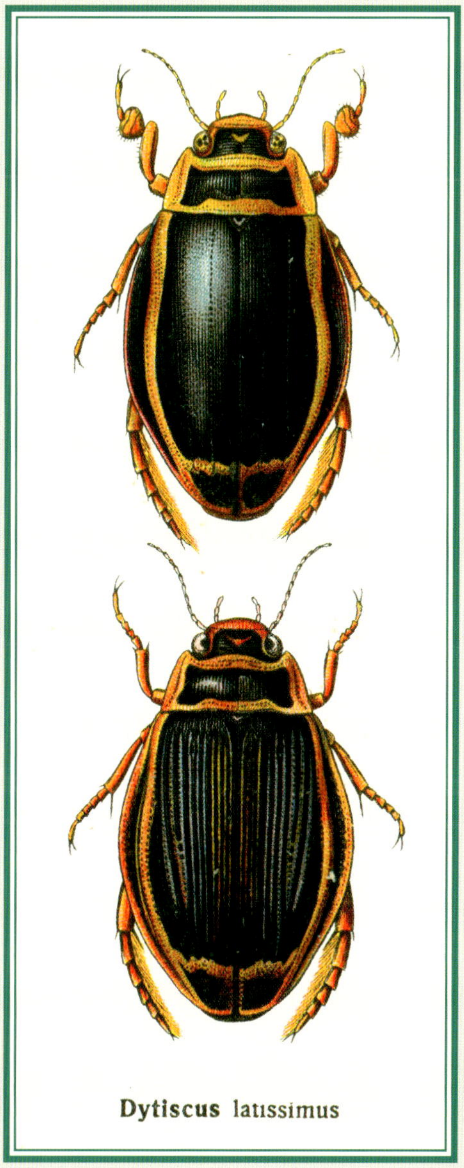

At 4.5 centimeters long, *Dytiscus latissimus* is almost as impressive as its giant Brazilian cousin. These aquatic predators were once found in much of Europe. In the nineteenth and early twentieth centuries, they were observed in northeast France, Belgium, the Netherlands, and throughout Germany, but they are now found only in the Baltics, pockets of northern Germany and Poland, Scandinavia, and Russia. They have been disappearing from the southern and western edges of their range since the nineteenth century due to fish farming, changes in pond management, water pollution from agricultural runoff, climate change (the species dates back to the Ice Age), and declines in caddisfly larvae, their main food source. The common factor in all these changes is, of course, human impacts on the environment.

Top left: Female *Dytiscus latissimus*.

Top right: Male (top) and female (bottom) compared.

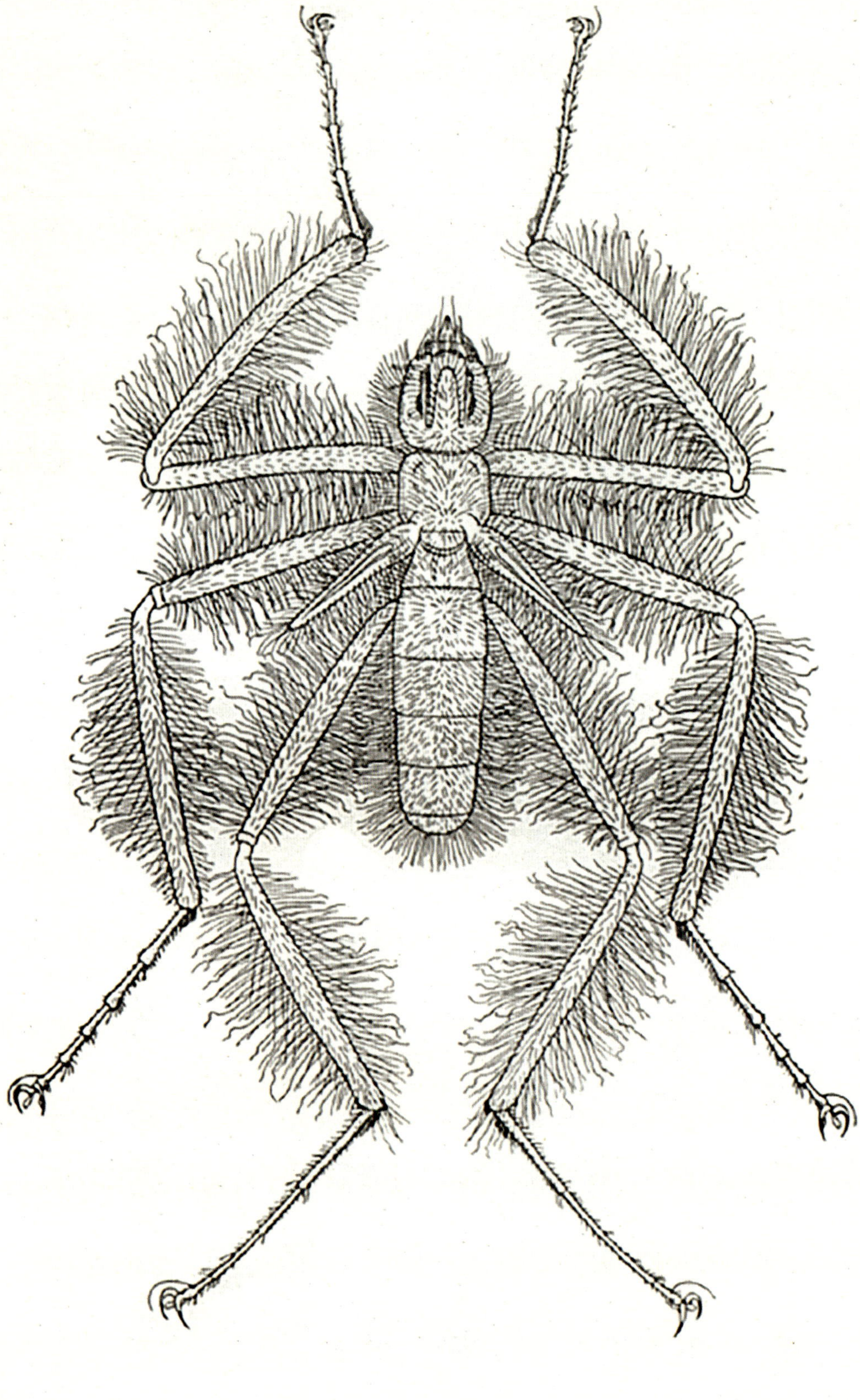

The terrible hairy fly (*Mormotomyia hirsuta*) was described in 1936 by English entomologist Ernest E. Austen (1867–1938). The species proved hard to classify, as it looks nothing like any of its cousins and is the only member of the family Mormotomyiidae. Its evolutionary relationship to other flies remains unknown.

THE TERRIBLE HAIRY FLY

MORMOTOMYIA HIRSUTA
(DIPTERA: MORMOTOMYIIDAE)

In 2010, two American entomologists, Robert Copeland and Ashley Kirk-Spriggs, rediscovered one of the strangest insects on the planet: the terrible hairy fly of Kenya. At the time, these mysterious creatures were only thought to live in one narrow rocky cleft of Ukasi Hill, an inselberg in an arid region about 200 kilometers east of Nairobi.

The terrible hairy fly, or frightful hairy fly, had only been spotted twice before: first in 1933, when two males were captured and used to describe the species; then in 1948, when the female and immature stages were discovered. A dozen other expeditions to their remote habitat were all unsuccessful.

The adults are about a centimeter long, with tiny heads and eyes. The male's long legs probably help with mating. The bodies of both sexes are covered in the yellowish hairs that give the species its name. The flies' wings and halteres are small and nonfunctional, so they cannot disperse by flying, and for a long time they were believed to live solely on the site where they had first been found. An analysis of specimens captured in 2010, however, showed genetic variation that suggested there must be other populations. Later studies led to terrible hairy flies also being discovered on Makilu, Ngauluka, and Mbuinzau, three hills nearly 200 kilometers from the original site but close to one another. It remains unclear how the flies disperse, unless they cling onto bats. But that has never been observed, and the flies do not have claws to grip onto bat fur . . . so the mystery persists.

The terrible hairy fly lives in clefts or fissures in rocky inselbergs that are also home to bat colonies. The larvae were discovered close to the cleft opening, in bat guano moistened by rainwater during the wet season, but it is possible that they can develop year-round in guano that accumulates deep within the clefts and so stays moist in all seasons. The adults appear to feed on secretions from bat skin and have been observed in great numbers on rock walls and bat guano.

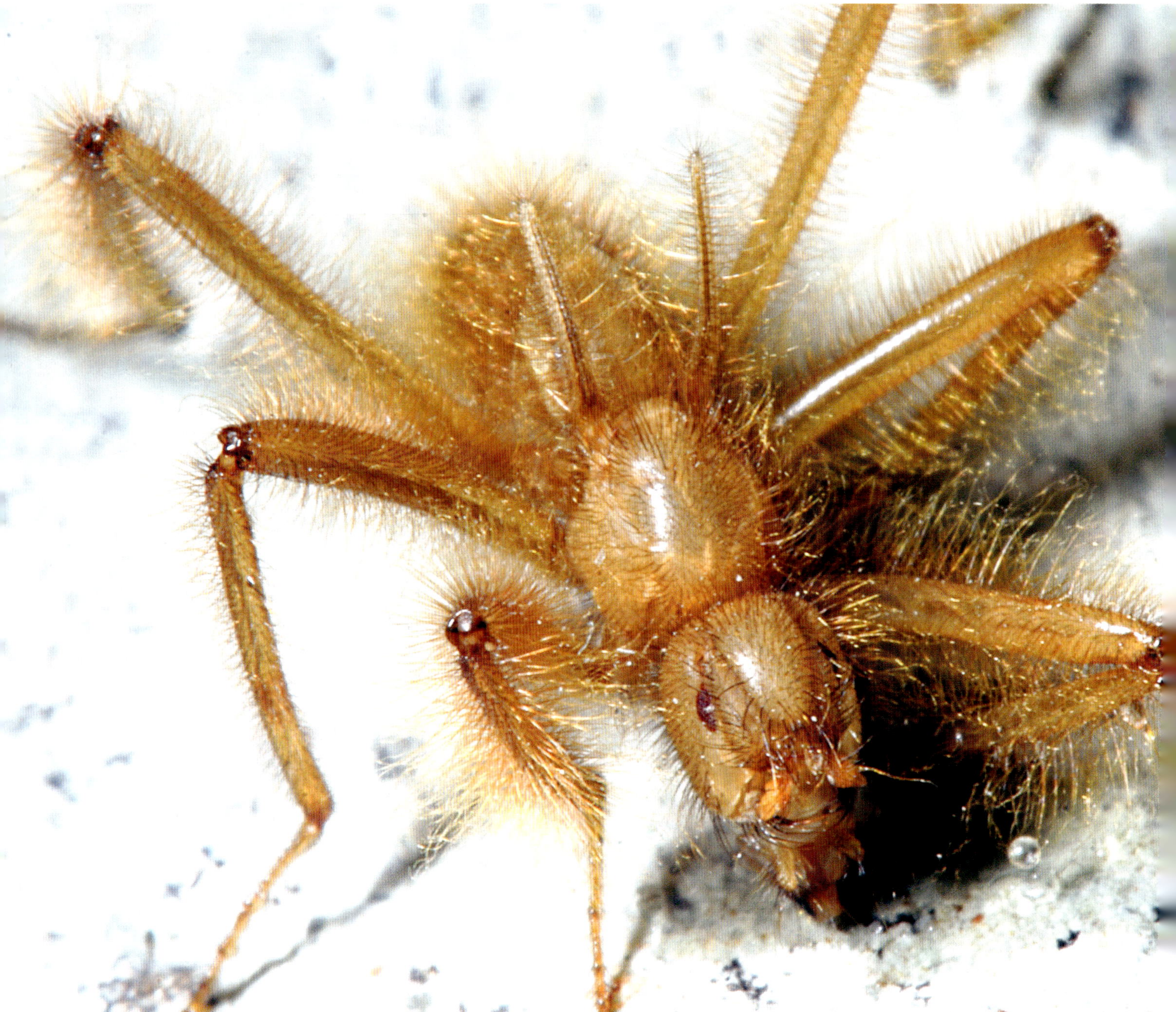

With its stumpy wings, long legs, and hairy body, *Mormotomyia hirsuta* looks more like a spider than a fly!
© Robert S Copeland

Males guard over the females once they have been fertilized and remain close by them until they lay their eggs. Both sexes avoid light and direct sun. They may become prey for lizards if they wander too close to the cleft opening.

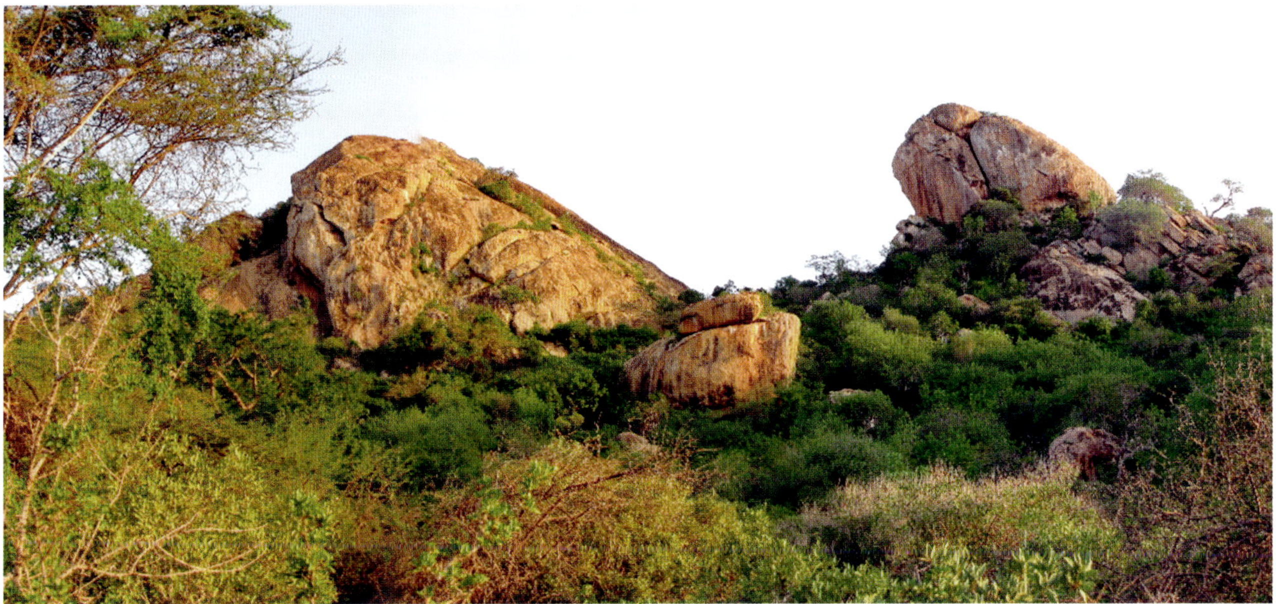

The terrible hairy fly lives in dry, rocky environments like Ukazi Hill in Kenya, where it was discovered in a narrow cleft that is also home to a bat colony. How this species disperses to new locations is a mystery.

© Robert S Copeland

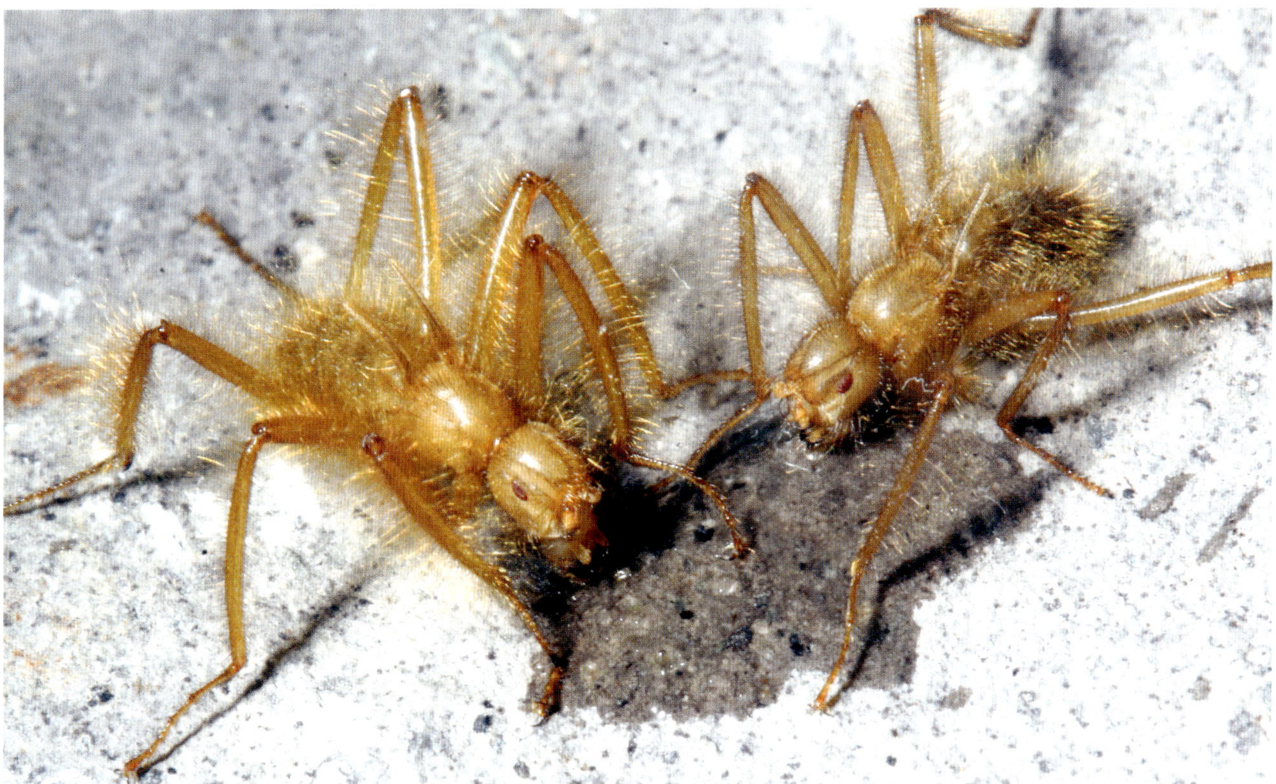

Two male terrible hairy flies.

© Robert S Copeland

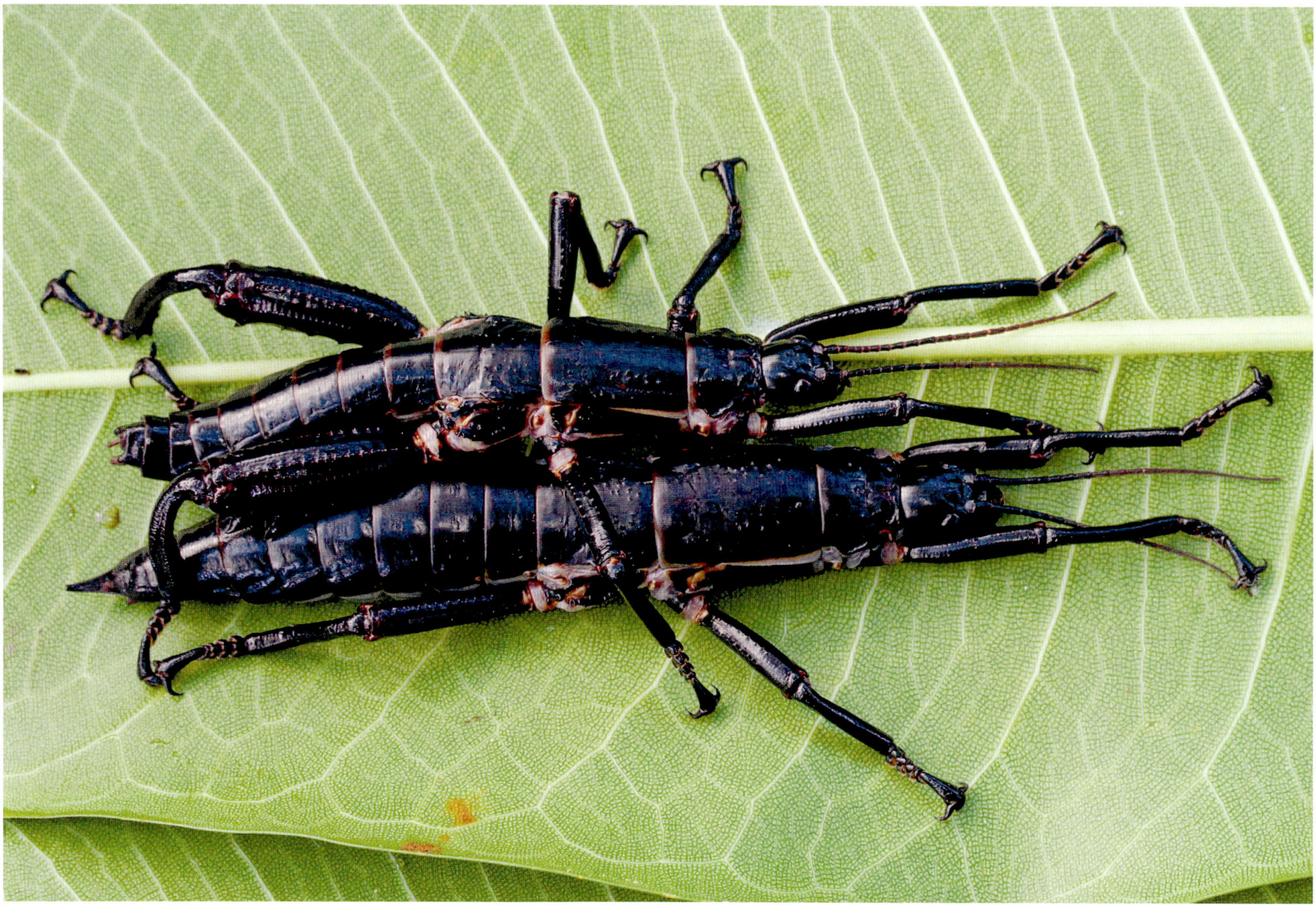

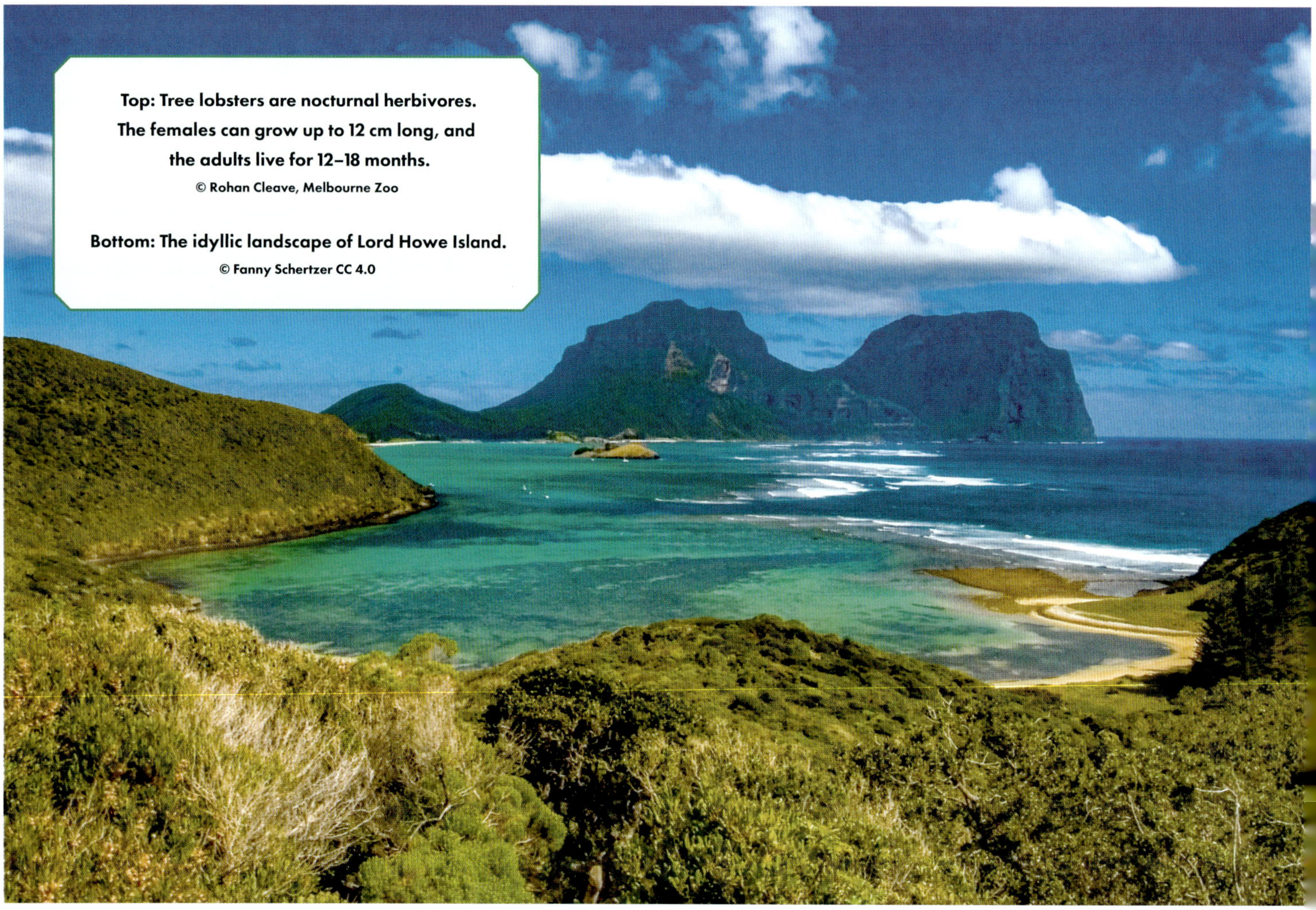

Top: Tree lobsters are nocturnal herbivores. The females can grow up to 12 cm long, and the adults live for 12–18 months.

Bottom: The idyllic landscape of Lord Howe Island.

THE RETURN OF THE TREE LOBSTER

DRYOCOCELUS AUSTRALIS

(PHASMATODEA: PHASMATIDAE)

Lord Howe Island, a 14-square-kilometer volcanic remnant in the Tasman Sea nearly 600 kilometers from mainland Australia, is home to several plants and animals that are found nowhere else. Among them is an extraordinary insect commonly known as the tree lobster or the Lord Howe Island stick insect, first described in 1855 by French naturalist Xavier Montrouzier (1820–1897).

These giant stick insects may look intimidating, but they are completely defenseless. They proved easy prey for black rats, which escaped from a ship that wrecked on the island in 1918 and were quick to feed on the slow-moving tree lobsters, whose numbers declined so rapidly that they were thought to be extinct by the 1930s. Their story might have ended there, like that of the Saint Helena earwig (page 175). But doubts started to emerge in the 1960s, when what looked like freshly dead tree lobsters were found on Ball's Pyramid, an uninhabited islet 23 kilometers southeast of Lord Howe Island. Still, no living specimens had been observed. Finally, in 2001, two Australian biologists, David Priddel and Nicholas Carlile, found tree lobster droppings on Ball's Pyramid, under a tea tree (*Melaleuca howeana*) endemic to the Lord Howe Island group that was growing on a natural terrace overhanging the ocean. When Priddel and Carlile came back after dark, they spotted three live tree lobsters crawling on the leaves. An expedition the following year identified a total of twenty-four individuals.

Currently, wild tree lobsters appear to live exclusively on a few square meters of moist ground on Ball's Pyramid, making them one of the rarest and most restricted insects in the world. How the species got to the islet is a mystery. The most likely hypothesis is that they were carried there from Lord Howe Island by birds, either as food or because the birds mistook them for sticks to use in their nests. Those that survived the trip could have colonized the islet, or a dead female may have been carrying viable eggs.

In 2003, researchers from the New South Wales National Parks and Wildlife Service collected four tree lobsters from Ball's Pyramid. One pair (named

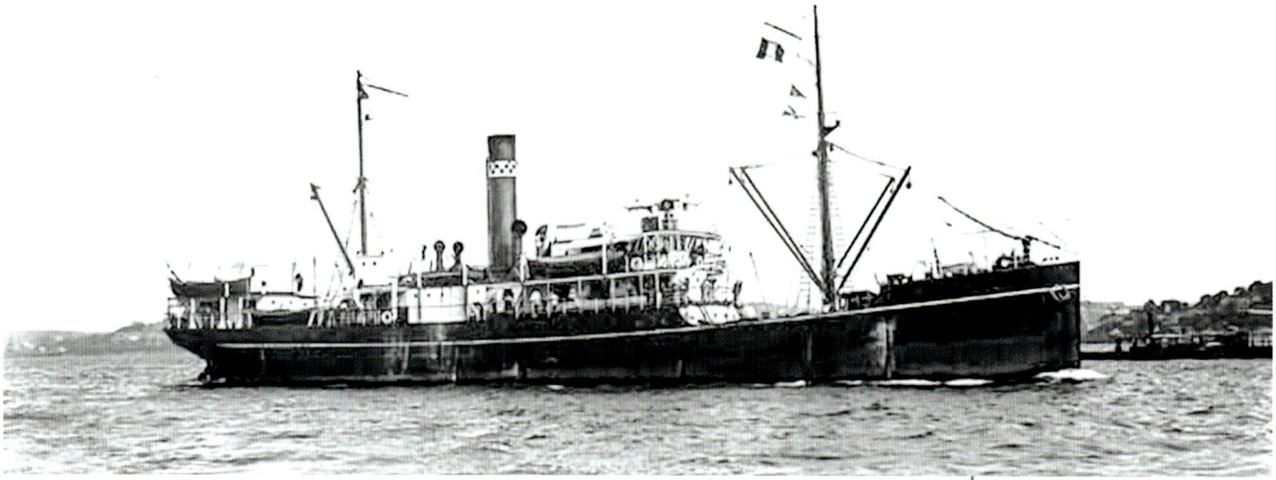

In 1918, rats escaped from the steamship *Makambo* when it ran aground on Lord Howe Island. They soon drove the Lord Howe Island stick insect, which was endemic to the island, to extinction. But a happy surprise was in store. . . .
© Samuel J. Hood Studio Collection

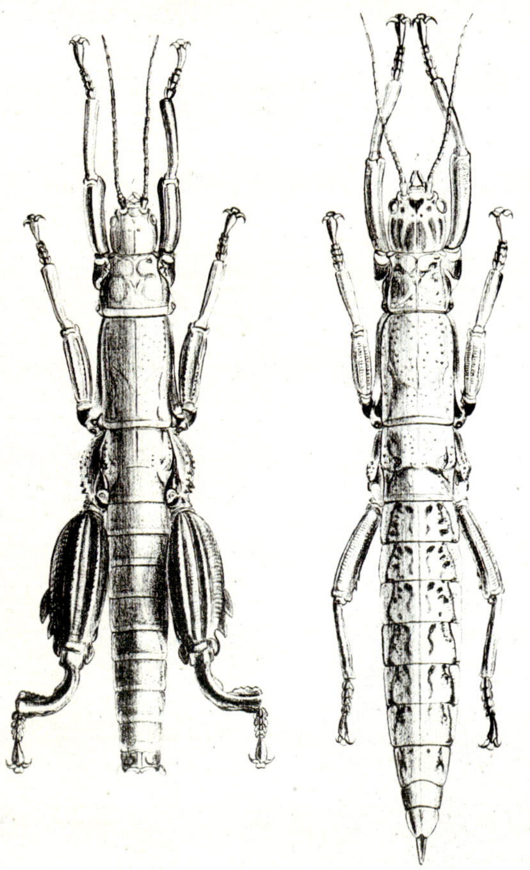

Pair of tree lobsters illustrated by John O. Westwood in his book *Catalogue of Orthopterous Insects in the Collection of the British Museum* (1859). The male (left) is smaller than the female (right) and has longer, thicker antennae, a slimmer abdomen, and thicker hindlegs covered in spines.

Adam and Eve) were sent to the Melbourne Zoo, and the other to an insect breeder in Sydney. The plan was to increase the gene pool by breeding the species in captivity so that it could eventually be reintroduced to Lord Howe Island, genetic tests having shown that the Ball's Pyramid population was the same species. Successful breeding programs have since been carried out in San Diego, Toronto, and Bristol. The next step was to eradicate rats and other invasive rodents from Lord Howe Island: in 2019, 43 tons of poisoned food was airdropped by helicopter and 28,000 ground traps were set to rid the island of its rats. (Any birds at risk of being harmed were trapped and taken to safety beforehand.) One day, tree lobsters will reclaim their place in the island's ecosystem.

AN ULTRARARE CRICKET UNDER THREAT

Another surprise survivor is found on the most populous island in the Seychelles: the Mahé boulder cricket (*Phalangacris alluaudi*). The species was rediscovered in 2014 after not being seen for over a century. It was long thought to be extinct and is now listed as critically endangered by the IUCN. These flightless crickets live under and among granite boulders, and appear to survive only in two locations, a range of less than 10 kilometers square.

Insects like the Mahé boulder cricket can subsist in very small areas that are easily destroyed by humans, meaning a cricket population that has existed for centuries can be wiped out in a moment. There are several factors behind the boulder cricket's extremely limited range: mass tourism; predation by nonnative birds, rats, and other mammals; competition from invasive ant species; and the spread of nonnative plants like the Ceylon cinnamon tree (*Cinnamomum verum*) and especially soapbush (*Miconia crenata*). The use of pesticides for agriculture and to "clean up" tourist areas also threatens these ultrarare insects.

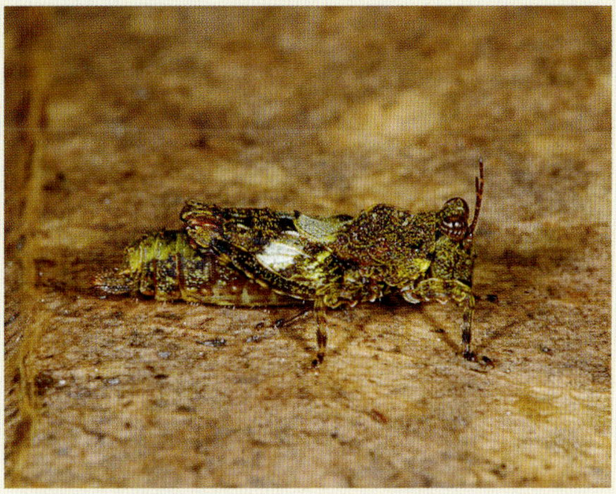

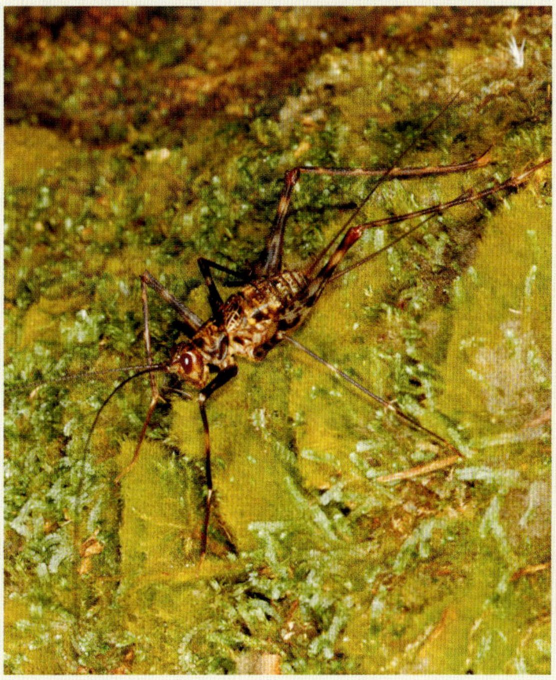

Top: *Amphinotus nymphula*, a grasshopper endemic to the Seychelles, is also on the endangered species list. It lives on mossy tree trunks in cloud forests and is threatened by invasive plants that have transformed its habitat.

Bottom: The Mahé boulder cricket was rediscovered in Morne Seychellois National Park in 2014.

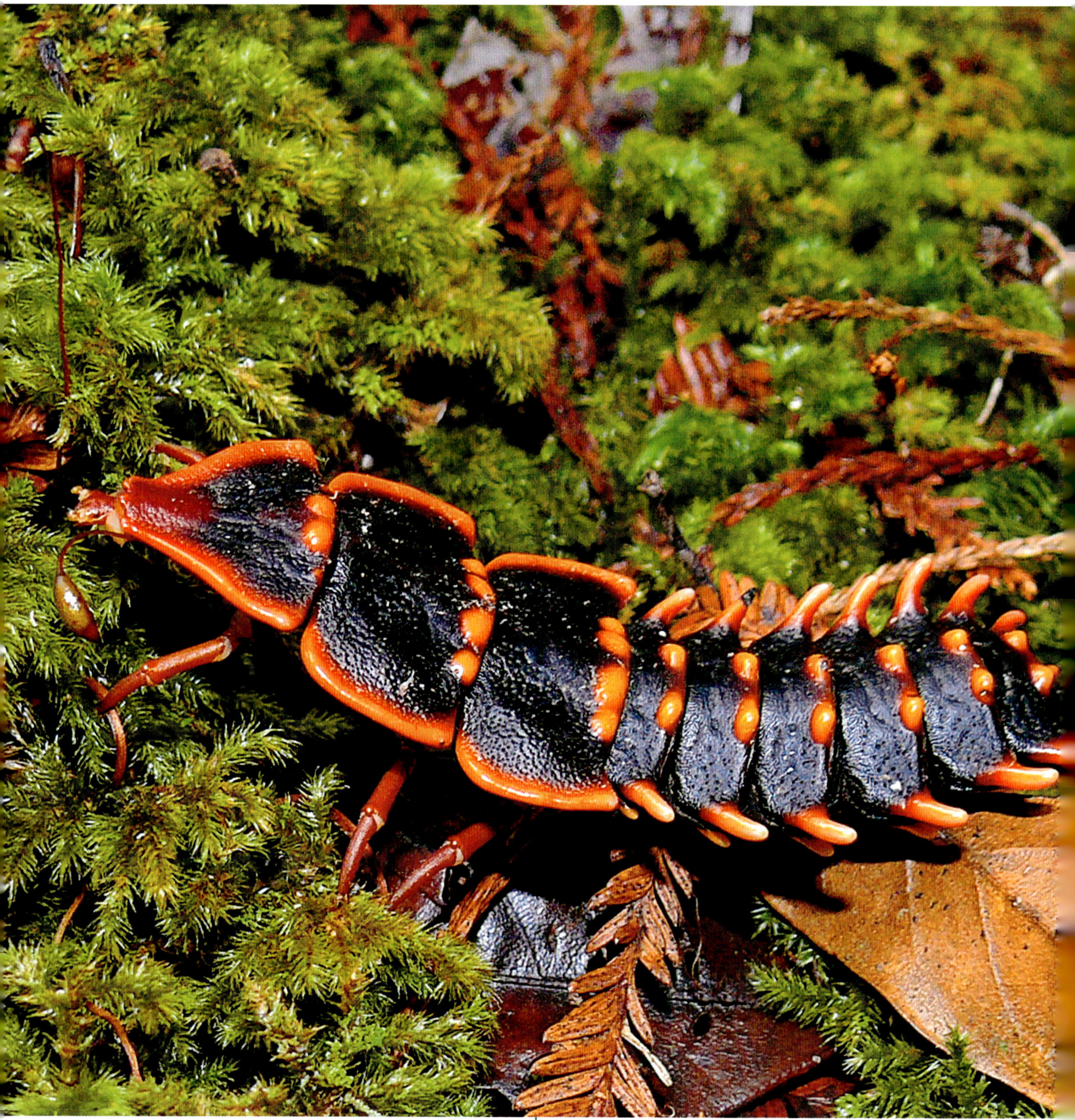

Trilobite beetles live in the jungles of Southeast Asia, mainly in Indonesia. They come in a variety of colors—purple, green, or black with bright orange points—and can draw their tiny heads into their bodies like turtles. This female *Platerodrilus paradoxus* from Borneo is around 8 cm long.

TROPICAL TRILOBITES

GENUS PLATERODRILUS AND COUSINS

COLEOPTERA: LYCIDAE

These bizarre-looking insects have legs that end in points and flat, colorful thoracic extensions like plated armor over their backs. Because of their extraordinary resemblance to trilobites—marine arthropods that lived on the seafloor 250 million years ago and are now found only as fossils—they are commonly known as trilobite beetles.

Because of their strange appearance, for a long time, trilobite beetles were mistakenly considered "living fossils." (The term itself is misleading, because it suggests that the species in question has not evolved over time. But while living fossils are morphologically similar to their extinct ancestors, genetically speaking, they are always different species. See page 137.) In fact, these beetles only appeared about 47 million years ago, more than 200 million years after trilobites went extinct.

The first trilobite beetle larva was discovered on the island of Java and described in 1831 by German entomologist Josef Maximilian Perty (1804–1884), who named it *larva singularis*, the "singular larva." A few years later, British naturalist John O. Westwood (1805–1893) classified these strange beetles as members of the Lycidae family. The genus *Platerodrilus* contains about twenty known species, all of which live in Southeast Asia.

The oddest part in the history of these odd insects is that, despite their attention-grabbing appearance, it took nearly a century for naturalists to identify a male. For a long time, only larvae—immature insects without sex organs, measuring 4–8 centimeters long—were known. Entomologists the world over were left to wonder: how did they reproduce? And what did the sexually mature adults look like? After spending two years studying insects in Sumatra, Swedish zoologist Eric Mjöberg (1882–1938) was determined to find a male and went to Borneo, where the beetles were more common, in 1922. Three years later, he described his extraordinary entomological adventure in an article for *Psyche* magazine in which he wrote of his

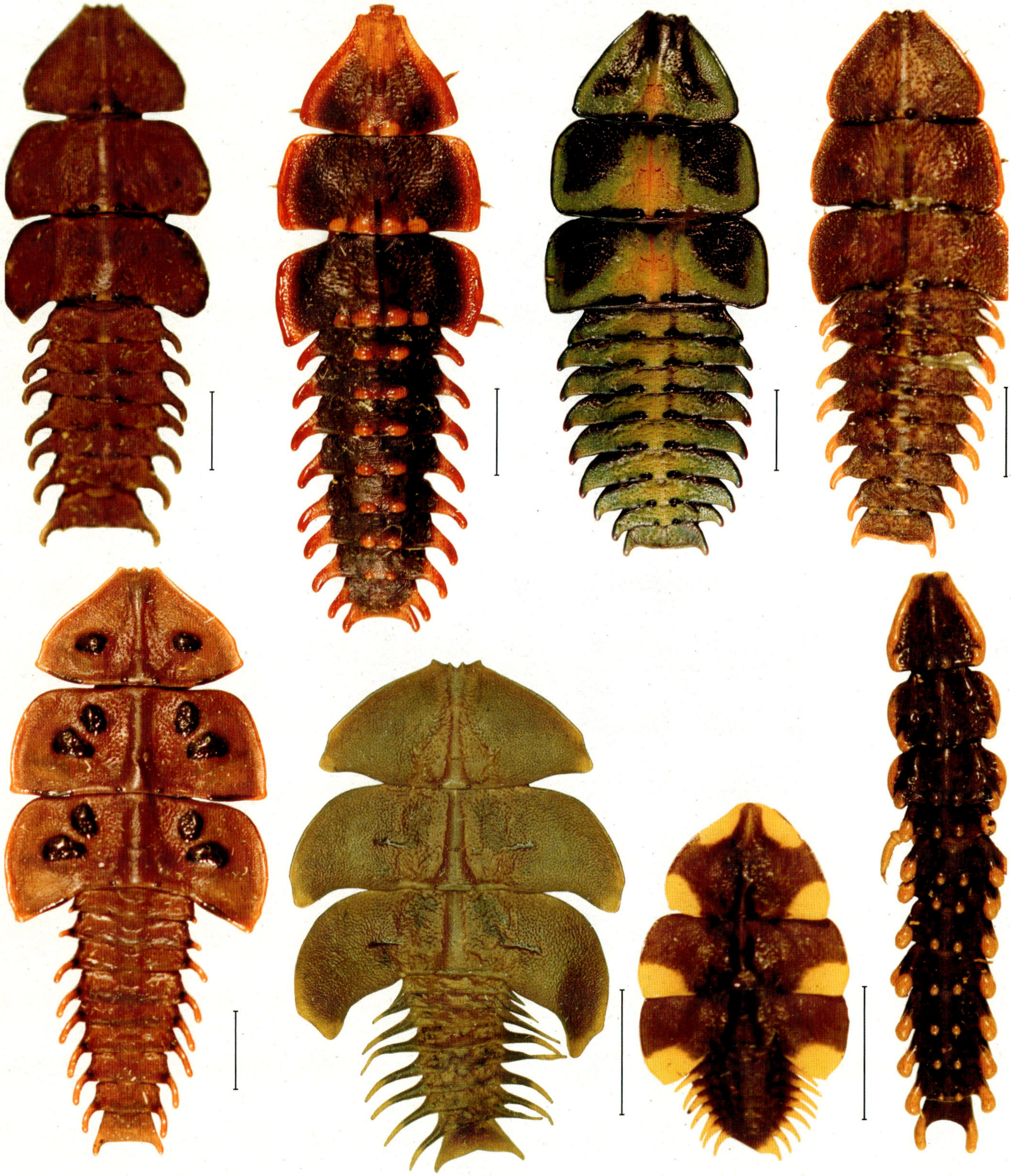

Various species in the genus *Platerodrilus* (black line = 1 cm).

© Ladislav Bocak

Trilobite beetle heads are tiny compared to their bodies, adding to their strange appearance. In this picture, a black simple eye can be seen just behind the short, forward-facing antennae.
© Nicky Bay

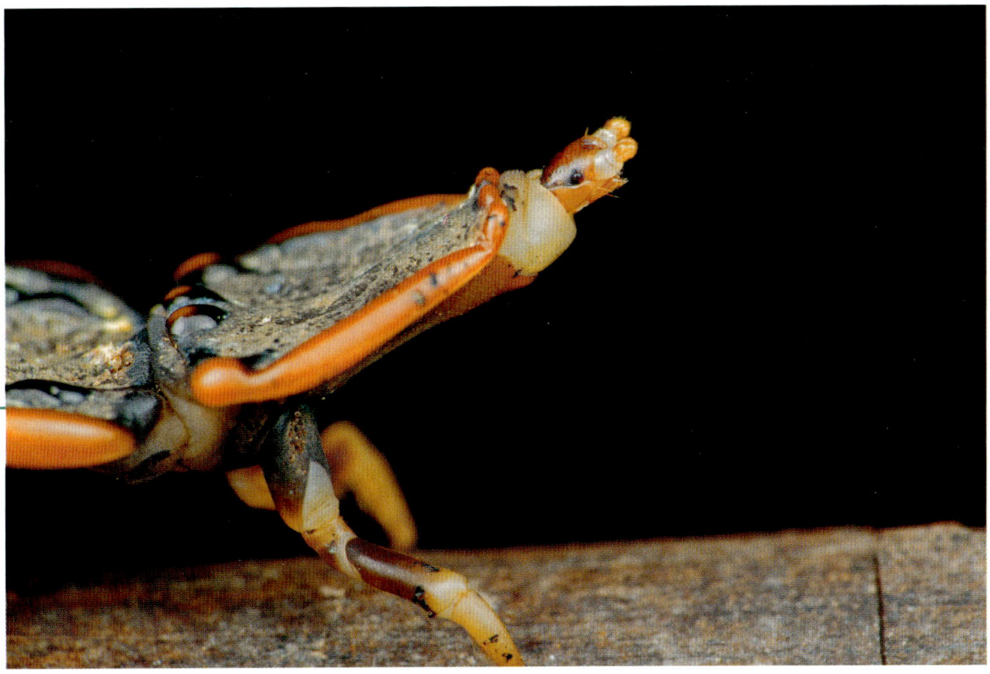

Frontal view of a female trilobite beetle observed in Borneo.
© Nicky Bay

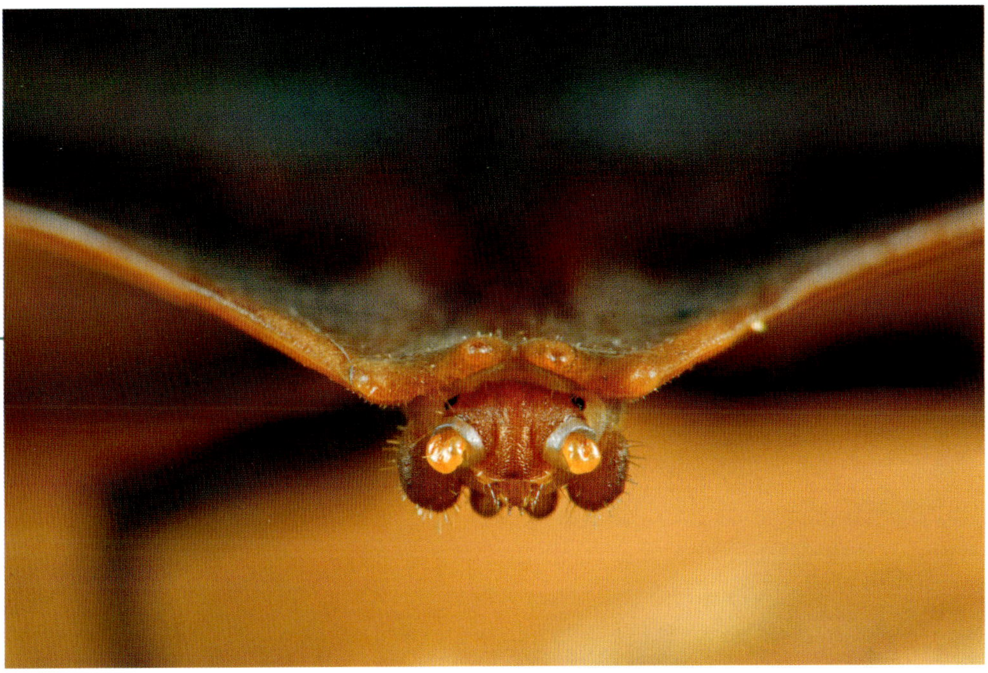

View of the same female laid on her back to show the size of the thorax (clearly divided into three segments), compared to the head and abdomen. The sex organ is visible at the end of the abdomen.
© Nicky Bay

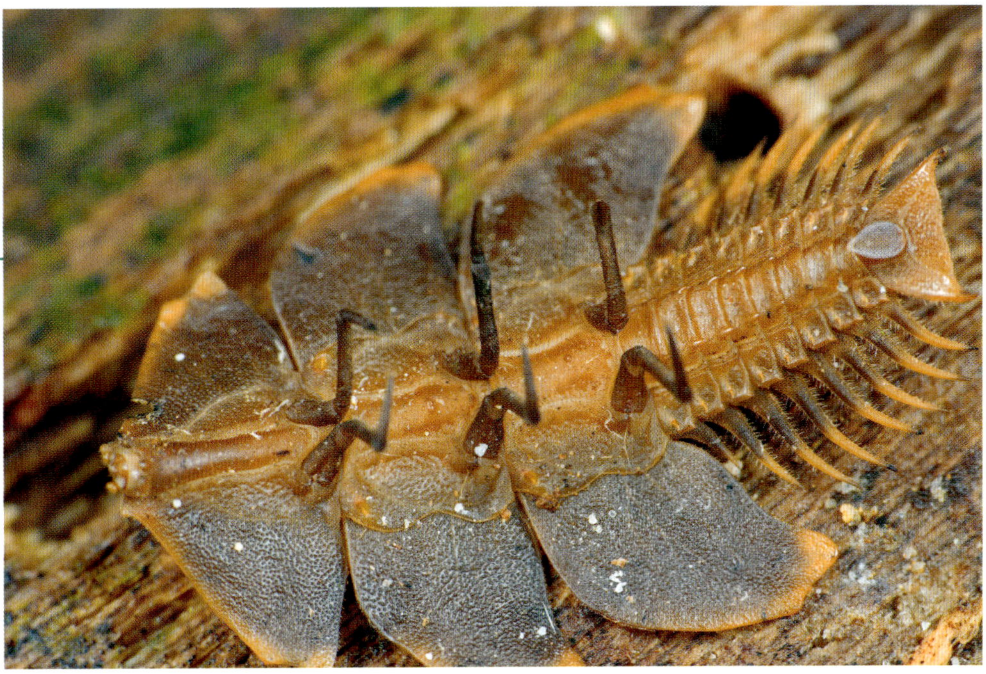

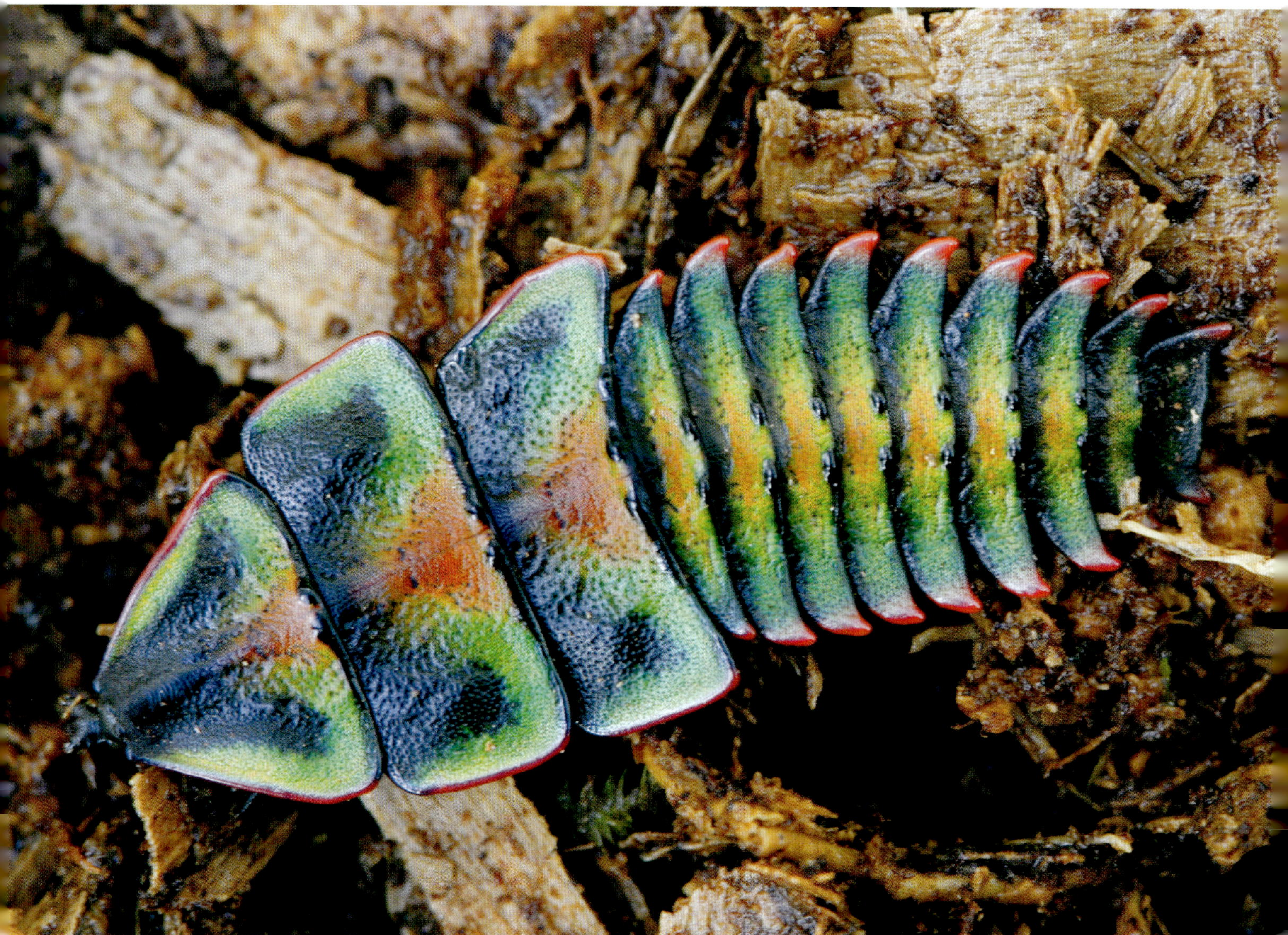

Female trilobite beetle observed in Borneo.
© Ladislav Bocak

perplexing quest: "Although having for years [. . .] turned every stone and split up thousands of pieces of decaying wood or heavy logs I have never been able to find a single fully developed female, in spite of the fact that full grown larvae were abundantly common thereabouts." But Mjöberg's perseverance paid off: one of the larvae he captured eventually rolled up and kept still for several days as if dead, then shed its skin, turned yellowish-white, and began moving again. The only difference after this metamorphosis was that it now had female sexual organs! Mjöberg finally had his hands on an adult female. Each morning, he found her holding up the tip of her abdomen to show she was ready to mate. But because he did not have a male to mate with her, the eggs she laid went unfertilized, and she died not long after.

But this gave Mjöberg an idea. He collected a number of sexually mature females and, once they began secreting pheromones, placed them in the forest tied to a string that gave them some degree of mobility. He watched them crawl back and forth at the end of their strings and waited for a male to appear—in vain. Far from giving up, he tried again the next year, this time with the help of locals, to whom he promised a cash reward for the first to bring him a male. At last, a man came to him one morning carrying a mating pair wrapped in a banana leaf. This was the first time an adult male had ever been observed. On the leaf, Mjöberg saw a dark, ordinary-looking beetle, only a tenth the size of his impressive mate. Now it was certain: the females retain their larval form as adults and acquire sex organs without ever becoming nymphs, a remarkable example of neoteny that allows them to save their energy for reproduction.

The two sexes are so different that, even today, it is difficult to know which belong to the same species without conducting genetic tests or catching them in the act of mating. It was a long time before another mating pair was observed, by Singaporean entomologist Alvin T. C. Wong in 1996. The reproduction of yet another trilobite beetle species, *Platerodrilus ruficollis*, was described in 2014. The males die only a few hours after mating. The next day, the females lay around two hundred eggs in leaf litter, then die in turn.

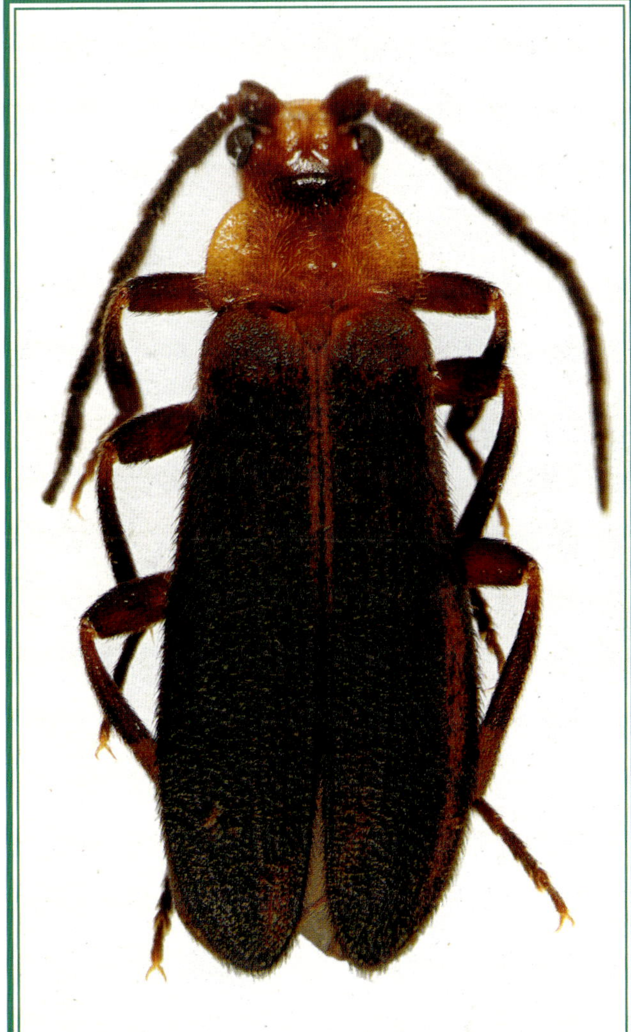

Male Platerodrilus *ruficollis*.

© Ladislav Bocak

Trilobite beetles live in humid, old-growth forests, where the female larvae spend their days crawling over dead leaves and rotting wood on the forest floor. Their diet is unknown, but they are probably fungivores that feed on the microorganisms in decomposing plant matter. All attempts to raise the beetles in captivity have failed, and the males' life cycle and behavior remain a complete mystery.

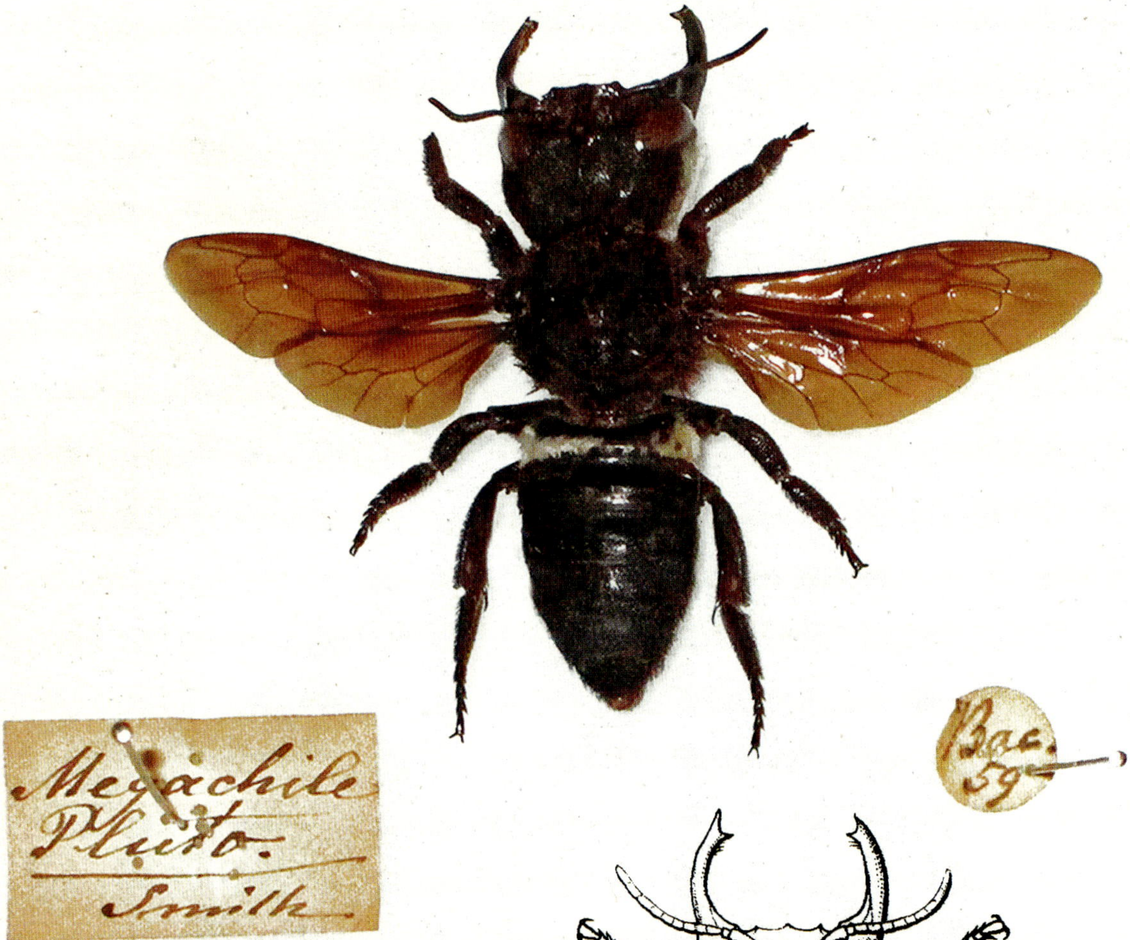

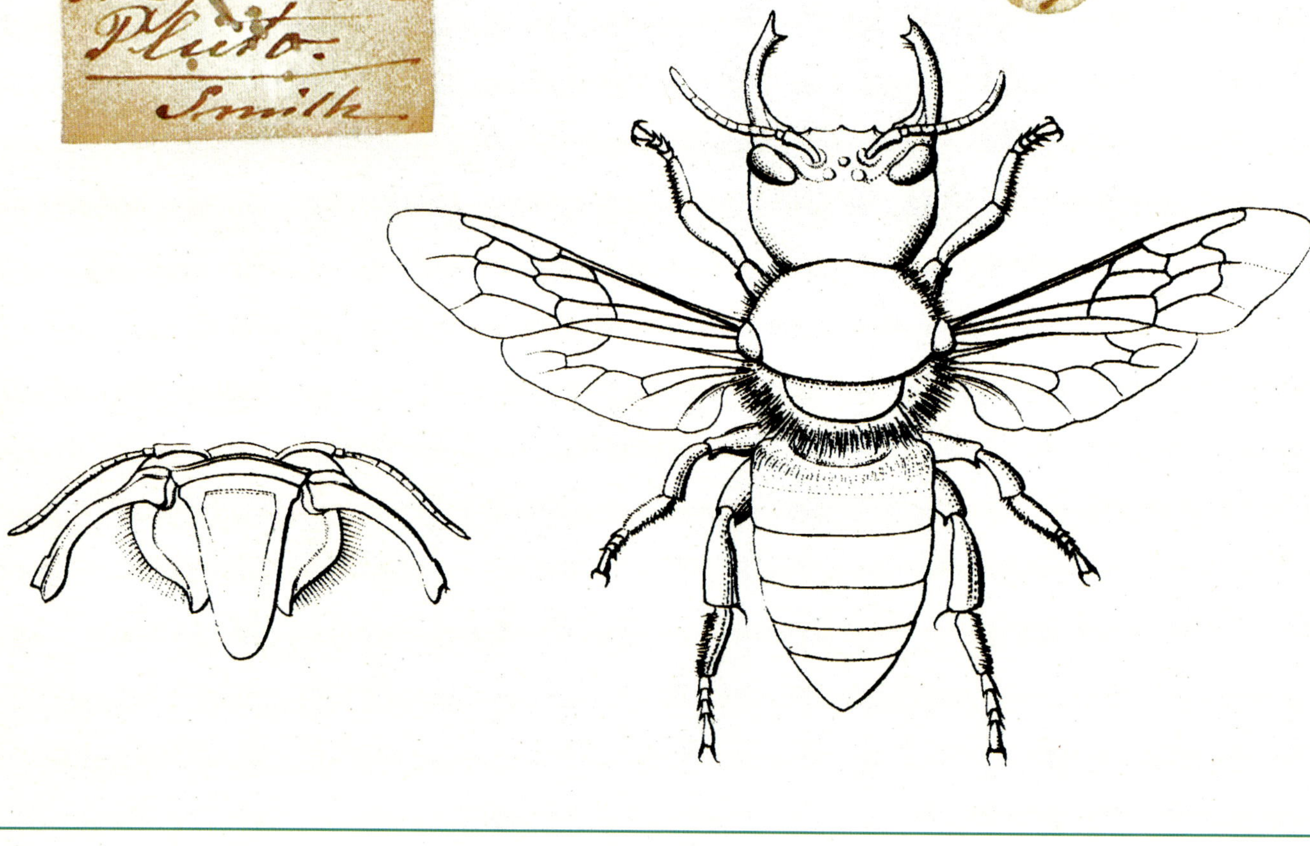

Top: Holotype (specimen used as the basis for describing and naming a new species) collected by Alfred Russel Wallace in 1859 on Bacan in the Maluku Islands, Indonesia.

Bottom: Engraving from *Catalogue of Hymenopterous Insects collected by Mr. A. R. Wallace in the Islands of Bachian, Kaisaa, Amboyna, Gilolo, and at Dory in New Guinea* by Frederick Smith (1860). Wallace's giant bee has only been found on a few Indonesian islands. It lives at low altitude in old-growth forests and plains.

EMPEROR OF THE BEES

MEGACHILE PLUTO

(HYMENOPTERA: MEGACHILIDAE)

Deep in the forests of Bacan, one of the northern Maluku Islands in what is now Indonesia, Alfred Russel Wallace first laid eyes on this giant bee in 1859—a discovery almost as exciting as that of the Wallace's golden birdwing in the same archipelago. The impressive specimen turned out to be the world's largest bee, known in the local language as *raja ofu*: "king of the bees."

Wallace wrote in 1873: "The giant *Megachile pluto* was only seen once, in the island of Batchian [Bacan]. It was obtained during an excursion to a tract of mountainous forests, and was watched flying round and round with a loud humming noise like that produced by a *Geotrupes*, till at last it was fortunately captured on the wing." English entomologist Frederick Smith (1805–1879), a specialist in Hymenoptera at the British Museum, took a particular interest in what would come to be known as Wallace's giant bee. Smith named and described the species in 1860, calling it "the giant of the genus to which it belongs, and the grandest addition which Wallace has made to our knowledge of the family Apidae."

Nevertheless, Wallace's giant bee remained shrouded in mystery. Bacan was rarely visited by naturalists, and study of Indonesian fauna was focused mainly on butterflies. There were no reported sightings of *M. pluto* for over a century, until a specimen was captured on Obi, an island near Bacan, in 1953. Scientists would later consider the species to be extinct.

At last, in 1981, American entomologist Adam C. Messer found *M. pluto* nests on three of the Maluku Islands and managed to observe the bees' singular behavior. They build their nests inside the active colonies of a tree-dwelling termite common to Southeast Asia, *Microcerotermes amboinensis*, with which they have a symbiotic relationship. The termites protect the bees from attackers and provide a consistent microenvironment. It is unknown just how social the bees are among themselves: their nests contain only a few females, although the males remain nearby. The females dig galleries inside the termite nest that they coat and divide

Wallace's giant bees are up to four times larger than domestic honey bees.
© Clay Bolt

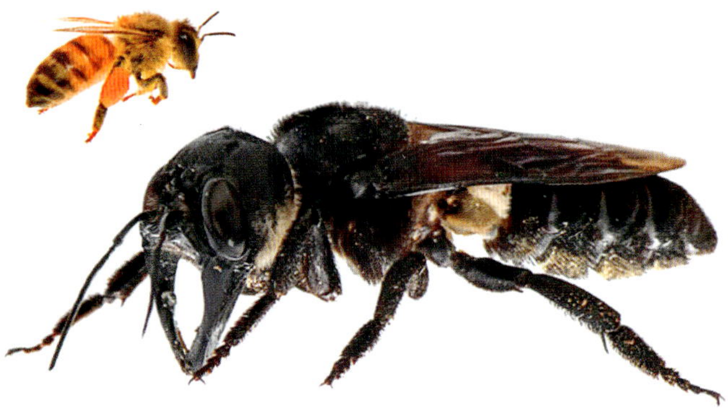

into compartments using a mix of resin and wood fibers collected from various trees. Once dry, the mixture turns black and hardens, preventing the termites from entering.

Wallace's giant bee, which is already rare, is increasingly under threat from deforestation by palm oil producers and other human impacts on the Maluku Islands. Recently, it has also been hunted by unscrupulous individuals hoping to sell specimens online.

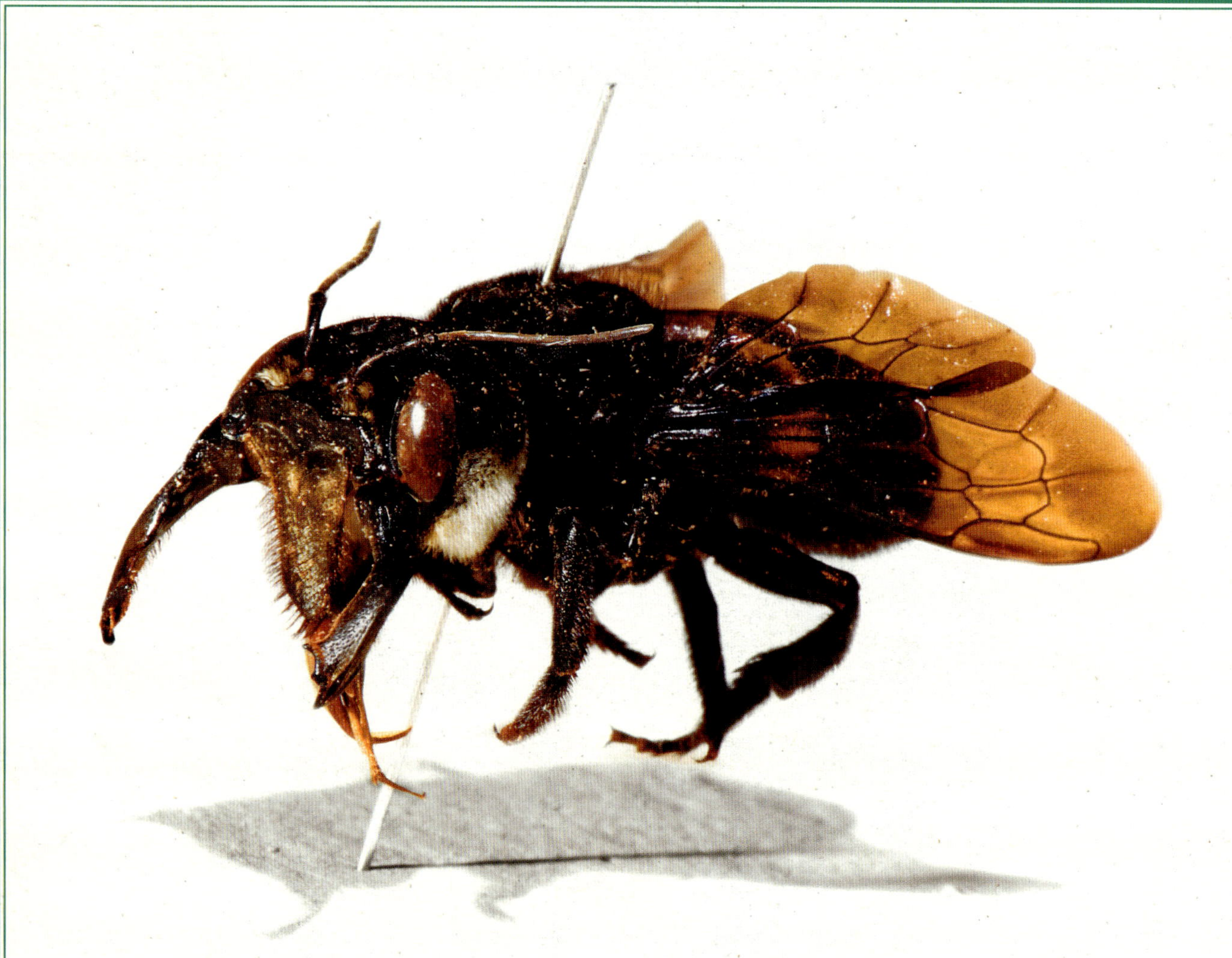

Females measure up to 4 cm long, with a wingspan over 6 cm. Their massive heads are 1.3 cm wide, and they have large, notched jaws for collecting resin and bits of wood, which they roll into balls up to 1 cm across. Males are much smaller and do not have the same impressive jaws.
© SPL - Science Photo Library/Biosphoto

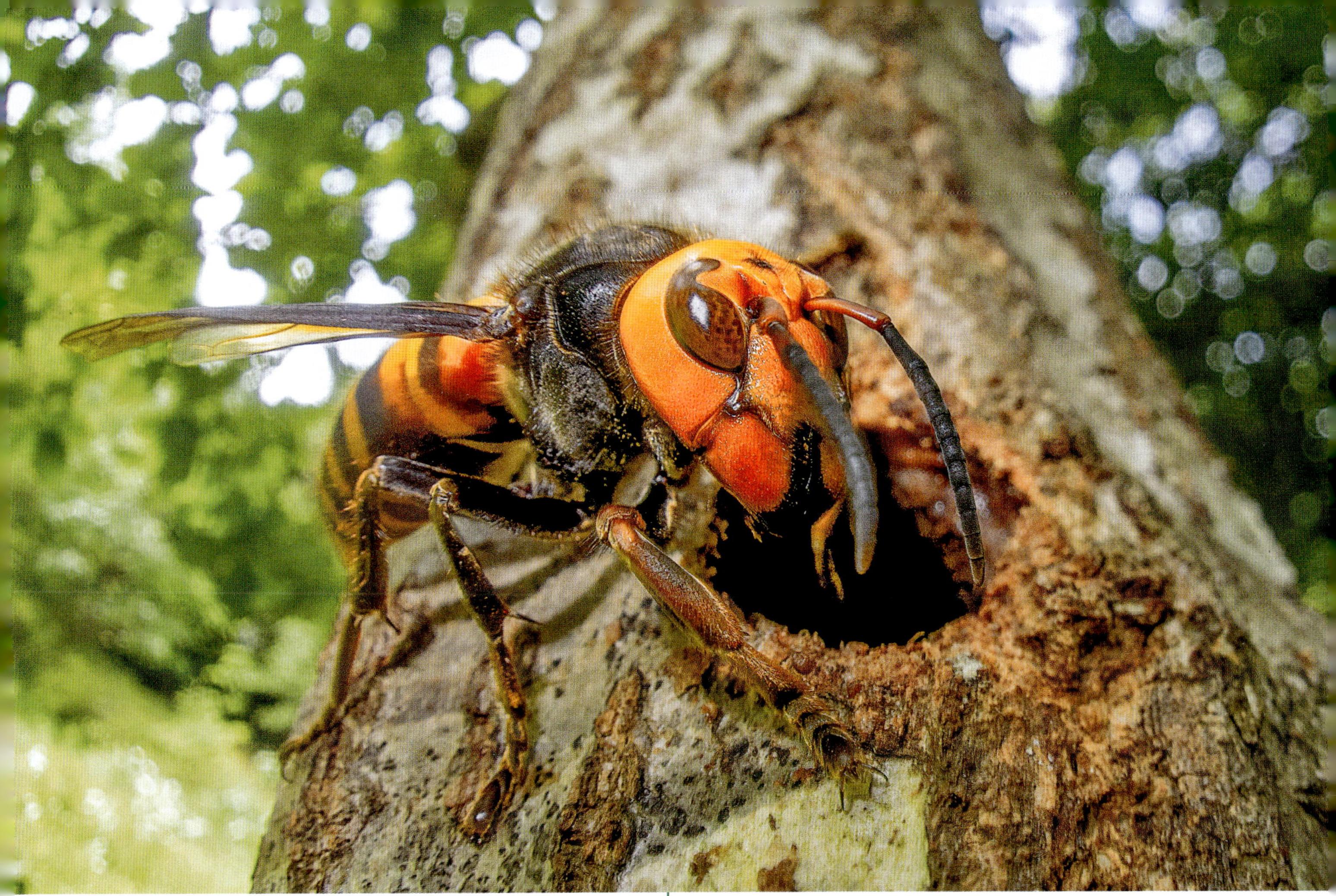

Another large hymenopteran, the northern giant hornet or "murder hornet" (*Vespa mandarinia*) can grow up to 5 cm long (or 6 cm for the queen), making it the largest social insect. They are predators, sometimes hunting as a group and killing all the adults in a nest of bees, wasps, or smaller hornets, then feeding on the larvae. The species was accidentally introduced to North America in 2019; the first nest was discovered and destroyed in northern Washington state in 2020. A similar invasion occurred in Europe in the early 2000s, when the yellow-legged hornet (*Vespa velutina*) colonized most of the continent.

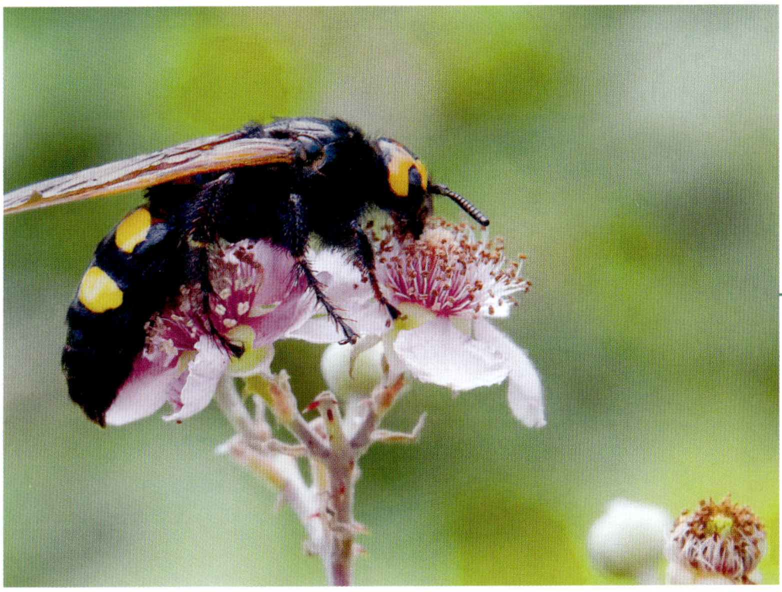

The mammoth wasp (*Megascolia maculata*) can grow up to 5 cm long with a wingspan of 9 cm, making it the largest hymenopteran in Europe. Despite its imposing size, it is completely harmless to humans. The females lay their eggs inside the larvae of the European rhinoceros beetle (*Oryctes nasicornis*), which the wasp larva consumes before emerging as an adult. As rhinoceros beetle populations decline, mammoth wasps are also becoming rarer.

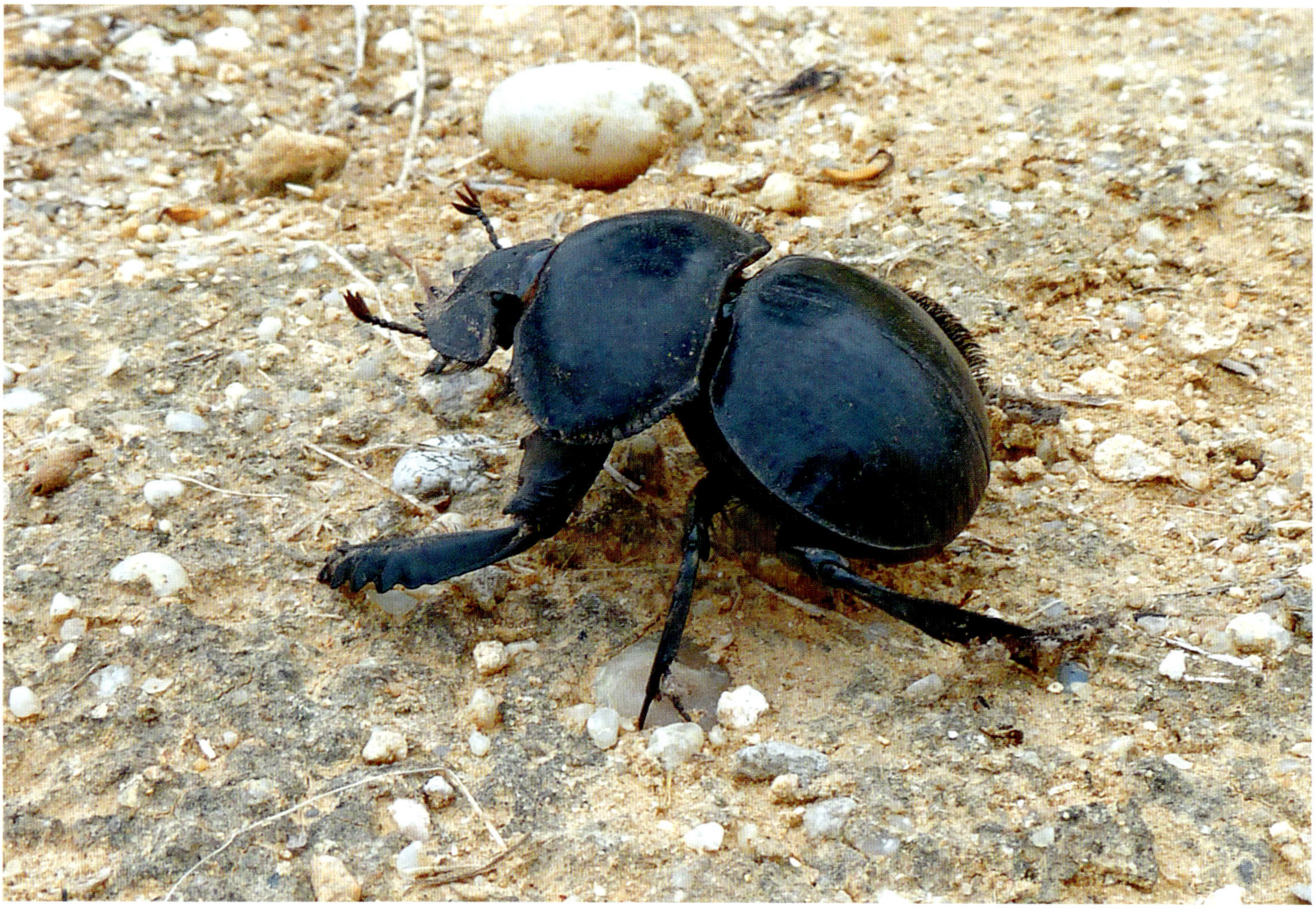

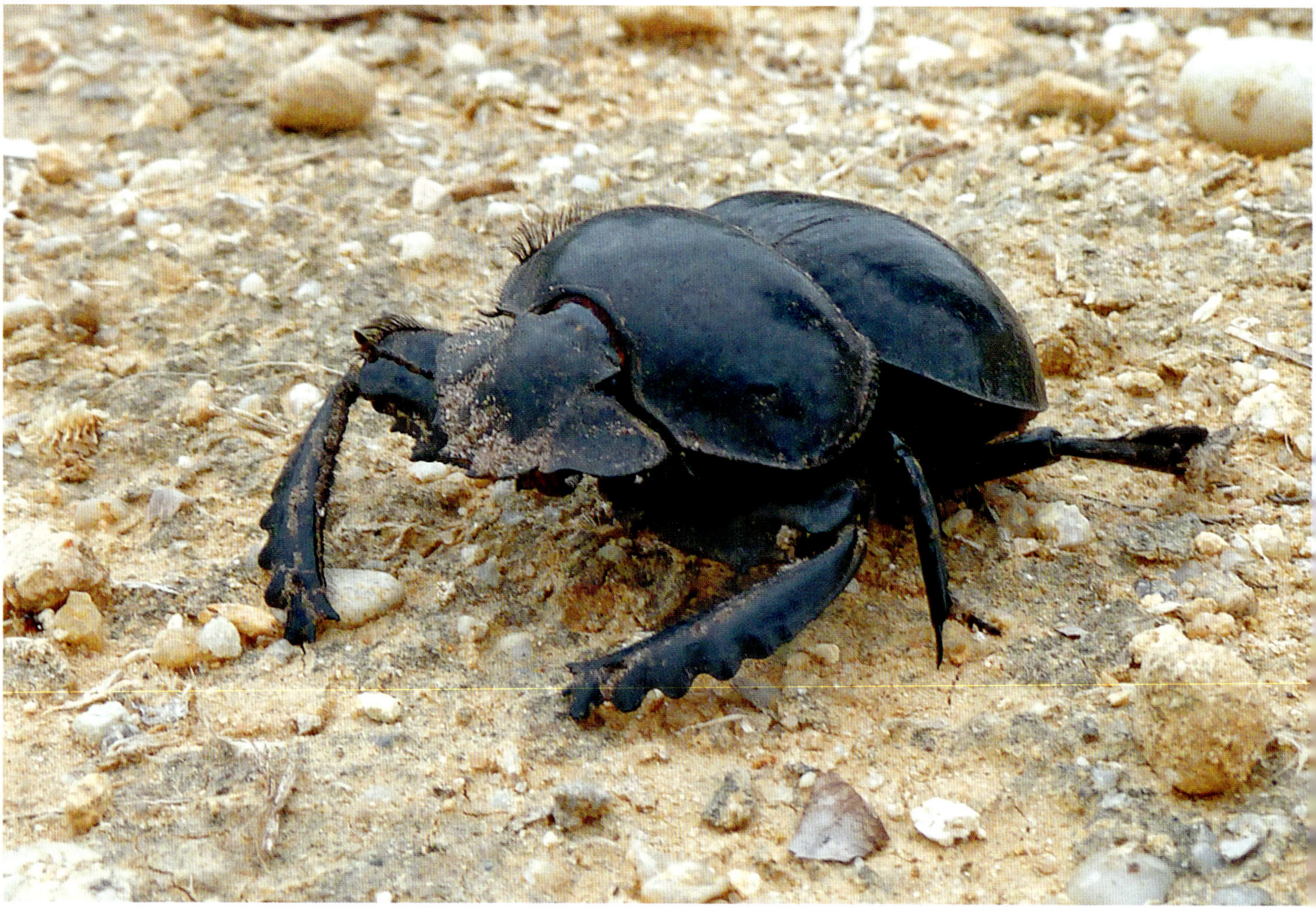

A SURVIVOR OF TWO WARS

SCARABAEUS (MNEMATIUM) CANCER
(COLEOPTERA: SCARABAEIDAE)

Until recently, this large, enigmatic dung beetle was only known from a few rare specimens held in collections. It was thought to be extinct, having last been spotted in southeast Angola in 1949. But in fact, the beetle had survived decades of devastating warfare and was rediscovered in 2015.

Elephant dung is a hot commodity—as soon as it hits the ground, dozens of dung beetle species make off with their share of the prize as fast as they can. Some bury it in the ground, some lay their eggs in it while it is still wet, and others form it into a ball, which they roll away to bury farther off. In short, speed is of the essence in the dung beetle world! It is a race in which *Scarabaeus (Mnematium) cancer*, described in 1919 by Gilbert J. Arrow (1873–1948), has a serious disadvantage: it has no wings. While being flightless is likely an advantage in terms of conserving water in a hot climate, it also means they are much slower than their winged cousins. That was not a problem when elephants and other large herbivores were still living and defecating in large numbers on the savannah, but their decline has led to stiff competition among Africa's dung beetles.

Based on the rare specimens held in collections, entomologists deduced that *M. cancer* fed on elephant dung like its cousins in the genus *Pachysoma* and dug galleries in the sand where it buried the dung balls in which it laid its eggs. But for decades that hypothesis was impossible to confirm, because the species was only known in Angola, which was waging a war of independence from 1961 to 1975, followed by a devastating civil war that lasted until 2002. Cuito Cuanavale, where the first specimen

The male *Scarabaeus (Mnematium) cancer* spotted by Keith Philips making its way along a path in the Cuito Cuarnavale region of Angola.

© Keith Philips

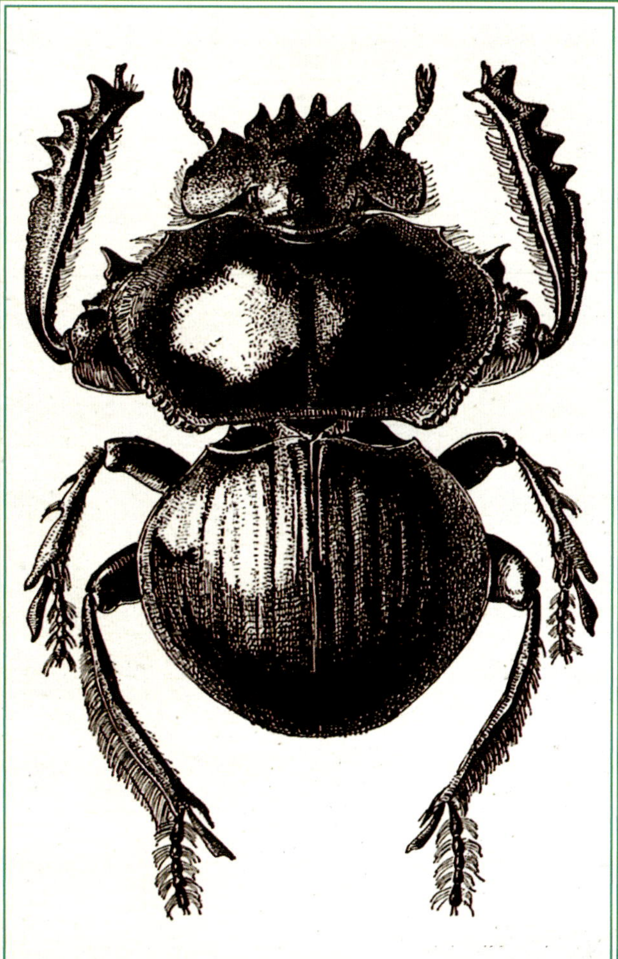

Engraving of a 5-cm-long specimen by Germaine Boca (1904–2002), an illustrator associated with the French National Museum of Natural History. The illustration was made in the 1950s based on a specimen brought back by French explorer Jacques de Rohan-Chabot (1889–1958), who guided a group of naturalists through southern Africa in 1912 and 1913.

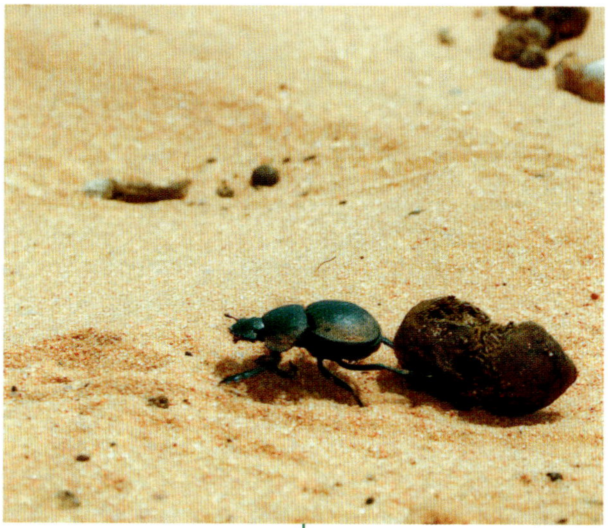

All thirteen species of dung beetle in the genus *Pachysoma* (pictured: *P. striatum*) are found on the northwest coast of South Africa. They are unusual in that they grip their dung balls with their hindlegs and drag them—instead of rolling them—over the hot sand.
© Marcus Byrne

had been collected, was the scene of particularly heavy fighting and a five-month-long battle that left the entire region riddled with mine blasts.

It was not until 2015 that the IUCN sent two entomologists, Bruce D. Gill (a Canadian) and Keith Philips (an American) to look for the beetle, which was thought to be extinct. After weeks of searching, just when Gill and Philips were ready to give up, they spotted an enormous dung beetle strolling placidly along the side of a path. The species had survived! The precious specimen was carefully examined and a tissue sample taken before it was released back into the wild. Later observations gave a clearer picture of the beetle's ecology: it is an opportunistic feeder and will readily accept rabbit or antelope droppings in a pinch—probably the key to its survival in a region where elephants are in sharp decline. Further study will show the extent of its range and teach us more about its life cycle and behavior.

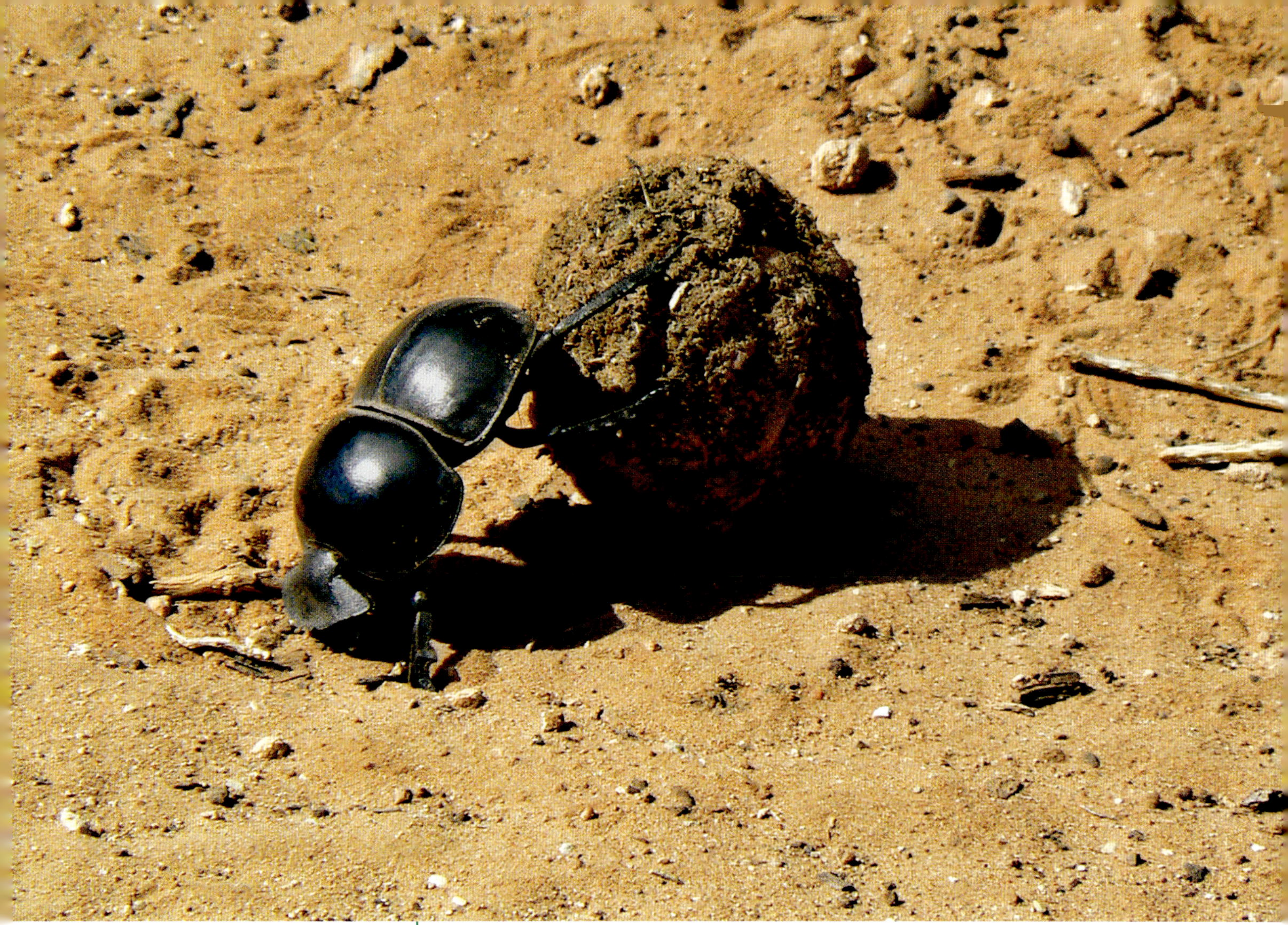

Circellium bacchus is another large flightless dung beetle with a preference for elephant dung. Like *Scarabaeus (Mnematium) cancer*, the species is suffering as elephants become rarer. It is highly endangered, with the largest population found in Addo Elephant National Park.

Sign encouraging drivers to avoid crushing beetles or the dung they rely on for food.

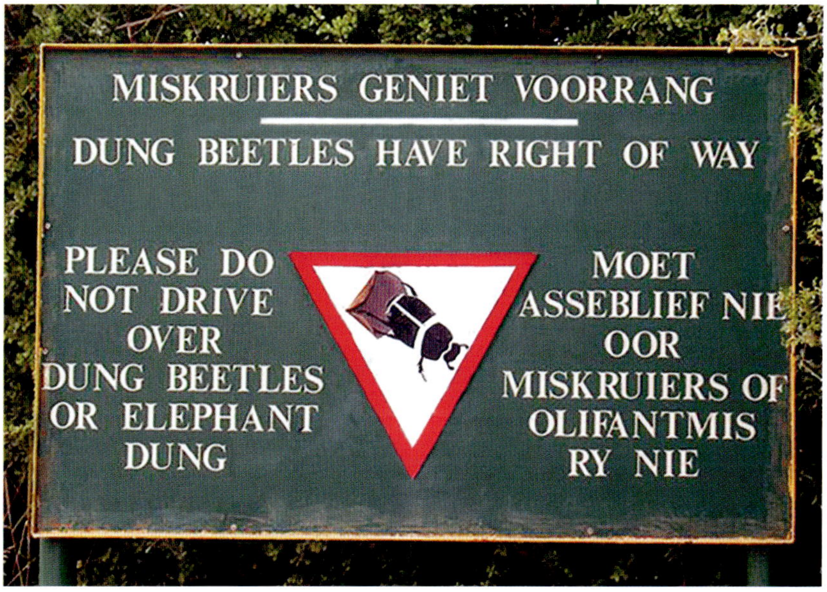

THE DUNG BEETLE PROJECT

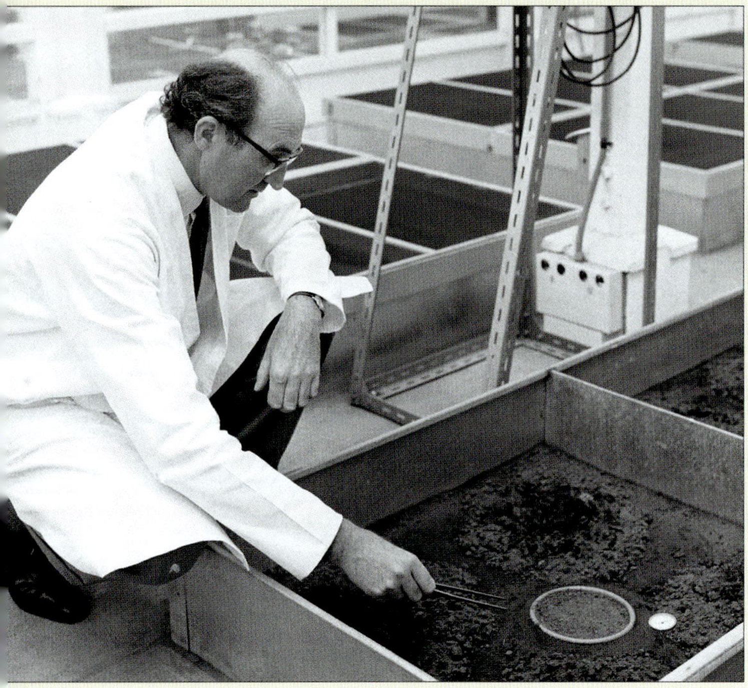

Some parts of the globe have few native coprophagic insects. The islands of Oceania, including Australia, had no large herbivores until they were introduced by humans. The introduction of large herds of cattle—with no dung beetles to clean up their manure—has created a textbook case of ecological imbalance. Prior to the arrival of English colonists in the late eighteenth century, the largest herbivores on the continent were kangaroos, whose dry, fibrous droppings are smaller than a golf ball and were consumed by some 250 native species from the subfamily Scarabaeinae, maintaining a satisfactory balance.

The situation shifted when animal agriculture exploded in the twentieth century. (There were over 30 million head of cattle in Australia by the end of the 1960s.) The local dung beetles did not care for cow manure, meaning it could only be broken down by rain, termites, or trampling by the cattle themselves. Each year, manure accumulated on another 7.4 million acres of pasture, making it unsuitable for grazing, since cows avoid eating grass near manure so as not to reingest parasites.

To solve the problem, new dung beetle species were introduced to Australia starting in 1968. The Dung Beetle Project was the brainchild of Australian entomologist George F. Bornemissza (1924–2014). First, beetle eggs were washed and disinfected to avoid the risk of introducing zoonotic diseases. Once they hatched, the beetles were kept in quarantine and raised in captivity for breeding. The second generation was then bred to produce beetles that were released into

Top: A Hungarian-born Australian, George F. Bornemissza, had the idea of introducing large numbers of beetles that feed on cow manure to restore ecological balance in Australia.

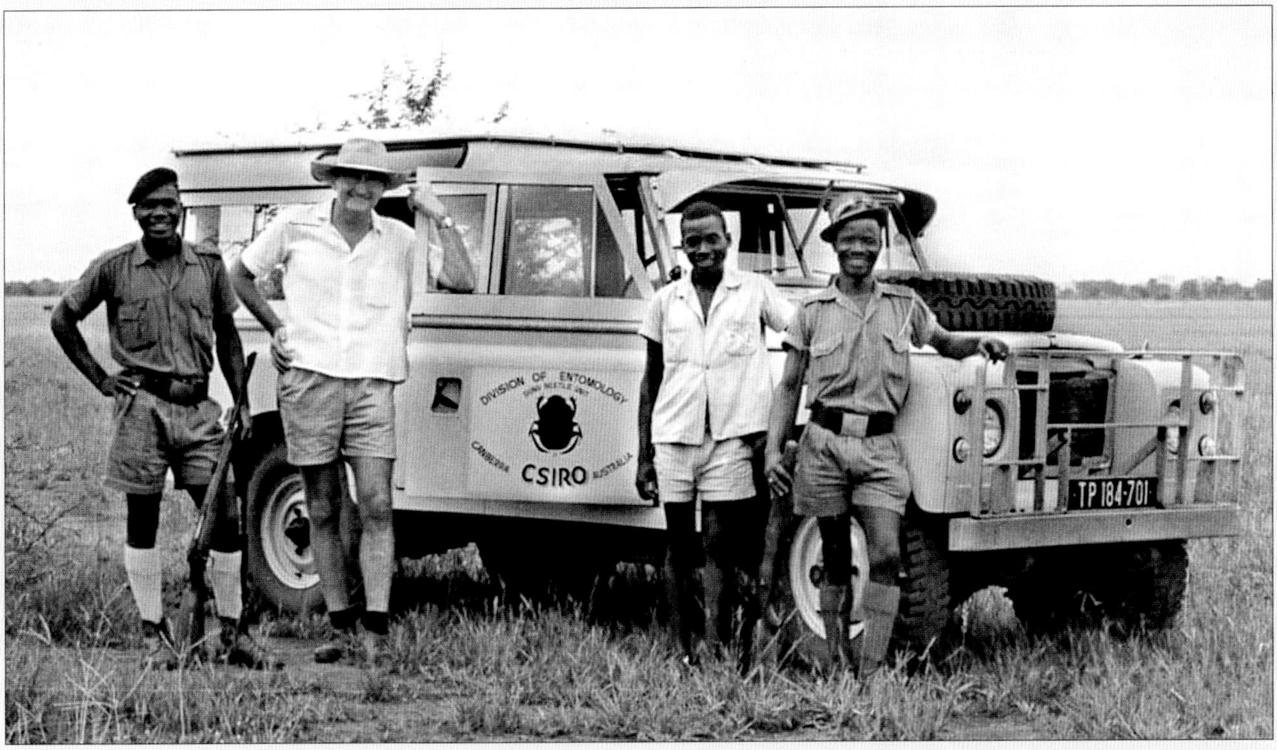

Above: Bornemissza in South Africa in the 1970s. He successfully introduced a number of South African dung beetle species to Australia.
© CSIRO

cow pastures in large numbers. The first release took place in Queensland in 1968. Some 275,000 individuals from four different species were introduced. In two years, the brown dung beetle (*Digitonthophagus gazella*) had multiplied by the millions and doubled its range to nearly 1,000 kilometers along the Queensland coast. The project's overall success rate was uneven but promising: by introducing complementary species that are active at different times of year, the biting fly population was significantly reduced. Nearly fifty species from South Africa, Europe, and Asia (a total of 1.7 million individuals raised in captivity) were introduced in total, of which twenty formed sustainable populations. Although it was abandoned for a time, the project resumed in the 2000s as the Queensland Dung Beetle Project.

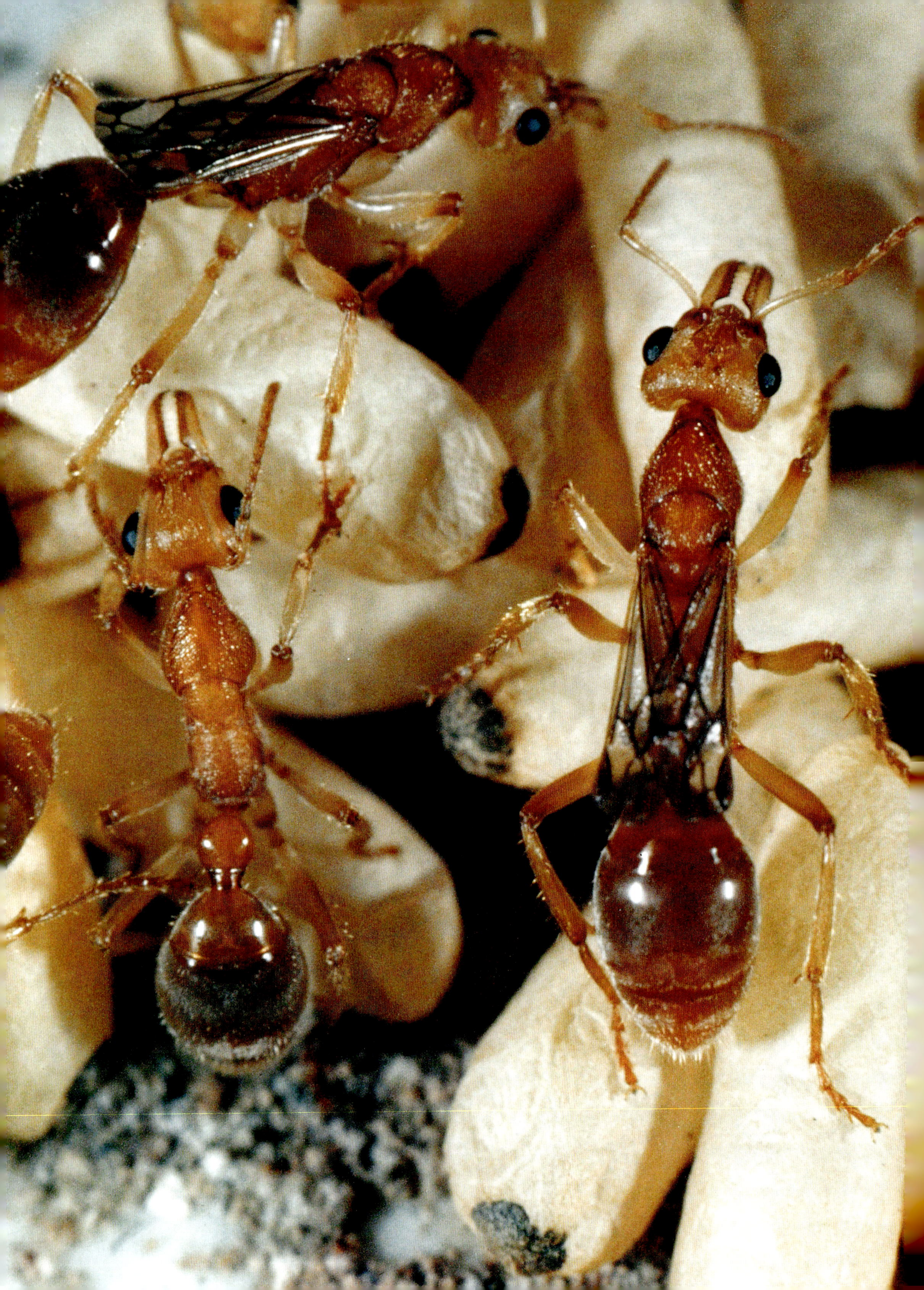

THE DINOSAUR ANT

NOTHOMYRMECIA MACROPS
(HYMENOPTERA: FORMICIDAE)

You may have heard of the coelacanth—a large fish discovered in the 1930 off the coast of South Africa—as the quintessential "living fossil." The term is actually misleading, since coelacanths are not prehistoric monsters that have somehow survived to the current day, but rather a species whose closest cousins are fossils dating back 250 million years. For entomologists, the best-known living fossil is the dawn ant or dinosaur ant.

In 1931, an expedition traveling on horseback between Balladonia and Esperance in the state of Western Australia was collecting insect specimens at the request of an artist and amateur entomologist associated with the Melbourne Museum. Members of the expedition picked up any insects they came across and stuck them into bottles of alcohol without dating or labeling them. This hodgepodge collection then ended up at the museum, where myrmecologist John S. Clark (1885–1956) was going through the specimens three years later when he came across two ants from a species as yet unknown to science. They were shaped like small wasps and most resembled fossil ants that lived over 60 million years ago.

Clark gave up his work around this time, but American entomologist William L. Brown, Jr. (1922–1997) recognized the species' importance to understanding how all ants had evolved. He set about trying to locate dinosaur ants in the wild so he could observe their social structure and perform studies that would be impossible using the damaged specimens at the museum. In 1951, Brown followed the same itinerary taken by the original

The dinosaur ant (*Nothomyrmecia macrops*) is the most primitive extant ant species known to science.

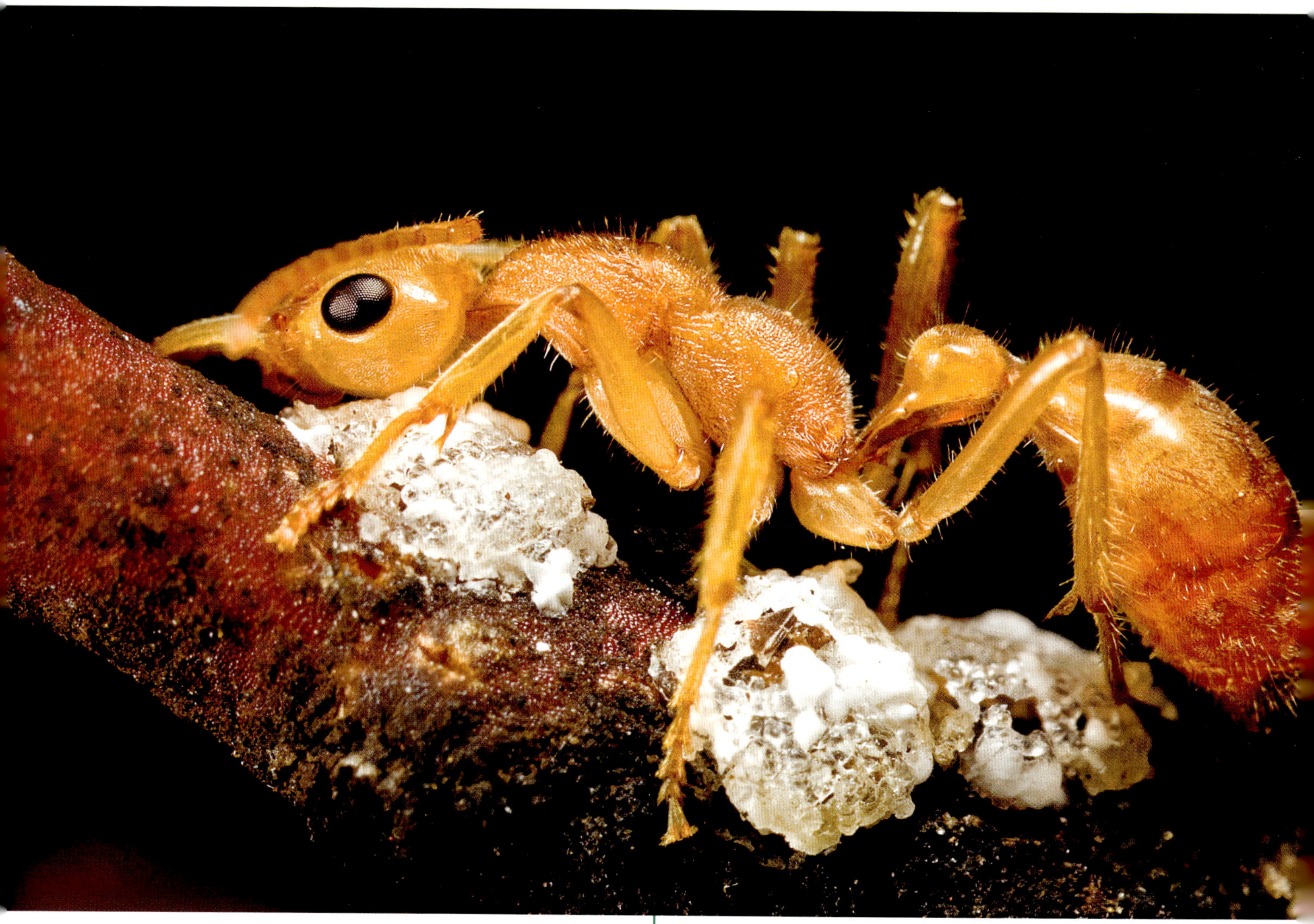

Dinosaur ant worker with scale insects covered in honeydew.
© Mark Moffett/Minden Pictures/Biosphoto

expedition but found no trace of the mysterious ants. Four years later, another American, Edward O. Wilson, spent an entire week in the field without success. Years passed, but all searches were fruitless. At last, in 1977, Australian entomologist Robert W. Taylor (Wilson's former student) led yet another expedition—this time starting over a thousand kilometers east of Esperance and following the arid coastline of the Great Australian Bight. Only a few days into the trip came an incredible stroke of luck: their vehicle broke down near Poochera, South Australia, forcing them to camp among some eucalyptus mallee. When the temperature dropped that night, most of the party stayed close to the fire, but Taylor went for a walk in the bush. Soon he was back, bursting with excitement. Only a few feet from camp, his flashlight had landed on a worker ant climbing up a eucalyptus trunk!

Dinosaur ants are as unusual in terms of behavior as anatomy. They are only active at night, when the air is cool, but not at all in winter. The entrance holes to their nests are particularly hard to detect, which explains why they slipped under the radar for decades. Their social structure is rudimentary: they form underground colonies composed of about a hundred individuals and a short-winged queen who does not look much different from the others. The workers are unspecialized and do not work together; they forage and hunt individually for prey to feed their larvae. Although they do groom each other, they do not communicate by trophallaxis (mouth-to-mouth exchange of food) the way other ants do. Instead, they use simple chemical signals to recognize members of their own colony and to signal danger.

These rare ants have only been found in some twenty sites near Poochera (but never between Balladonia and Esperance). The IUCN listed them as critically endangered in 1996. While it is possible that they also live elsewhere in Australia, Poochera is proud of its dinosaur ants, which draw biologists from all over the world.

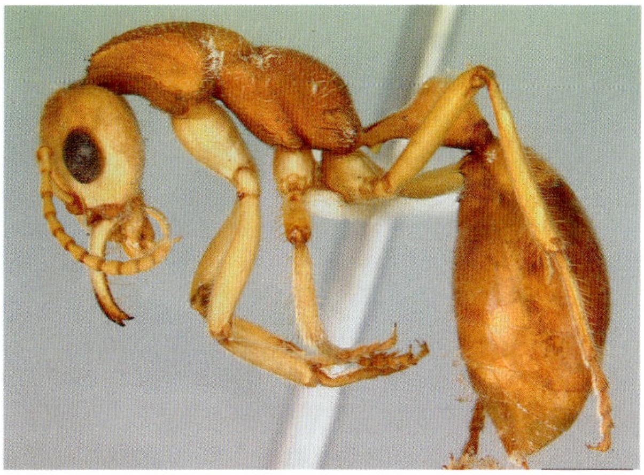

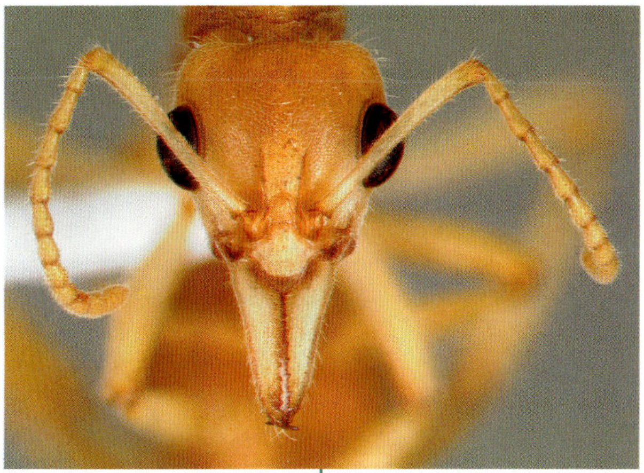

The dinosaur ant has only been found in a few places in southern Australia.
© Atlas of Living Australia

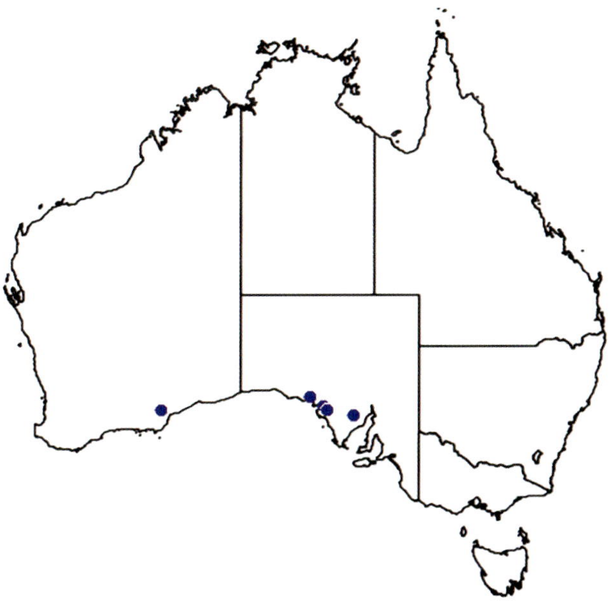

Close-up frontal view of a dinosaur ant head. For a long time, these ants were among the most mysterious on the planet.
© April Nobile, © AntWeb.org, CC 3.0

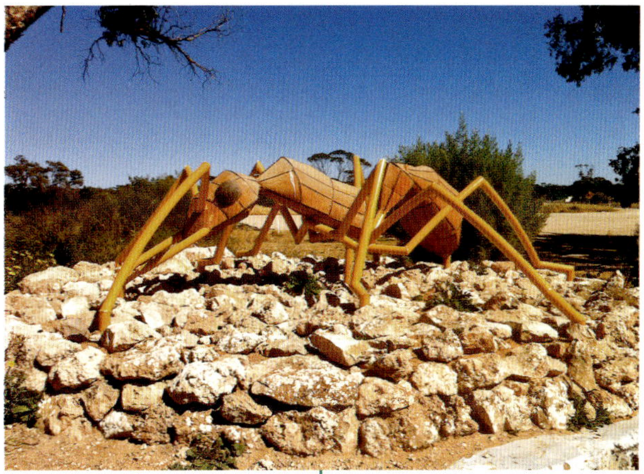

Dinosaur ant sculpture in Poochera.
© Unaimedplaya CC 4.0

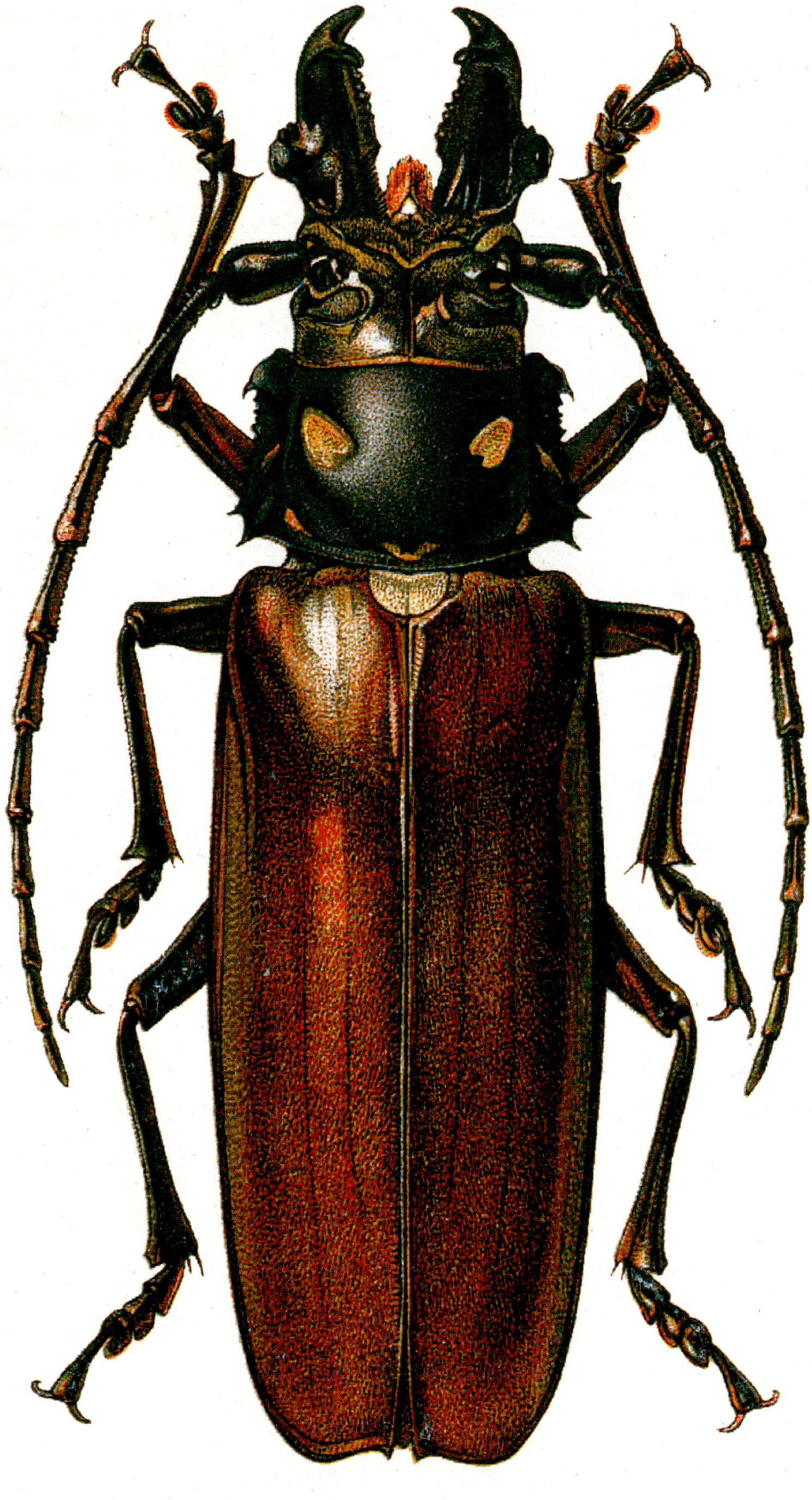

Illustration of *Callipogon relictus* in *Beetles of Russia, Western Europe and Neighboring Countries* (1905), a masterwork by Russian entomologist Georgiy Jacobson (1871–1926).

AN OLD-WORLD RELICT

CALLIPOGON RELICTUS
(COLEOPTERA: CERAMBYCIDAE)

The largest Palearctic beetle is unique for more than just its size. While all the other members of its genus live in the tropical forests of Central and South America, this rare species is only found in the northeastern extremity of Asia.

Callipogon relictus was described in 1898 by Russian entomologist Andrey Semyonov-Tyan-Shansky (1866–1942). Females can reach up to 9 centimeters long, and males up to 11 centimeters. Of the nine species in its genus, *C. relictus* is the only one found in Eurasia. In addition to far-eastern Russia, it is also present in northeastern China (Heilongjiang, Shaanxi, Shanxi, and Inner Mongolia) and the Korean peninsula.

To understand how this beetle ended up so far from its cousins, we have to think back to the time when the Old and New Worlds were still connected. *Callipogon* beetles probably moved north from what is now Latin America during warm periods of the Paleogene (66–23 million years ago) or Neogene (23–2.6 million years ago), when the climate in North America and Eurasia was quasi-tropical. Relict species often have a patchwork range: their habitat expands during periods of global warming, then shrinks into separate patches when global temperatures cool. A given species might survive only in areas with the right conditions or adapt into a new species better suited to the new climate.

C. relictus has been endangered by forest management practices and intense logging (especially in Korea, where keyaki trees are the preferred host for its larvae). Unscrupulous collecting has also contributed to the decline of these iconic insects, which the Republic of Korea named a natural monument in 1968.

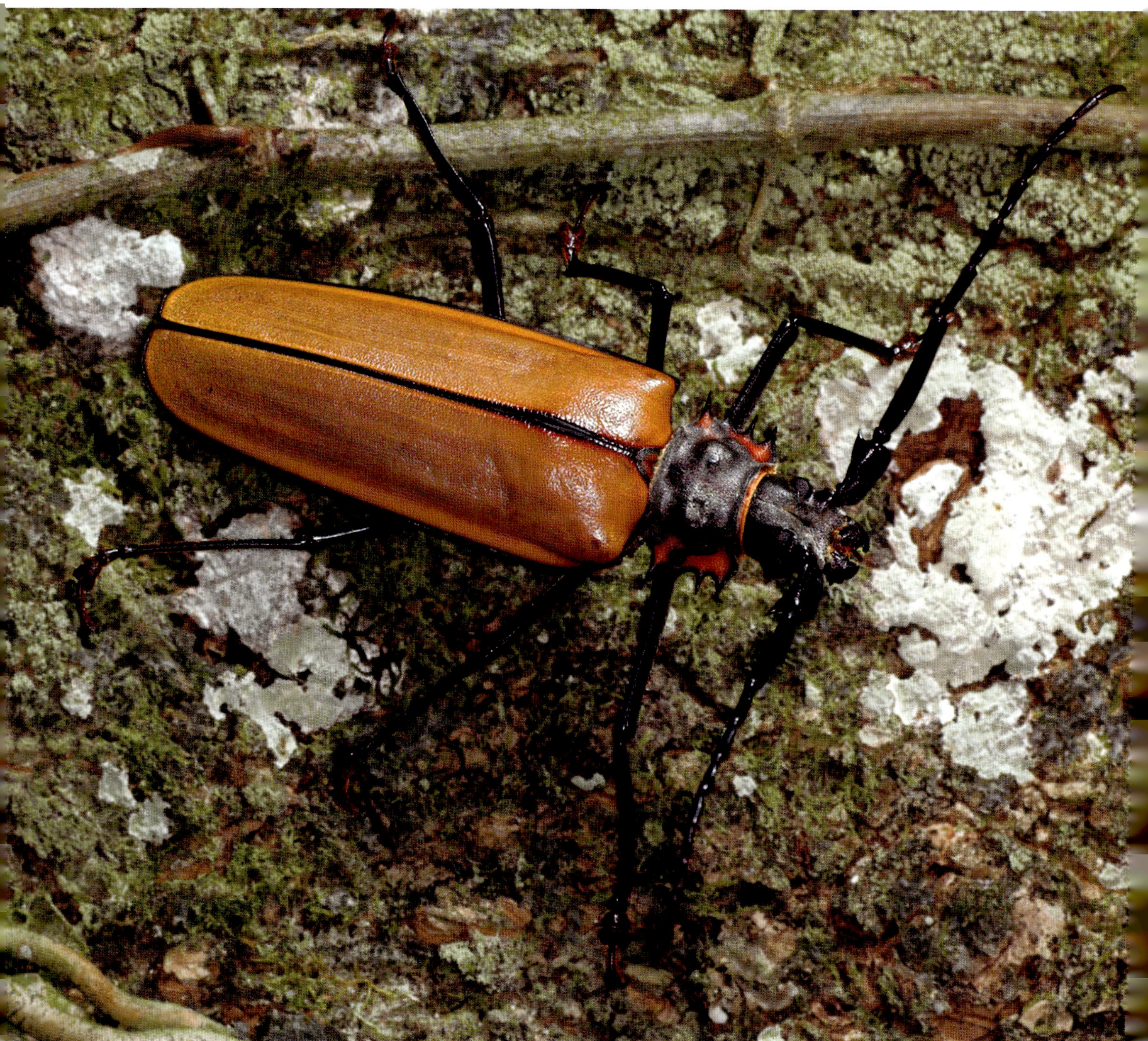

Callipogon armillatum, a 12- to 13-cm-long cousin of *C. relictus*, is a near relative in terms of genetics but not geography—it lives in the American tropics.
© Nikolay Ivshin

SPEEDING UP THE CYCLE

The various threats facing *C. relictus* have made conservationists eager to increase its numbers by breeding the beetles in captivity, then releasing them back into the wild. But because they spend such a long time as larvae (up to several years), captive breeding can be tricky. Biologists have managed to accelerate their life cycle by feeding the larvae sterilized Mongolian oak shavings enriched with oyster mushroom mycelium. This special diet makes them grow much faster, producing large adults (over 10 centimeters) in just one year and showing that, like other saproxylic insects, how fast they develop depends on the amount of fungal matter in their food.

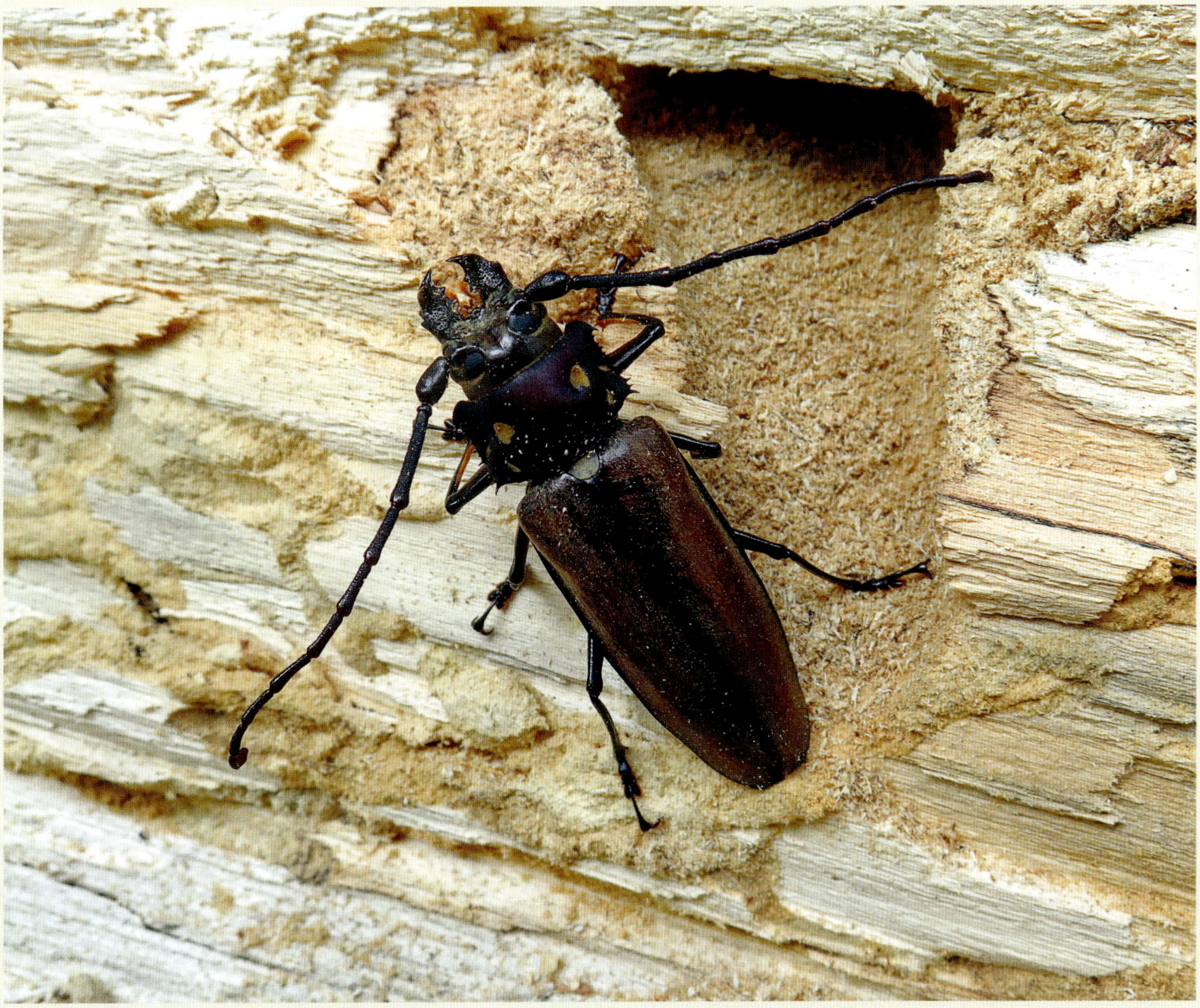

C. relictus **male emerging from the cradle where it pupated.**

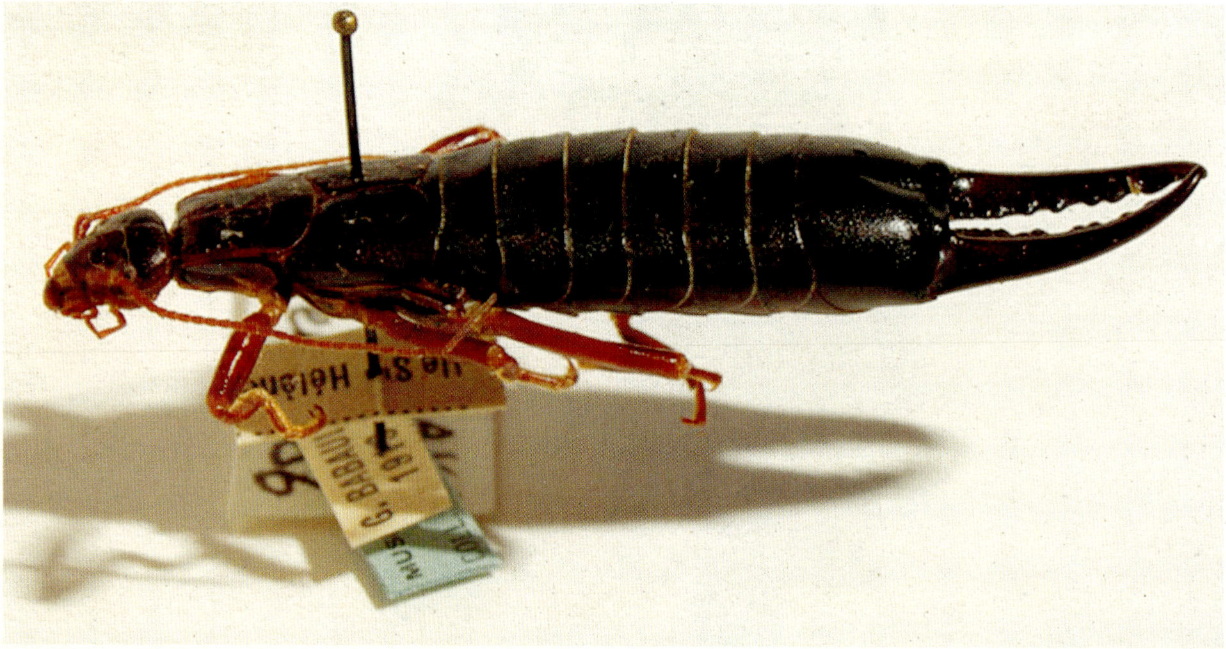

Female *Labidura herculeana* specimen conserved at the French National Museum of Natural History in Paris.

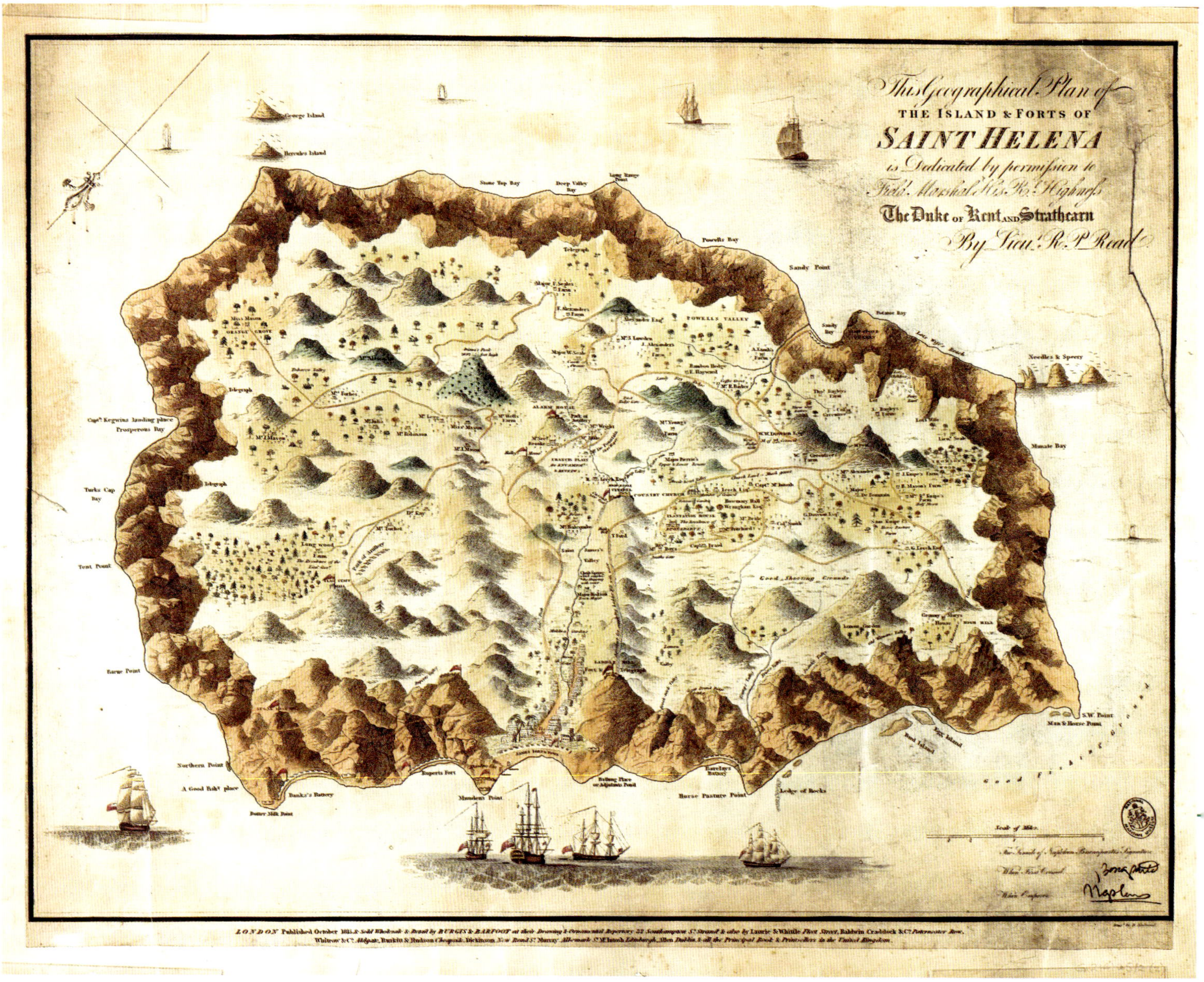

THE EARWIG AT THE ENDS OF THE EARTH

LABIDURA HERCULEANA

(DERMAPTERA: LABIDURIDAE)

The Saint Helena earwig—a giant measuring up to 8 centimeters long—was described in 1798 by Danish naturalist Johan Christian Fabricius (1745–1808). It was more or less forgotten until 1959, when researchers studying birds on the remote island of Saint Helena found the remains of enormous pincers on Prosperous Bay Plain. Entomologists would later discover these giant earwigs living in burrows under large rocks on Horse Point Plain.

On May 24, 1967, Belgian entomologist Narcisse Leleup (1912–2001) captured six Saint Helena earwigs not far from Longwood House, where Napoleon Bonaparte spent his final years in exile. The date became a sad marker in insect history: *Labidura herculeana* has not been observed alive since. A search organized by the London Zoo in 1988 and subsequent searches in 1993, 1995, 2000, and 2003 were all in vain. (In 1995, only pincers were found.) The IUCN declared the species extinct in 2014.

Saint Helena is an island of volcanic rock located in the South Atlantic Ocean, roughly 2,000 kilometers from the African coast and 3,500 kilometers from Brazil. It was never part of the African or American continents, and its flora and fauna either evolved from species that landed there by their own means or were introduced by humans. The Saint Helena earwig falls into the first category. Its morphology is close to that of the shore earwig (*Labidura riparia*), and it was mistaken

The island of Saint Helena was once a famous place of exile for enemies of the British Crown. Notable residents included Dinuzulu kaCetshwayo (the last king of the Zulu nation), Khalid bin Barghash (the sixth sultan of Zanzibar), and, of course, Napoleon, who lived there from 1815 until his death in 1821. In addition to making it a good place to send exiles, the island's extreme remoteness also explains its wealth of endemic plants and animals.

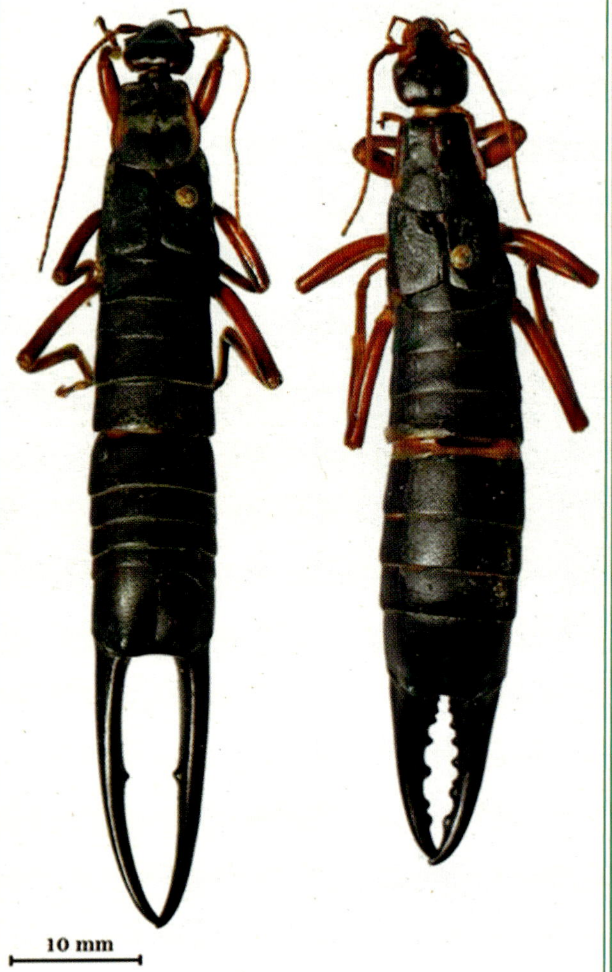

Pair of Saint Helena earwigs (*Labidura herculeana*).
© Piotr Naskrecki CC 2.0

for a subspecies of *L. riparia* for many years. The Saint Helena earwig likely evolved from the shore earwig when it adapted to fit a new ecological niche: while shore earwigs live on sandy beaches, Saint Helena earwigs lived in burrows (from which they only emerged at night) on coastal plains or rocky areas near bird colonies.

Why did this insect disappear from a landscape that remained relatively well preserved for centuries, even after being colonized by humans? Like other island insects (see pages 93 and 147), the Saint Helena earwig fell victim to animals intentionally or accidentally introduced by colonists starting in the sixteenth century: goats, cats, rats, and other predators, including an invasive centipede (*Scolopendra morsitans*). The earwig also suffered from deforestation and—in what was probably the final straw—the construction of an airport in Prosperous Bay, its last known habitat, in 2012.

Prosperous Bay Plain—the last place the Saint Helena earwig was found alive, in 1967—is now home to an airport.
© Kevstan CC 4.0

MATERNAL INSTINCT

The Saint Helena earwig was closely related to the shore earwig and probably had similar reproductive behavior. Shore earwigs are predators and occasionally cannibals, so the male runs no small risk when courting a mate. The female lays her eggs in a burrow where she remains without feeding to watch over her eggs, licking them and keeping them clean of mold. She even continues to care for the larvae after they hatch; she keeps them in a group, protects them from predators, and feeds them or at least guides them to food. This happy family splits up as soon as the larvae undergo their first molt, however. Then the mother earwig does not hesitate to eat her own offspring if the opportunity arises.

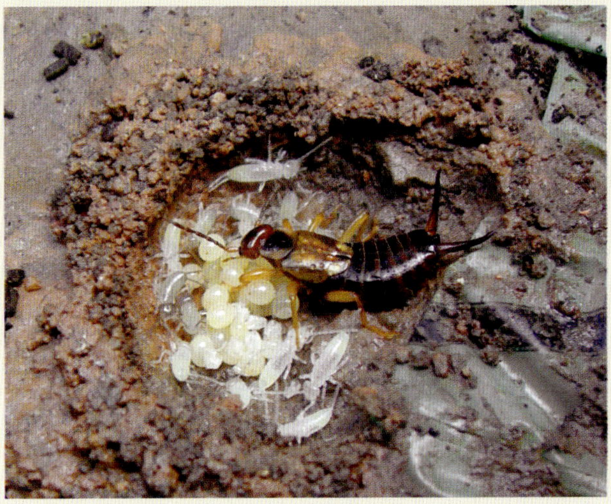

Female shore earwig (*Labidura riparia*) watching over her eggs.

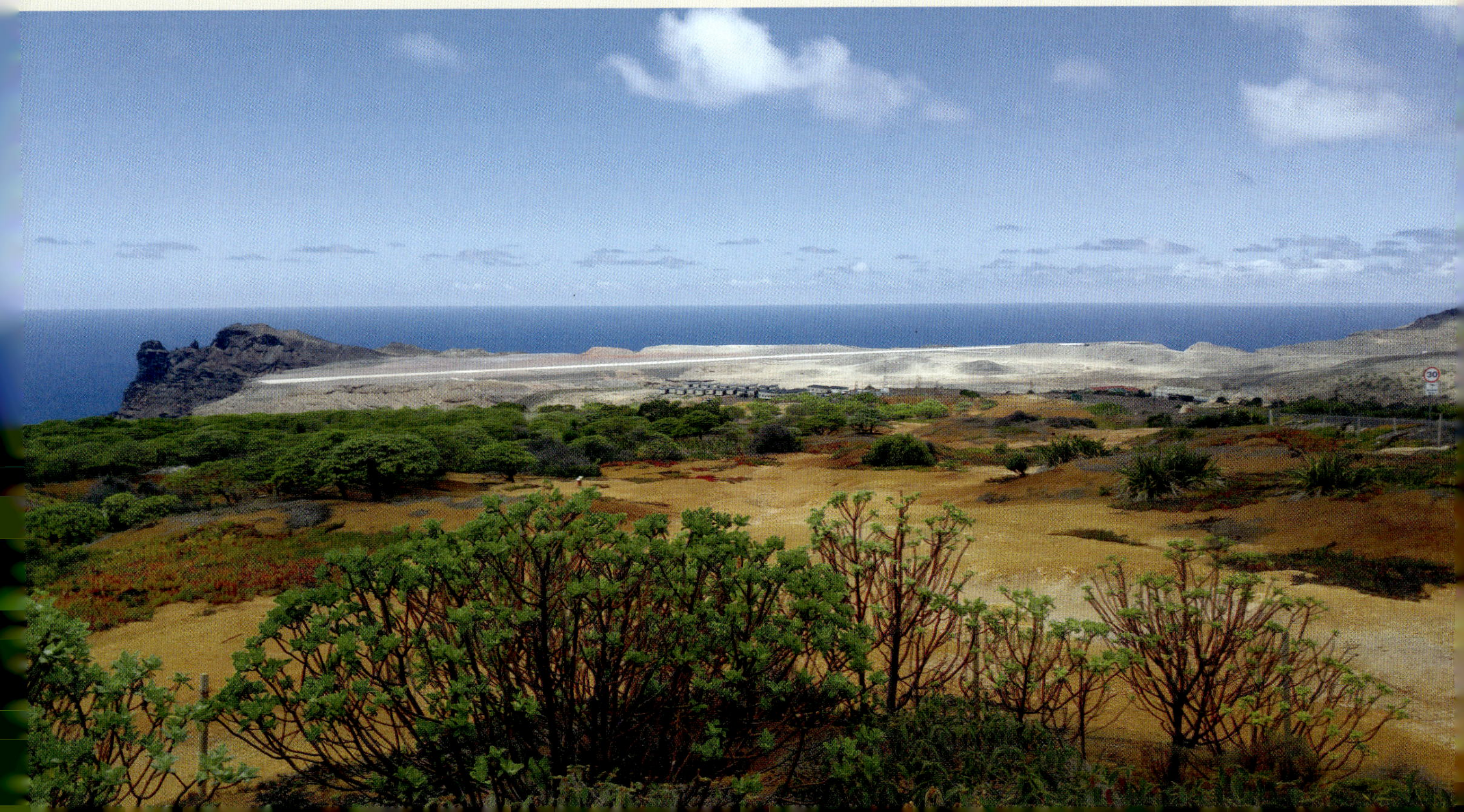

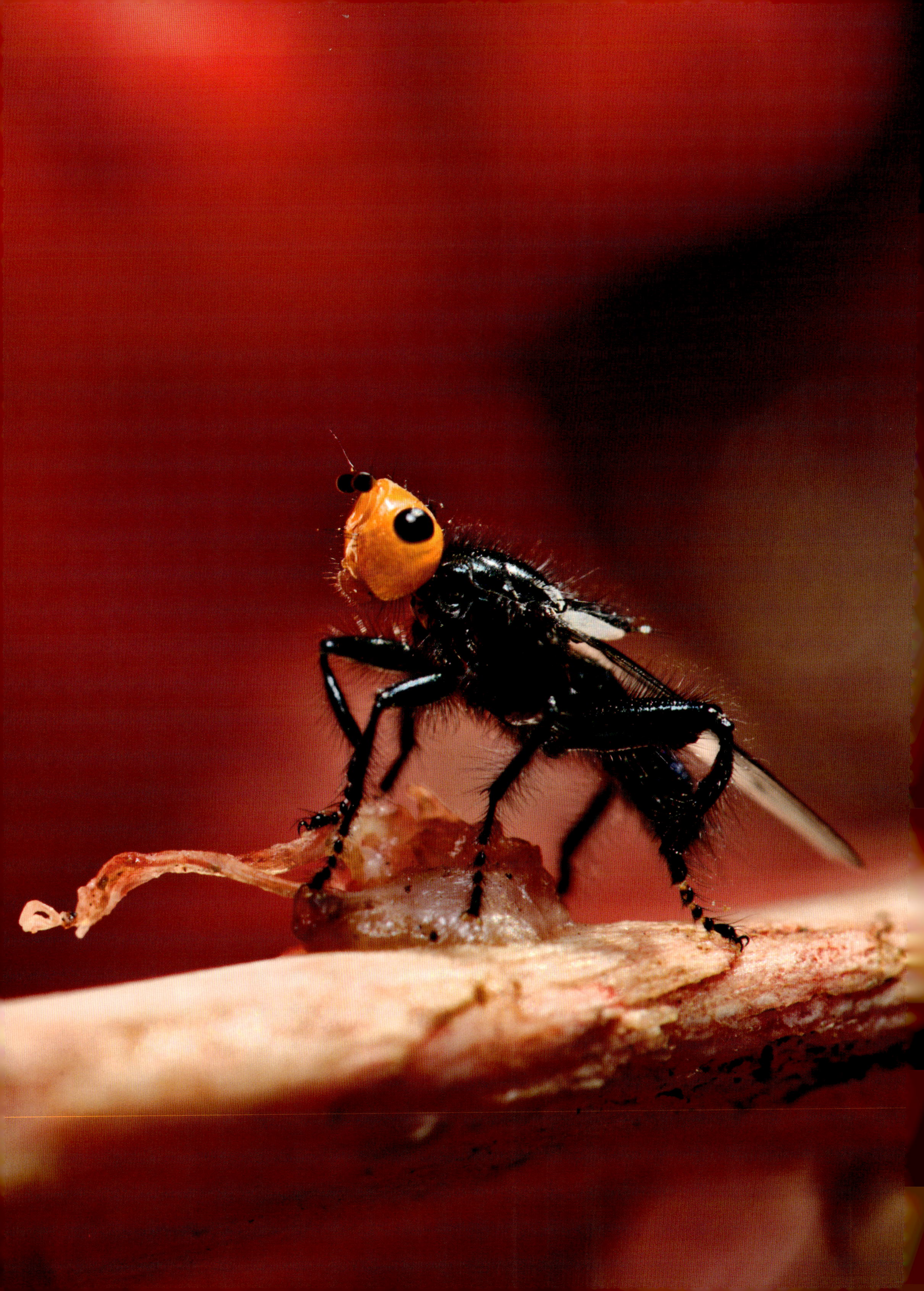

BACK FROM THE DEAD

THYREOPHORA CYNOPHILA

(DIPTERA: PIOPHILIDAE)

The fly known as the bone skipper was described by German naturalist Georg W. F. Panzer (1755–1829) in 1798. Panzer named the species *cynophila* ("dog lover") because he captured the first specimen from a dog carcass in Mannheim. Bone skippers were later observed in Germany, Austria, and various parts of France, including by Jean-Baptiste Robineau-Desvoidy, who spotted some on a horse carcass near Paris in 1849, for what would prove to be the last time.

. . . Until the winter of 2007, that is. Spanish entomologist Daniel Martín-Vega was studying insects that feed on carrion in the countryside outside Madrid when he found six bone skippers in one of his traps. The incredible discovery added to the sixteen collected specimens scattered among a few European museums. It had been over 150 years since humans had caught a glimpse of this strange, pumpkin-headed fly.

Since then, bone skippers have been found in the Sierra de Cebollera nature reserve and other sites in the northern Iberian peninsula. A citizen science initiative located some in Ariège, France, in February 2019 and parts of the Pyrenees in the winter of 2019–20. The elusive fly could very well be living elsewhere in Europe—people just need to look in the right places at the right time!

Not much is known about the bone skipper's biology. The flies are nocturnal and active from November to March. Adults are drawn to the rotting carcasses of large mammals, where they spend the daylight hours hiding in eye sockets and other cavities. The larvae develop over fifteen to twenty days in the bone marrow and move by curling and

[The bone skipper (Thyreophora *cynophila*) is 6–10 mm long. Its legs and body are metallic blue and contrast with its bright orange head.

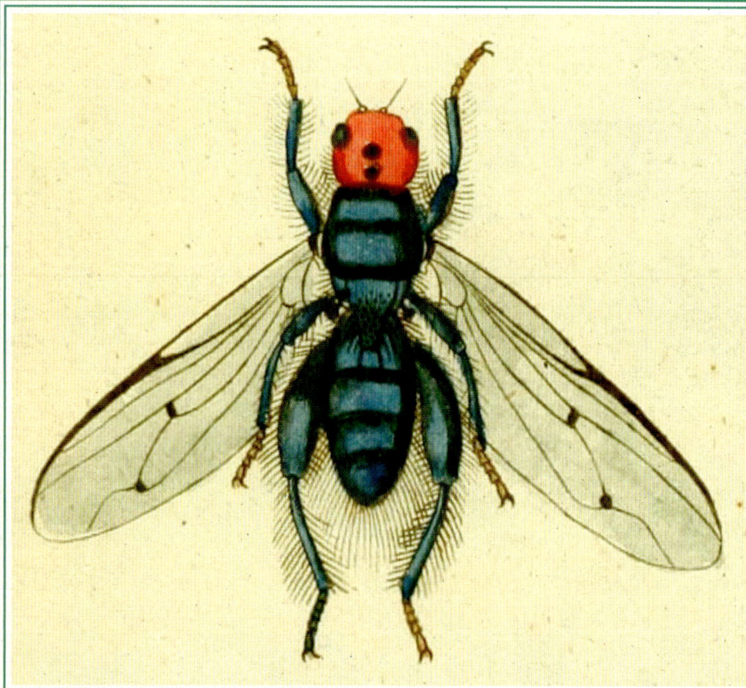

French entomologist Justin Macquart (1776–1855) claimed that the bone skipper's head could glow in the dark. While that proved to be false, his description in *Histoire naturelle des insectes diptères* (1835) still makes for excellent horror movie material: he claimed the fly "dwells among shadows and desiccated corpses. By the dark light of its phosphoric head, it flocks to fleshless bones and gorges on the last remains of animality."

Engraving from *Fauna Germanica* (1794) by Georg W. F. Panzer.

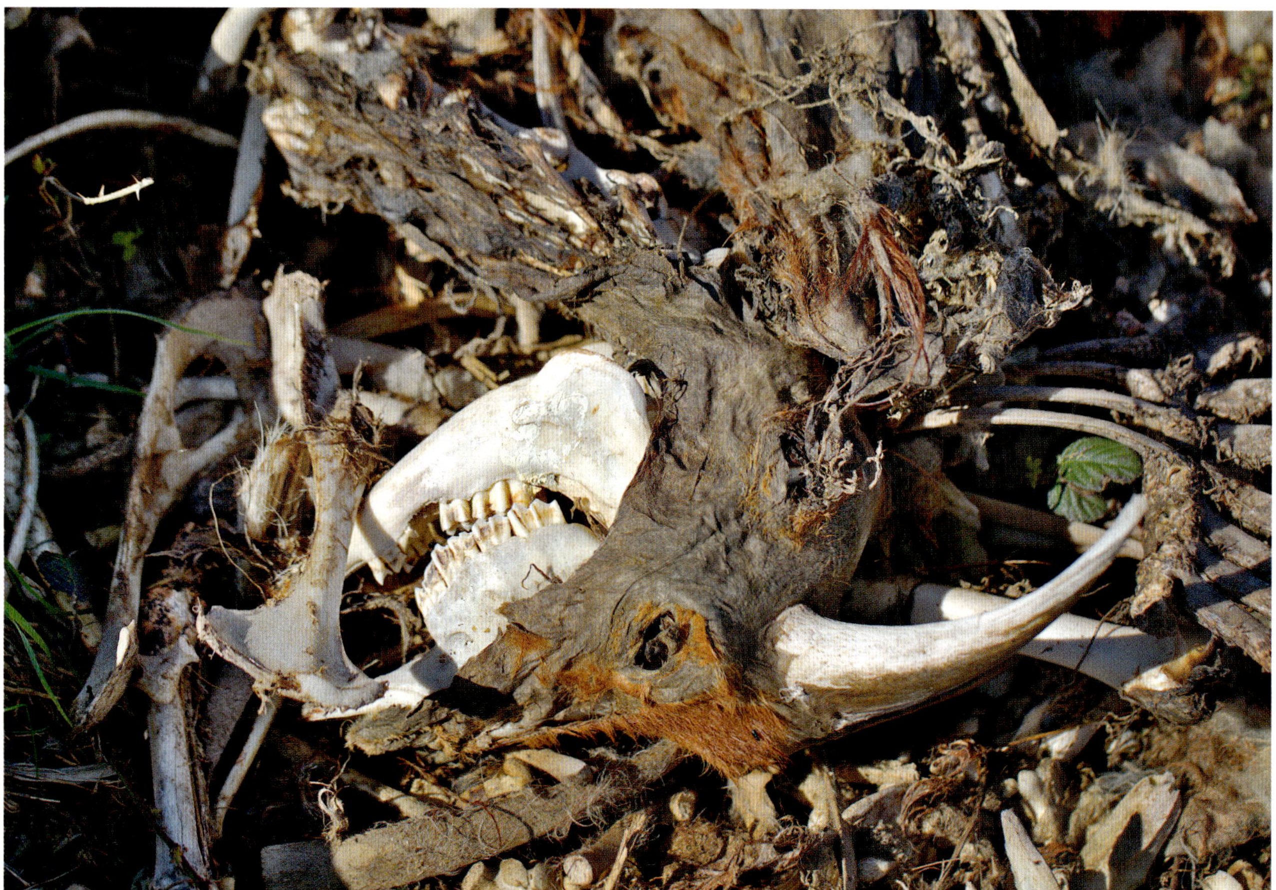

This goat carcass in an advanced stage of decomposition is an ideal microhabitat for bone skippers.

© Frédéric Azémar

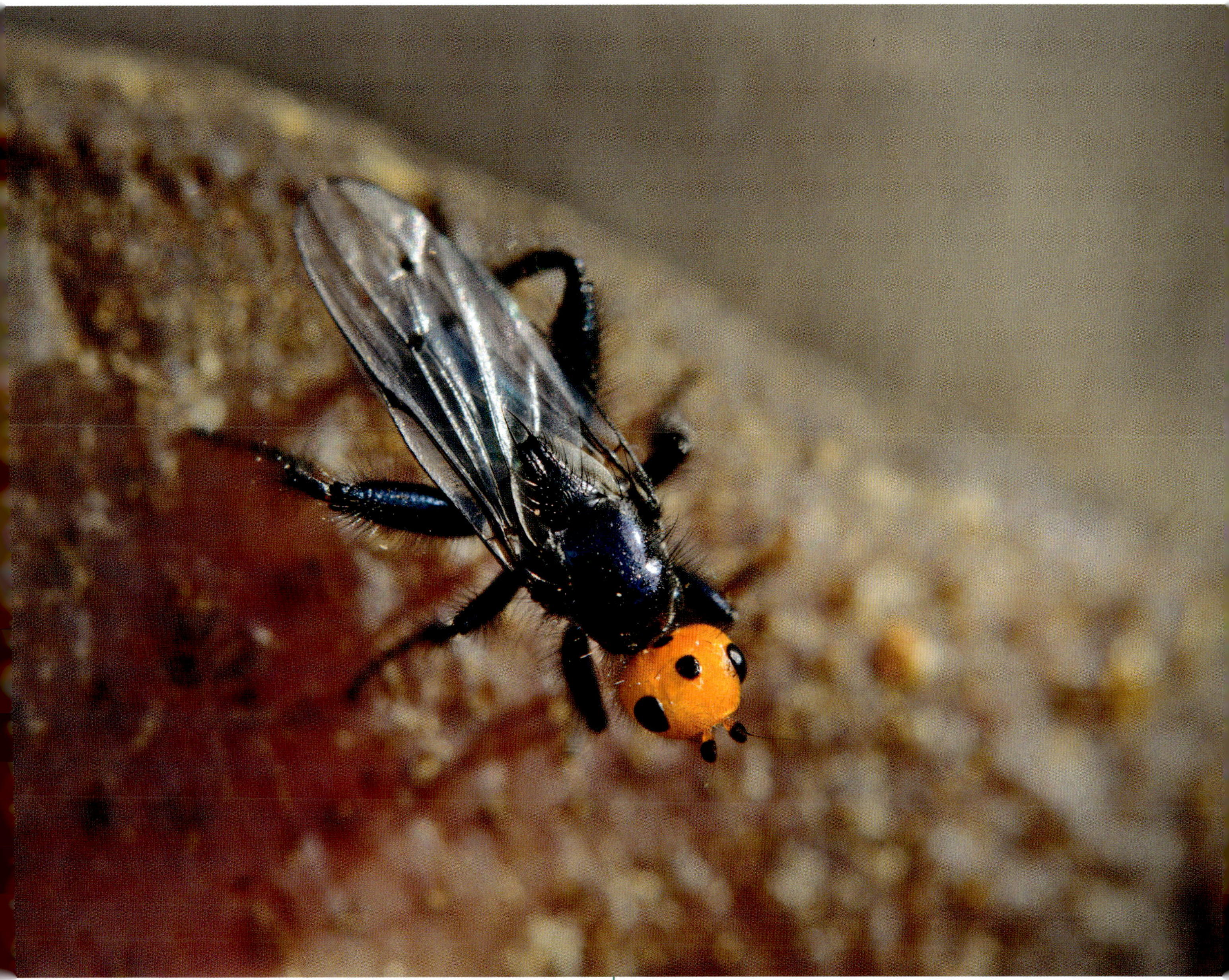

A bone skipper perching on a piece of rotting flesh.
© Frédéric Azémar

uncurling their bodies in a "skipping" motion, the source of their common name. The flies metamorphose underground, where they also stay dormant in summer, and produce two generations per year, one at the end of winter and one at the end of autumn.

There are several factors that might explain why bone skippers have so rarely been observed: fewer wolves and other large predators capable of breaking open the bones of animal carcasses, the systematic eradication of scavengers, and habitat fragmentation, to name a few. Also, entomologists tend not to peer into the orifices of rotting horse and donkey carcasses in winter. Whatever the reason, now that the bone skipper is back from the dead, it is time to study whether its populations can be sustained and how it can be protected.

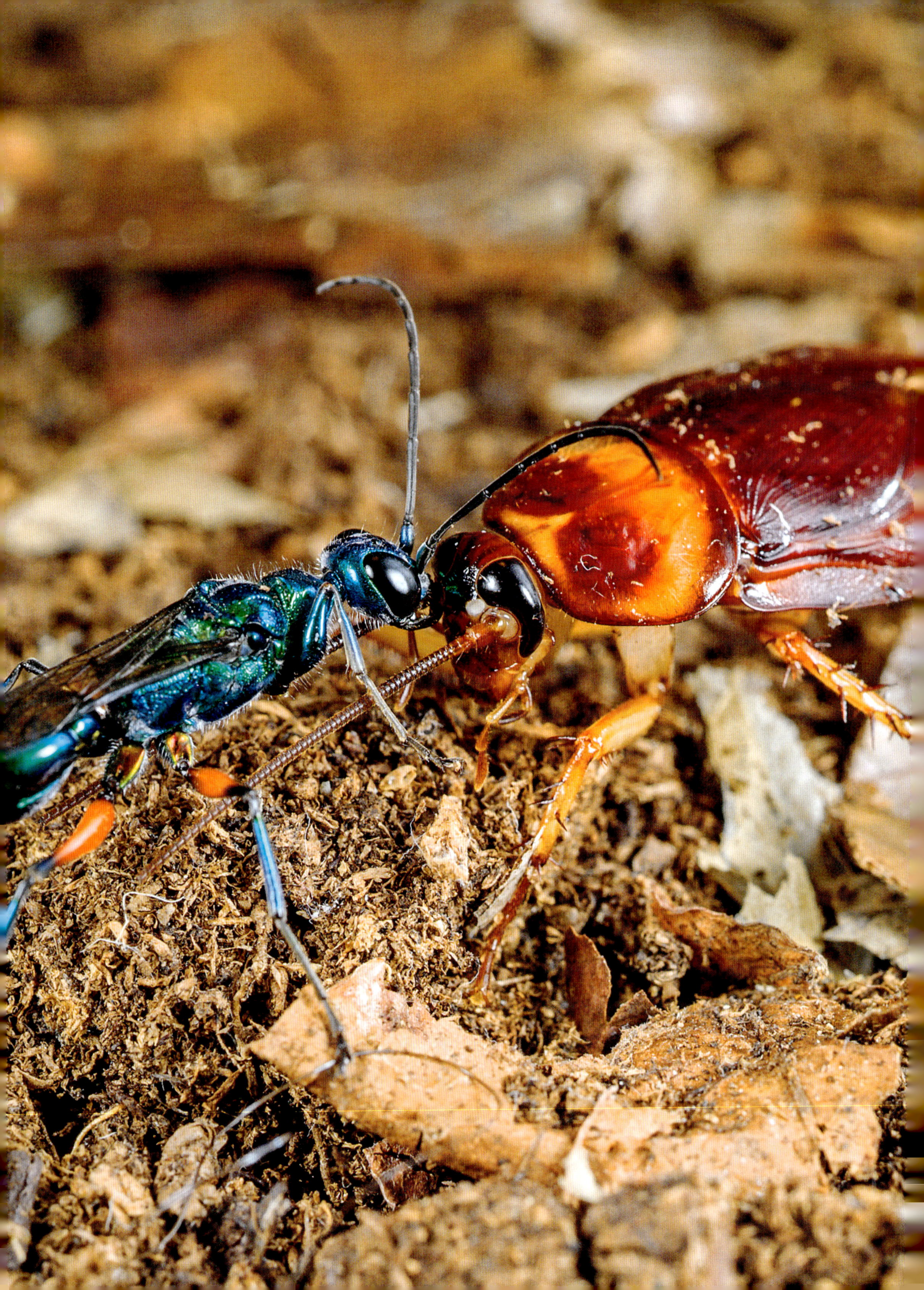

MIGRANTS AND INVADERS

Insects are astonishingly good at conquering new territory—their malleable genetics, small size, and adaptability have allowed them to establish populations in the unlikeliest of places. They have colonized remote islands after crossing the ocean on floating rafts of vegetation or being swept off course by the wind. They have adapted to the desolate cold of the Antarctic. They have even taken advantage of human migration and globalized commerce to make a home for themselves on every continent on Earth. And their travels have left a mark on human history: think of the swarms of locusts that have terrorized farmers since the dawn of agriculture, or the unstoppable advance of the Colorado potato beetle across much of the planet in the space of fifty years.

Other insects are seasonal travelers. Some, like the monarch butterfly, migrate over vast distances—becoming stars in the process. With species like the monarch facing dire threats to their survival, urgent and well-tailored action is needed to protect these transcontinental nomads.

The emerald cockroach wasp (*Ampulex compressa*) has followed the American cockroach (*Periplaneta americana*) to nearly every tropical region of the globe. The wasp, a parasitoid, turns the cockroach into a zombie by stinging it in specific parts of its ganglia and taking control of its motor functions. The wasp then leads the much larger cockroach by the antennae to its nest, where the roach will serve as food for the wasp's larvae.

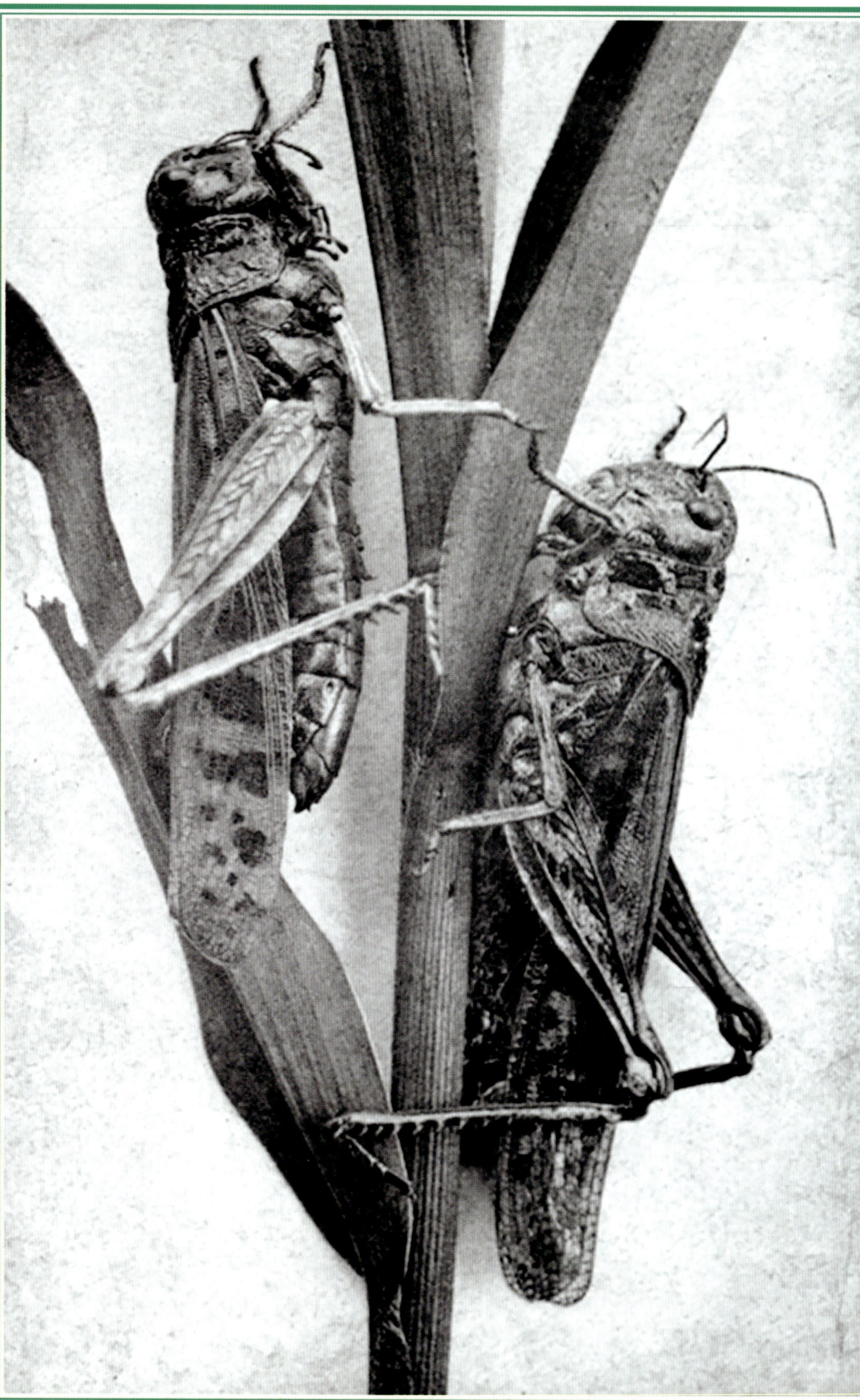

This photograph of Rocky Mountain locusts from 1870 is one of the few ever taken.

A SWARM FROM THE WEST

MELANOPLUS SPRETUS

(ORTHOPTERA: ACRIDIDAE)

The Rocky Mountain locust, once one of the largest insect populations in the world, is now extinct. It was known and reviled throughout the western United States and parts of western Canada, but only reproduced regularly in the Rockies. Every other year, the adults took to the air in swarms to feed on prairie plants and crops east of the mountains.

Melanoplus spretus was described in 1866 by American entomologist Benjamin D. Walsh (1808–1869). It once gathered in swarms larger than any of its African cousins, including the migratory locust and red locust. The species became known to European settlers in the eighteenth century, when farmers moving west began to encounter them. People lived in terror of the moment when, having left their reproductive habitat, the locusts formed immense whitish clouds up to 3,000 kilometers long and 200 kilometers wide, blocking out the sun for three or four days straight. In 1875, a swarm of Rocky Mountain locusts made up of 12.5 trillion insects and weighing a total of 27 million tons was reported to cover 510,000 square kilometers: an area larger than the state of California! Wherever it landed, this superorganism devoured more than just crops: garden covers, sheep's wool, wooden fences, leather saddles . . . nothing was safe. Although the locusts did lay eggs in the Great Plains, they never or hardly ever developed there, as they were ill adapted to the habitat.

Less than thirty years after the great swarm of 1875, the species had disappeared. On July 19, 1902, Norman Criddle (1875–1933), a Canadian entomologist specialized in pest control, captured a pair in his family's garden in Treesbank, Manitoba. How could he imagine that they would be the last ever to be observed alive? The Rocky Mountain locust was so abundant in the nineteenth century that no one thought to collect them—for this reason, almost none have been preserved.

A combination of factors led to the locust's extinction. In addition to nineteenth-century campaigns to eradicate the "plague" by poisoning or crushing Rocky Mountain locusts, changes in

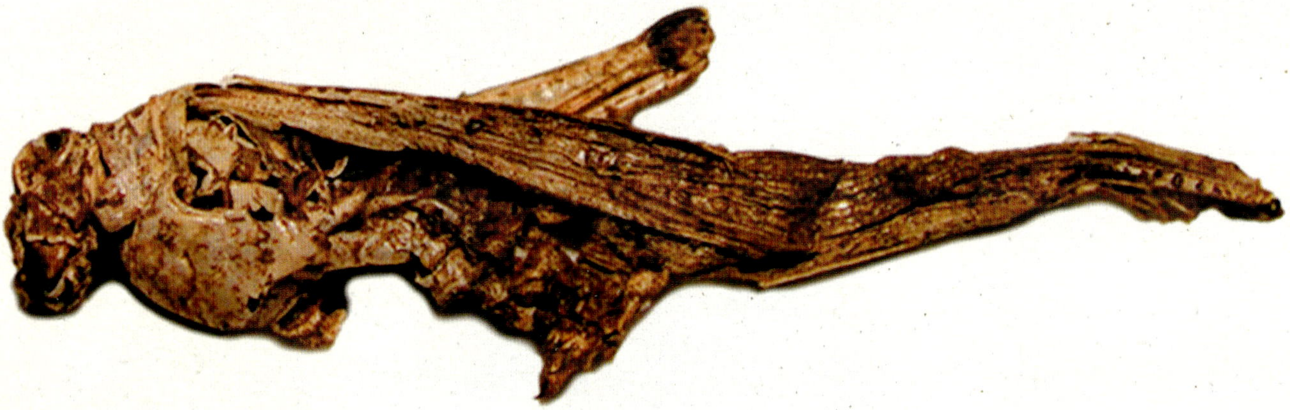

Grasshopper Glacier in Montana is named for the millions of grasshoppers preserved in its ice, where they were probably driven off course by the wind hundreds or thousands of years ago. While many are unrecognizable (especially as melting ice has caused them to decompose) some are well preserved enough to be identified as Rocky Mountain locusts, including this "mummified" specimen.

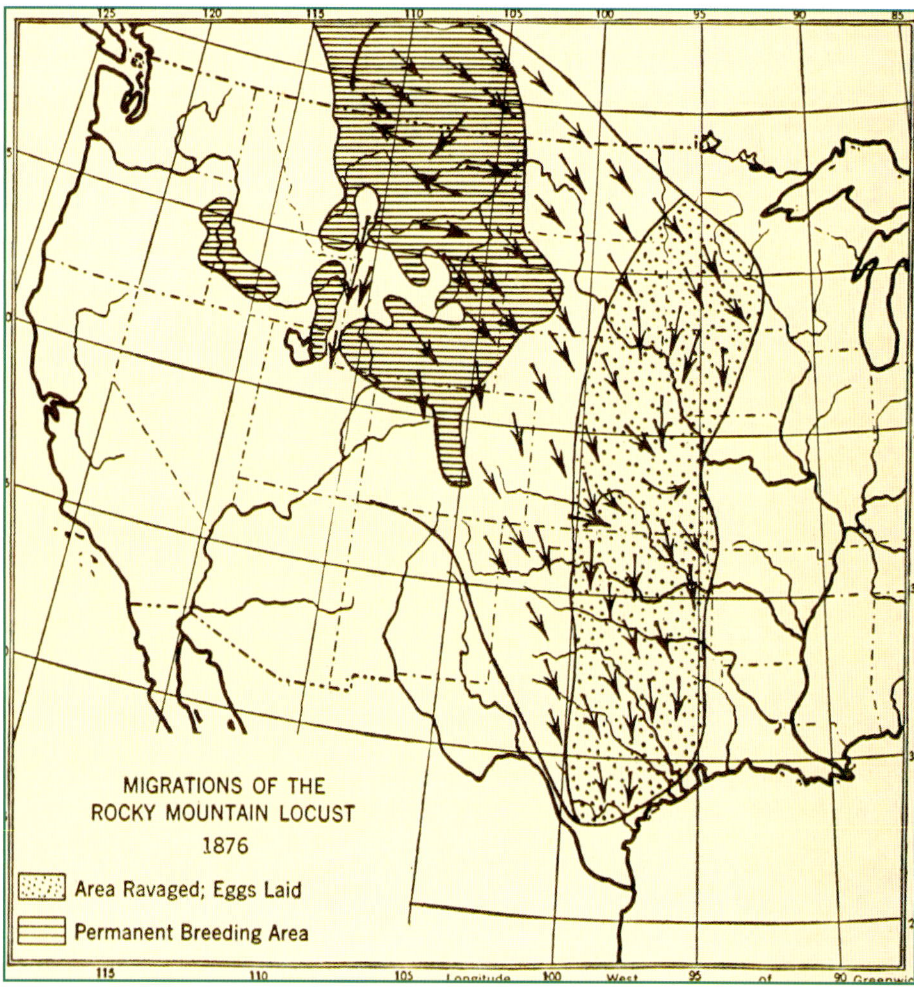

The Rocky Mountain locust left its reproductive habitat to swarm over the Great Plains roughly every other year, as shown in this map from 1876.

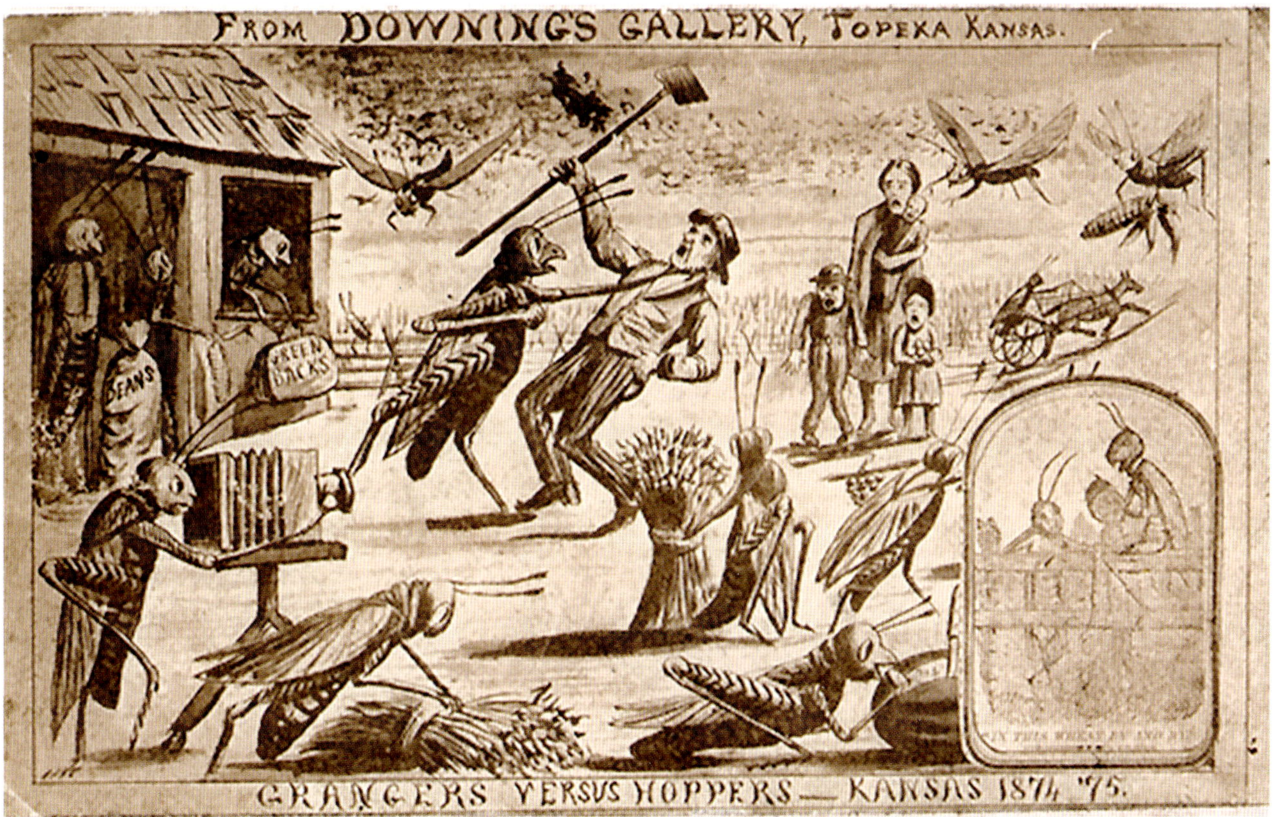

Farmers waged war on Rocky Mountain locusts in the nineteenth century, as parodied in this 1874 cartoon by Henry Worrall (1825–1902).

agricultural practices also accelerated their decline, including the introduction of winter wheat, which was harvested before their migration period, and alfalfa, which they were unable to digest. More importantly, the expansion of farming to their permanent breeding area—moist, sandy riverbanks in the Rockies—meant their eggs were massively and regularly destroyed.

Because locusts are a form of grasshopper that only appear when the population reaches a certain density, some entomologists have suggested that individual *Melanoplus spretus* may have survived in the Rockies for over a century in their solitary phase. The mystery remains to this day. Whatever the case may be, the IUCN declared the Rocky Mountain locust extinct in 2014.

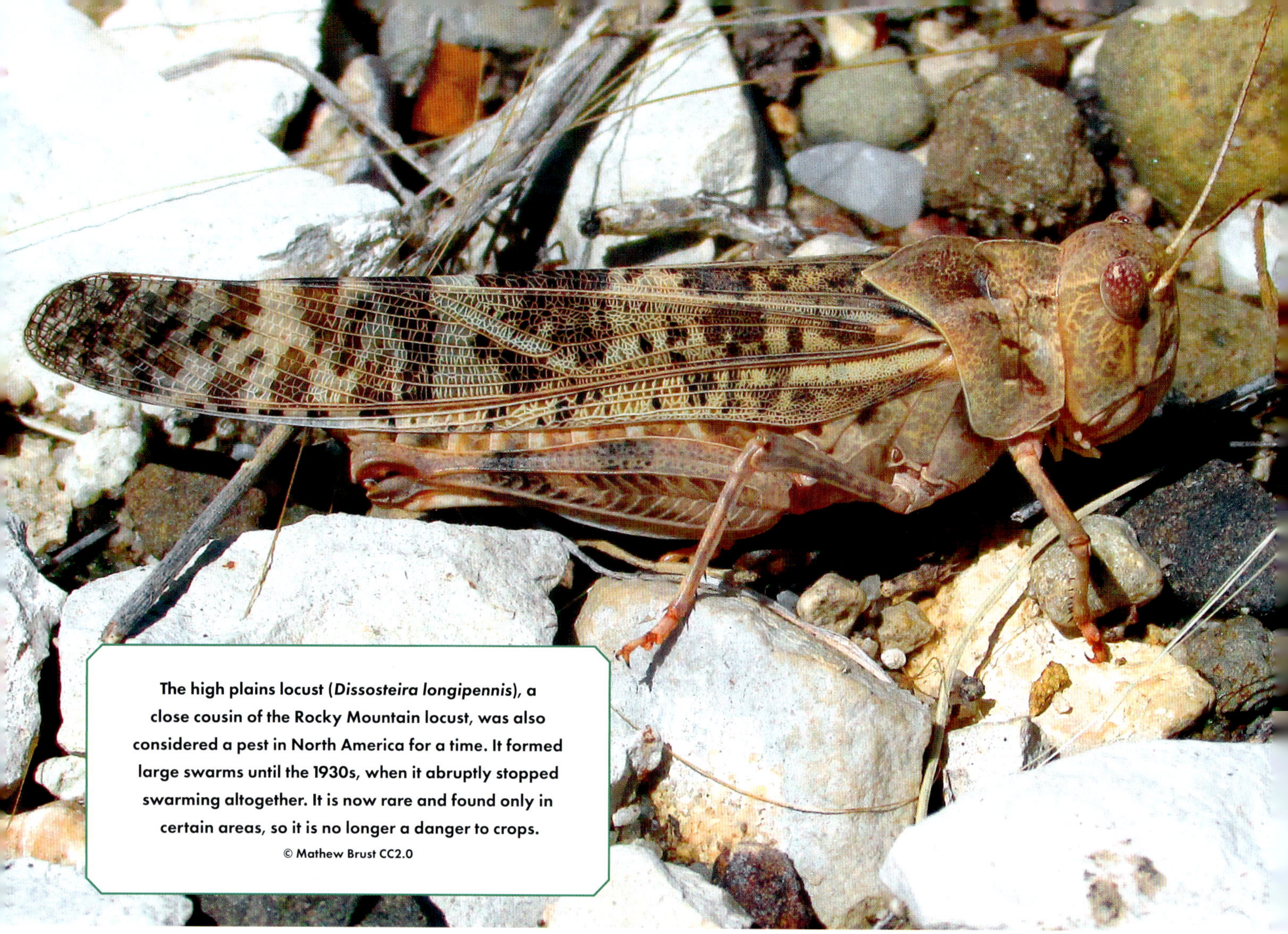

The high plains locust (*Dissosteira longipennis*), a close cousin of the Rocky Mountain locust, was also considered a pest in North America for a time. It formed large swarms until the 1930s, when it abruptly stopped swarming altogether. It is now rare and found only in certain areas, so it is no longer a danger to crops.

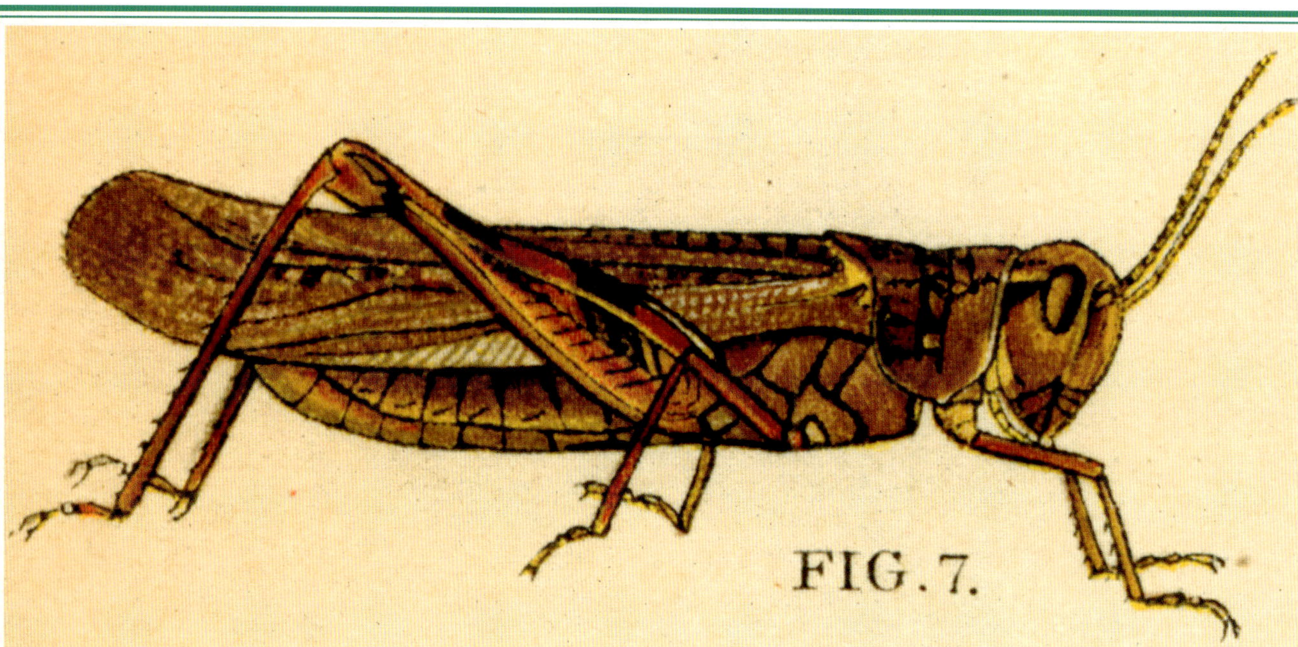

Illustration of the Rocky Mountain locust from 1902. Now extinct, these locusts once gathered in the most impressive swarms ever observed.

IT'S JUST A PHASE

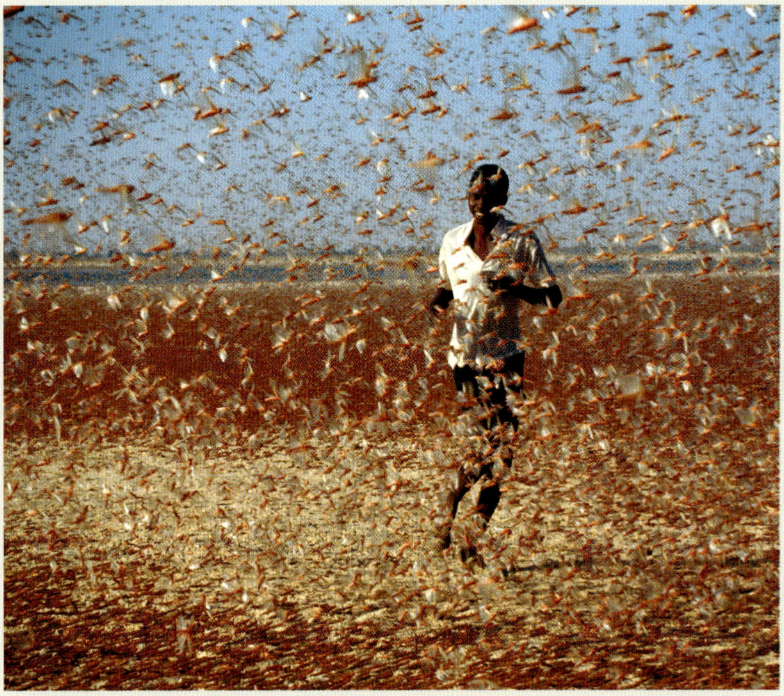

The term "locust" applies to any species of grasshopper that periodically migrates in swarms for hundreds or thousands of kilometers. What sets locusts apart from other grasshoppers (which can also exhibit gregarious behavior and cause damage to crops) is that their color, size, and body proportions—as well as their behavior and habits—change so much in their swarming phase that they have sometimes been mistaken for a different species. Locusts have solitary, gregarious, and intermediary phases. How susceptible they are to phase transition depend on their species, sex, life experiences, and group conditions. The desert locust (*Schistocerca gregaria*) begins to show signs of transitioning to the gregarious phase when the density of winged individuals reaches five hundred per hectare; for the migratory locust (*Locusta migratoria*), it is two thousand per hectare. When large numbers are gathered together, the effects are immediately visible: the insects change in color and behavior, and their offspring will have a slightly different body shape and physiology. The transition is just as rapid in reverse. When locusts in the gregarious phase are isolated from one another, their offspring quickly revert to the solitary phase.

The phenomenon is a survival mechanism. Locusts gather in swarms when environmental conditions, such as a drought, force them to migrate in search of food. The desert locust is able to roam the farthest: in 1988, swarms crossed the Atlantic Ocean from Africa to reach the Caribbean and South America!

Top: Locusts are grasshoppers capable of proliferating into massive swarms to migrate, as in this picture taken in Senegal.

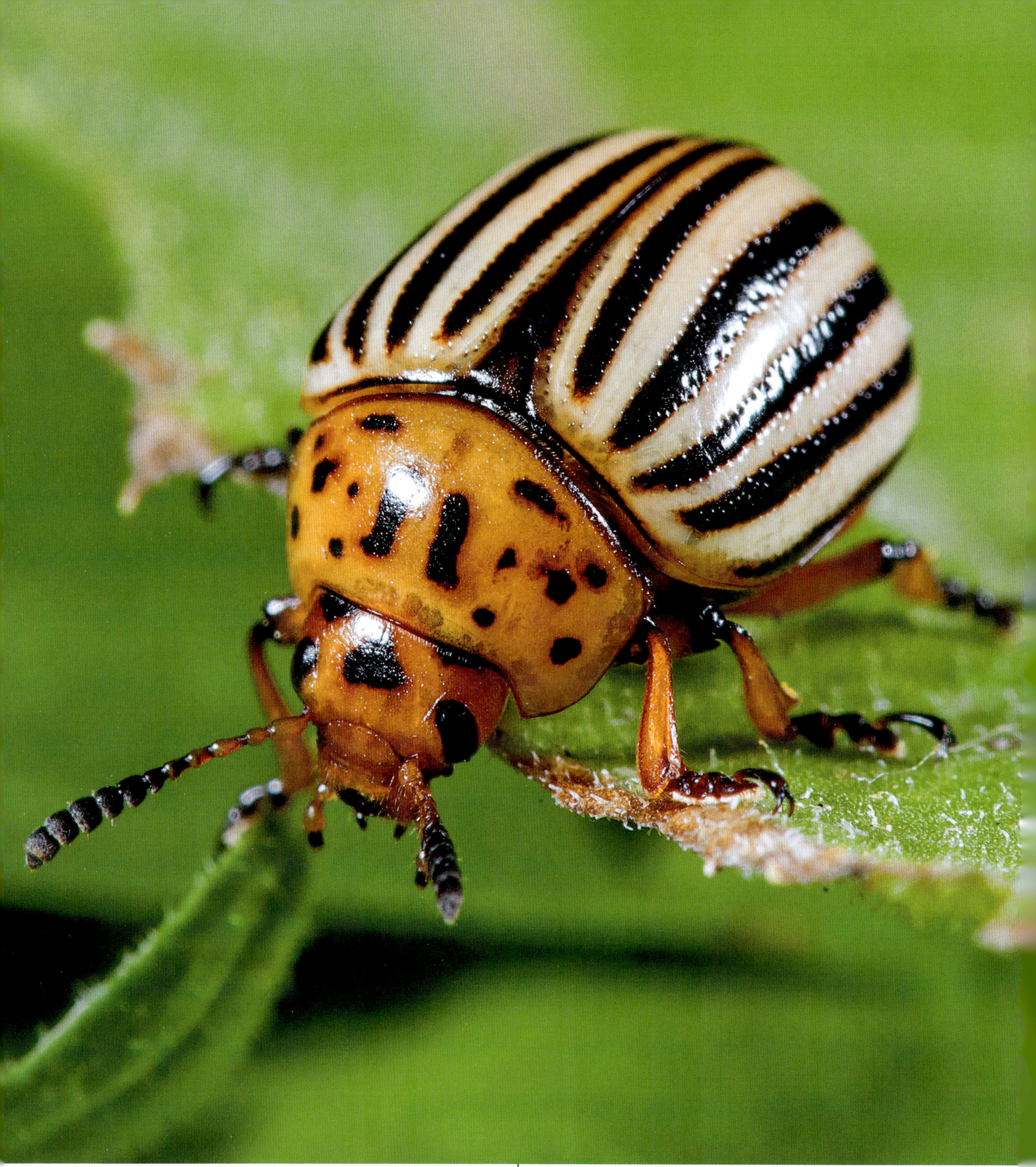

The Colorado potato beetle is roughly 10 mm long and instantly recognizable by the elegant pattern of ten stripes on its elytra (whence its species name, *decemlineata*, and common names like "ten-striped spearman"). Its fat, pink, rounded larvae are also easy to identify. Both adults and larvae can be found in great numbers in potato fields. Like its close cousins, the beetle produces leptinotarsin, a potent neurotoxin that protects it from most predators.

WILL TRAVEL FOR POTATOES

LEPTINOTARSA DECEMLINEATA

(COLEOPTERA: CHRYSOMELIDAE)

What is so special about this small beetle with a taste for potato plants? Undoubtedly the incredible lengths it has gone to eat them, which gives it pride of place alongside the *Phylloxera* and Rocky Mountain locust as one of the most famous agricultural pests in history.

Despite its name, the Colorado potato beetle originally comes from the remote plateaus of Mexico, where it fed on wild nightshade plants. It is also known as the ten-striped spearman or ten-lined potato beetle, for the distinctive dark stripes on its elytra. It is a species of leaf beetle, first observed in the Colorado Rockies in 1811 by English naturalist Thomas Nuttall (1786–1859), who found it feeding on a wild nightshade, the buffalo bur (*Solanum rostratum*). Both beetle and plant were likely introduced to the region accidentally by Mexican herders. The species was described in 1824 by American entomologist Thomas Say (1787–1834) based on specimens collected in the Rockies, where the beetles lived quietly for three decades without drawing much attention to themselves and developed on various nightshades.

The story might have ended there. But the beetle's destiny changed forever when it discovered a new nightshade from South America that was being planted farther and farther west in the 1840s and '50s: the potato. It was love at first bite. Stories of ravaged potato fields began to pour in, starting with Nebraska in 1859. The beetles could strip 80 percent of the vegetation from a potato field in addition to spreading pathogens that attacked the plants. Flying from one field to the next, within twenty-five years they had conquered the entire United States east of the Rockies. Then they took the West Coast as well, advancing at an average rate of 8 kilometers per hour. In 1869, the Detroit River was covered with a layer of drowned potato beetles, and newspapers reported swarms so large they caused trains to skid on their tracks. The beetle reached Canada in 1870,

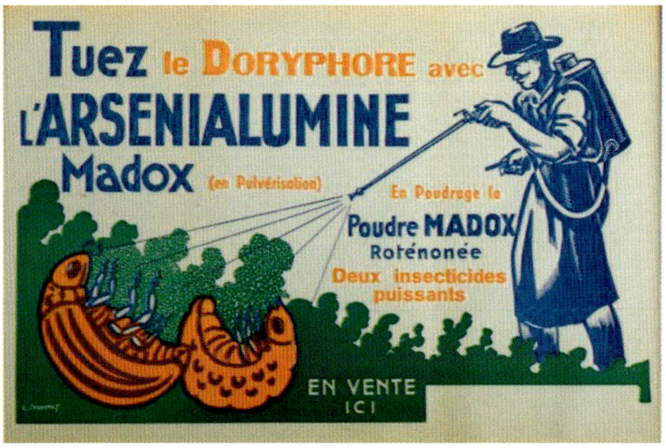

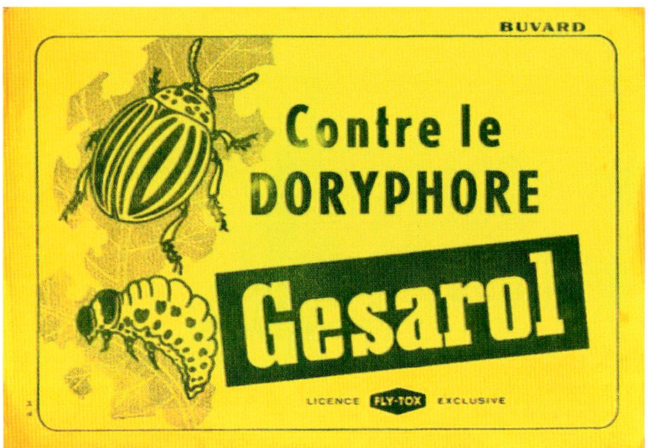

Arsenic compounds were commonly used as insecticides from the late nineteenth century to the modern era. Aluminum arsenate, in particular, was sprayed onto potato plants to prevent the spread of Colorado potato beetles. Other chemical insecticides, like Gesarol (a trade name for DDT), were used on a massive scale against the beetles. Besides being carcinogenic to humans, DDT also caused environmental pollution. It is now banned in the United States and Europe.

and by 1910, it was present everywhere potatoes were grown in North America.

Colorado potato beetles arrived in Europe in 1870. For years, they would turn up only occasionally in German, English, and Dutch ports. That changed in 1922, when they were suddenly discovered to have invaded huge swaths of the Médoc region in France—having likely stowed away in sacks of American potatoes shipped to Bordeaux during the First World War. The beetles had gained a lot of ground fast and undetected, and they proved impossible to eradicate even using arsenic-based pesticides. Twenty years later, they were all over Europe, and a continent-wide response was mounted to fight them. A special conference was held in Brussels in 1936, and the European Plant Protection Organization (EPPO) was formed in 1951 partly to combat the potato beetle.

Countless insecticides—no matter how toxic—have proven useless against the Colorado potato beetle, because the species develops resistance easily and reproduces at a massive rate: a single female can lay over three thousand eggs per year. Biological control measures (the introduction of natural predators or parasites) have also been ineffective. Genetically modified potatoes, which produce a protein toxic to the beetles, were tested in the 1990s but failed to deliver the results promised by the companies promoting them. Only crop rotation has been helpful, in addition to being a natural and sustainable solution.

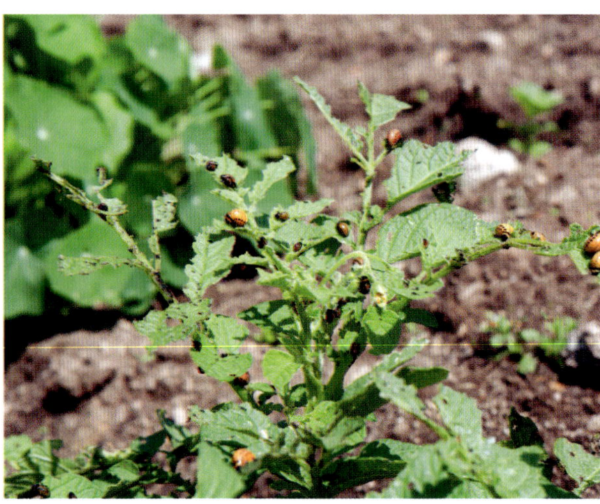

The reddish-pink larvae are easy to spot on potato plants.

During the First World War, French infantrymen nicknamed their German foes *doryphores* (the French word for potato beetles) because of the round helmets they wore. The name originally referred to Persian soldiers armed with spears who guarded the king's chariot, inspiring the genus name *Doryphora* initially assigned by Nuttall in reference to the beetle's spear-like mouthparts.

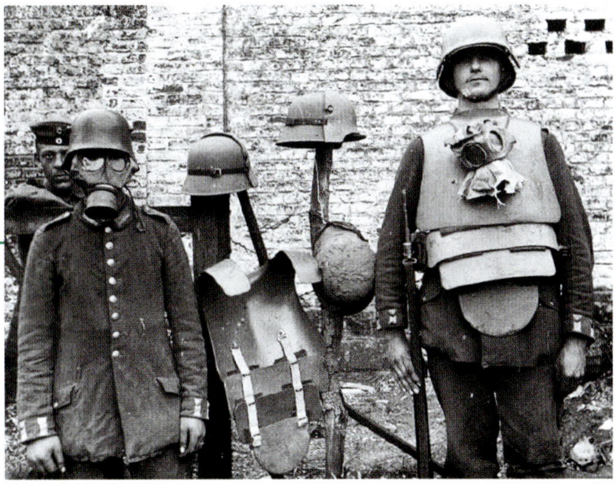

The proliferation of Colorado potato beetles in East Germany during the Cold War was so damaging that it inspired a propaganda campaign: in 1950, the authorities accused the United States of having airdropped the beetles to destroy Soviet agriculture.

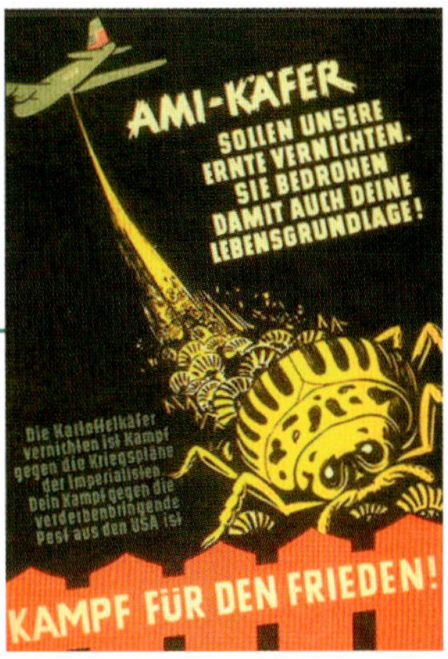

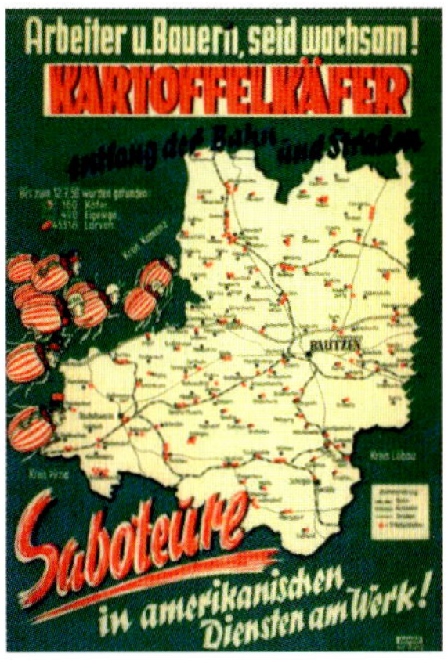

Starting in the 1940s, DDT was the go-to insecticide for pests like the potato beetle. Despite its being highly toxic to humans and the environment, industrialized countries did not start to ban it until the 1970s.

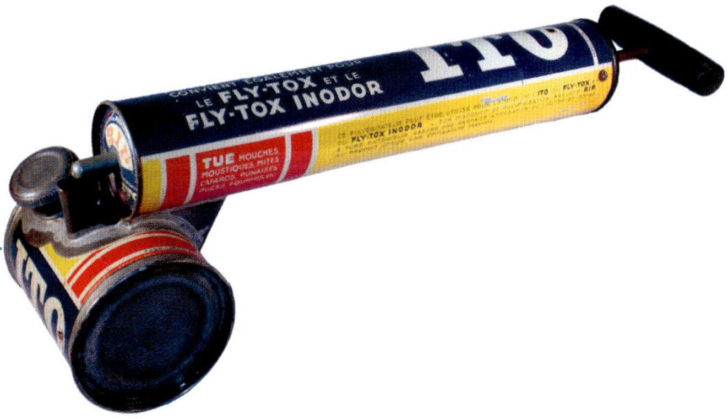

The Colorado potato beetle can feed on various other domestic nightshades (eggplants, tomatoes, bell peppers, etc.) as well as wild plants like black nightshade and groundcherry. It has also adapted to different habitats: populations in Russia, for example, have a shorter life cycle, grow larger, and hide deeper into the ground in winter than those in warmer climates. The beetle's amazing adaptive and phenotypic plasticity has allowed it to conquer practically the entire planet. It remains a concern for potato farmers in many countries even as it has become less common in Western Europe, probably due to unfavorable genetic changes.

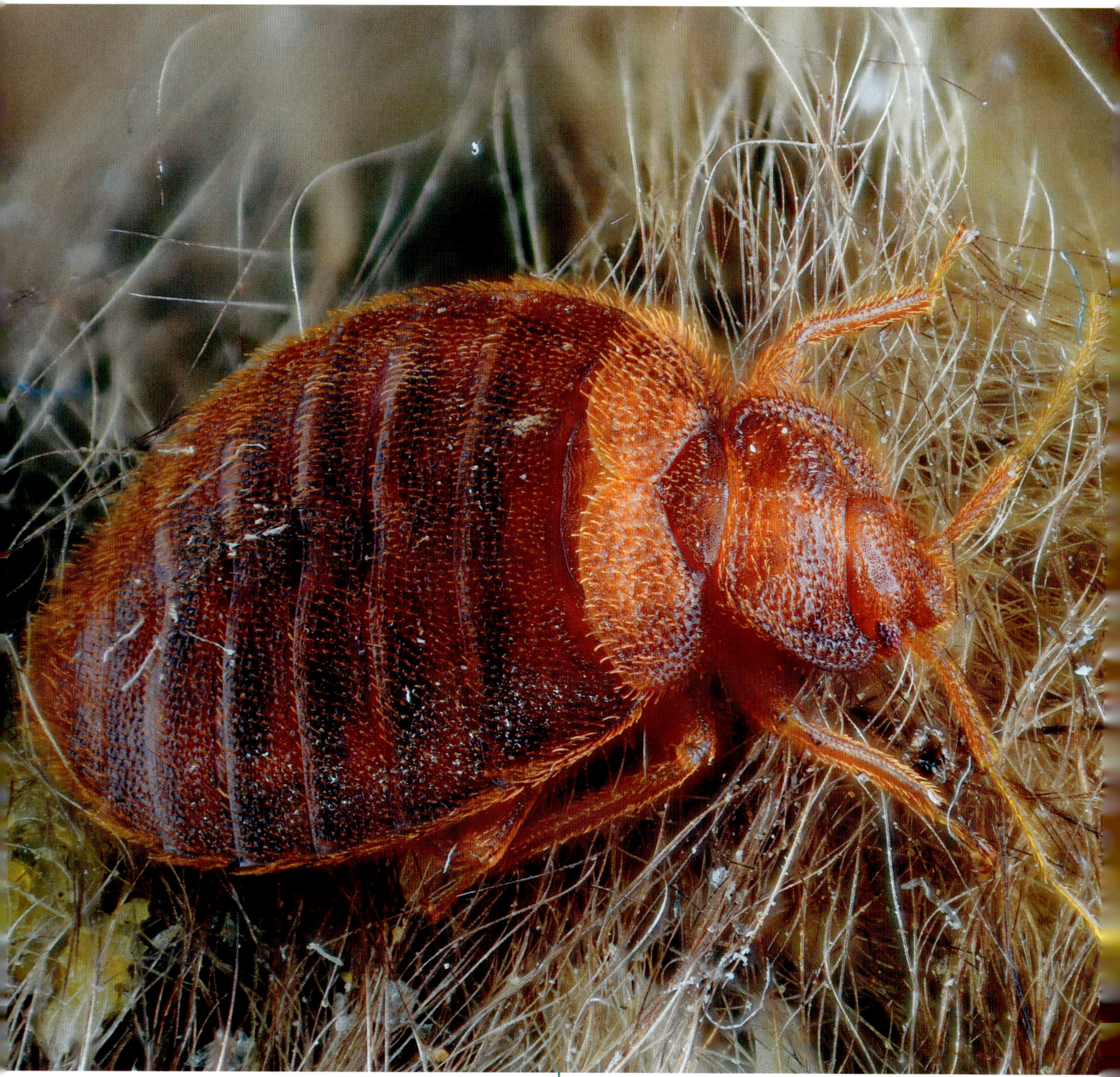

Common bedbug photographed on a bat, one of its natural hosts.
© Gilles San Martin

INVASION OF THE BEDBUGS

CIMEX LECTULARIUS AND COUSINS
(HEMIPTERA: CIMICIDAE)

The term "bedbugs" can refer to several related species but is usually reserved for *Cimex lectularius*, the common bedbug. Their behavior differs significantly from their fellow true bugs in the suborder Heteroptera, which feed on sap and plant matter. Not so for these parasites. They feed exclusively on the blood of warm-blooded animals . . . including humans.

Bedbugs are good at making themselves scarce during the daytime. Their flattened bodies slip easily into cracks in the floorboards, baseboards, and furniture. They can also hide inside upholstery, mattresses, pillows, and clothes, or behind wallpaper, picture frames, and electrical outlets. Once night falls, they emerge to feed on the house's sleeping inhabitants. They tend to leave stains and fecal spots on bedding when they feed, not to mention red welts on the victim's skin: sometimes up to ninety bites from a single adult bug over the course of each ten- to twenty-minute meal. Then, having eaten their fill, they hide again to digest over the next several days.

The adults are reddish brown and measure 5 to 8 millimeters long. They look like apple seeds and can neither jump nor fly, but they are prolific and hard to kill. Females are fertilized several times and lay between two hundred and five hundred eggs, each of which hatches into a tiny bedbug that immediately sets off in search of heat and blood. The young bugs develop into adults after five molts that take place three to fifteen days apart. If they cannot feed, they cannot molt, and simply remain in their current instar for up to a year. Adults can also survive for months without feeding.

Although the common bedbug and its cousins do not appear to transmit infectious diseases (unlike mosquitoes, for example), they are still considered a public health problem because of their painful, itchy bite and the psychological distress they cause. In the 1950s, bedbugs had all but disappeared from developed countries. But they came back with a vengeance in the late 1990s, probably for a number of reasons: DDT and similar insecticides were banned, the bugs developed resistance to other commonly

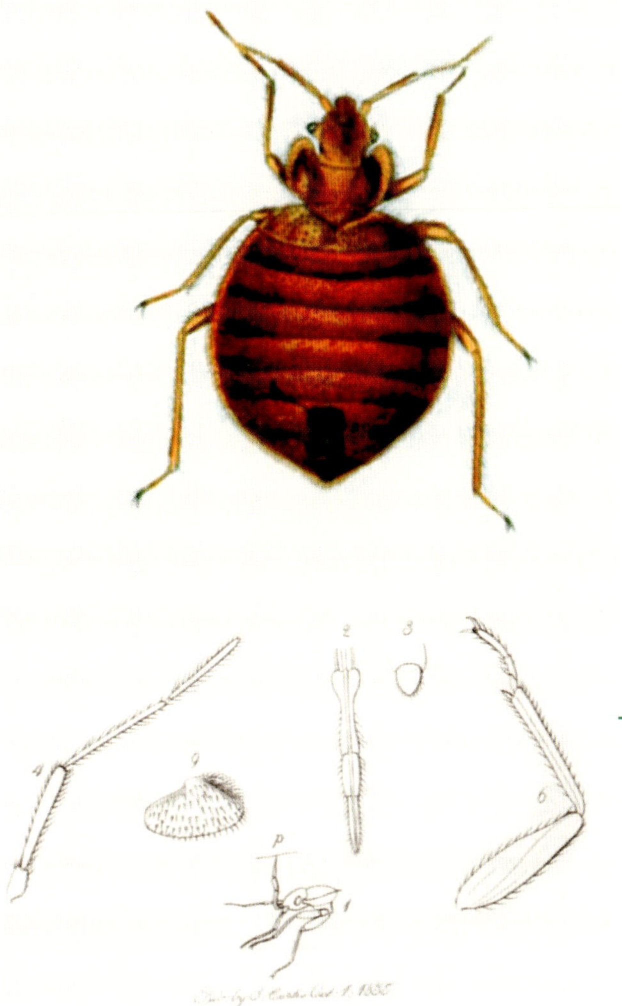

Did you know that bedbugs were once used in medicine? In 1554, Italian physician Pietro Mattioli (1501–1578) wrote that the Greek pharmacologist Dioscorides recommended swallowing seven bedbugs wrapped in fava bean skins to stop a fever from rising (or, without the bean skins, to treat viper bites). Despite being ugly, bothersome, and foul-smelling, Mattioli wrote, bedbugs still had their uses. He pointed out that some doctors of his day took Dioscorides' advice and placed live bedbugs in the urethras of patients struggling to urinate, writing: "This appears to be very good counsel, as the live bugs walking upon their legs tickle the urinary passages, causing them to open and flush the bugs out."

© John Curtis, *British Entomology*, 1836

used insecticides, trade and tourism became more globalized, climate change allowed them to multiply in greater numbers, and some sanitary measures were no longer applied.

Eradicating bedbugs from a home requires chemical treatments (insecticide) and nonchemical control measures (heat, cold, vacuuming, etc.). Worldwide, the number of infestations increased by more than 4,500 percent in the early twenty-first century, and in 2020 it was estimated that one in five Americans had either experienced infestation or knew someone who had.

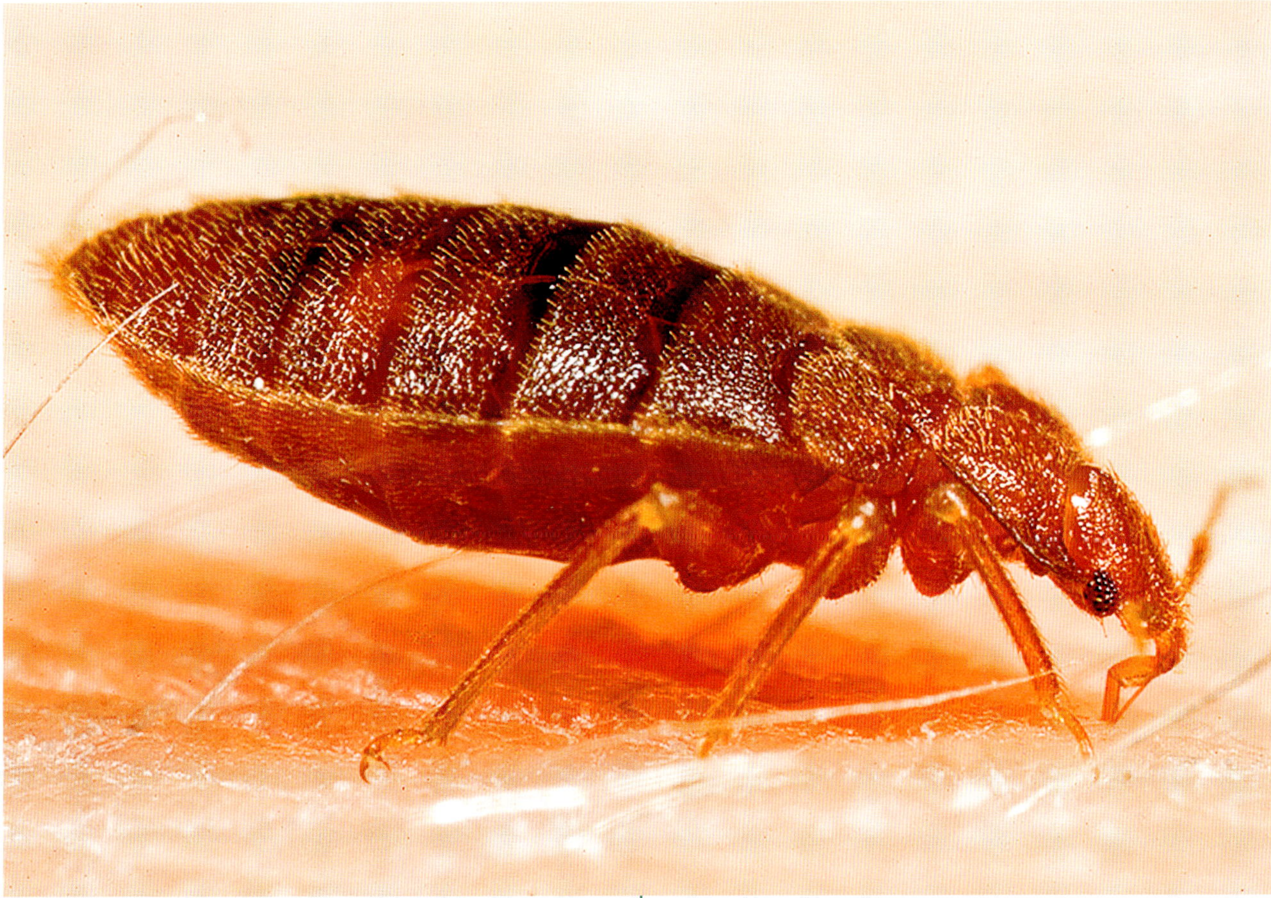

A bedbug feeding on human blood. Bites usually occur on exposed parts of the body and look similar to mosquito bites but are grouped together in threes or fours, sometimes in a line. Bedbug bites can be extremely itchy, cause allergic reaction, and become infected if scratched.

© CDC image bank

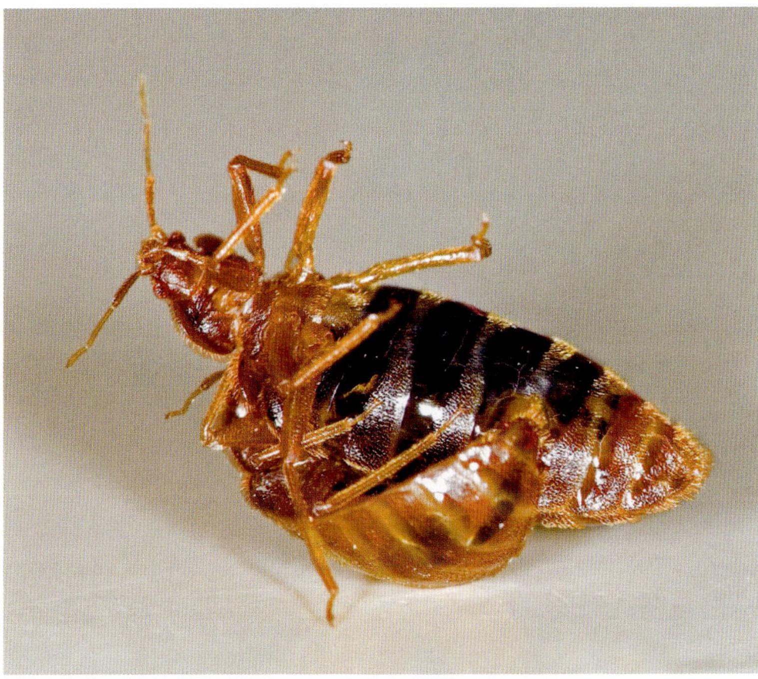

The common bedbug and its cousins have a surprising way of mating, known as traumatic insemination. The male pierces the female's abdominal wall with his spiked sex organ in an area where the wall is thinner, called the spermalege, then injects his sperm (as shown in this photograph). Many females die from the wounds and resulting infections inflicted by this process.

© Rickard Ignell, Swedish University of Agricultural Sciences

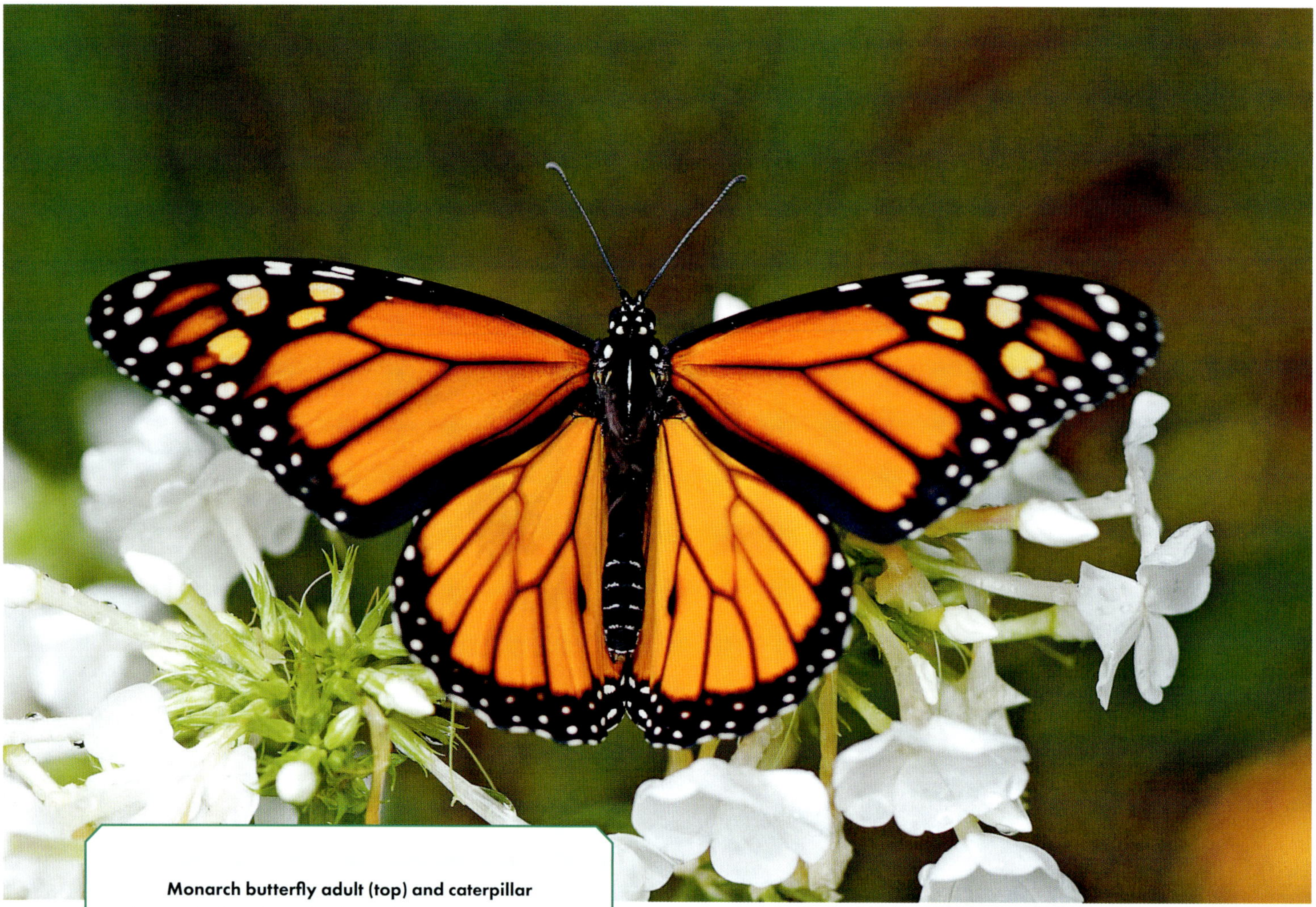

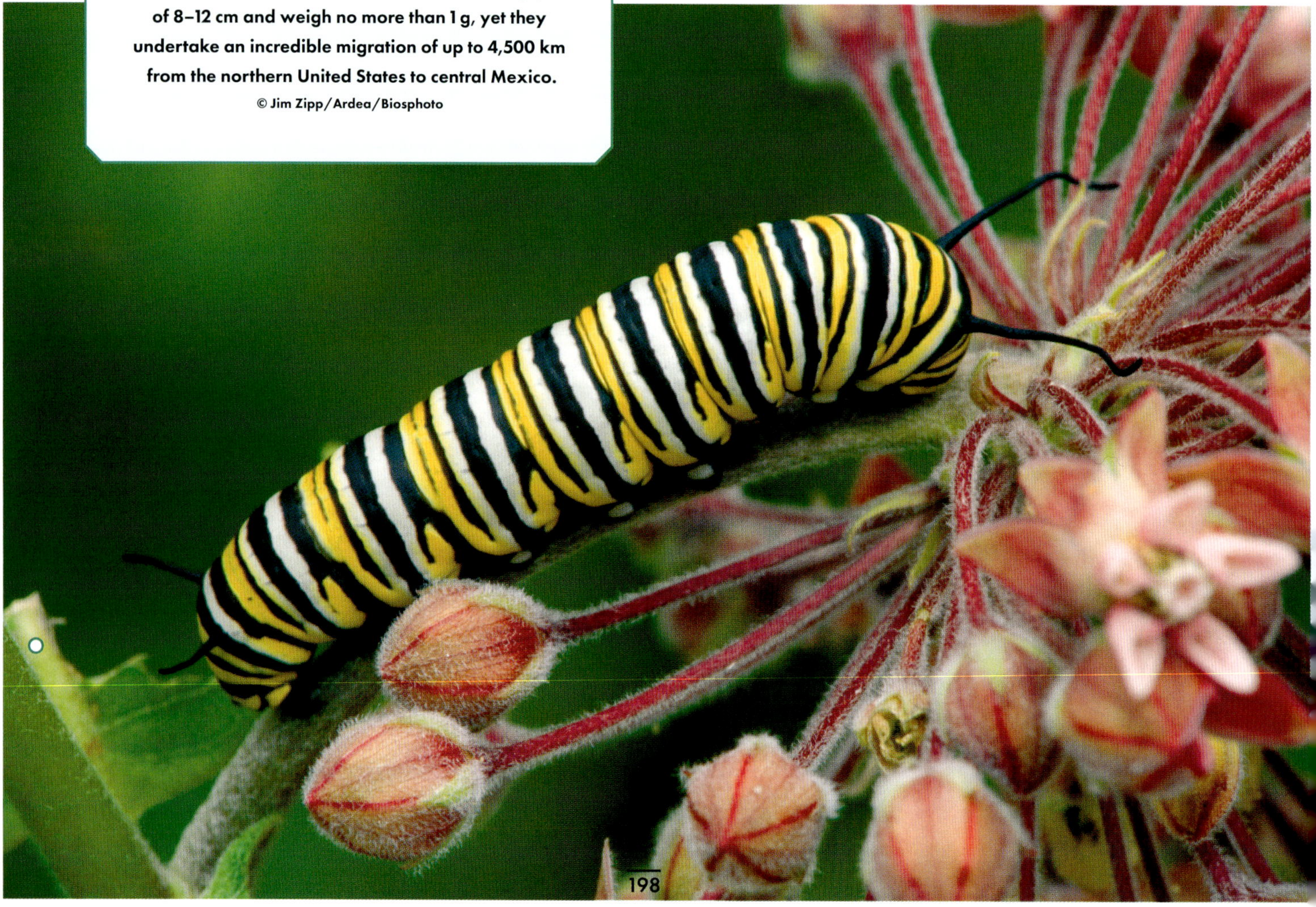

Monarch butterfly adult (top) and caterpillar (bottom). These beautiful butterflies have a wingspan of 8–12 cm and weigh no more than 1 g, yet they undertake an incredible migration of up to 4,500 km from the northern United States to central Mexico.

THE END OF THE MONARCH'S REIGN?

DANAUS PLEXIPPUS

(LEPIDOPTERA: NYMPHALIDAE)

The monarch butterfly is famous all over the world for its epic autumn migration, which has been immortalized in photographs and films. But the days when their orange-and-black clouds once filled the skies seem to be over. The western populations, which were once welcome winter visitors in California, have shrunk drastically. And the monarchs that migrate from the northeastern United States and Canada to Mexico each year are not doing much better—their numbers have declined by 80 percent.

According to the Xerces Society for Invertebrate Conservation, 4.5 million monarchs from the western slopes of the Rockies used to spend November to March in California's Marin and San Diego counties in the 1980s. That number dropped to one million in 1997, to 192,000 in 2017, to less than 30,000 in 2019 and 2020. On the eastern side, it is estimated that one *billion* monarchs migrated to and from Mexico in the early 1990s, but only 35 million took the trip in 2014.

The monarch's decline has outstripped even the most pessimistic predictions. It probably stems from several factors, including climate change, which has resulted in cold snaps in the southeast United States and drought in the regions where the caterpillars develop, leading to scarcity of their preferred host plant, milkweed. Moreover, the rise of industrialized agriculture and monoculture has meant that there are fewer nectar-producing plants during the summer months, plants that the adults rely on for nutrients during their long flight and breeding season. Monarchs have also been affected by shifting bloom seasons and human impacts on their winter habitat, not to mention the wildfires that now regularly ravage California.

Other threats to this iconic species are less visible. Spreading salt on roads in winter can contaminate what few milkweed plants still grow along the roadside despite the use of agricultural herbicides. Caterpillars that feed on milkweed containing too much salt grow much slower, and as butterflies they have underdeveloped muscles and poor vision that impedes flight. Some conservation efforts are aimed

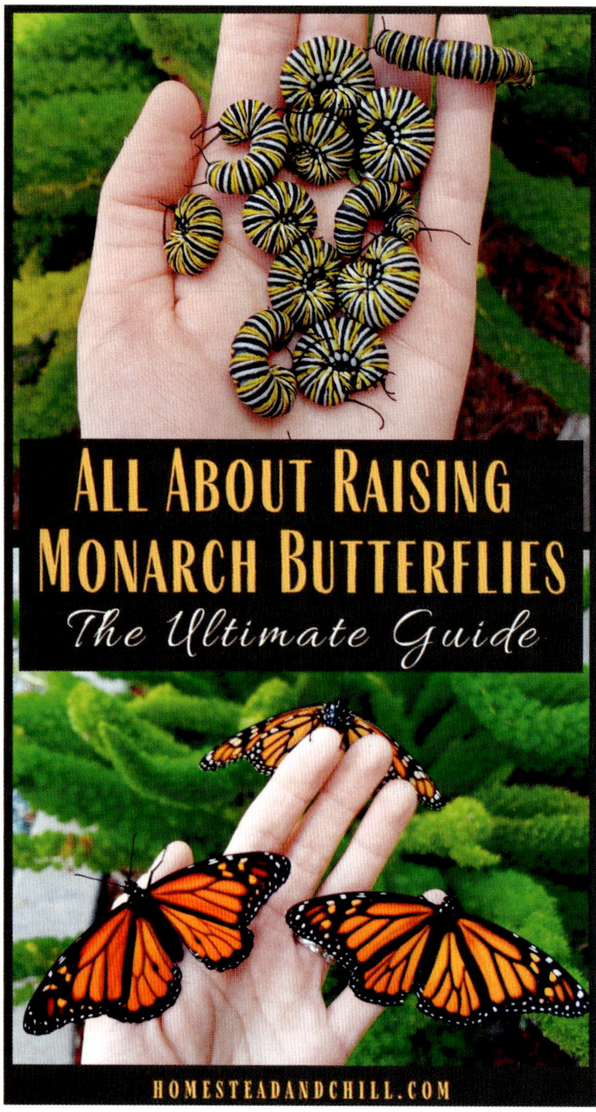

How-to guides like this one promote breeding monarchs in captivity. While raising butterflies has obvious educational value, it is controversial as a conservation approach.
© www.saveourmonarchs.org

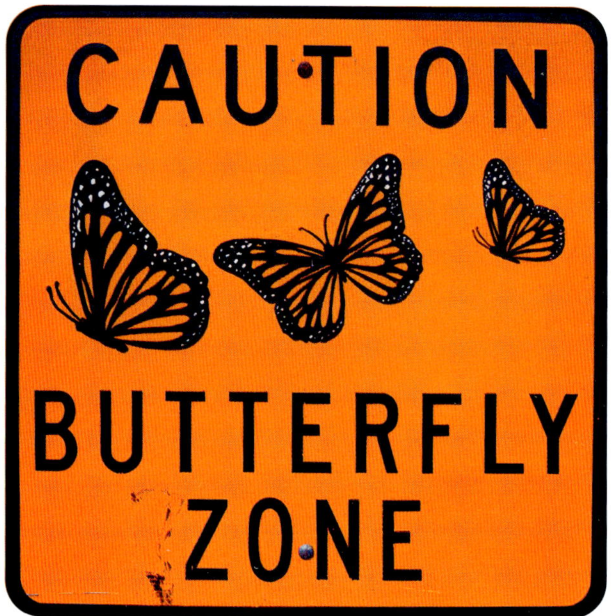

Sign posted along the monarch's migration route and wintering areas.
© www.saveourmonarchs.org

at encouraging monarchs to choose plants farther away from roads, such as by regularly cutting the vegetation on roadside berms. Another subtle threat comes from a protozoan parasite, *Ophryocystis elektroscirrha*, which affects female monarchs in particular, leading to a gradual increase in the number of males and thus an unbalanced sex ratio.

Even well-intentioned efforts can backfire. Butterfly enthusiasts and schoolchildren have raised monarchs in captivity and released them into the wild to bolster populations, but over the course of generations, it is possible (though not proven) that the descendants of captive butterflies lose the ability to migrate. Even monarchs descended from wild stock but raised in an insectarium where the light and temperature constantly simulate summer conditions cannot figure out how to migrate. Captive breeding is therefore not the solution—and may be harmful, as the loss of migratory instinct seems to be passed down to offspring even when captive-raised individuals mate with wild butterflies. If monarchs are raised outdoors or in an environment that simulates autumn conditions, however, they retain the instinct to migrate.

WHEN DID MONARCHS START MIGRATING?

Apart from the monarch, the 150 or so species in the genus *Danaus* all live in the tropics of Southeast Asia, Africa, Central and South America, and the Greater Antilles. Several other *Danaus* butterflies also migrate between the wet and dry seasons, though for much shorter distances. This shared behavior suggests that monarchs have been migrating for a very long time. Repeated glacial cycles during the Pleistocene epoch (also known as the Ice Age) displaced North American flora, including more than 100 species of milkweed, to the north and south. The monarch probably followed its favorite food source, which would have been possible because its genus had acquired the ability to move between habitats. Because monarchs cannot survive harsh winter conditions, natural selection would have favored individuals that migrated southward at the end of summer. With the passage of time, that relatively simple migratory mechanism evolved into the complex, sophisticated migration that monarchs undertake today.

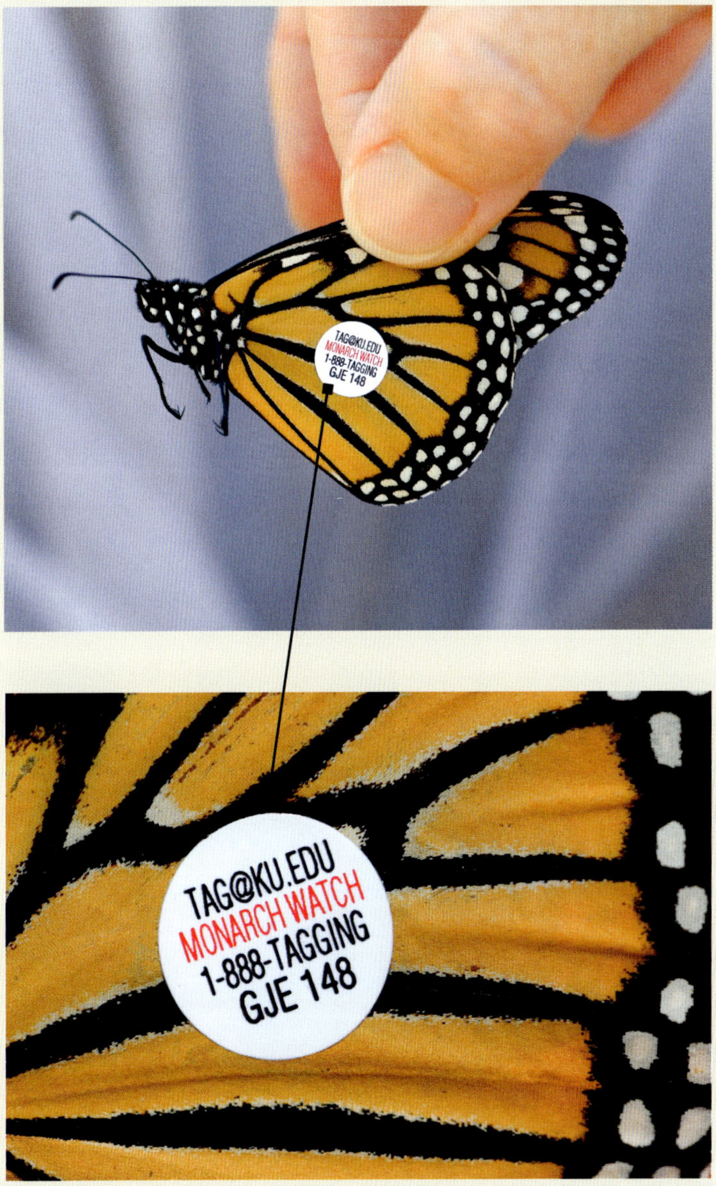

Scientists tag monarch butterflies to study their migration patterns. This allows them to keep track of where the monarchs go, with help from an army of amateur butterfly spotters.
© Ingo Arndt/Minden Pictures/Biosphoto

EAST VS. WEST

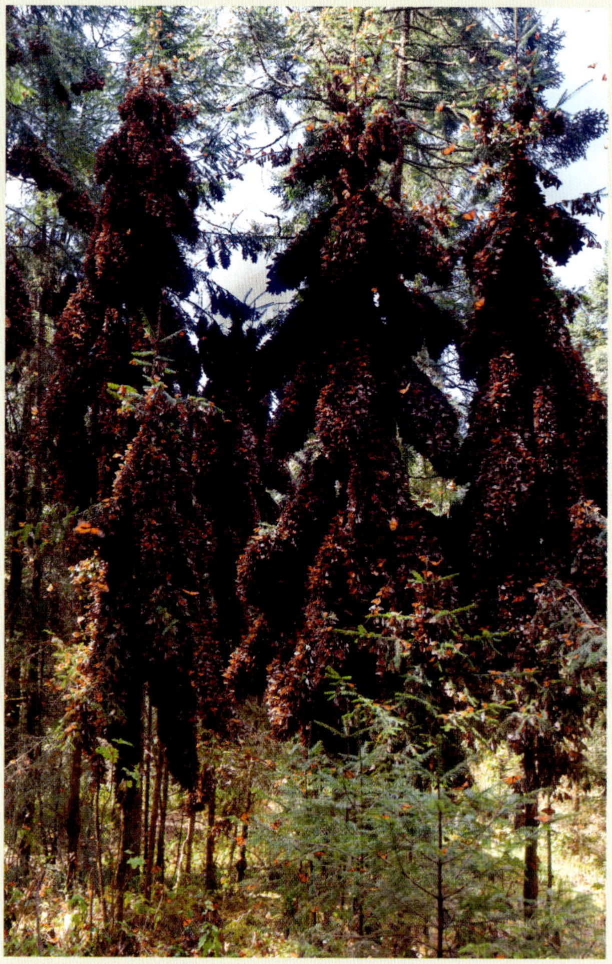

There are two distinct monarch butterfly populations in North America, both of which migrate using receptors in their antennae that sense the cycle of days and nights and the direction of the sun.

Western monarchs winter in a few locations along the California coast. They arrive in autumn and leave again in spring to reproduce farther inland, at higher altitude.

Eastern monarchs fly between 2,000 and 5,000 kilometers from the Great Plains and southern Canada to their wintering grounds in central Mexico. A single individual completes the entire southward trip, but the trip back north takes place over two to four generations. After wintering for about four months in central Mexico, the monarchs fly to the US–Mexico border region to lay their eggs. As soon as this first generation emerges from their chrysalises, they head north to lay their own eggs, with each subsequent generation hatching farther north. If they emerge early enough, some even produce a fourth generation that gets as far as Canada. The third and fourth generations live longer than the first and second, up to nine months instead of two. They do not reproduce right away, and instead fly back to the point of origin in Mexico, where they spend the winter before starting the cycle all over again.

Above: Eastern monarchs spend the winter in the Monarch Butterfly Biosphere Reserve, on the border between Mexico's Michoacán and Mexico states. The reserve was named a World Heritage Site in 2008. Monarchs were once so numerous here they formed masses that bent the branches of trees.
© Sylvain Cordier/Biosphoto

Perhaps as unknowing stowaways on a ship, or blown off course at high altitude, monarchs appeared in Hawaii in 1845, the Marquesas Islands in 1860, and New Caledonia and the west coast of Australia in 1870. From there, they spread to New Zealand, India, and Southeast Asia. Monarchs probably reached Europe and northern Africa via the Azores, Madeira, and the Canary Islands, where they became established in the late nineteenth century. For the past forty years, monarchs have made a home for themselves in parts of southern Spain and Portugal where tropical milkweed (*Asclepias curassavica*) and narrow leaf cotton bush (*Gomphocarpus fructicosus*) have been introduced and are abundant in the wild. Monarchs are also regularly sighted in the United Kingdom, France, and the Netherlands.

MONARCH MIGRATION PATTERNS IN THE AMERICAS

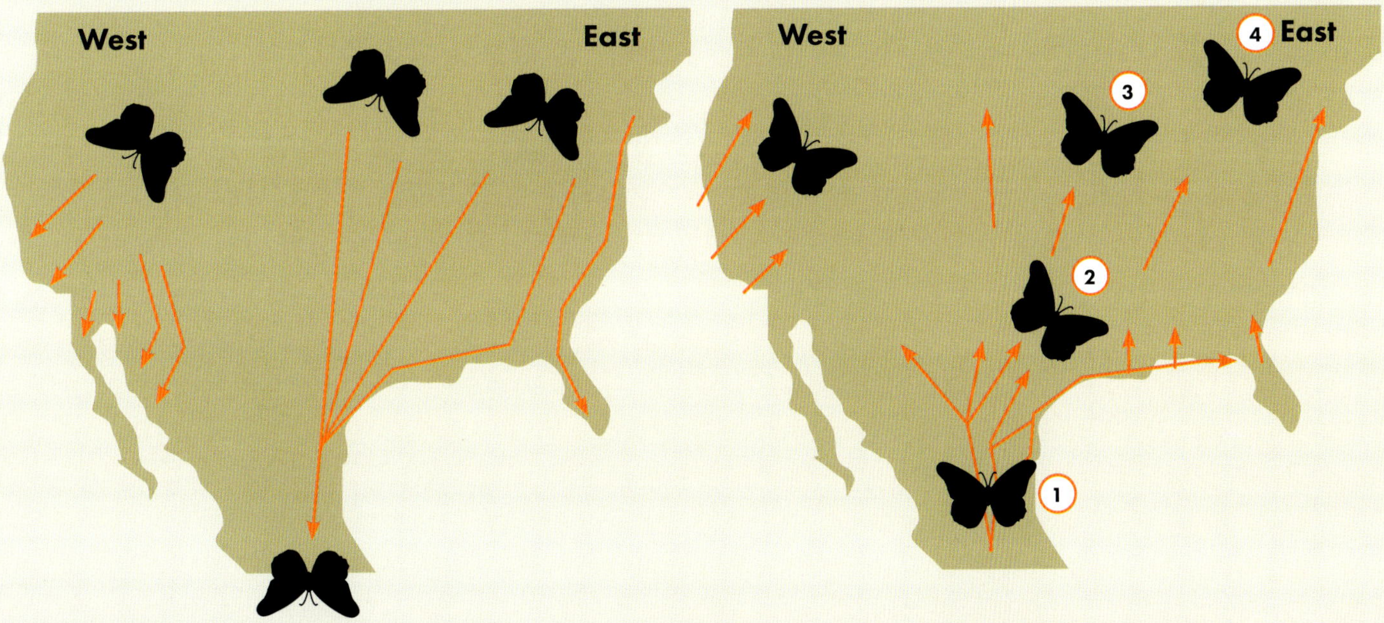

While the western monarchs' migration route is relatively straightforward, in the east things get more complicated. Eastern monarchs migrate south in autumn from where they hatched in the Great Plains, eastern United States, and southern Canada (left). They fly thousands of kilometers, without stopping to reproduce, to spend the winter in Mexico or, in some cases, Florida. The northward migration (right) is a different story. Monarchs that wintered in Mexico only make it part of the way before they stop to reproduce and die. Successive generations (numbered 1 to 4 on the map) complete different stages of the trip north, reaching as far as Canada. The last generation will, come autumn, fly south again in a single trip.

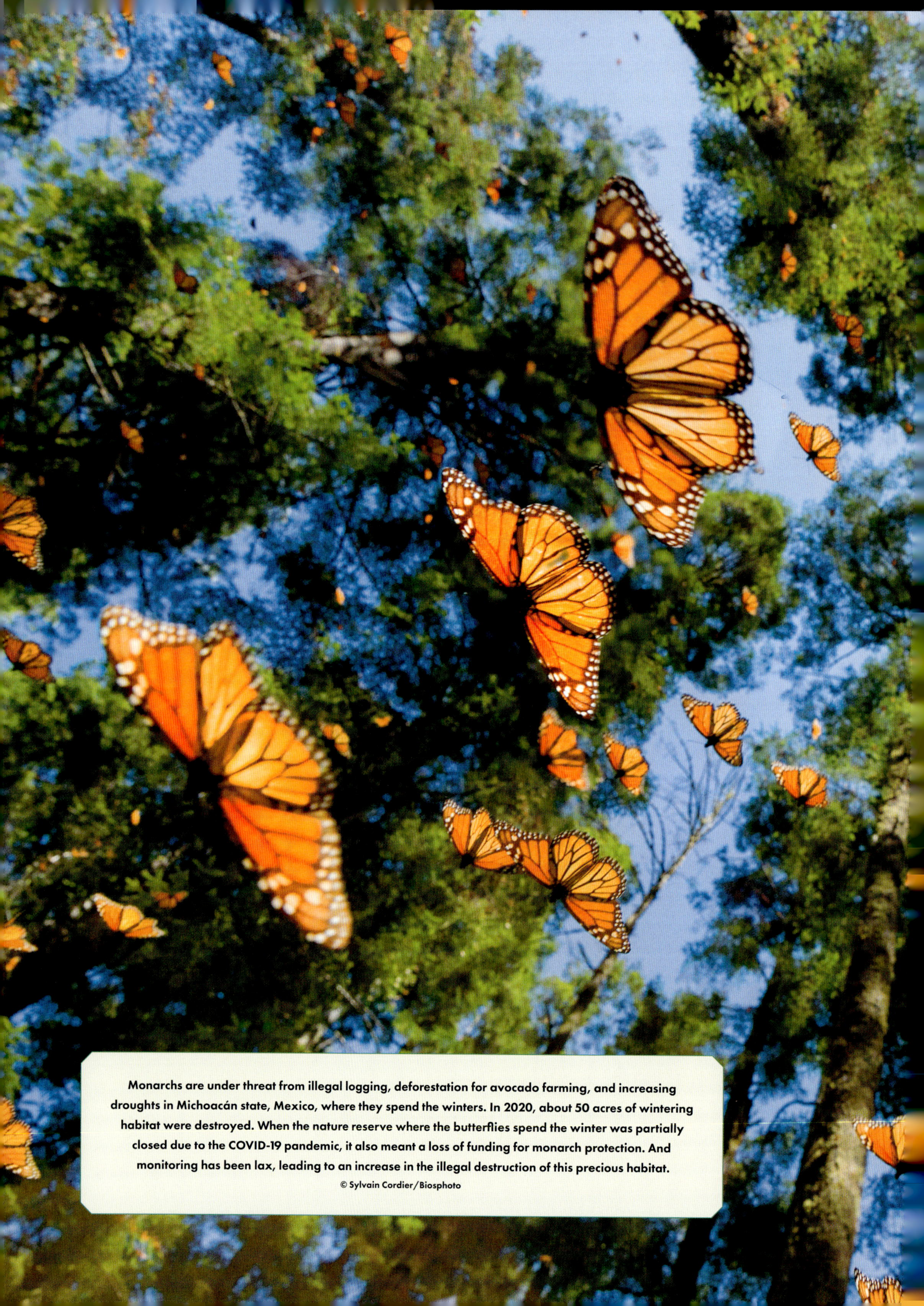

Monarchs are under threat from illegal logging, deforestation for avocado farming, and increasing droughts in Michoacán state, Mexico, where they spend the winters. In 2020, about 50 acres of wintering habitat were destroyed. When the nature reserve where the butterflies spend the winter was partially closed due to the COVID-19 pandemic, it also meant a loss of funding for monarch protection. And monitoring has been lax, leading to an increase in the illegal destruction of this precious habitat.

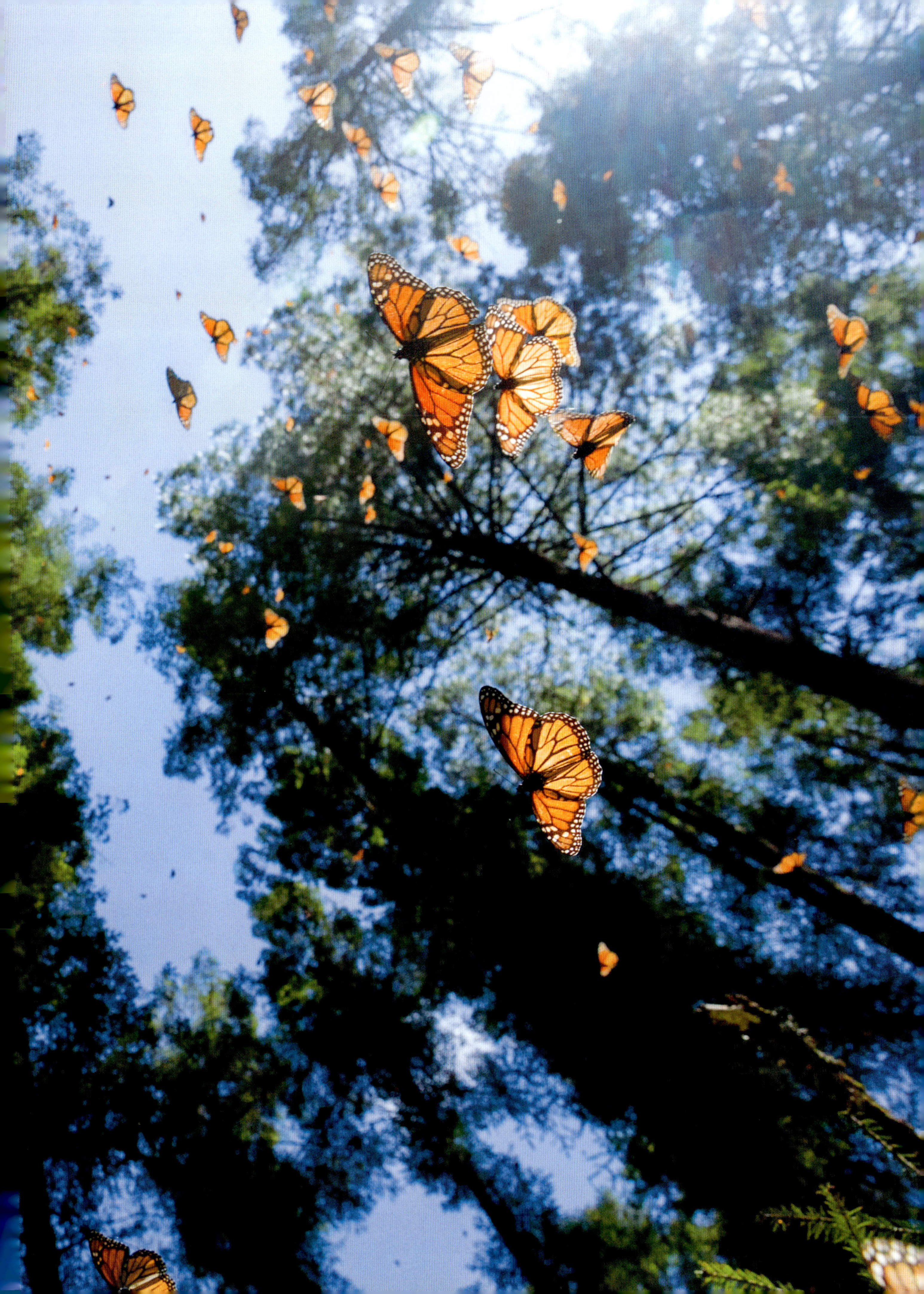

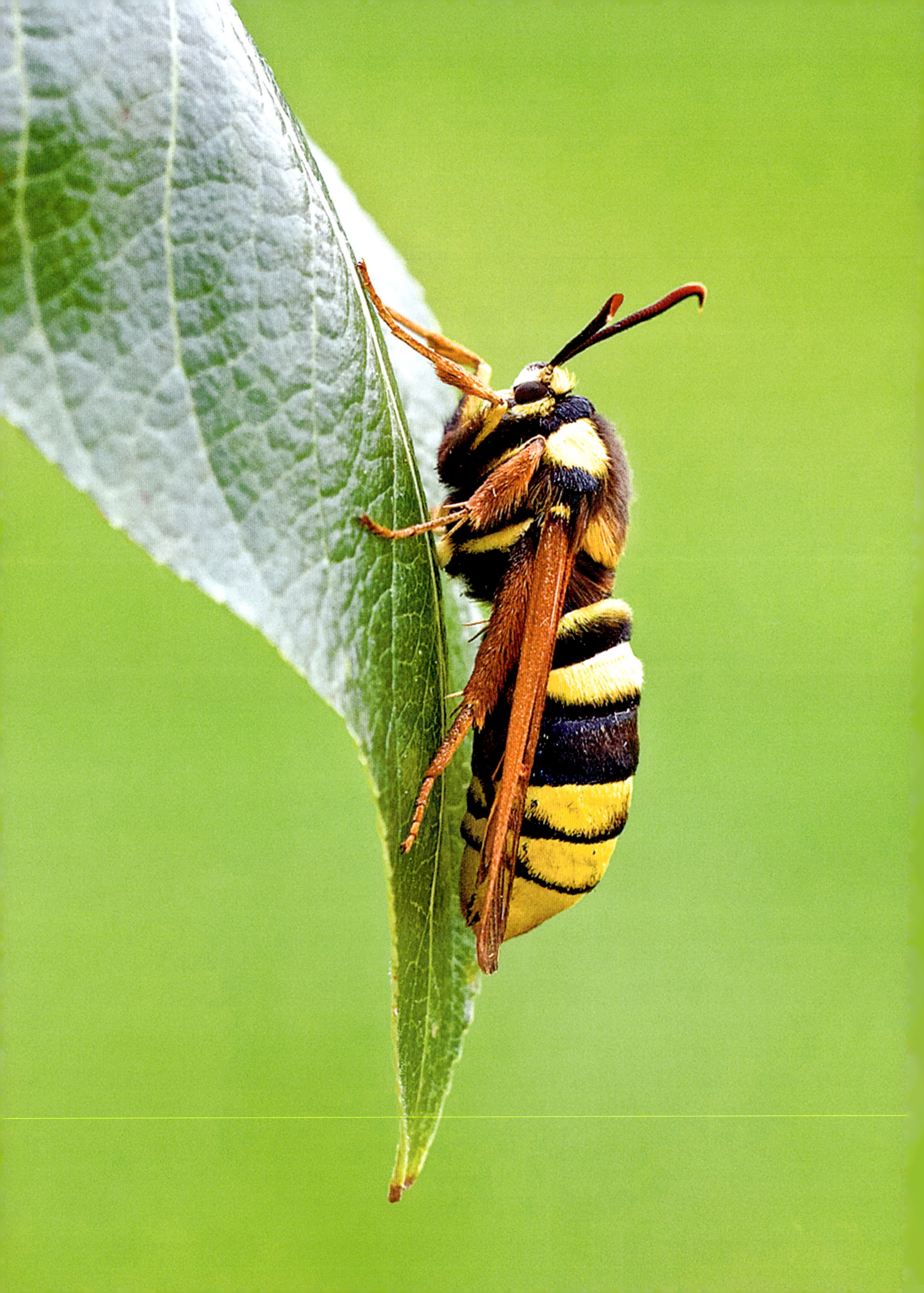

WEAPONS AND DEFENSES

Life is all about survival, and many insects—as larvae, at least—are remarkably good at doing just that. Some have evolved to produce deadly toxins, mimic more dangerous relatives, or prey on other creatures . . . either directly or as parasites. (For example, insect larvae sometimes grow and develop inside another animal, which they eventually kill.) These protective mechanisms can be as violent as they are sophisticated and have helped insects to survive in every habitat on Earth.

How do you stay safe when you have no defensive weapons? By imitating someone more dangerous than you are! This remarkable insect is not a hornet or a wasp . . . but a moth. *Sesia apiformis*, commonly known as the hornet moth, is native to Europe and the Middle East. Its larvae live under the bark of poplars and aspens.

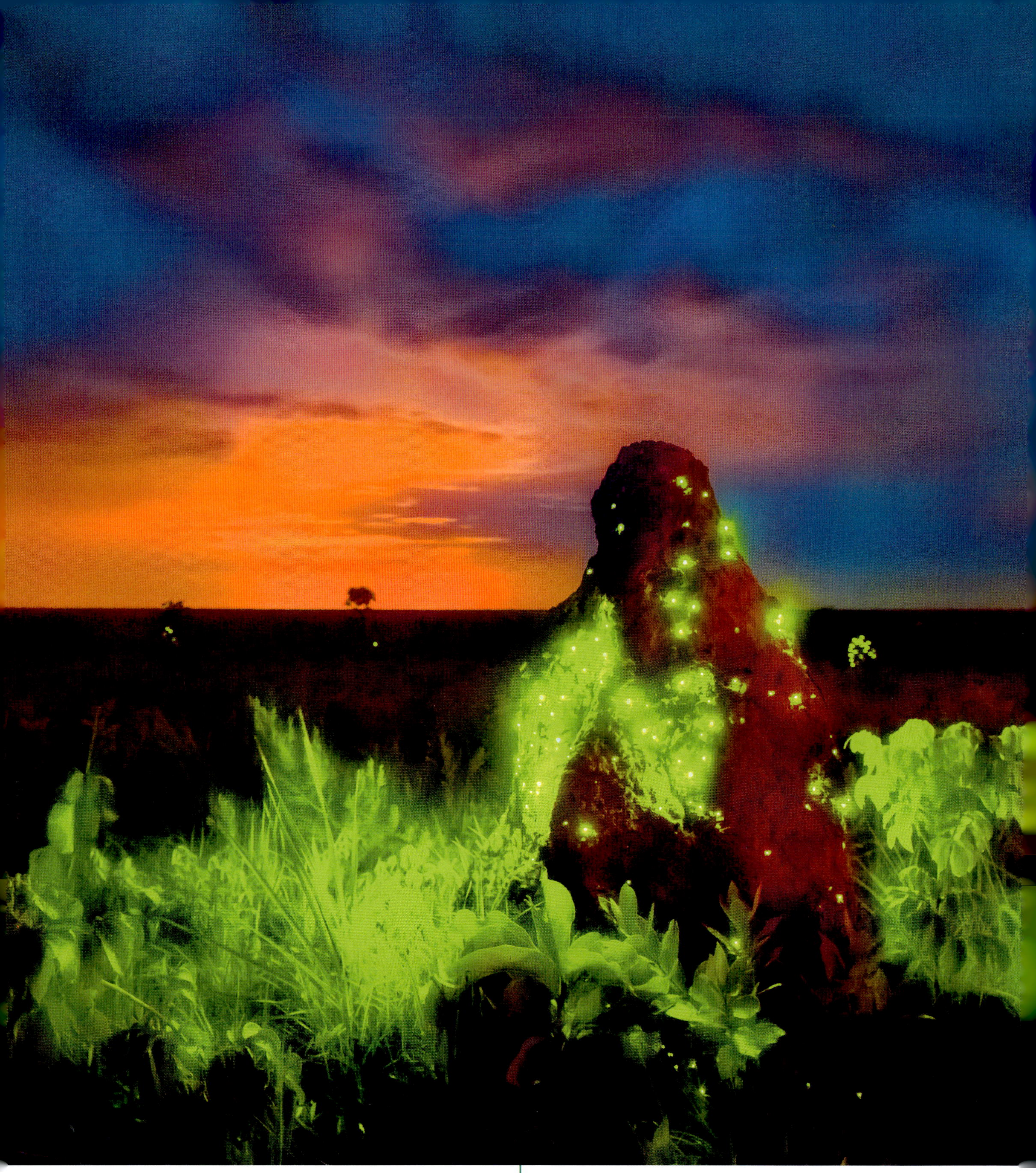

Emas National Park, some 500 km southwest of Brasília in Goiás state, Brazil, features spectacular glowing termite mounds for about two weeks each year. Although the effect is actually caused by beetle larvae, early European colonists thought they were seeing thousands of tiny ghosts. Related beetle species produce a similar effect in other parts of the Brazilian savannah.
© Marcio Cabral/Biosphoto

GLOWING FORTRESSES

PYREARINUS TERMITILLUMINANS

COLEOPTERA: ELATERIDAE

Late September to early October marks the start of the wet season in central Brazil—a special time when the large termite mounds dotting the tropical savannahs of the Cerrado light up with thousands of tiny bioluminescent lanterns. The source of this otherworldly effect? Click beetle larvae hidden inside the walls.

When examined closely, the glowing termite mounds contain larvae of the click beetle species *Pyrearinus termitilluminans*, described in 1982 by Cleide Costa, an entomologist at the University of São Paulo. The 2-centimeter-long larvae dig galleries into the walls of mounds made by termites in the genus *Cornitermes*; at night, they stick out their bioluminescent heads and the first segments of their thorax to attract prey, winged termites and other arthropods that are drawn to their glow. The result is an ethereal lightshow first described in 1847 by French naturalist Francis de Castelnau (1810–1880) during an expedition to Brazil.

The *P. termitilluminans* larvae metamorphose into adults within the termite mound. Fully grown, they are roughly 16 millimeters long and can be seen flying around the mounds or in the surrounding savannah in search of a mate. Once the females have been fertilized, they lay their eggs at the base of a termite mound. The minuscule larvae are already luminescent when they hatch by the thousands to form a glowing green halo around the base of the mound. They start out eating microorganisms on the ground until they have grown large enough to dig shallow galleries into the walls of the mound.

The clouds of insects flying around, and crawling over, these glowing termite mounds attract various predators: spiders, scorpions, centipedes, and amphibians that come to feast on creatures drawn to the larvae's glow (while the larvae themselves stay safely hidden in the walls). These predators themselves become prey for nocturnal birds, bats, and other animals, who leave droppings containing plant seeds around the mounds. The luminous skyscrapers of the Cerrado thus form the bedrock of an entire ecosystem.

DEADLY DECORATORS

New Zealand glowworms, or *titiwai* in Māori, are larvae of the species *Arachnocampa luminosa*, which produce an enzyme in the excretory organs in their abdomens that causes them to glow. They use their luminescence to lure small flies toward the silk strands lined with sticky droplets that they hang from the ceilings of caves. Adult *A. luminosa* somehow manage to avoid falling into their own larvae's traps. Other *Arachnocampa* species exhibit similar behavior in Tasmania and mainland Australia, and some cave-dwelling flies in North America also have luminescent larvae.

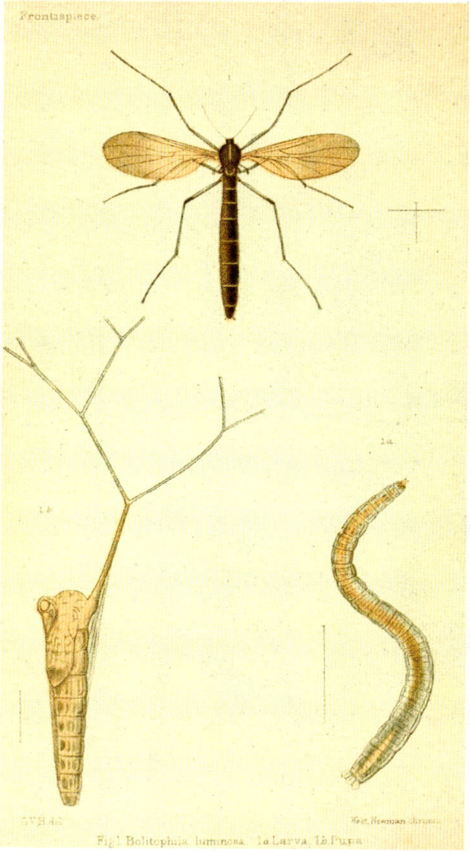

Arachnocampa luminosa **are glowworms endemic to New Zealand. This 1892 engraving from *An Elementary Manual of New Zealand Entomology* by George V. Hudson shows the adult (15–18 mm), pupal, and larval forms.**

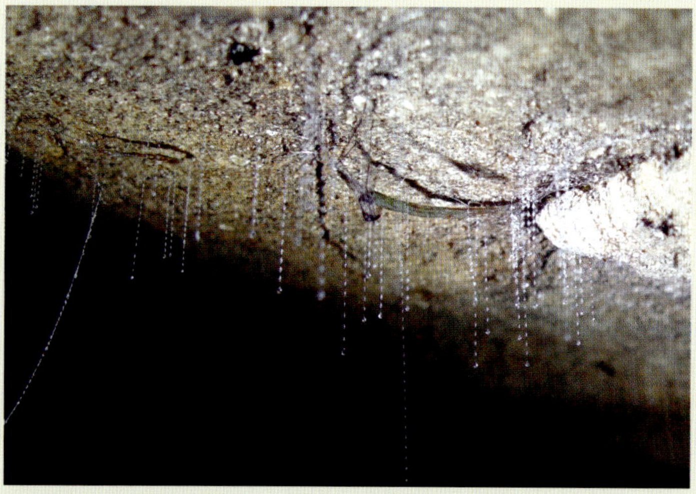

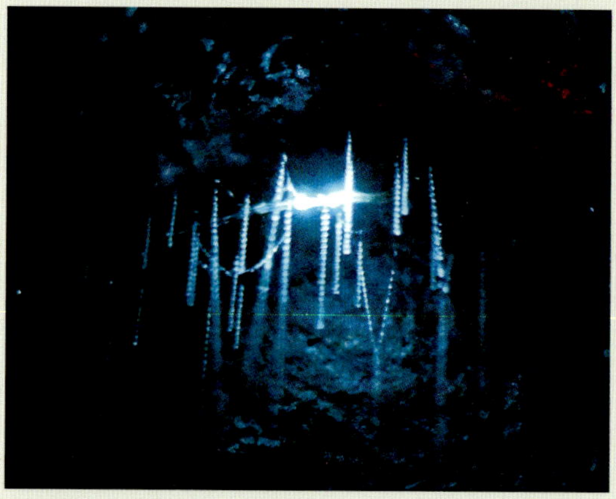

Top: Fully developed *Arachnocampa luminosa* larvae are 3–4 cm long and can be found in caves, crevices, mine tunnels, and sometimes the cavities of trees and tree ferns. They put on a particularly good show in the Waitomo caves on New Zealand's North Island.

Right: The eerie glow of *Arachnocampa* larvae in a cave.

LET THERE BE LIGHT!

The light produced by fireflies and some click beetles is a source of delight, and even veneration, in many parts of the world. In North America and Asia, for example, the annual emergence of tens of thousands of fireflies results in a breathtaking aerial courtship dance. Sadly, habitat destruction and nighttime light pollution have driven many species into decline, and it is becoming increasingly rare to see them gather in large numbers.

Explorers and naturalists were also dazzled by glowing South American beetles, which emit a sustained or pulsing cold light (less than 20 percent thermal radiation) of varying intensity, in colors ranging from green to greenish-yellow to orange. The glow is produced by enzymes that cause a chemical reaction in specific parts of the insect's body. Depending on the species, eggs, larvae, nymphs, and adults may all emit a glow of varying strength, or in some cases none at all. Luminescence plays a role in mating but also serves as a warning to predators: many of these insects are toxic.

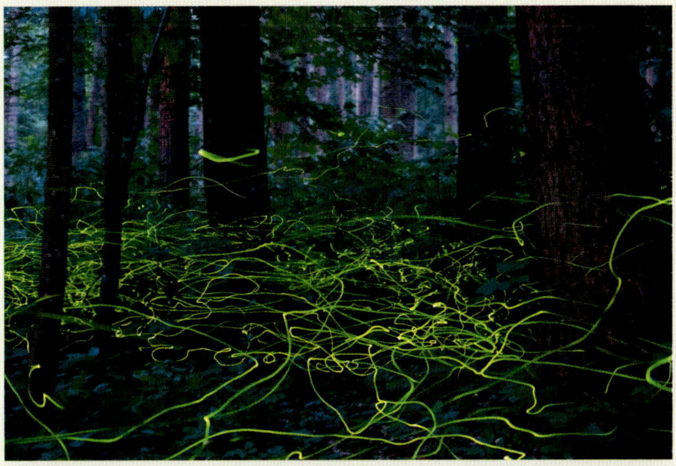

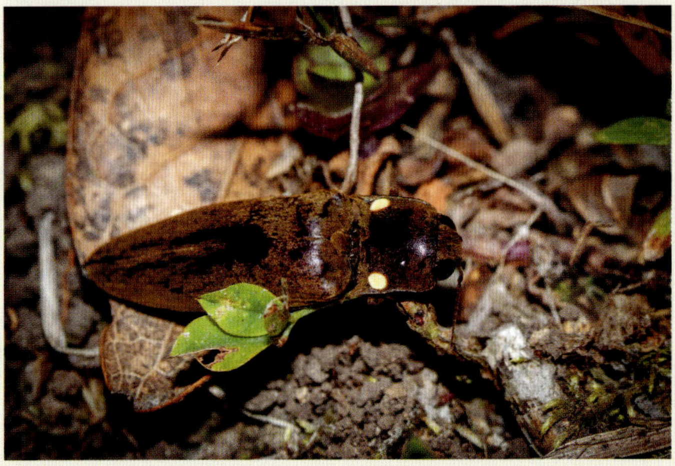

Top: Fireflies in a German forest. Long-exposure photography shows the dazzling dance of these tiny luminescent beetles in all their glory.

Bottom: With a luminance of 45 millilamberts, the fire beetle or headlight elater (*Pyrophorus noctilucus*) is the brightest insect in the world. These beetles are commonly found from South America to Florida and the Caribbean. They are 20–40 mm long and emit a constant glow from two eyespots on their thorax that is bright enough to read by.

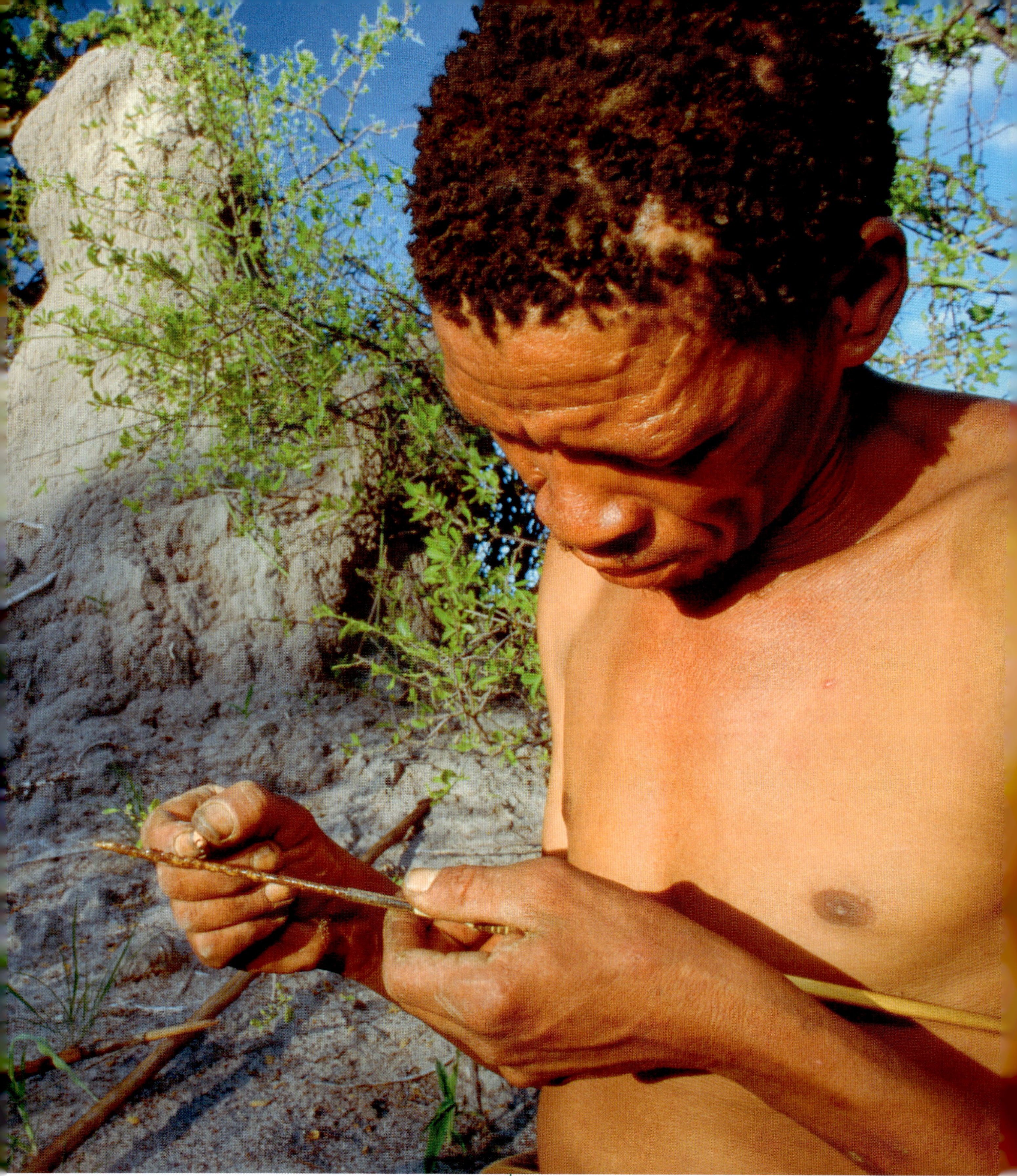

Hunter poisoning an arrow using a *Diamphidia nigroornata* pupa.

THE ARROW-POISON BEETLE

DIAMPHIDIA VITTATIPENNIS AND RELATIVES

(COLEOPTERA: CHRYSOMELIDAE)

Indigenous hunter-gatherers of the Kalahari Desert in southern Africa have traditionally hunted using poison arrows made with toxin from a humble insect. In the eighteenth century, Finnish explorer Hendrik Wikar (1752–1779) described these deadly beetle larvae as "poisonous worms."

But that was not the whole story, of course. British explorer Thomas Baines (1820–1875) recognized the "worms" as beetle larvae, and Swiss botanist Hans Schinz (1858–1941) identified African myrrh (Burseraceae) as their main host plant and documented how they were used to make poison arrows. In 1958, South African entomologist Charles Koch (1904–1970) showed that among the many species used, all of them toxic, one was from the genus *Diamphidia* and another from the genus *Polyclada* (family: Chrysomelidae). More surprising, three of the larvae examined turned out to be from the genus *Lebistina* (family: Carabidae): parasitoid beetles that prey on poisonous species and absorb their toxins.

The Ju|'hoansi, one of the peoples that use beetles for arrow-making, call the cocoons (a mix of silk and sand) *hatshu* and the larvae *!oan*, meaning "poison." The cocoons are found 50 to 100 centimeters underground at the foot of the host plant, each containing either a larva, a pupa, a freshly emerged adult, or the larva of a parasitoid carabid beetle. Only chieftains and shamans collect the cocoons, which they store in ostrich eggs for future use or trade as currency. Juice from the crushed insects is smeared on a section of the arrow shaft (not the tip, for safety), then the arrow is dried in smoke. It takes about ten cocoons to obtain enough poison to cause the red blood cells to break down, followed by slow paralysis and acute kidney failure. Animals pierced with the poison arrows die a few hours later (sometimes days, for large mammals); the hunters therefore have to follow their game for some time.

Studies of the toxin's structure in the 1970s and '80s revealed that it works by increasing the permeability of red blood cell membranes. It is only dangerous to mammals and only when it enters the bloodstream—it is perfectly safe to ingest. *Diamphidia* larvae probably use it for self-defense. (The concentration in adults is only a tenth as strong.)

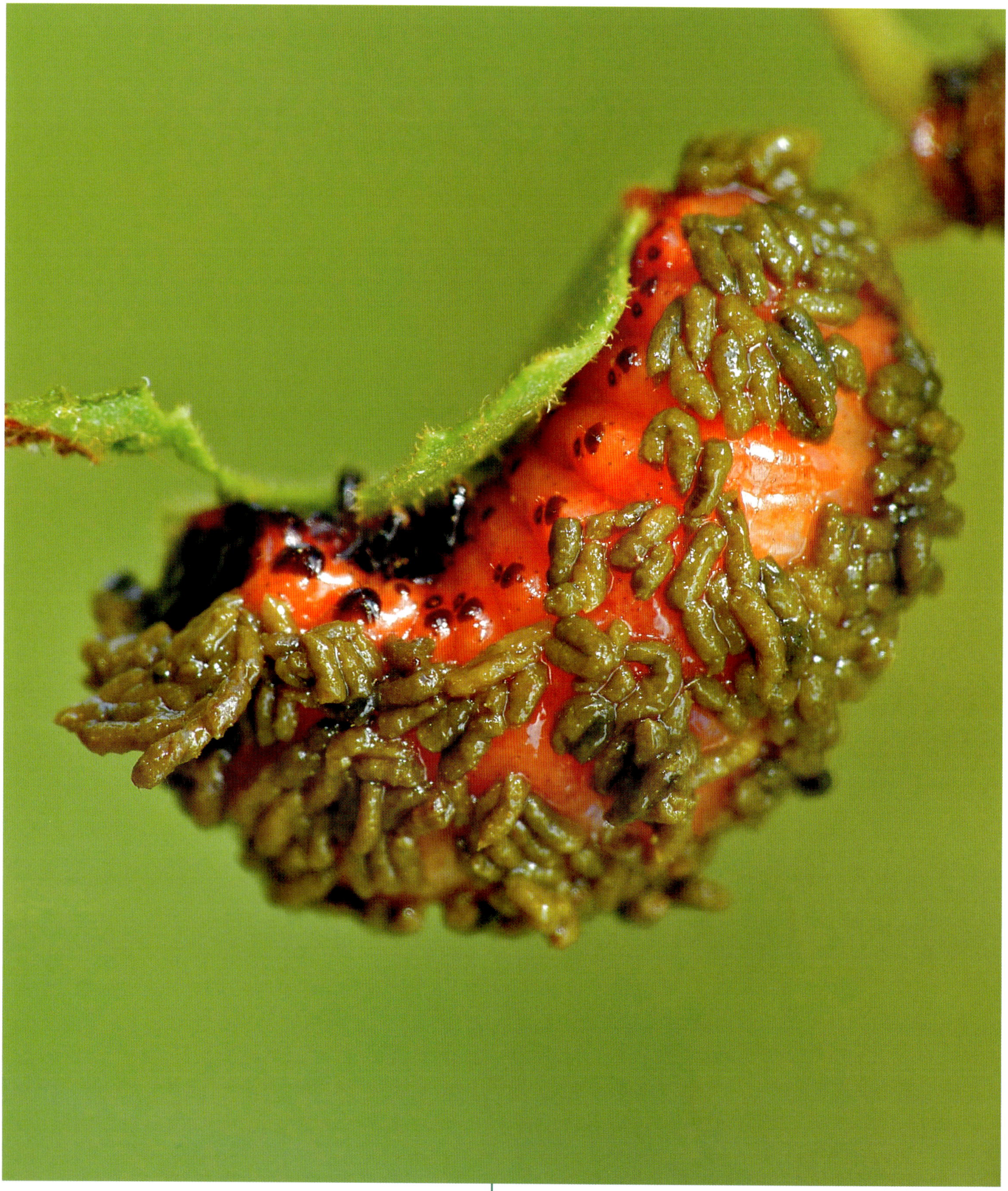

Beetle larvae in the genus *Diamphidia* (pictured: *D. vittatipennis*) cover themselves in their own excrement for camouflage.

© Bernard Dupont

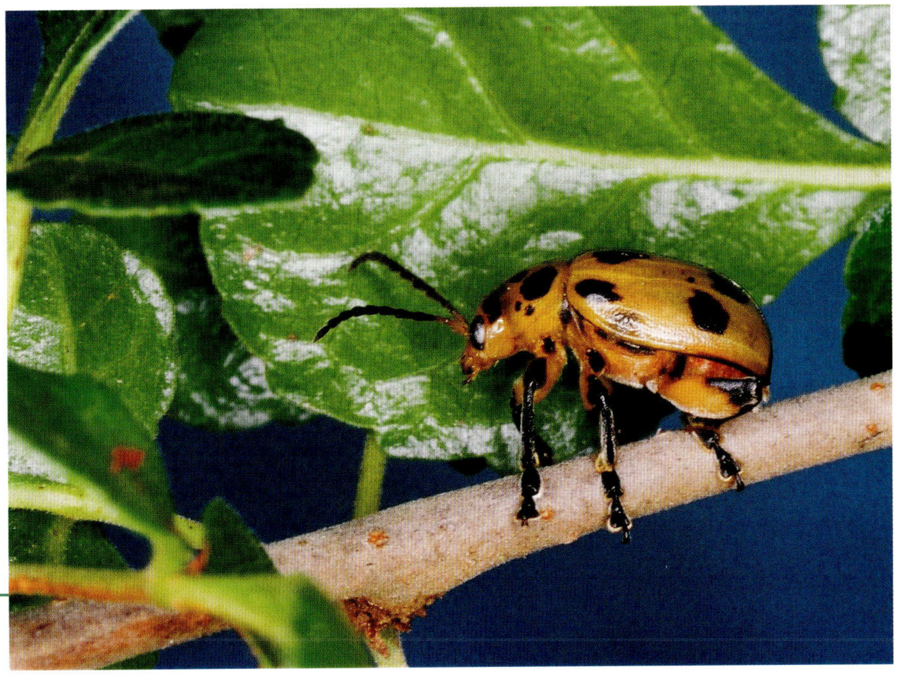

Adult *Diamphidia vittatipennis*.
© Caroline S. Chaboo

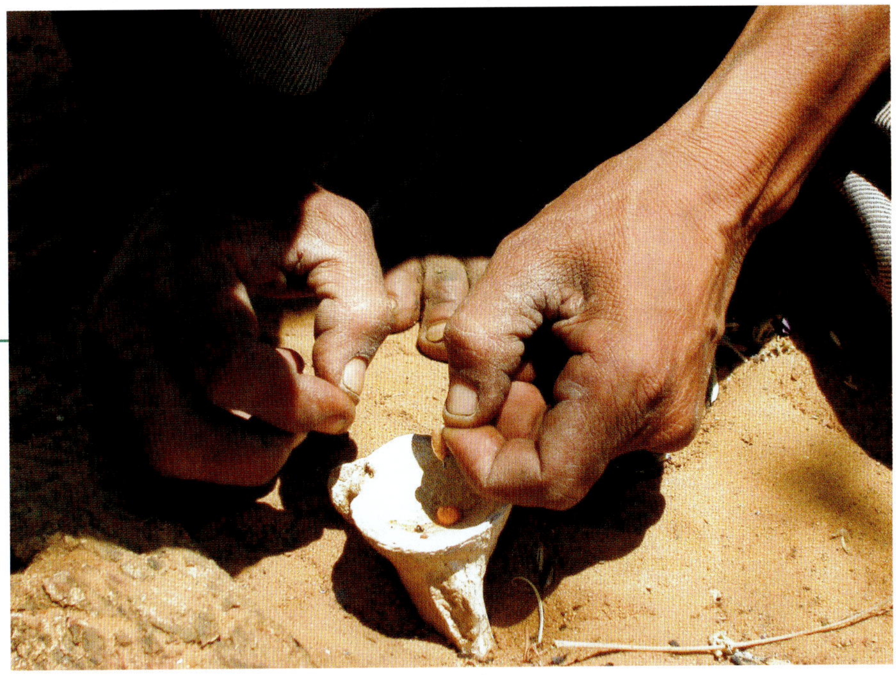

Preparing arrow poison
in a giraffe vertebra.
© Caroline S. Chaboo

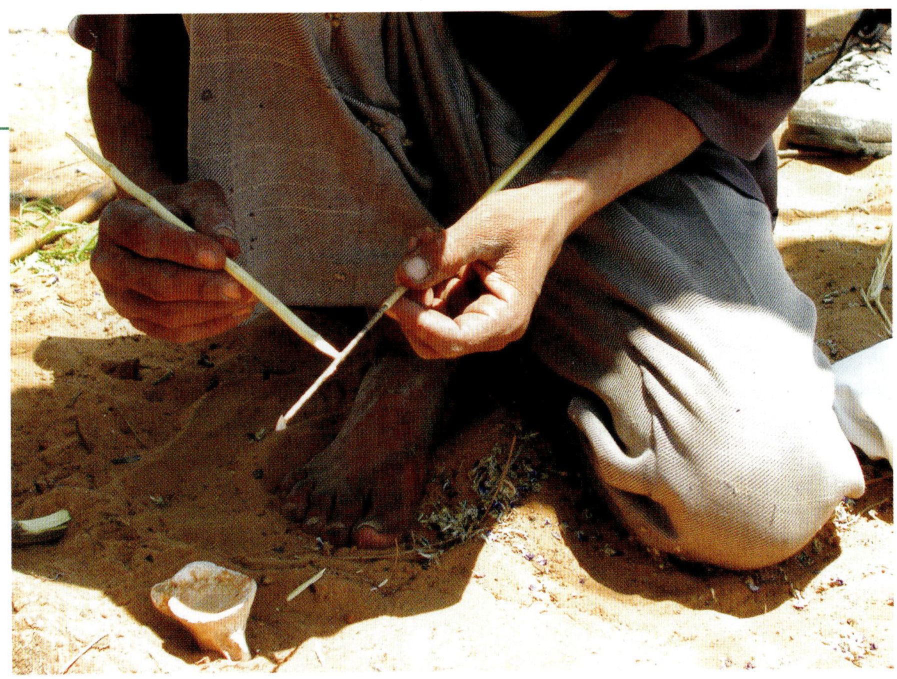

For safety, the poison is always
applied to a section of the shaft,
not the tip of the arrow.
© Caroline S. Chaboo

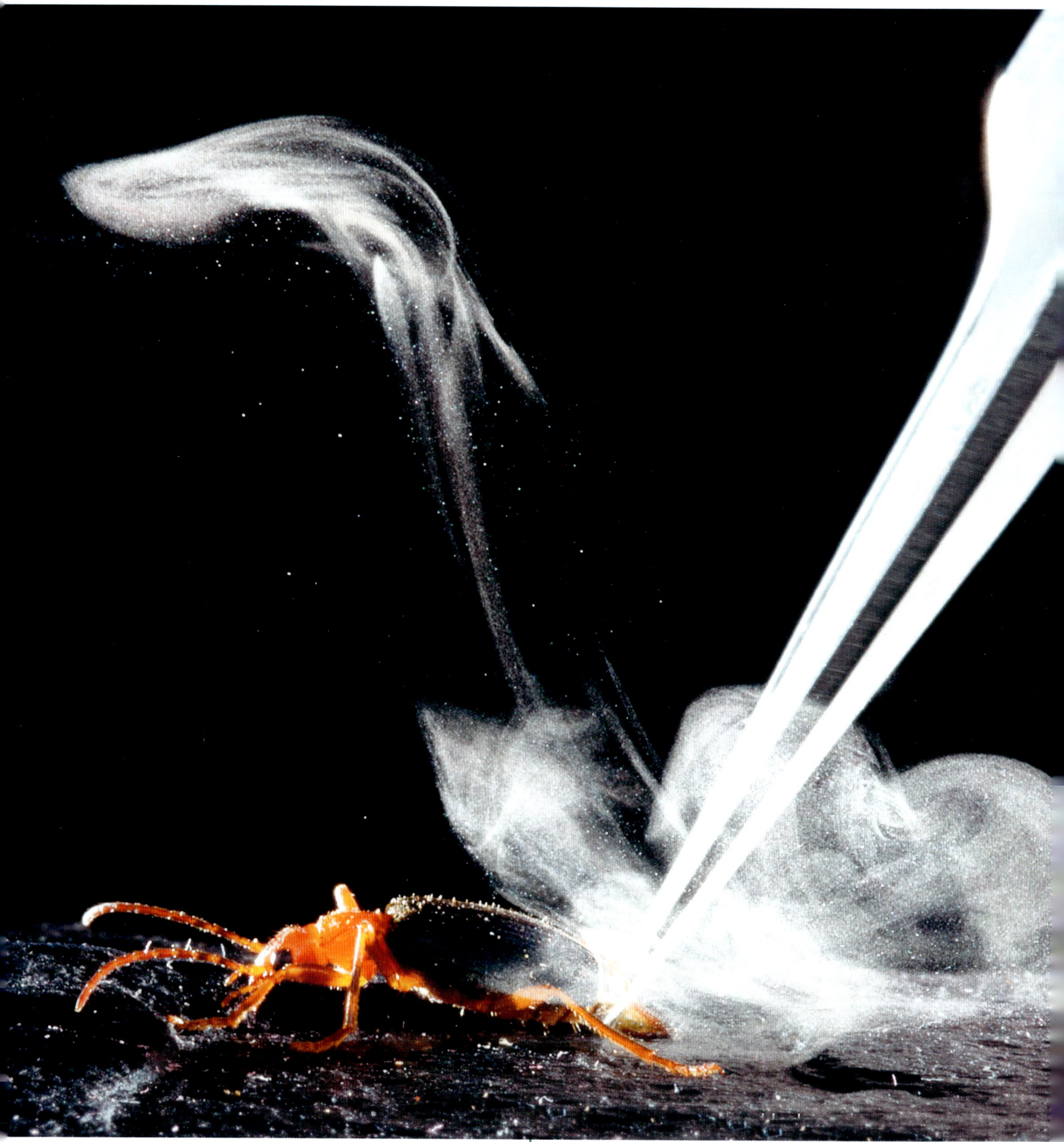

A video shot at 2,000 frames per second captured a bombardier beetle shooting caustic liquid from its abdomen.

TINY EXPLOSIONS

GENUS *BRACHINUS* AND COUSINS
(COLEOPTERA: CARABIDAE)

Hidden under stones or in the grass at the foot of trees, there lurk tiny insects that pack an explosive punch: bombardier beetles. They inhabit almost the entire planet, with more than forty species found in the United States. The group's common name comes from their remarkable defense mechanism: they can shoot a burning, corrosive substance at attackers that explodes upon release.

English entomologist John O. Westwood (1805–1893) observed the formidable defenses of a South American bombardier beetle in the nineteenth century, but it was German chemist Hermann Schildknecht (1922–1996) who discovered how the mechanism worked in 1957. The corrosive spray is produced from the reaction of two chemical compounds, hydroquinone and hydrogen peroxide, which are stored in separate cavities in the beetle's abdomen. When combined in a third, particularly strong-walled "firing chamber" (where enzymes help to break down the hydrogen peroxide and oxidate the hydroquinone), the hydrogen peroxide rapidly decomposes into oxygen and boiling water, while the hydroquinone oxidizes into benzoquinone, producing heat that brings the mixture to nearly 100 °C (212 °F). A gas then explodes out of the beetle that can be shot up to 30 centimeters from the tip of its abdomen. Some bombardier beetles can fire fifteen, twenty, or fifty times using a system of valves; others (like *Pheropsophus insignis* from Africa) release a spray of rapid-fire blasts. The beetles aim with precision by twisting their abdomens, burning would-be predators' eyes and mucous membranes with a blue-white vapor. And if some foolhardy frog chances to swallow a bombardier, the beetle can fire its caustic liquid from within the frog's stomach, causing it to vomit the beetle back out . . . alive!

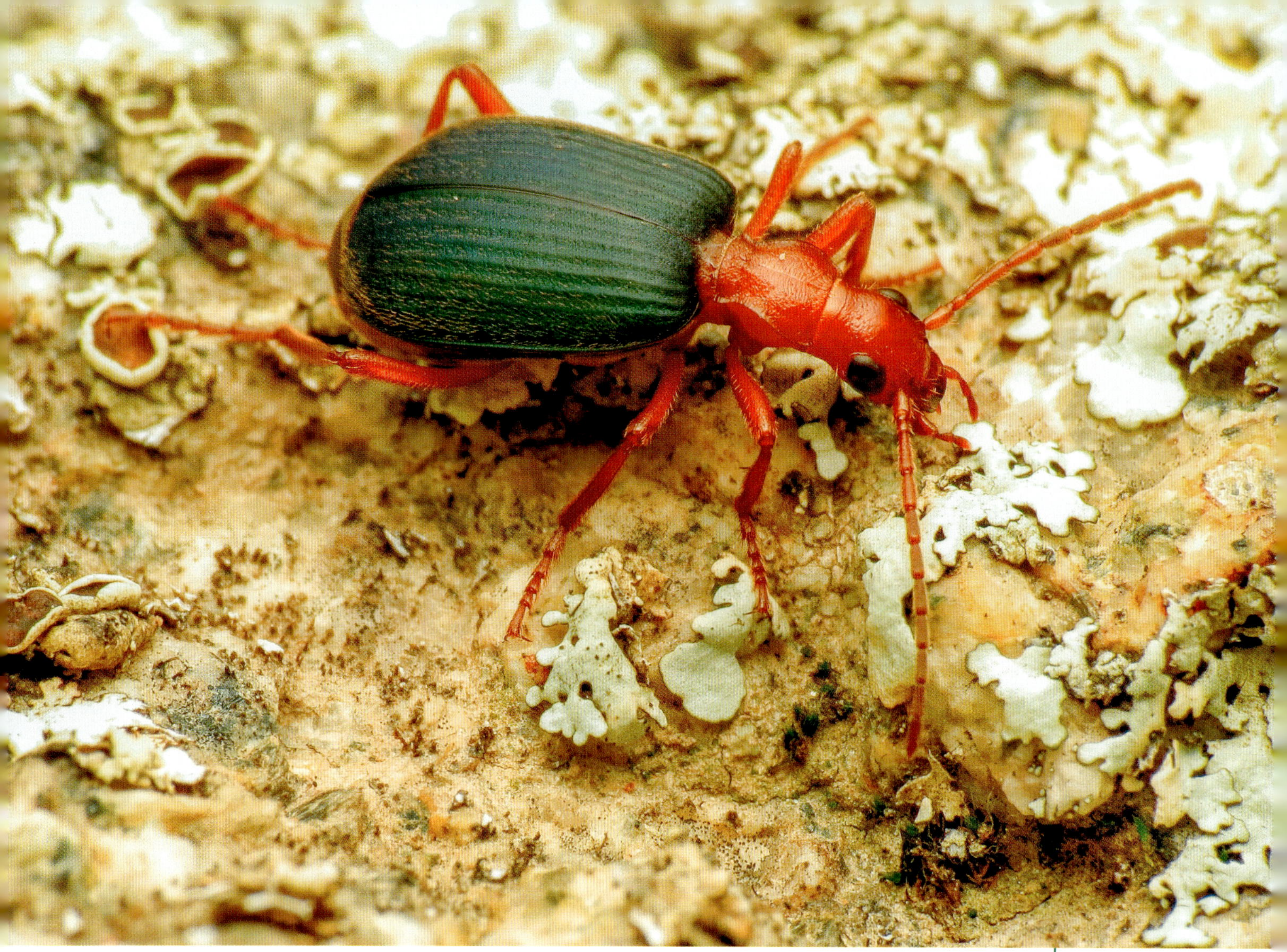

The eighty or so species of bombardier beetles in the genus *Brachinus* are found almost everywhere in the world. Pictured here: a *Brachinus fumans* from North America.

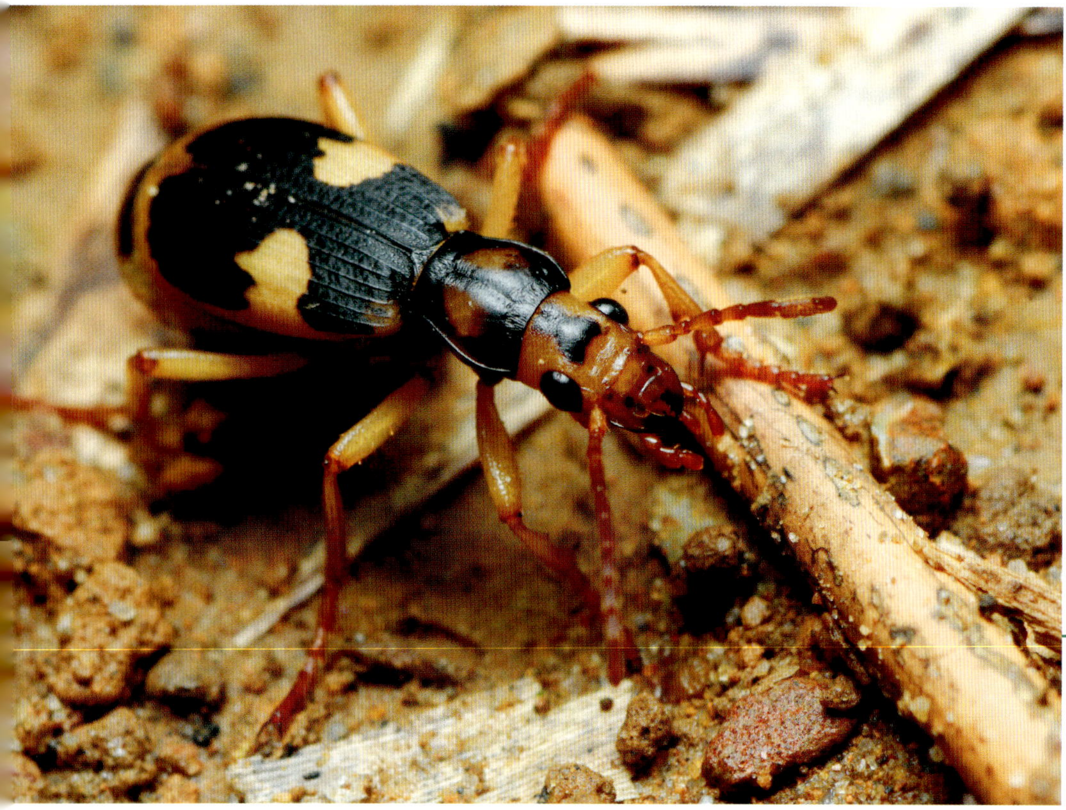

The genus *Pheropsophus* is made up of close cousins of the genus *Brachinus*, including this species from East Asia.

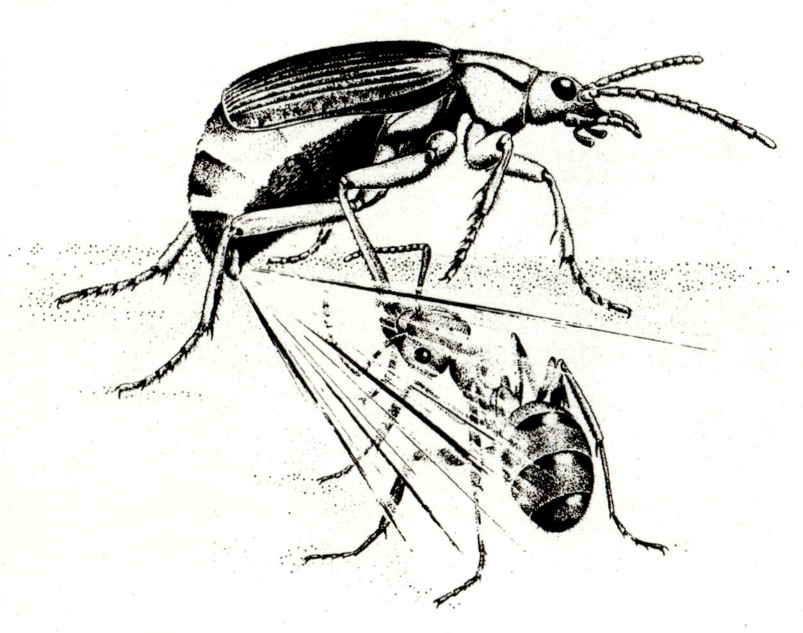

Bombardier beetles can target attackers with precision.

© Jacobs & Renner, *Biologie und Ökologie der Insekten: Ein Taschenlexikon* (1988)

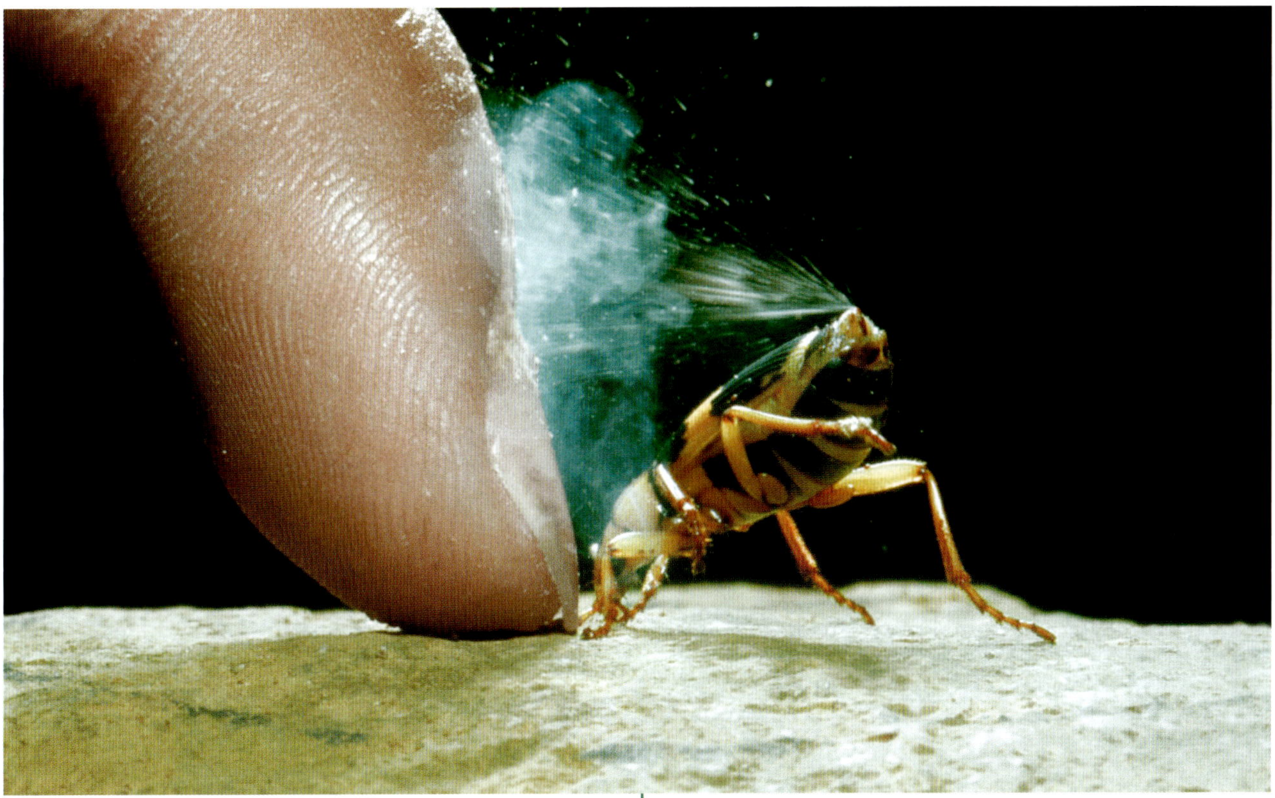

When threatened, bombardier beetles like this *Pheropsophus jessoensis* release a caustic spray.

© Ayaan Sheikh CC 4.0

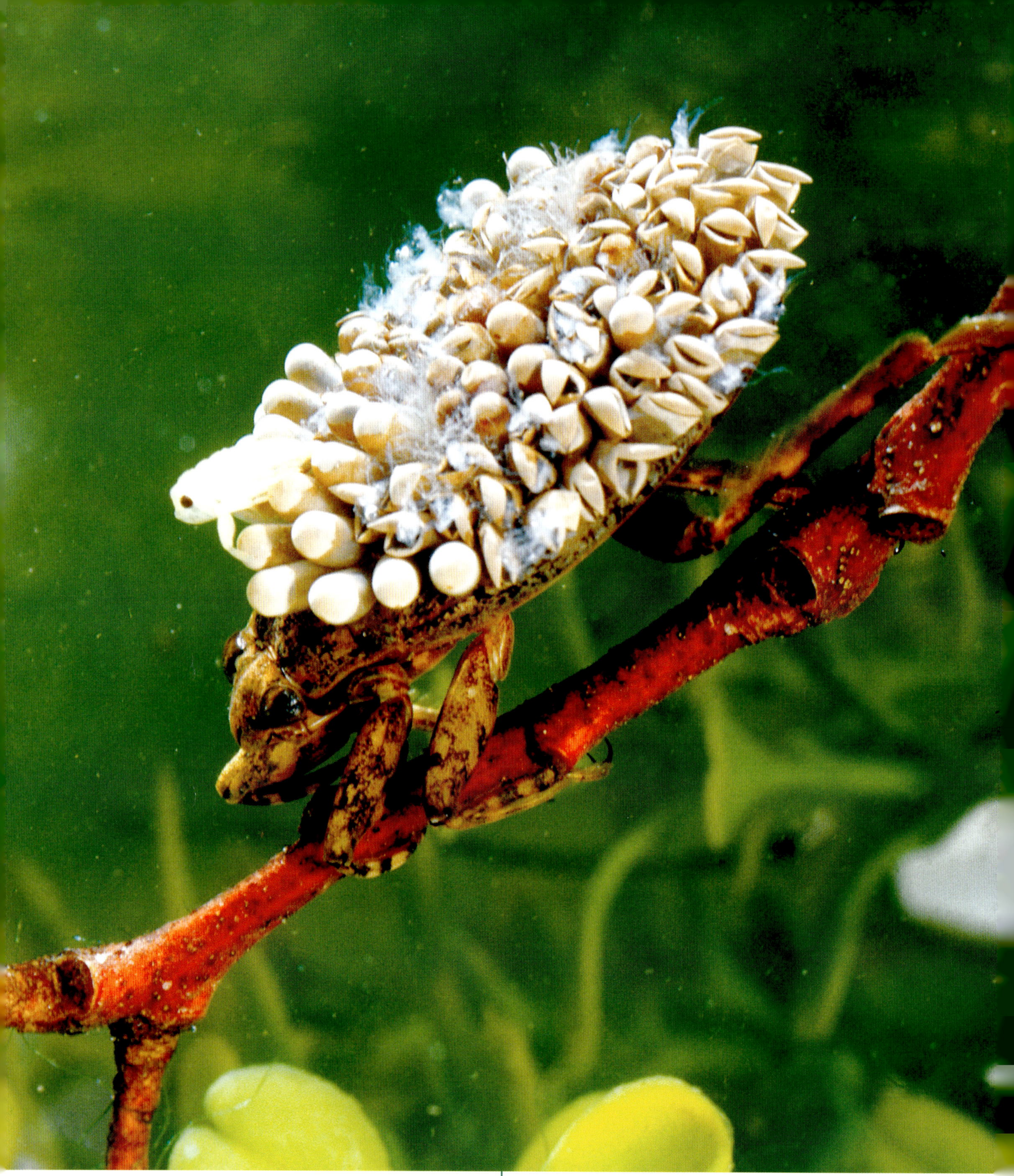

Male giant water bug with his eggs on his back.

KILLER DADS

LETHOCERUS *GRANDIS* AND RELATIVES

HEMIPTERA: BELOSTOMATIDAE

Giant water bugs are the great white sharks of aquatic insects . . . even if some only measure one or two centimeters long. The largest species in the genera *Lethocerus*, *Kirkaldyia*, and *Belostoma* do live up to the name—frequently reaching lengths of 8 centimeters, with some exceeding 12. Surprisingly, these ferocious predators are also attentive fathers.

The family Belostomatidae is made up of around 170 species of predatory hemipteran insects found in the Americas, Africa, and Southeast Asia, where they live in freshwater ponds, slow-moving streams, and rice paddies. They prey on crustaceans and other aquatic arthropods, fish larvae, amphibians, and small aquatic reptiles, which they stab with their proboscis and inject with digestive toxins, then suck out the victim's liquified body fluids. Their bite is probably the most painful of any insect, as their saliva attacks the subcutaneous tissues and can leave a lasting scar. The bites are also susceptible to infection.

Giant water bugs sometimes leave the water at night and may be drawn to light while flying. Males attract females by making regular undulating movements near the surface of the water. After mating, each female lays one to four eggs, then mates again, repeating the sequence up to thirty times. This strategy provides assurance of paternity and has led the males in some species—including some of the largest—to take part in caring for their young. Many species (including those in the genus *Lethocerus*) lay their eggs on stones, wood, or leaves. But females in the genus *Belostoma*, for example, lay their eggs on the father's back. Males in both categories will watch over the eggs until they hatch, by bringing them to the surface to receive oxygen or by keeping eggs laid on land moist. The eggs hatch after about three weeks, releasing baby water bugs that immediately start hunting prey appropriate to their size.

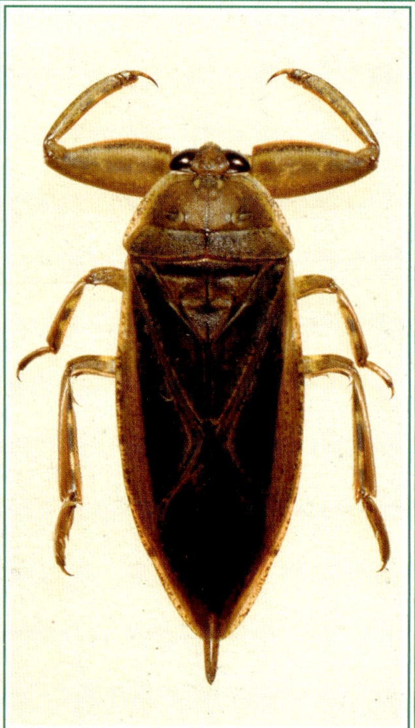

Lethocerus (Kirkaldyia) deyrollei, a large species native to Asia.

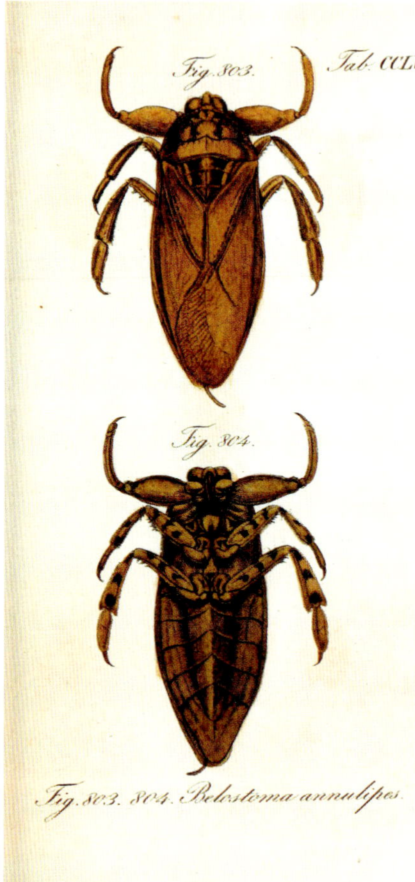

Illustration of another giant water bug, *Lethocerus annulipes*, from *Die wanzenartigen Insekten: Getreu nach der Natur abgebildet und beschrieben* (1839) by German entomologist Gottlieb Herrich-Schäffer (1799–1874), who described the neotropical species in 1845.

6-cm-long adult *Kirkaldyia deyrollei* attacking a baby turtle in a rice paddy in Hyōgo prefecture, Japan.

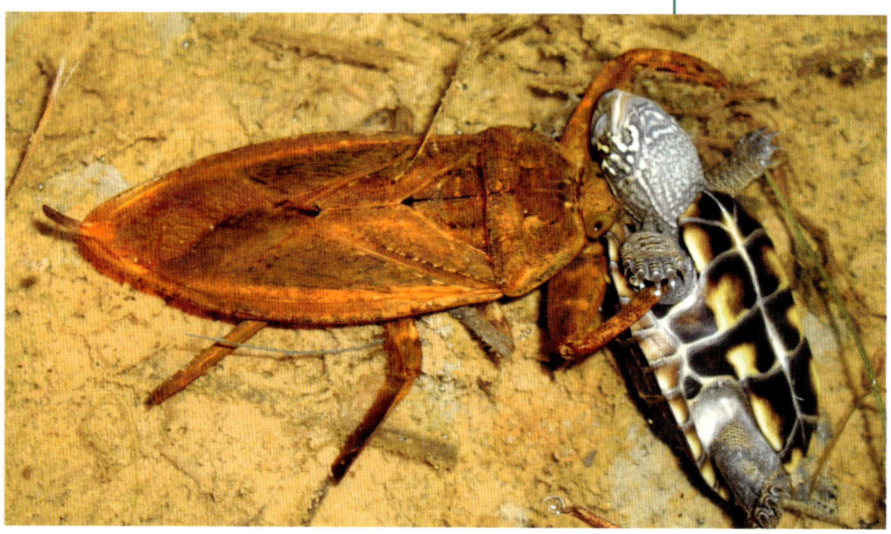

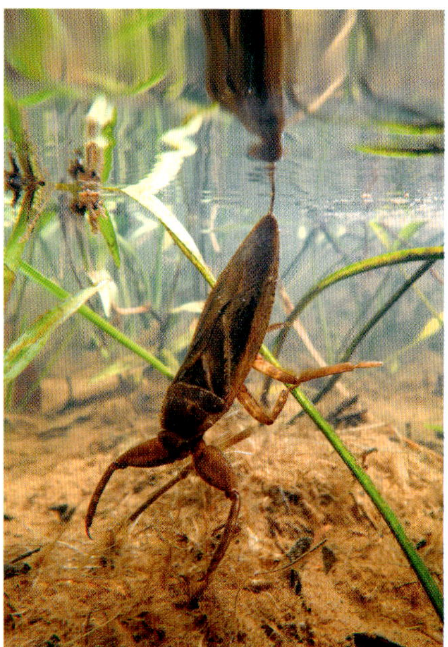

Giant water bugs, like this *Kirkaldyia deyrollei*, breathe underwater using a "snorkel" at the end of the abdomen. Heads down, they scan the water for potential prey.

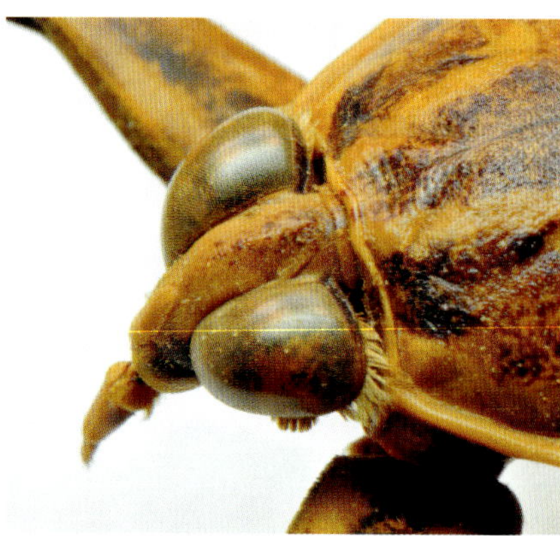

Giant water bugs use their rostrum (or proboscis) like a straw to suck out their prey's insides after liquifying them with digestive enzymes.

BUGS ON THE MENU

In some countries, giant water bugs are considered a delicacy. They are collected using floating traps that draw them in with lights, then sold in street markets. The most commonly eaten species is *Lethocerus indicus*, which is found throughout Southeast Asia and is known in Vietnam as cà cuống. A pheromone produced by the male is extracted from its glands and used parsimoniously as a condiment. As the threatened insects become more rare, this substance—often sold in tiny glass bottles—can fetch a high price, and much of what is sold is counterfeit. Giant water bugs are also eaten in the region around Yangon, Myanmar, where they are caught while flying around street lights and grilled over hot coals. In Thailand and Cambodia, they are fried with kaffir lime and garlic chives and eaten with hot sauce.

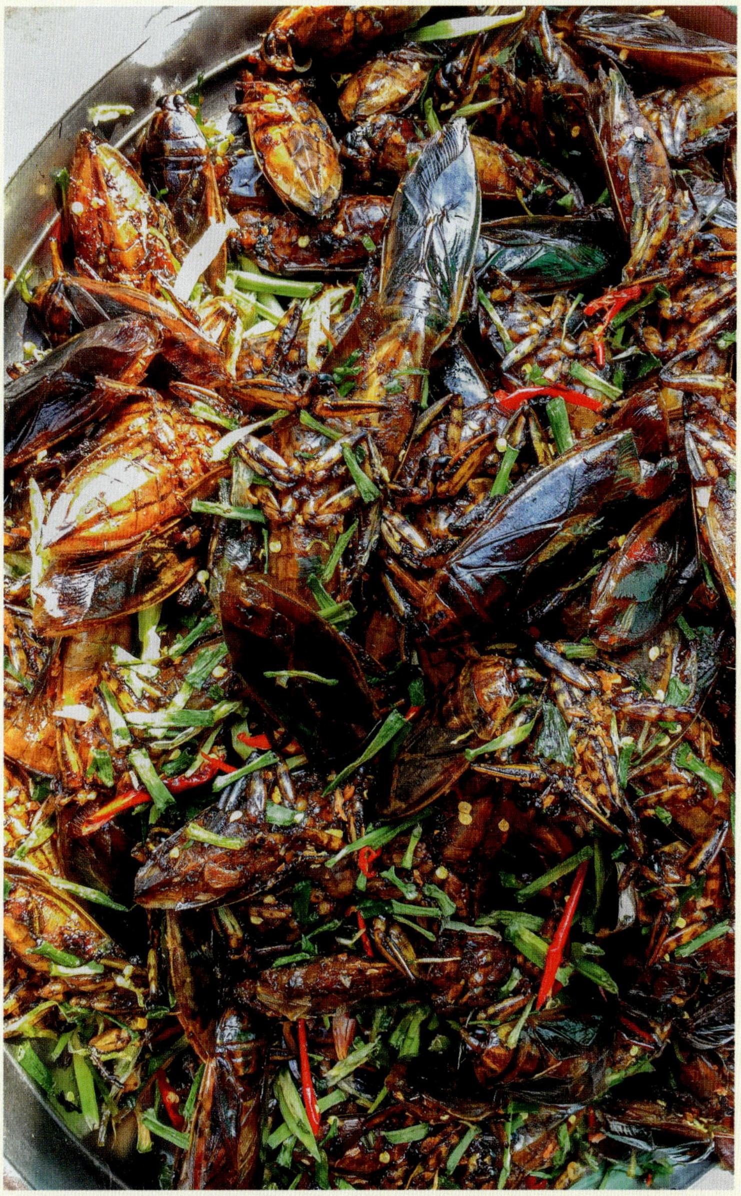

Fried giant water bugs for sale at a market stand in Phnom Penh, Cambodia.

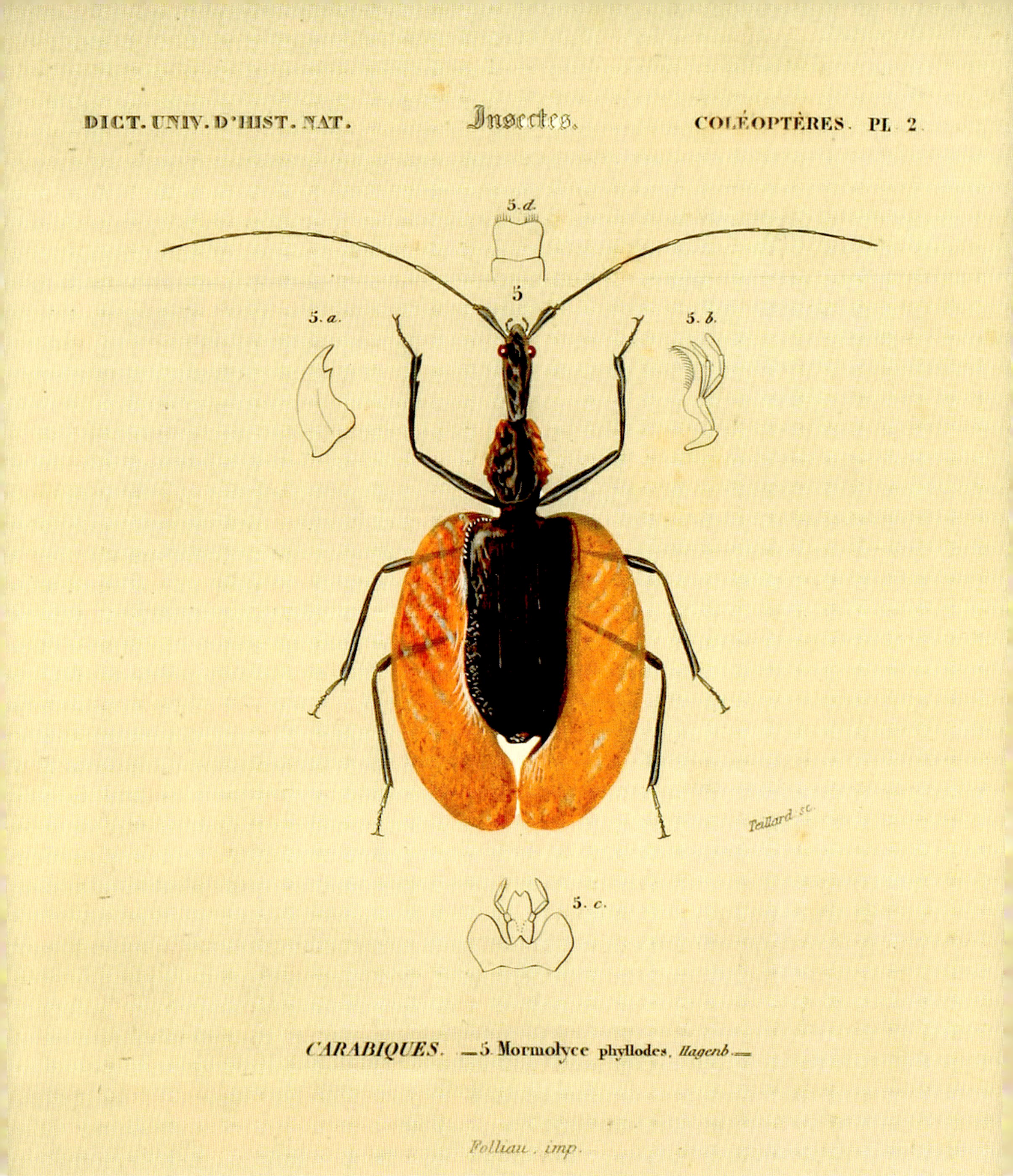

Illustration of *Mormolyce phyllodes* in *Dictionnaire universel d'histoire naturelle* by Charles d'Orbigny (1849).

THE ART OF CAMOUFLAGE

MORMOLYCE PHYLLODES
(COLEOPTERA: CARABIDAE)

The spectacular violin beetle has a flattened body that is vaguely shaped like the instrument in its name. Among several other defense mechanisms, it uses camouflage to hide from predators and can quickly slip away into narrow cracks and crevices.

This unusual-looking ground beetle was described by Swiss entomologist Jacob Johann Hagenbach (1802–1825) and greatly intrigued naturalists of his day. Its broad, flat, translucent elytra mimic a dry leaf (the species name *phyllodes* means "leaflike"), allowing it to blend in with the forest floor. A fine fungal coating over most of its body completes the effect. Its flat body shape allows it to slip under the bark of trees and fallen logs, or into rocky fissures or cavities. It can even fit within the layers of tree fungus (conks) growing on dead or dying trees, which is where its larvae develop. Like other ground beetles, it defends itself by secreting butyric acid when threatened. Violin beetles are active at night and attracted to light. They are good fliers, although they have to take off from a tree trunk to build up speed. Both the larvae and adults are carnivorous and feed on small arthropods and gastropods.

There are six species of violin beetle, all of which are native to the tropical forests of Southeast Asia (including parts of Thailand, Malaysia, Indonesia, and the southern Philippines). For a long time, they were rare in collections. English entomologist Robert C. Shelford (1872–1912) recounted in a posthumous work published in 1916 that, in the late nineteenth century, the French National Museum of Natural History in Paris offered up to a thousand gold francs for a specimen captured on Java. Nowadays, these beautiful beetles are threatened by mass tourism and the clearing of forests for agriculture.

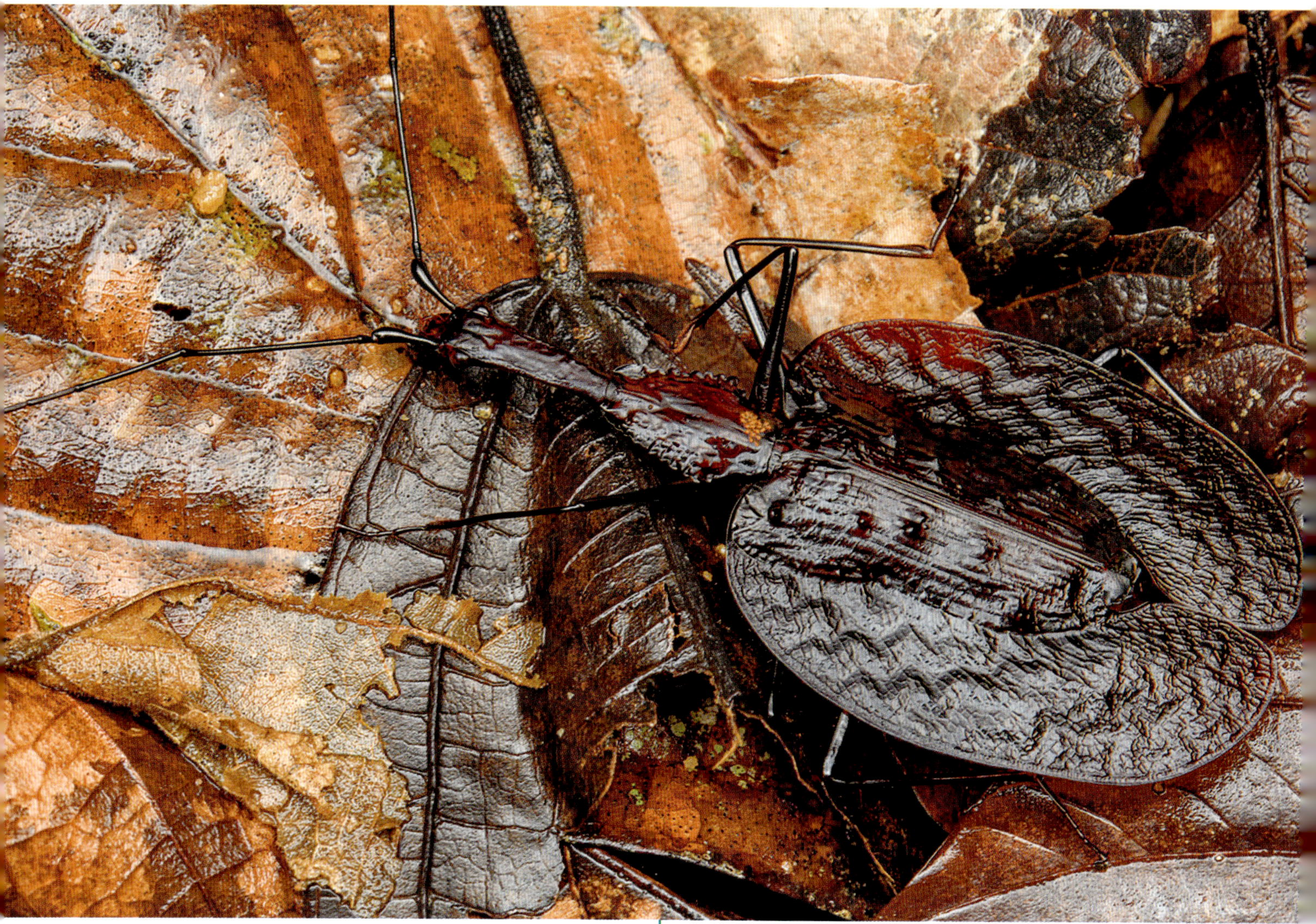

Violin beetle moving over the tropical forest floor on the island of Borneo. These rare beetles are 6–10 cm long.
© Chien Lee

The giant Malaysian leaf insect (*Pulchriphyllium giganteum*), like the violin beetle, hides by mimicking a leaf. Its forest habitat makes this an ideal defensive strategy. Leaf insects can be found from India and China throughout the Malay Archipelago to Australia.
© Kazuo Unno/Oasis/Biosphoto

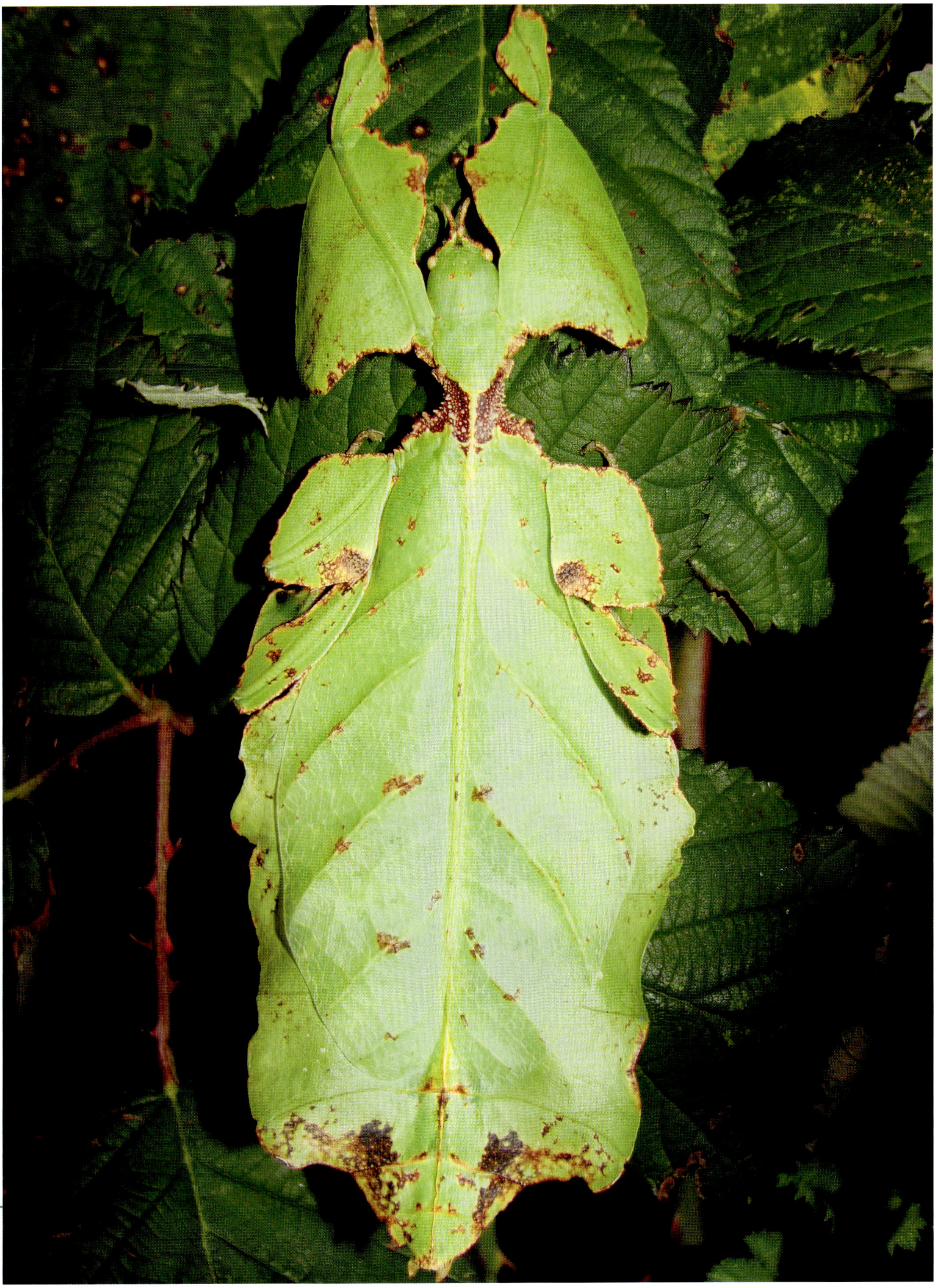

DRESSED FOR DEFENSE

LACEWINGS IN DISGUISE

The larvae of green lacewings and certain other net-winged insects (order: Neuroptera) have small bumps and hairs on their backs that they use to cover themselves in debris—egg remnants, the bodies of their prey, cast-off pieces of exoskeleton, plant litter, dirt, etc.—all wrapped up in silk. It is not entirely clear what this covering is for. Camouflage? Retaining heat or moisture? Protection from ants, ladybugs, and other predators? Revealingly, lacewing larvae that do not cover themselves are often more voracious, aggressive, and mobile, and they develop more quickly. All lacewing larvae also have a chemical defense mechanism to discourage predators (and their own cousins) from eating them.

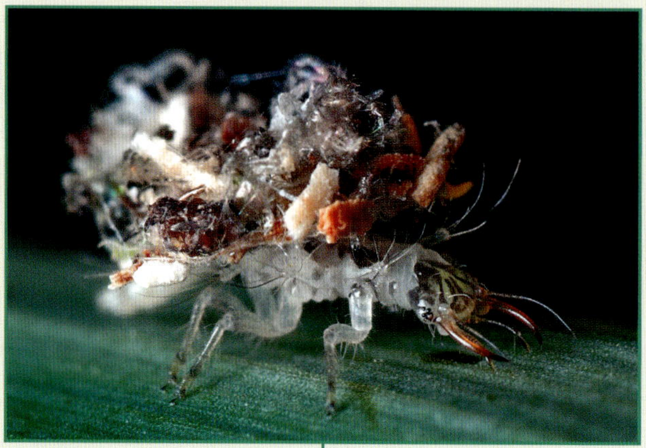

Green lacewing larva covered in the bodies of ants and other debris.

CADDISFLY ARTISTS

Trichopterans, commonly known as caddisflies, are a diverse order of insects whose larvae are famous for making underwater structures in which to hide on lake- and streambeds. These structures may take the form of tubular body cases or stationary domes that they construct using their strong, flexible silk and various other materials (such as sand, gravel, plant debris, bits of shells) or sometimes silk alone. They have even been encouraged to make beautiful art pieces by giving them bits of gold or silver leaf to build with. Some species only build protective structures for use during metamorphosis. In all cases, the larvae's creations are not just useful for themselves: the structures also benefit the geomorphology of the entire aquatic habitat when caddisfly populations are large enough.

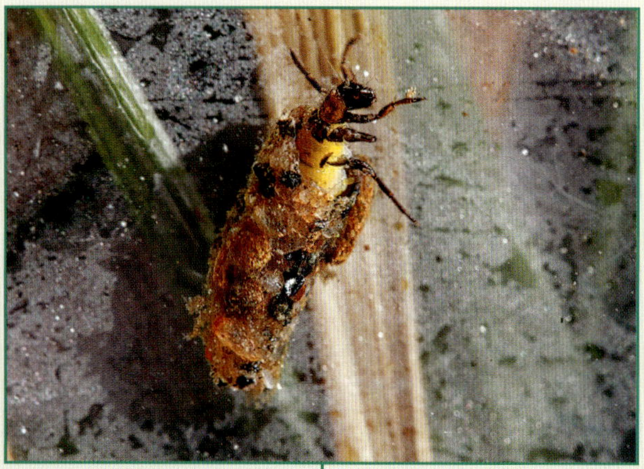

Caddisfly larvae build protective cases from various materials. This *Neophylax consimilis* from North America used colorful gravel.

CATERPILLARS IN CABINS

Some caterpillars also dress up for defense: bagworms in the family Psychidae build armor out of wood! These protective cases are made using twigs, thorns, or other woody debris to form precise structures, some of which look like tiny log cabins. The caterpillars never leave their cases entirely and simply remodel them as they grow.

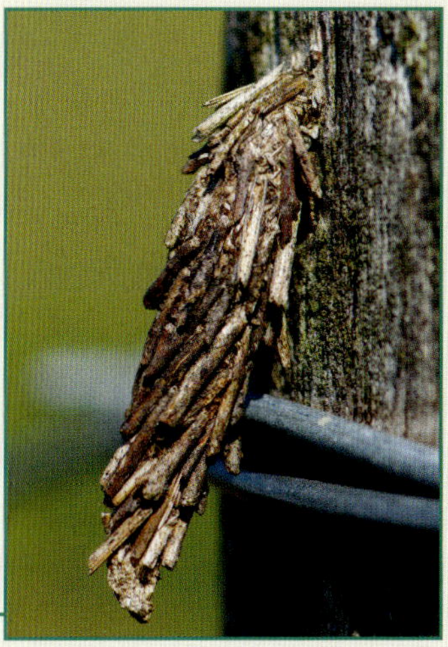

Protective wooden case built by a bagworm caterpillar.

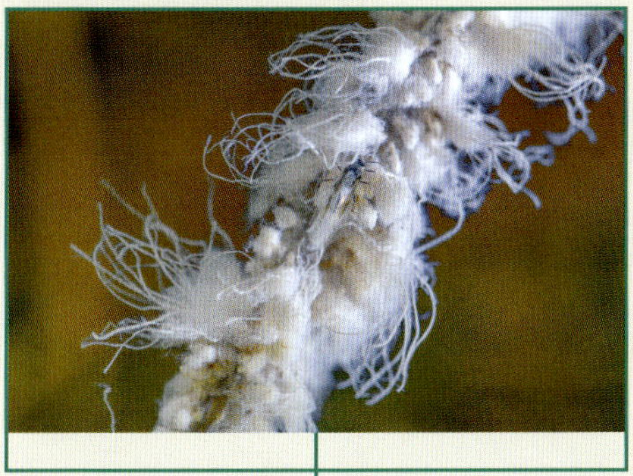

Woolly apple aphids (*Eriosoma lanigerum*).

WOOLLY, WAXY APHIDS

Instead of collecting material to build a defensive shelter, some insects prefer homemade. For example, woolly apple aphids (order: Hemiptera) shelter under a cottony white secretion of wax that protects them from predators and UV radiation and keeps humidity levels stable. This "wool" looks similar to the furry coating on some plants, so it may also serve as camouflage. Or it may be the other way around, and the plants are mimicking the aphids . . . to dissuade new arrivals by giving the impression that the plant is already infested.

FOAMY HOMEMAKERS

Spittlebugs, also known as froghoppers (Hemiptera: Cercopoidea), are found all around the world. Their common name comes from the fact that the nymphs of many species protect themselves from predators and changes in temperature and humidity by hiding in a nest of "spittle": viscous liquid excrement into which they blow air to make foam. The nymphs remain inside their foamy nests until adulthood. Some species can even adjust the size of the bubbles based on the intensity of the light, as smaller bubbles offer more protection.

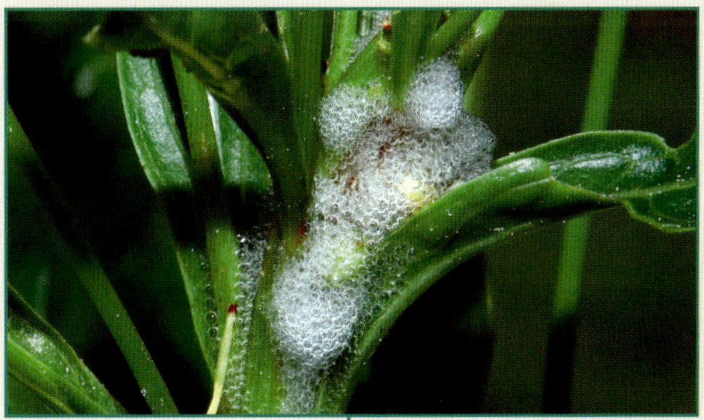

The meadow spittlebug (*Philaenus spumarius*) is native to the Palearctic realm but has been introduced to the United States, where it is now common. The nymphs produce a froth of iridescent bubbles colloquially known as "cuckoo spit," "frog spit," or "snake spit."

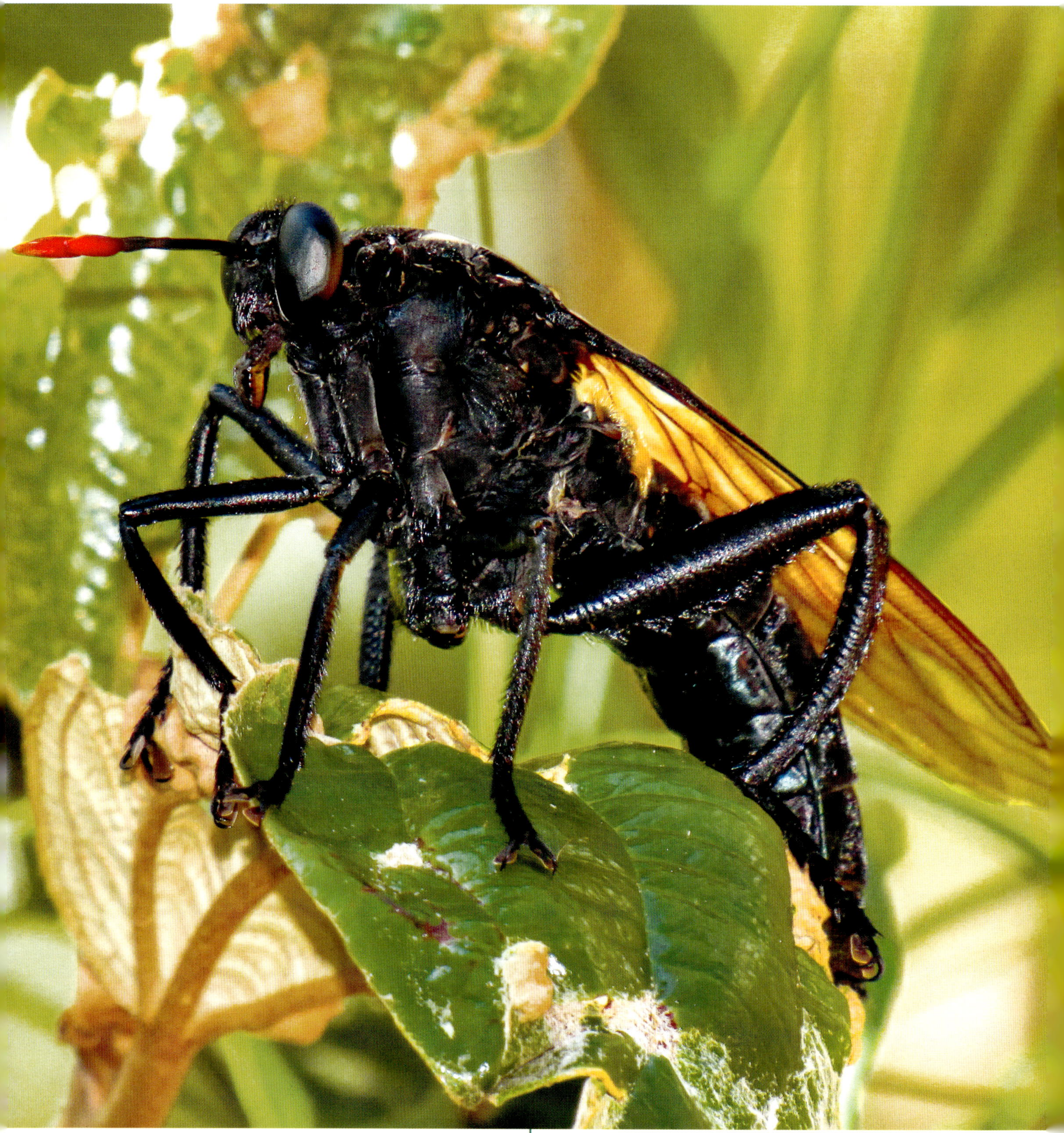

Rare photograph of a live *Gauromydas heros* fly.

A FLY IN WASP'S CLOTHING

GAUROMYDAS HEROS
(DIPTERA: MYDIDAE)

Although it certainly stands out, this giant fly from southeastern Brazil and Paraguay has rarely been observed. It can grow up to 8 centimeters long, with a wingspan of 10 centimeters across, and has oversized, arched hindlegs ending in spines. Its appearance mimics spider wasps in the genus *Pepsis*, which have a sting powerful enough to kill tarantulas that the wasps feed to their larvae.

From 1817 to 1835, a team of naturalists traveled to Brazil in an expedition organized and financed by the Austrian Empire to study the country's flora, fauna, and Indigenous cultures, still largely unknown in Europe. During eighteen years of field work, the team collected thousands of specimens, most of which are now held at the Deutsches Museum in Munich. Based on specimens brought back by a member of the expedition, Johann Baptist von Spix (1781–1826), German naturalist Maximilian Perty (1804–1884) described some twenty new species of fly, including the largest known to science: *Gauromydas heros*.

G. heros is a remarkable example of Batesian mimicry (named after English naturalist Henry Walter Bates), in which a harmless species imitates the warning signals of a more dangerous species to frighten off predators. This fly takes the deception even further by imitating not only the appearance but also the behavior of spider wasps: fluttering just over the surface of anthills, wiggling its antennae, and constantly rubbing its wings.

The giant fly was studied in depth by Jose Francisco Zikán (1881–1949), an entomologist born in Czechoslovakia who emigrated to Brazil in 1902 and spent the next forty years studying the fauna of Itatiaia National Park, on the border between the states of Rio de Janeiro and Minas Gerais. The adult males feed on nectar, and the females do not feed at all. The latter can be seen flying around leafcutter ant nests (genus: *Atta*), where they lay their eggs near the fungi cultivated by the colony, apparently unbothered by the ants. *G. heros* maggots develop within the anthill and grow to over 4 centimeters long. They feed on beetle larvae: symbionts of the ants that develop in the chambers of the colony

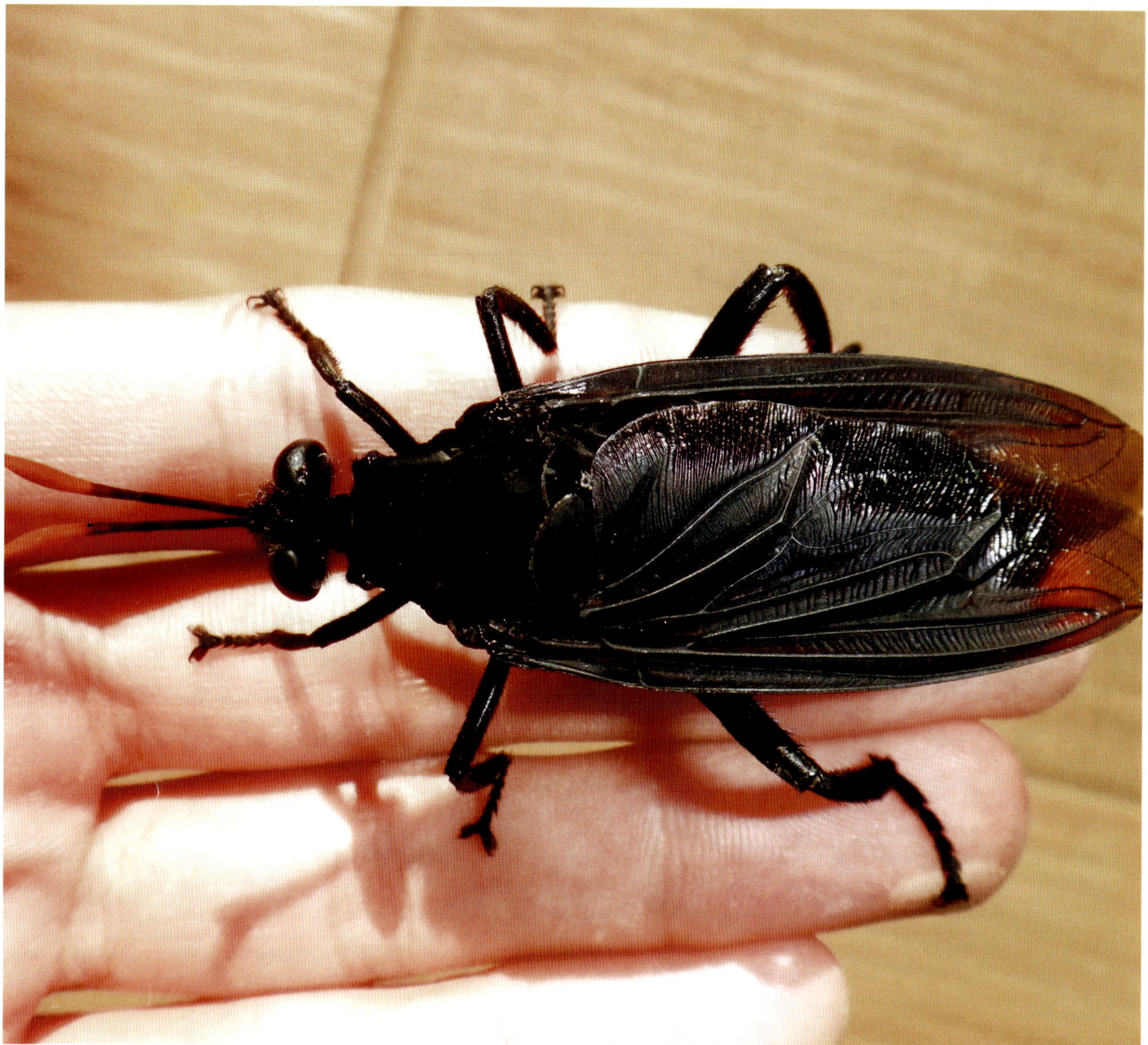

A human hand for scale shows the impressive size of *Gauromydas heros*.
© André Alves

where the ants store their waste. It is unknown how long the *G. heros* maggots take to fully develop, but once they are ready to metamorphose, they dig a 10- to 20-centimeter-deep gallery into the soil that ends in a chamber where they pupate. Males tend to emerge before the females and are highly territorial, fending off rivals with their spiny hindlegs as they wait near leafcutter anthills for the females to emerge and mate.

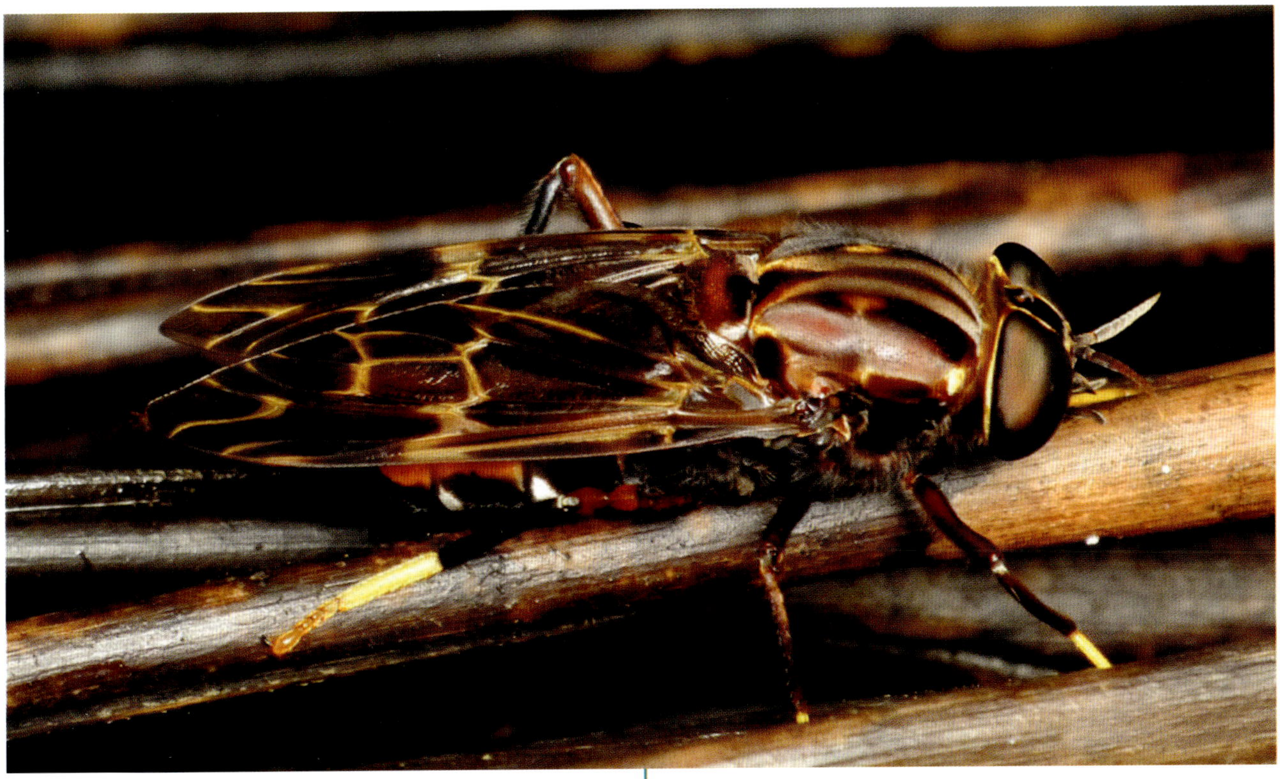

Flies from the family Pantophthalmidae are also among the largest in the world, reaching 6 cm in length with a wingspan of 10 cm. Their larvae feed on decomposing wood, the source of their common name: timber flies. They are native to the Amazon basin and have rarely been observed. This *Pantophtalmus* pictus was photographed in Ecuador.

© Andreas Kay

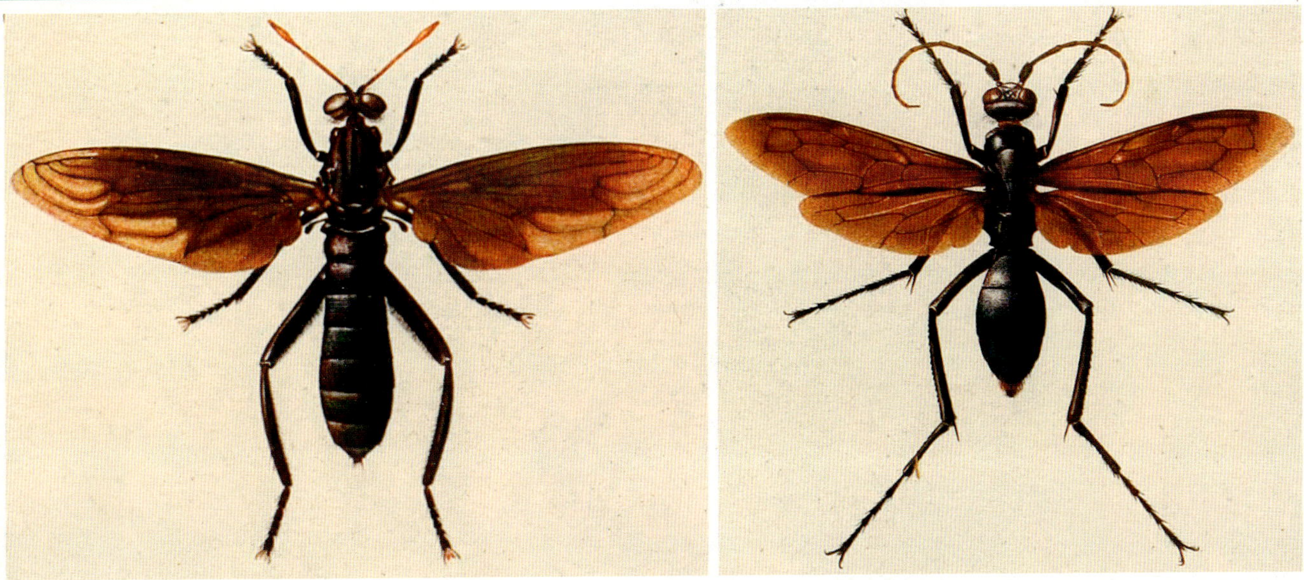

Gauromydas heros (left) are flies that mimic spider wasps, also known as tarantula hawks (right). This illustration comes from a 1910 article by Australian entomologist Ernest E. Austen (1867–1938).

© Austen, "A new species of the dipterous genus Achias Fabr. (Family Ortalidae)," *Novitates Zoologicae*, 1910

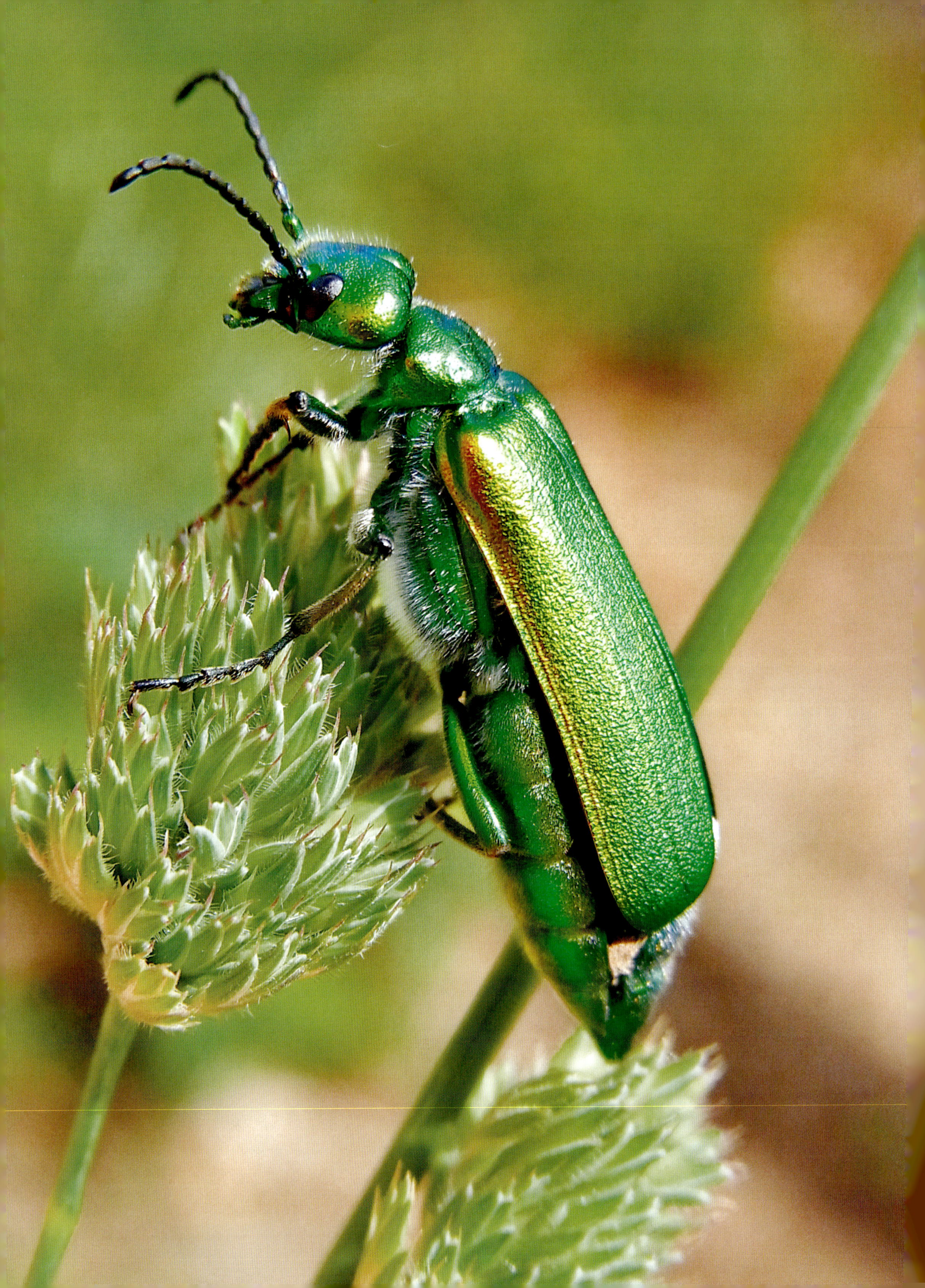

THE SADISTIC SPANISH FLY

LYTTA VESICATORIA

(COLEOPTERA: MELOIDAE)

The Spanish fly is not actually a fly at all but a beetle. It was famously used for centuries in medicine as a blistering agent in apothecary preparations, as well as a supposed aphrodisiac.

The Spanish fly has had a significant role in medicine—and therefore considerable economic significance—dating back to ancient history. In 1798, during the First French Republic, physicians were urged to collect the insect and exploit it for its therapeutic virtues. French pharmacist Pierre Robiquet (1780–1840) isolated its active component, cantharidin, in 1810. The highly toxic substance remains active for a long time and can be as poisonous as strychnine. Horses and other livestock have died from eating hay containing Spanish flies. If ingested, cantharidin causes severe damage to the gastrointestinal and urinary tracts, diarrhea, fever, accelerated breathing and heartbeat, dehydration, hypersalivation, and even death—a lethal dose for humans is between 10 and 80 milligrams. If touched, it irritates the skin and mucous membranes, causing blisters and lesions. The Spanish fly and other cantharidin-producing insects are not hurt because, while within their bodies, the compound is linked to molecules that keep it within their hemolymph (the insect equivalent of blood), which prevents it from entering their cells.

For centuries, Spanish flies were used in medicine as a local irritant or diuretic. Collecting and sun-drying the beetles was once a lucrative business in Spain, Italy, the south of France, and other Mediterranean countries. And they were not hard

***Lytta vesicatoria*, the Spanish fly, is actually an iridescent green beetle measuring 10–22 cm long. It is native to central and southern Europe, the Mediterranean Basin, and much of Asia. If its unpleasant smell is not enough to warn off predators, it can exude a toxic substance, cantharidin, from its leg joints.**

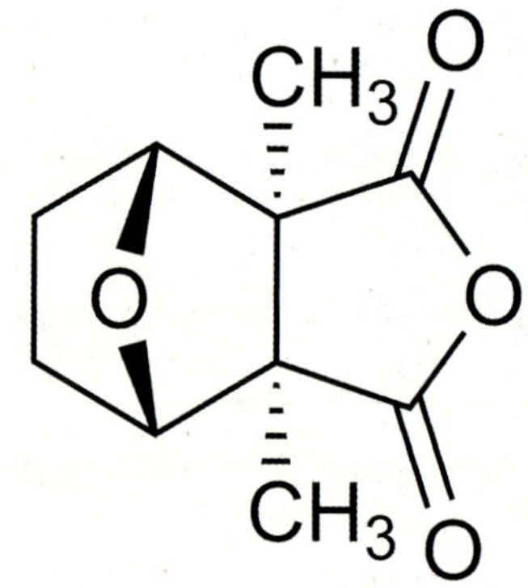

The name of the toxin produced by the Spanish fly, cantharidin, comes from the insect's name in ancient Rome (*cantharis*) and ancient Greece (κᾰνθᾰρῐ́ς, kantharís). Many other species produce or "collect" cantharidin (by eating the insects that produce it) as a defense mechanism at various stages of development. It is highly damaging to the cellular metabolism and is still used to this day in some wart-removal creams.

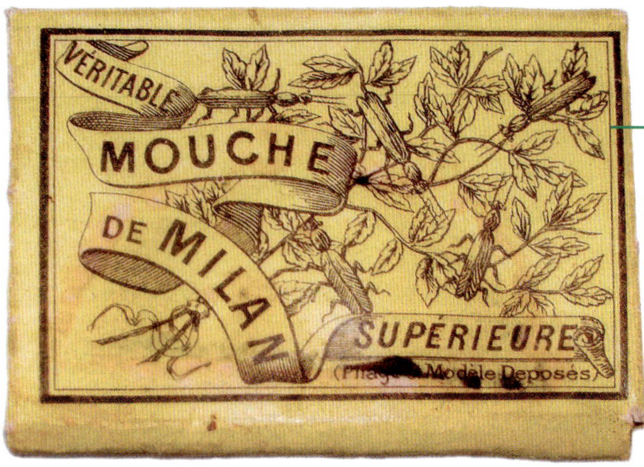

The Spanish fly is also known as *la mouche de Milan* in French. The name was trademarked as a pharmaceutical brand in 1858.

© Pierre-Olivier Maquart

to find: in 1848, English botanist Giles Munby (1813–1876) described seeing a willow tree near Dijon, France, that was so covered with Spanish flies that their droppings darkened the ground and they could be smelled from a hundred feet away. Munby also noted that the dry beetles sold for six shillings per pound.

But the Spanish fly is perhaps best known for its use throughout history as an aphrodisiac, under the name cantharides. Because its toxin irritates the urinary tract, the effect can be mistaken for sexual arousal; it also dilates the blood vessels, causing

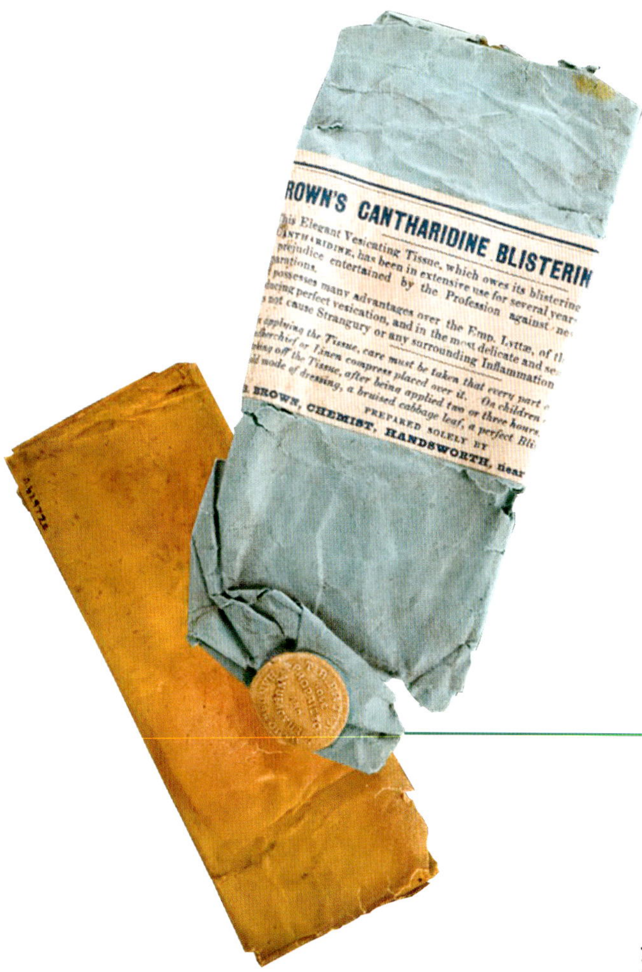

Cantharidin, often mixed into resin or wax, was once used as a topical irritant and applied to plasters and bandages for treating inflammation of the skin and joints.

© Wellcome Collection CC 4.0

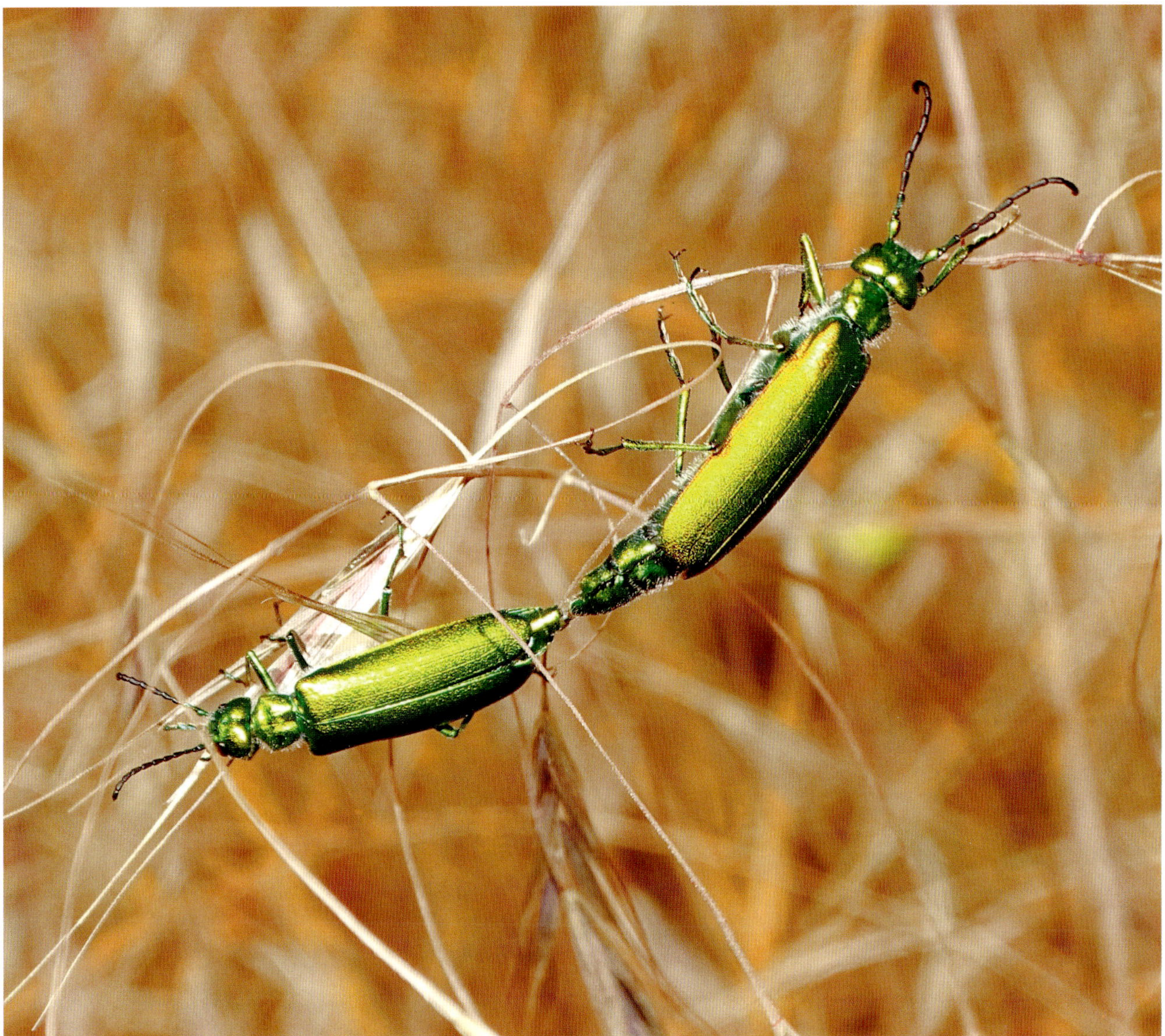

Only male Spanish flies produce cantharidin, which they synthesize from farnesol, a natural alcohol found in many plants. Females acquire it from the males as a "nuptial gift": the spermatophore (an organic capsule containing sperm) that males give to females also contains cantharidin that they then stock in their ovaries. A sample taken in Sicily showed that male Spanish flies contained about 1.8 percent cantharidin, and females 1 percent.

priapism in men that can irremediably alter erectile function. An effective dose is dangerously close to a fatal one, and there are many recorded cases of accidental or intentional poisoning with cantharides. Sweets laced with the substance were said to have been distributed by the notorious libertine Maréchal de Richelieu (1696–1788) to women he hoped to seduce. And in 1772, the Marquis de Sade (1740–1814) gave aniseed-flavored pastilles laced with cantharides to two prostitutes in Marseille. Both fell critically ill. One of them, Marguerite Coste, realized what had happened and denounced Sade, who was condemned to death in absentia, having fled to Italy. (The sentence was reversed in 1778.)

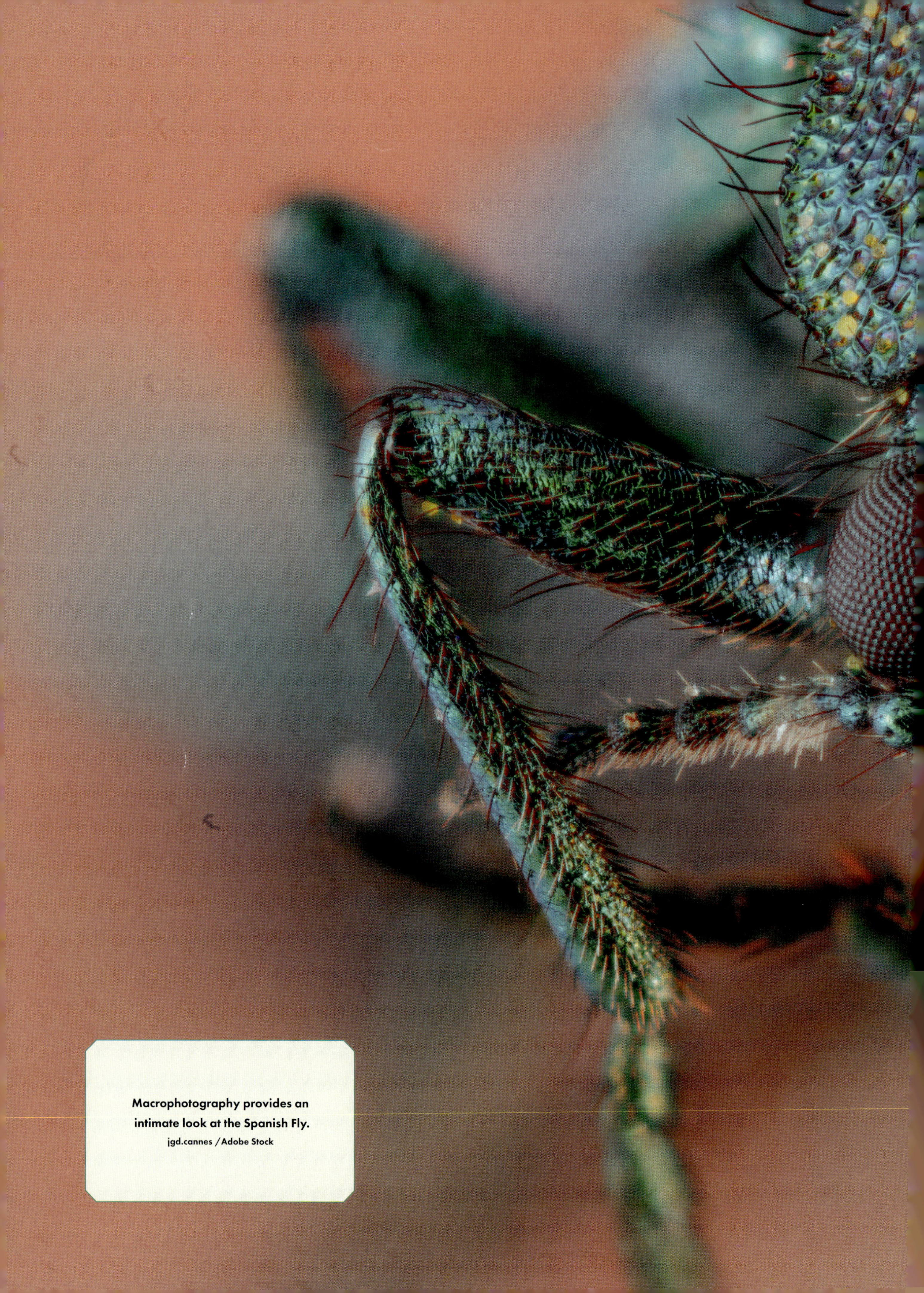

Macrophotography provides an intimate look at the Spanish Fly.
jgd.cannes / Adobe Stock

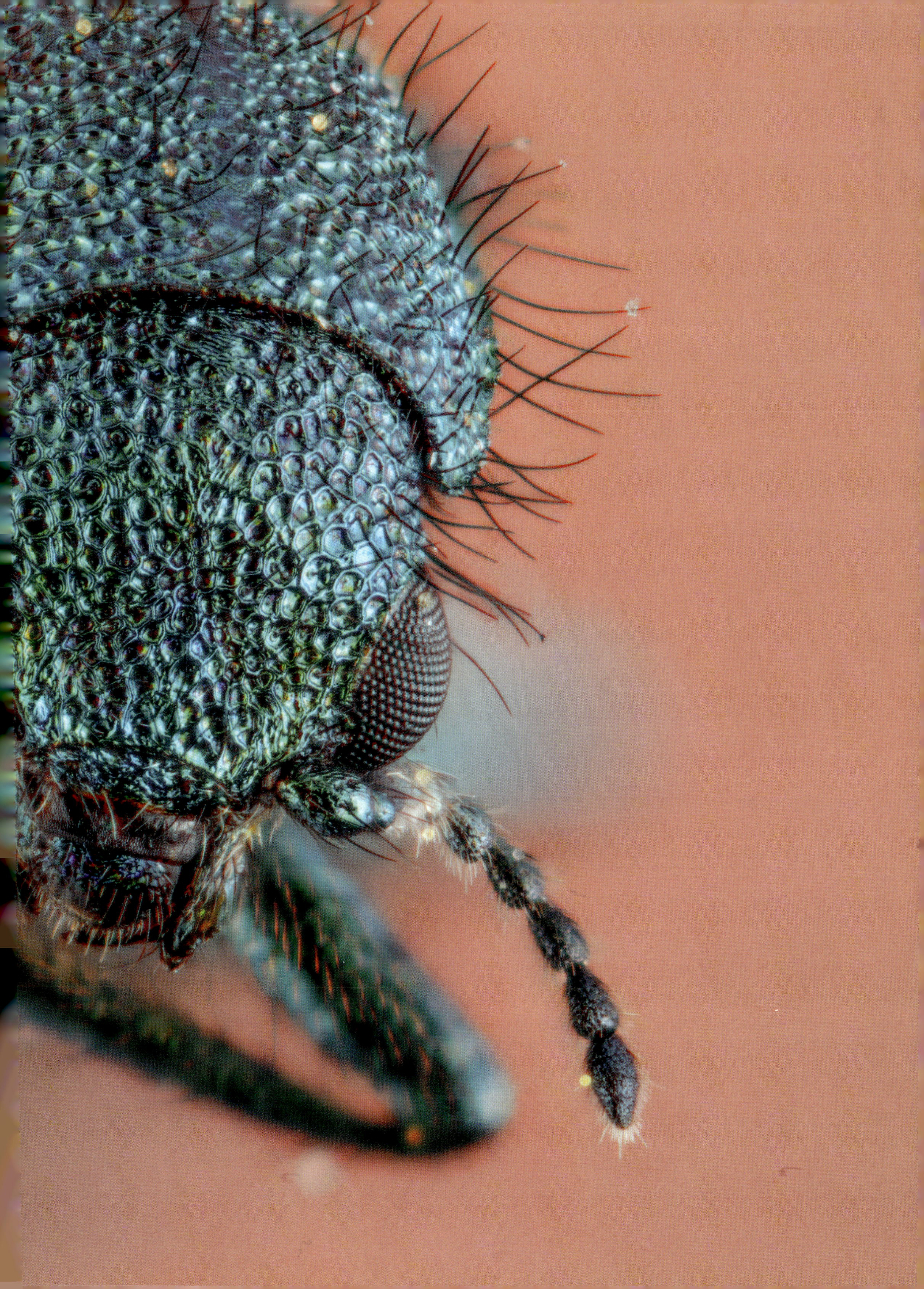

THE WONDER CABINET OF FABULOUS INSECTS

English-language design: Benjamin Brard

Library of Congress Control Number: 2024943700
ISBN: 978-1-4197-7976-3

Originally published in French in 2021 as *Fabuleux insects* by Delachaux et Niestlé. This English-language edition first published in 2025 by Cernunnos, an imprint of ABRAMS.

Printed and bound in China
10 9 8 7 6 5 4 3 2 1

ABRAMS The Art of Books
195 Broadway, New York, NY 10007
abramsbooks.com